THE STRUCTURE AND PERSUASIVE POWER OF MARK

**THE SOCIETY OF BIBLICAL LITERATURE
SEMEIA STUDIES**

Vincent L. Wimbush, Editor

THE STRUCTURE AND PERSUASIVE POWER OF MARK
A Linguistic Approach

by
John G. Cook

Scholars Press
Atlanta, Georgia

THE STRUCTURE AND PERSUASIVE POWER OF MARK
A Linguistic Approach

© 1995
The Society of Biblical Literature

Library of Congress Cataloging in Publication Data
Cook, John Granger.
    The structure and persuasive power of Mark : a linguistic approach / by John G. Cook.
        p. cm. — (The Society of Biblical Literature Semeia studies)
    Includes bibliographical references.
    ISBN 0-7885-0027-9 (alk. paper). — ISBN 0-7885-0028-7 (pbk. : alk. paper)
        1. Bible. N.T. Mark—Criticism, interpretation, etc.
2. Linguistics. I. Title. II. Series: Semeia studies.
BS2585.2.C62   1995
226.3'06—dc20   95-8489
                                    CIP

Printed in the United States of America
on acid-free paper

To my wife

ACKNOWLEDGEMENTS

This book is a revision of a doctoral dissertation completed at Emory University in 1985 under the direction of William Beardslee and David Hellholm (of the University of Oslo). I would like to thank them for their guidance and friendship. I am also indebted to Hendrik Boers for his extensive work on the manuscript and for first introducing me to the exciting world of linguistics. Carl Holladay and Fred Craddock have also made many helpful comments. Martin Buss was very helpful in finding English terms for text linguistic concepts. Vernon Robbins has generously offered his able editorial guidance in preparing this manuscript for publication. He was a wonderful mentor during my two years of post-doctoral work in the department of religion at Emory. The editor of *Semeia Studies*, Vincent L. Wimbush, has spent many hours editing the manuscript. I owe him a debt of gratitude.

TABLE OF CONTENTS

FOREWORD xii

INTRODUCTION 1

Chapter 1
MARK: STRUCTURE, MESSIANIC SECRET, AND GENRE 11
  1.1. Introduction 11
  1.2. Structure 13
    1.2.1. Introduction 13
    1.2.2. Invariants in the Markan Structure? 17
    1.2.3. Extra-Textual Models 18
    1.2.4. Text-Internal Approaches 25
      1.2.4.1. Thematic Methods 25
        1.2.4.1.1. Stories about the Disciples 26
        1.2.4.1.2. Themes Concerning Jesus and Other
                    Dramatis Personae 28
        1.2.4.1.3. Christological Themes 30
      1.2.4.2. Literary Methods 33
        1.2.4.2.1. Summaries 33
        1.2.4.2.2. Literary Forms and Types of Stories 37
      1.2.4.3. Markers 39

1.2.4.4. Methods Combining Thematic and Spatial Changes 47
1.2.4.5. Multiple Structures 50
1.3. The Messianic Secret 52
   1.3.1. William Wrede and Rudolf Bultmann 52
   1.3.2. The Determination of the Evidence 55
   1.3.3. The Explanation of the Motif 56
   1.3.4. The Diachronic Issue and the Motif's Definition 56
   1.3.5. Two Attempts to Evaluate the Facts: Heikki Räisänen and Jack Dean Kingsbury 58
   1.3.6. The Reader 60
      1.3.6.1. Martin Dibelius 61
      1.3.6.2. G. Minette de Tillesse 62
      1.3.6.3. Elias Bickerman 63
      1.3.6.4. Hans J. Ebeling and Nils Dahl 63
      1.3.6.5. Kingsbury 64
      1.3.6.6. Summary 64
   1.3.7. Messianic Secret and Salvation History 65
      1.3.7.1. Hans Conzelmann 65
      1.3.7.2. Georg Strecker 66
   1.3.8. Conclusion 66
1.4. The Text's Effect on the Audience 68
   1.4.1. Norman Perrin and the Function of Mark 68
   1.4.2. William Beardslee 69
   1.4.3. Hendrikus W. Boers 70
   1.4.4. Other Scholars on Mark's Effect on the Audience 70
1.5. The Question of Genre 72
   1.5.1. Pearls on a String: Karl L. Schmidt 72
   1.5.2. Kerygmatic Literature: Bultmann and Dibelius 73
   1.5.3. The Gospel as Aretalogy 77
   1.5.4. The Gospel as Biography and Other Options 79
1.6. Interpretation and Linguistics 86

Chapter 2
A TEXT LINGUISTIC METHOD: SEMANTICS, PRAGMATICS, AND STRUCTURE 87

2.1. The General Approach 87
2.2. Semantics 89
    2.2.1. The Triangle 90
    2.2.2. The Trapezium 91
    2.2.3. Lexicography 97
    2.2.4. Semantic Presuppositions 99
2.3. Pragmatics 101
    2.3.1. Pragmatic Presuppositions 101
    2.3.2. Pragmatics and the Trapezium 105
    2.3.3. Speech Acts 106
    2.3.4. Individual Gospel Stories as Speech Acts 110
    2.3.5. Textual Written Acts 115
2.4. The Outline or Structure of a Text 118
    2.4.1. Communication Frames 123
    2.4.2. Narrative Markers 126
        2.4.2.1. Meta-Communicative Markers 129
        2.4.2.2. Substitution Markers 130
        2.4.2.3. Speech Act Markers 132
        2.4.2.4. Episode Markers 133
        2.4.2.5. Character Markers 133
        2.4.2.6. Syntactic Markers 133
    2.4.3. Establishing a Structure 134

Chapter 3
A LINGUISTIC OUTLINE OF MARK 137
3.1. Introduction 137
3.2. The Frames of Communication 138
    3.2.1. Frame 00 138
    3.2.2. Frame 0 140
    3.2.3. Frame 1 140
    3.2.4. Frames 2–4 141
    3.2.5. The Dynamic Interaction of the Frames 142
3.3. The Markers 149
    3.3.1. The Inscriptio (^{00}TP) 149
    3.3.2. The Title: Mk 1:1 (^{0}TP) 151
    3.3.3. The Major Episodes (^{1}TP) 157

3.4. Comparison with Other Outlines..............................164
3.5. Abbreviations: Communication Frames...................165
    3.5.1. Explanation of the Subdivisions: OT, SOT, PN, ON......167
3.6. Abbreviations: The Markers......................................168
3.7. Using the Frames and Markers to Produce an Outline...........169

Chapter 4
THE GOVERNING SPEECH ACT AND THE EXEGESIS OF MARK..............285
4.1. Introduction..285
4.2. The Governing Speech Act of Mark.........................286
    4.2.1. Mk 1:2–13, 14–15 and the Governing Speech Act............289
    4.2.2. Mk 8:27–9:1 and the Governing Speech Act...................295
4.3. The Governing Speech Act and the Genre of Mark...............302
    4.3.1. Form or Text-Syntactic Elements of a Gospel.................304
    4.3.2. Content or Text-Semantic Elements of a Gospel.............304
    4.3.3. *Sitz im Leben* or Text-Pragmatic Elements of a Gospel..............304
    4.3.4. The Content and Function of the *Vita Apollonii* and Mark..............306
    4.3.5. Conclusion...309
4.4. The Messianic Secret and the Governing Speech Act in Mark..............311
    4.4.1. Semantics and the Motif..312
    4.4.2. The Definition of the Motif in Mark...........................315
    4.4.3. A Dynamic Understanding of the Motif......................318
    4.4.4. A Pragmatic Understanding of the Motif....................323
    4.4.5. Concluding Remarks on the Messianic Secret...............328

Chapter 5
CONCLUSION..331
5.1. The Thesis of the Work...331
5.2. Semantics and Pragmatics.......................................333
5.3. Text Linguistics and Exegesis..................................335

APPENDIX 1..339

Appendix 2
SUMMARY OF THE OUTLINE IN CHAPTER THREE 343

GLOSSARY 349

BIBLIOGRAPHY 353

LIST OF FIGURES
    1. The Triangle 90
    2. The Trapezium 93
    3. The Triangle as an analysis of a *signeme* on the *parole* level of abstraction 95
    4. The motif-proposition as a complex sign 314
    5. The motif as a sign 315

    N.B. The abbreviations are in conformity with the guidelines of the *Journal of Biblical Literature* and Liddell-Scott-Jones' *Lexicon*. Other abbreviations can be found in 3.5 and 3.6, including "TP" for "Text Part." "TLG" is the *Thesaurus Linguae Graecae* CD Rom.
    The fonts, Graeca and Hebraica, are from Linguists Based Software. The text of Mark in Chapter Three is from the United Bible Societies text (third edition), published electronically by Linguists Based Software (Box 580, Edmonds, WA 98020-0580). It is used with the permission of the German Bible Society.

FOREWORD

During the last two decades, New Testament scholarship has shifted from a discipline in which textual and hermeneutical practices were subdisciplines of history to an interdiscipline in which language, on the one hand, and society, on the other, stand in unremitting relation to one another. This shift has wrought significantly new practices with texts at the same time that it has modified many of the disciplinary practices that have characterized historical-critical analysis and interpretation for more than a century. A pressing question for the New Testament scholar at present is the relationship of the previous disciplinary practices to the new practices of interpretation. What are the relationships between textual criticism, source criticism, form criticism, redaction criticism, history of religion, history of tradition, history of theology, structuralist criticism, literary criticism, social-scientific criticism, rhetorical criticism, linguistic criticism, feminist criticism, African-American criticism, and ideological criticism? The pertinent focus in this context is on linguistic criticism. What is its relationship to other forms of analysis and interpretation?

Central to the issue of interpretation in New Testament study today is disciplinary versus interdisciplinary analysis. The common mode until the 1970s was disciplinary interpretation. There are two primary characteristics of a disciplinary approach. First, this mode of analysis uses tools and results of other disciplines in a "subdisciplinary" manner. This means that other disciplines are allowed to enter the arena of interpretation only on the terms of the reigning discipline, not on their own terms. Second, a discipline regularly establishes a "polar" relation to another discipline; this polarity excludes other disciplines from the arena of "serious" or "authoritative" interpretation.

In New Testament interpretation, the reigning discipline has been "history" and the polar discipline has been "theology." The manner in which historical criticism, with its polar relation to theology, has set the agenda for German analysis and interpretation is well exhibited in Martin Hengel's recent presidential address for the Studiorum Novi Testamenti Societas.[1] The tasks in view do not include serious engagement with sociology, anthropology, modern and postmodern forms of literary criticism, feminist criticism, ideological criticism, or psychology. The tasks are "historical" with "theological" interests in mind. In fact, the seminars of the Studiorum Novi Testamenti Societas themselves reach far beyond this polar orientation. In addition, the wide range of activities in the Society of Biblical Literature reach deeply into other disciplines to develop resources for analysis and interpretation. What, then, of John G. Cook's linguistic analysis in this book?

Cook's opening formulations place his use of linguistics in a subdisciplinary relation to historical criticism. The mood at this point is simply to clarify and supplement the great achievements of historical analysis and interpretation. Linguistic criticism submits to the boundaries of historical criticism through a polarity between "diachronic" and "synchronic" analysis. Within this polar relation, however, linguistic criticism creates a space for synthetic analysis of language, texts, and society. Then it breaks the polarity by introducing a linguistic spectrum of syntactic, semantic, and pragmatic modes of analysis and interpretation that move freely back and forth across the boundaries of diachrony and synchrony. Chapter One, accordingly—distinguishing among syntactic, semantic, and pragmatic analyses of Mark—makes excellent observations about

---

[1]Hengel 1994.

previous interpretations of Mark. In this mode, however, linguistic analysis and interpretation simply clarify and supplement historical criticism in a subdisciplinary manner.

In Chapter Two, Cook brings the resources of speech-act theory into syntactic, semantic, and pragmatic analysis and interpretation. This begins to change the function of linguistic criticism from a subdiscipline of historical method to a "discipline" that uses resources from historical, social, and cultural analysis on its own terms. No longer does linguistic criticism simply clarify and supplement historical criticism; Cook's discourse begins to launch its own theses about the nature of the Gospel of Mark.

After a display in Chapter Three of the complete text of Mark that identifies the frames of communication, linguistic markers, and some of the types of speech-acts, Chapter Four contains an analysis of the Gospel of Mark on the basis of the "governing speech act" at its beginning, the nature of its genre, and the function of the "messianic secret" in the context of the governing speech act. In this chapter, the strength of Cook's method comes to the fore as he shows how the text attains its linguistic power, yet many interpreters in late antiquity resisted that power. Also he shows that views of the genre of Mark regularly differ according to their focus on syntactic, semantic, or pragmatic aspects of the text.

To understand more specifically what Cook has achieved in this essay, I will point to the particular networks of signification in the Gospel of Mark that have captured his attention. At present, the field of New Testament interpretation is seriously engaged in analysis and interpretation of four networks of signification in texts, which I call arenas of texture: (a) inner texture; (b) intertexture; (c) social and cultural texture; and (d) ideological texture.[2] A fifth arena, namely psychological texture, hovers on the horizon, but interpreters do not at present appear to be ready to engage the psychological texture of New Testament texts in a disciplinary manner.

---

[2] Robbins 1992, xix-xliv; 1994b.

The strength of Cook's work lies in its analysis and interpretation of both inner texture and intertexture in Mark. He calls the arena of inner texture *parole*, and he divides the arena of intertexture into *langue* (the relation of Mark to all texts in Hellenistic Greek) and *langage* (the relation of Mark to all texts and speech in all languages). On the level of *parole*, which he calls "text-internal," he performs "syntactic" analysis—the relation between signs—and "semantic" analysis—the relation of a sign to its meaning. The beautiful thing, so to speak, about this approach is that it immediately begins to break the boundary between text-internal and text-external phenomena. It is not possible to perform semantic analysis without what Cook calls "semantic presupposition." This means, as he says, that semantics deals with signs "not included in the text," namely propositions or groups or propositions which the interpreter can "infer" to be present. This functions as an important corrective to new-critical and formalist literary approaches that have drawn a solid boundary around texts, as though it were possible to interpret the signs in a text apart from "external" phenomena functioning in relation to them.

Modern linguistic criticism has played a significant role in biblical interpretation for more than thirty years.[3] Yet this method has not, in my opinion, had the substantive impact on analysis and interpretation that it should have. There are many reasons, not least of which has been the preference by linguistic critics for technical vocabulary where more conventional words would carry the meaning. Another reason has been the advent in biblical interpretation, during the last two decades, of forms of literary criticism that focused on theological discourse at the expense of culturally based discourse from linguistics and anthropology. South African biblical scholarship has developed a highly nuanced ability to use linguistic criticism in the context of other accepted modes of analysis and interpretation.[4] Cook's analysis, using European-American scholarship, introduces

---

[3] Barr 1961.
[4] Botha 1994.

linguistic criticism in a manner that should make it accessible to many scholars who previously have been unable to see its importance in analysis and interpretation of the Bible.

Vernon K. Robbins
Emory University

INTRODUCTION

Text linguistics has had a difficult time finding acceptance among New Testament scholars. Part of the reason for this is that linguistics itself is a field full of a bewildering number of different theories about language. It shows promise, however, of increasing the battery of tools that exegetes can use in their work. It may not be as revolutionary as the advent of form criticism was in exegesis, but it is the contention of this work that a text linguistic method can provide a modest addition to historical critical exegesis. The name "text linguistics" itself originates from the fact that entire texts instead of single sentences are analyzed.[1] There is no claim here that the text linguistic method in this work is complete in itself. There are many other linguistic methods that are promising for the field of NT studies.

To achieve the goal of showing the potential usefulness of one text linguistic method for exegesis, I will first review in Chapter One certain problems in Markan interpretation from a linguistic point of view. The chapter will justify itself if it shows

---

[1] The bibliography in Chapter Two will include references to many researchers in the field. On the American scene, the linguist and scholar of Canaanite, Zellig Harris, was one of the early scholars interested in a linguistics that went beyond the bounds of a sentence. He was also interested in the connection between language and behavior or social situation (Harris 1970).

that some linguistic categories can helpfully illuminate exegetical problems. The second chapter will be a summary of the text linguistic method to be used in the work. The third chapter will offer a linguistically oriented structural outline of Mark.[2] The fourth chapter will have three sections. Those sections will relate a conception of the function of Mark to some Markan texts, to the genre of Mark, and to the Messianic Secret motif. A brief conclusion (Chapter Five) will review the results of the work.

Before an analysis of some aspects of Markan interpretation can proceed, several linguistic terms need to be introduced to orient the reader to the fundamentals and assumptions of text linguistics. One useful distinction, made by Ferdinand de Saussure, is between the synchronic and diachronic approach to language. A synchronic approach considers a language at one point in its history over its entire breadth. A diachronic approach considers a language's development through time.[3] In terms of text linguistics a synchronic interpretation of Mark looks at the meaning of Mark as the text stands without asking questions about the historical development of a given Text Part in Mark. "Text Part" will be used to refer to a given sequence of text. A diachronic interpretation of Mark looks at the historical development of the Markan text and asks questions about the redactional additions to the tradition. The diachronic approach leads to consideration of the meaning of a Markan Text Part (TP) in Jesus' ministry (if the Text Part is judged to be historically accurate), the meaning of the Text Part in the life of the early church, and the meaning of the Text Part at the stage of the gospel itself. A synchronic approach to Mark could consider Mark in relation to other texts that are examples of the gospel genre. In this work I shall concentrate on Mark as a single text. This approach is mainly synchronic, but it is not primarily

---

[2] Sometimes called "macrostructure" or "superstructure."

[3] Ferdinand de Saussure 1960, 114, 135ff.; more recently, see Hubert Frankemölle 1982, 62ff. David Hellholm 1991, 137, n.1 refers to the originator of the distinction, Georg von der Gabelentz 1901/1984, 3, 8–9, 49f., 59, 138–39, and to the discussion in Eugenio Coseriu 1984, 3–35.

interested in establishing the nature of the genre "gospel," although this question will be addressed.

Three further abstractions aid the linguist in analyzing the nature of signs: *parole*, *langue*, and *langage*. A sign on the level of *parole* is used in an actual context, such as a word in a sentence of the Gospel of Mark. A sign on the level of *langue* includes all possible meanings of the sign in a given language. An example would be the possible meanings of a given word in Hellenistic Greek. The level of *langage* is the system of all languages. An example of an investigation on the level of *langage* would be the consideration of the meaning of a sign such as "evil eye" in ancient Hebrew and Greek.[4]

Using the concepts above one can investigate a text on the level of *parole*. Here one would consider the relationships between the signs of a text such as Mark, and other signs in the text with reference to extra-linguistic reality. This would be a text-internal approach to semantics. A *langue* internal semantics considers the relationships between signs and other signs in the texts of a given language with reference to extra-linguistic reality. An example of such an approach would be the investigation of the text of Mark by using the entire system of Hellenistic Greek. A *langage* internal semantics considers the relationships between signs and other signs in texts on the level of *langage* with reference to extra-linguistic reality. An example of this kind of approach is an investigation of the text of Mark by using texts in Greek, Hebrew, and other ancient languages.[5]

Another set of concepts that will be useful in the survey of Markan interpretation has been developed by David Hellholm, who synthesized the work of several linguists in order to understand the use of signs in a language.[6] In this approach,

---

[4]For a discussion of these three abstraction levels, see Stephen Ullmann 1957, 27, 28, 261, 164.

[5]For a discussion of the these methods of semantics, see Hellholm 1980, 37, 38.

[6]Hellholm 1980, 23–24; for a very simple introduction, see Frankemölle 1982, 62.

syntax is the relation between signs.[7] Semantics is the relationship between a sign and its meaning.[8] "Meaning" includes both the sense or connotation of a sign and the reference or denotation of a sign.[9] A word such as "angel," for example, can have the sense of a "supernatural messenger," but its reference may be to an angel such as Gabriel as in Lk 1:26, or to any member of the set of "angels." Pragmatics can then be defined as the relationship between a sign, its meaning, and the users of the sign,[10] and includes both the sender(s) and receiver(s) of the sign. Pragmatics can concentrate on the sender of the signs (Mark the person in our case), the receivers of the signs (Mark's audience), or the contemporary receivers of the signs (hermeneutics). The communication situation between sender and original receivers is consequently a part of pragmatics. The distinction between semantics and pragmatics is important in Markan scholarship. Interpretations based on lexicography and other forms of semantic analysis should be kept distinct from those based on hypotheses about the cultural background of the Text Parts in Mark (pragmatics of author and original audience). Often pragmatics determines semantics.

The border between semantics and pragmatics can sometimes be hazy. For example, an expression such as "anointed one" (χριστός) used for a person may be (and likely is) confined to Jewish and Christian texts.[11] Assuming this is the case,

---

[7]Or in symbols R(S,S') where "R"="Relation" and "S"="Sign" and " S' " is another sign.

[8]Or R(S,M) where "M"="Meaning."

[9]The investigation of the denotata of signs is sometimes called "sigmatics."

[10]Or R(S,M,U) where "U"="Users."

[11]Compare Walter Grundmann's statement in Grundmann et al. 1974, 495 that the word is never related to people outside the LXX, the NT and dependent sources. A search on the *Thesaurus Linguae Graecae CD* (*TLG*) reveals about 25,000 uses of the word in Greek literature (not including those in letters, gravestones, inscriptions, ostraca, etc., which are not yet on the disk. In addition, the literary texts are not all recorded yet). The texts on the

one is hard pressed to distinguish precisely between semantic and pragmatic aspects of the word. This would be true because from a semantic point of view other usages of the expression in Greek, Hebrew and Aramaic (a *langage* internal semantics) illuminate it. But from a pragmatic point of view the expression would be understood as a distinct element of ancient Jewish and Christian culture (the users of the sign). The texts (semantics) that illuminate the word are confined to a particular element in Greco-Roman culture (pragmatics). Mark (8:28) might assume that readers were aware of the expression and of this shared cultural background. In this case the semantics of the word nearly collapses into pragmatics. The lexicographer (semanticist) would look at other texts to understand the term. A historian of religion (working with pragmatics) could try to determine the cultural background of the author and audience necessary to understand the word. These concepts will be used in the survey of several issues in Markan interpretation in Chapter One.

The first chapter will review, using the linguistic categories, work on the structure of Mark, the Messianic Secret, the function of Mark, and the genre of Mark. To review the different outlines of Mark, I shall distinguish between text-external and text-internal approaches to the gospel. Those approaches that make use of models from literature outside of Mark are text-external. Text-internal approaches include those based on themes such as discipleship and christology, literary methods that use features such as summaries, and methods that make use of changes of scene (time and place). The Messianic Secret will be approached from both its semantic and its pragmatic aspect. The semantic aspect comprises the content or definition of the motif and the

---

disk are listed in Luci Berkowitz and Karl Squitier 1990. As could be expected, the first texts in which the word is used to describe a person are from Hellenistic Judaism (LXX and *Sibylline Oracles*). The rest appear beginning with the NT. Marinus De Jonge also mentions a use in *Test. R.* 6:8 (MS b) in Grundmann et al. 1974, 512. The first appearance of the word used to refer to a person (Jesus) in a non-theological writer on the *TLG* disk is in the work of the engineer Heron, *De Mensuris* 60.11.2 (ca. 62 CE).

pragmatic aspect looks at the effect of the motif on the reader. Another pragmatic approach to Mark considers the entire text's function or its effect on an audience. Genre research on Mark involves syntactic, semantic, and pragmatic analyses of the entire text of Mark.

The second chapter gives an account of semantics, pragmatics, and the nature of a text linguistic structure of a narrative text. Semantics is an attempt to account for meaning in language. Using the two concepts, sense and reference, I shall show that they go back to the Stoics, even though they have often been ignored in NT studies. The triangle of word, sense, and reference (or thing) has been expanded into a trapezium (with four corners) by several linguists who want to give an explanation for the fact that a word (or larger sign) can have multiple meanings. The complete sense of a sign (*signifié*) includes all the possible meanings. Each of these meanings can be called a *sememe* of the word. In the NT, for example, the Greek word for "angel" can mean a "human messenger" or a "divine messenger" (cf. Lk 7:24, Mk 1:13). Each meaning can be divided into components (such as "divine" and "human") that the semanticists call *semes*. The chapter will also discuss the issue of a pragmatic approach to language.

One of the most difficult areas of exegesis is deciding what presuppositions an author and audience share. This concern is part of pragmatics because authors and audience have to be taken into account (not just signs and their meanings). Presuppositions include such things as common cultural beliefs and perceptions of socio-economic realities that author and audience share. Another important aspect of pragmatics is the capacity of speech to do things. This phenomenon has been named "speech acts" in this century, although ancient scholars were aware of the ability of language to act (see 2.3.3 below). "I baptize you" is an example of a speech act. The words themselves perform the act. An entire text can be viewed as a written speech act. Several criteria will be offered for analyzing an entire text as a written speech act. I shall argue that Mark is a speech act that can be called "gospel narrative " because it makes assertions about Jesus and makes a claim upon the allegiance of the reader.

After the discussion of semantics and pragmatics, I shall review a text linguistic understanding of what an outline is. An outline has a syntactic aspect that comprises text sequences that govern smaller text sequences. Each text sequence has a function. The semantic aspect of an outline includes the themes and subthemes that correspond to each of the text sequences. The pragmatic aspect of an outline includes understanding an entire text as a governing speech act (or "macro" speech act) that governs the smaller speech acts that make up the text. To do a text linguistic outline, I shall explain how Mark can be divided into different narrative levels or frames of communication. A communication frame is the context in which communication takes place. One frame would be that of an author and her or his audience. Another frame would be that between characters in the text who speak to each other. The characters' frame is included within that of the author and audience. If a character tells a story in which other characters have a conversation, then those characters' speech would be in a third frame. Each frame includes the smaller frame. One can imagine a large picture frame enclosing a smaller frame, which in turn encloses a still smaller frame. After setting out the text of Mark into its different frames of communication, I shall use a set of narrative markers to delimit the text into sequences (or Text Parts). A marker is an indicator or signal that helps a hearer to structure a speaker's communication by dividing it into its parts. The latter indicate that changes are being made in the linear flow of the text. A chapter title is an example of a marker that stands for or substitutes for a text sequence. Scene changes such as changes in time, place, and *dramatis personae* are also examples of markers. The structure in Chapter Three will use the communication frames and markers to understand Mark as a text.

In Chapter Three I shall first give an account of the different communication frames and large text sequences that are contained in the outline. Then the text of Mark will be divided into communication frames with an outline of the Text Parts on the facing page. The communication frame that is largest in Mark is the editor's title "Gospel according to Mark" or "According to Mark." The next frame is the author's title for the text (or part of the text) in Mk 1:1. The narrator's frame includes the reports about the actions of Jesus and the other characters. The next frame includes the words of Jesus and the other characters. There are two more frames, each of which is embedded in a larger frame. The frame that governs an embedded frame is called a "meta-frame." In the narrator's "Jesus said to them" (1:17), for example, the words "Jesus said to them " appear in Frame 1. The words "Follow me" appear in Frame 2. Frame 1 is the "meta-frame" for Frame 2. There are several interesting kinds of speech that appear in different frames that I have specifically tagged with abbreviations. The narrator in Frame 1 sometimes identifies scriptural authors, and their words (in Frame 2) can in turn quote the words of other characters (that appear in Frame 3). When a character becomes a narrator of events in the past, present, or future, I have tagged that speech. If a supernatural character speaks, I have also marked that kind of language. And when a character indicates his or her own speech with "I say to you," I have marked that kind of communication. Then I shall discuss the dynamic interaction of the communication frames. Next, the larger sequences of the text will be reviewed. They include the introduction (John and Jesus in the wildernesss, Mk 1:1–13), Jesus' ministry in Galilee and environs (1:14–8:26), Jesus' journey to Jerusalem (8:27–10:52), and Jesus in Jerusalem and environs (11:1–16:8). The outline follows.

Chapter Four has three parts, each of which develops the claim that Mark has a governing speech act. That and other speech acts are noted in the outline in Chapter Three. The governing speech act of Mark is indicated by Mk 1:1. It unifies the interpretation of the speech acts that appear in the text. Every speech act has a content (such as "the little girl rises"). The speech act ("little girl, I say to you, rise") in Mk 5:41 indicates the correct interpretation of the content. In a similar fashion the governing speech act of Mark that I have called "gospel narrative" indicates the correct interpretation of the content of

Mark's narrative world. In the first section I shall relate the governing speech act to the texts in Mark 1:2–13, 14–15 and 8:27–9:1. The speech acts contained in these texts are governed by the primary speech act in Mark. The second section will describe the implications of the governing speech act for the debate concerning the genre of Mark. Syntax, semantics, and pragmatics should all play a role in trying to understand genres. Occasionally, syntax and pragmatics are left out of the picture. An emphasis on the governing speech act is a concern of pragmatics. The third section comprises implications of the governing speech for interpretation of the Messianic Secret motif. Defining the motif and the texts that create the motif is an issue of semantics. Relating the motif to the governing speech act and consequently to readers is an issue of pragmatics. Scholars who have worked with the Messianic Secret's effect on readers have given independent confirmation of my approach. The work of these scholars (from Martin Dibelius to Jack D. Kingsbury) is summarized in 1.3.6 below. A text linguistic approach to Mark can, I believe, make a good contribution to the exegetical enterprise.

The concluding chapter will briefly summarize what I consider to be some of the contributions that a text linguistic method offers to Markan interpretation.

CHAPTER 1

MARK: STRUCTURE, MESSIANIC SECRET, AND GENRE

1.1. Introduction

In this chapter we shall look at several aspects of Markan scholarship from the linguistic perspective developed in the introduction—the structure of the text, the Messianic Secret, the effect of the text on its audience, and the genre of the text. From a semiotic perspective these issues involve syntax, semantics, and pragmatics. An outline delineates sequences of the text and, since it deals with the relations between signs and other signs it is syntactic. If, for example, Mk 1:1–8:2 is a sequence in an outline, then it relates all the signs in that Text Part to one another as belonging to one unit. When a scholar gives such a sequence a thematic title, then he or she is summarizing the content or meaning of the signs, and is thus working with semantics (signs and their meanings). Rarely do scholars making outlines bring in the question of the effect of the Text Parts on the reader, but if they do, they are then working with pragmatics (signs, their meanings, and the users of the signs). If it were claimed that Mk 1:1–8:2 had a catechetical function in the Markan community, then pragmatics would be involved.

The Messianic Secret is one of the most important elements of the content of the text of Mark according to many scholars. It is a concern of semantics. Some researchers have raised the issue of the effect of the Messianic Secret on the reader. They move from semantics to questions of pragmatics when they bring up the users of the language. A natural extension of their concern for the reader is the attempt to determine the effect of the entire text of Mark on the audience.

The question of Mark's genre demands an attempt to cope with the syntax, semantics, and pragmatics of the entire text. The outline of Mark, the Messianic Secret, and the effect of the text on the audience have played a role in attempts to define the genre of the gospel. In addition to the three semiotic categories (syntax, semantics, and pragmatics), we shall use the distinction between synchrony and diachrony to understand the issues in Markan research. Scholars who use the redaction/tradition distinction, for example, are working with a diachronic approach. Outlines are usually done with a synchronic approach. On the other hand, scholars often approach the Messianic Secret from a diachronic perspective, since they attempt to determine what belongs to tradition and what belongs to Mark's editorial hand.

The concepts of *parole, langue,* and *langage* will also be useful in sorting out issues in the research to be surveyed in this chapter. When Mark is approached as a text in its own right without comparing it to other texts in Hellenistic Greek, one works on the level of *parole*. If one needs to use other Hellenistic Greek texts to understand Mark, then one works on the level of *langue*. And when texts in other languages—such as Latin and Hebrew—are used, then one works on the level of *langage*. The outlines reviewed below are mainly done using synchronic methods on the level of *parole*. They have syntactic and semantic aspects, and occasionally pragmatics plays a role in understanding the function of the text sequences.

1.2. Structure

1.2.1. Introduction

After reviewing about ninety varying proposals for a Markan "structure" (or "outline"), one is left feeling skeptical.[1] Rudolf Bultmann claims that Mk 8:27 is the only structural break in the Gospel.[2] After reviewing several attempts, Howard Kee doubts that one can come up with a convincing outline.[3] According to Alfred Loisy,[4] Mark appears to be a group of memories without a vigorous structuring principle. In other words, Mark comprises a group of "pearls on a string."[5] Given this state of affairs, why bother with an outline or structure at all? One answer holds that an interpreter should attempt to discover an author's

---

[1]For the purposes of this chapter I will use "structure" and "outline" as synonyms. In the course of this chapter I will make use of the concept of different levels of an outline. For instance, in an outline the Roman numerals I, II, III would be on the first level and I.1 or I.2 would be on the second level. I.1.1 would be on the third level. In the so-called legal type of outline used in this text 1.1 would be on the second level, and 1.1.1 would be on the third level. See 2.4.3.

[2]Bultmann 1963, 350. 8:27–10:52 is a section. He does concede the existence of a preface and a Jerusalem section.

[3]Kee 1977, 64:

> It would appear that Mark no more lends itself to analysis by means of a detailed outline developed by simple addition of components than does a major contrapuntal work of music. In spite of illuminating and ingenious attempts to discover the one theme which provides the unity of meaning for the structure of Mark, none has been found.

Compare Dieter Lührmann's view (Lührmann 1987, 23): "Mk gibt freilich keine Gliederung seines Werkes."

[4]Loisy 1912, 9.

[5]Karl L. Schmidt 1923, 127, 128.

understanding of the structure of her or his work.[6] But even such an able commentator as Erich Klostermann presents an outline and then finds almost no use for it in his commentary, which focuses on the individual stories.[7] One can make the same claim about almost any other commentary such as those of Ernst Lohmeyer, Rudolf Pesch, Joachim Gnilka, Dieter Lührmann, et al.[8] Consequently, one needs to ask the following question: what is the usefulness of a proposed outline or structure? Any commentator can propose an outline, write a few paragraphs or pages summarizing the Text Parts and then get back to the individual stories. Does the outline actually illuminate one's understanding of the text, and most important, can it be justified by indications in the Markan text?[9] Compare the view of Mark in

---

[6]Compare Ludger Schenke 1986, 56:

> Das Aufbauprinzip des Evangeliums muß sich aus dem Text selbst ergeben. Es sind also für unseren Versuch allein die Signale und Hinweise des Textes zu beachten. Inhaltliche Überlegungen, sofern sie bereits Ergebnis der Interpretation sind, sollten möglichst zurückgestellt werden. Wir beginnen damit, daß wir nach der Technik der Evangelisten bei der Verknüpfung von Abschnitten und Perikopen fragen.

Chalmer E. Faw (1957, 19) writes:

> If that outline is well constructed it is one that grows naturally out of the book itself rather than one superimposed upon it by modern interests. It should be one which, as nearly as can be determined, the author himself, consciously or unconsciously, has followed in writing the book.

[7]Klostermann 1971, 1 and compare the extremely brief discussion of 8:27–10:52 in 1971, 78.

[8]Lohmeyer 1967, 7, 8; Pesch 1976, 32–40; Gnilka 1978, 30–32; Lührmann 1987, 23.

[9]See Schenke in note 6; Lohmeyer 1967, 8:

> Es ist nicht leicht, in dem Bericht des Mk, der Einzelgeschichten und Einzelworte der Überlieferung aneinanderreiht und sie nur

Klostermann and in the collaborative work of David Rhoads and Donald Mitchie. In Klostermann's work Mark is mostly disjointed stories, whereas in the work of Rhoads and Mitchie many interlocking motifs emerge.[10] A useful outline should help the reader draw the text together. Ancient writers could and did structure their texts.[11] So the major argument of this chapter is

---

selten durch summarische Bemerkungen verbindt, größere Abschnitte nach inneren oder äußeren Gesichtspunkten zusammenzufassen; jede Einteilung ist darum nur ein Versuch, der sich durch sein Gelingen rechtfertigt.

[10] Klostermann 1971; Rhoads and Mitchie 1982.

[11] See Dietrich-Alex Koch 1983, 158 n. 1 with reference to authors that overview their works using *prooemia* such as Diod. Sic. 1.4.6–5.3 and Pliny, *Hist. Nat.* 1. He also refers to the marking of units of meaning by new line beginnings or by punctuation signs (in ancient writings). Ancient drama and rhetoric are sometimes used to structure the text of Mark (see Benoît Standaert 1978), so I will summarize basic concepts to be used in evaluating some proposed structures of Mark. Compare Aristotle *Poet.* 12 on the Text Parts (μέρη δὲ τραγῳδίας) of tragedies : πρόλογος ([prologue] before chorus); ἐπεισόδιον ([epode] inbetween choral songs); ἔξοδος ([exode] no choral song after it); *Poet.* 18, δέσις ([complication] until the change of fortune); and λύσις ([unravelling]; compare Lausberg 1960, 569ff., sec. 1197). Aristotle analyzes the μῦθος ([plot] 10, 11) as ἀναγνώρισμος (change from ignorance to knowledge, Lausberg 1960, 585ff., secs. 1213–1215), περιπέτεια (change of situation to the opposite, Lausberg 1960, 584, sec 1212), πάθος (calamity, destructive or painful occurrence), and the ἁμαρτίαν μεγάλην (13, tragic flaw) in the hero. Also compare the discussion of the order (*dispositio*) of orations in the rhetorical handbooks (and see Lausberg 1960, 241, sec. 443). *Ad Herenn.* 1.2.4, (forensic speech): *exordium* (introduction), *narratio* (narration), *divisio* (division), *confirmatio* (proof), *confutatio* (refutation), *conclusio* (conclusion); 3.4.7–8, (for a deliberative speech) introduction, narration (if there is one), the division, proof, refutation, and conclusion. On the structure of epideictic speeches in this work see 3.6.11, 3.6.12, 3.7.13, and 3.8.15. The same parts in a judicial speech are discussed in 1.3.4 (compare Quint 3.9.1 without the *divisio*). Arist. *Rhet.* 3.1.3 (1414a,b) on any speech: πρόθεσις (statement), πίστις (proof), and in epideictic and judicial oratory a

that one should look for a Markan structure that will be useful in illuminating the text and that can be justified by the text itself. A refreshing example is the work of Mary Ann Tolbert, in which she develops an outline (discussed below in 1.2.3) and then uses it to great advantage in her commentary.[12]

Scholars apparently do not agree on the following principle: any outline or structure that is proposed for Mark needs to be argued for. Many commentaries simply present an outline with no further justification.[13] Such a fact shows how difficult it is to actually find a method for detecting an outline in a narrative text such as Mark. In the following survey of the literature we shall concentrate on the arguments used to delimit the text into sequences or Text Parts. Other surveys of the literature tend to classify the contributions based on how many Text Parts (three parts, four, etc.) scholars find in the text.[14] One can divide approaches into those that use models drawn from extra-Markan literature and those that look to the text itself for a structure without making use of other ancient literature. This distinction will help one understand the methods used by several scholars. One notices that, whatever method is used, certain texts appear frequently in many different outlines.

προοίμιον (proem) and ἐπίλογος (epilogue) with a διήγησις (narration) as part of the πίστις in judicial oratory. *Rhet. ad Alex.* on deliberative oratory: introduction (29), exposition (30), proof (32), anticipation of opposing arguments and recapitulation (33); and on forensic oratory (36) introduction, proof, anticipation of opposing arguments, recapitulation with the narration (1142b30) as part of an introduction or separately placed. Lausberg 1960, 148, sec. 262 gives a convenient summary of the elements of an oration. Compare Burton Mack and Vernon Robbins 1989, 54.

[12]Tolbert 1989.

[13]Outlines by *fiat* can be found in the majority of discussions and commentaries: e.g., A. E. J. Rawlinson 1927, ix; Julius Schniewind 1952, 41; Ernst Haenchen 1966, 34.

[14]Étienne Trocmé 1963, 60ff. (who does make some methodological comments); Rudolf Pesch 1968, 50ff; Heinrich Baarlink 1977, 75ff.

1.2.2. Invariants in the Markan Structure?

As far as I can determine, scholars have found no absolute invariants in their outlines of the text of Mark. Mk 8:27 and 11:1 do not always appear as breaks in the outlines that are discussed below, although 8:27 and 11:1 would certainly appear to be the most popular breaks in the text. In addition, breaks are often found in the following places: somewhere between 1:9–14; 2:1; somewhere between 3:6–20; 4:1, 4:35; somewhere between 6:6–14; and at 7:24; 10:1; 13:1; and 14:1. The sample of about ninety authors surveyed below is not exhaustive. Part of the reason for this multiplicty of structures is the desire to divide the text into equal parts (from two to six or more).

Scholars sometimes offer reasons for the divisions—if not, one has to guess the method used by looking at the titles that summarize the proposed division of the text. Unless extra-textual models (such as Greek tragedy) are used, the proposals work on the level of *parole* (the text of Mark only). They also are synchronic because they do not generally attempt to use the redaction/tradition distinction to find breaks in the text.

The limits of the smaller stories evoke much more agreement. Some ancient manuscripts (such as Codex Alexandrinus [A] and Codex Vaticanus [B]) divide the text into κεφάλαια (sections) as do some ancient commentators.[15] The κεφάλαια are still useful because scholars tend to focus their commentaries on "story units." The linguistic analysis in Chapter Three will hopefully clarify the reasons behind the general agreement on the limits of the smaller pericopes. Indications of change in geography, time,

---

[15]For a list of the κεφάλαια in A (48) and B (62) compared with Westcott and Hort, see Henry Swete 1913, liff. Swete also gives A's list of τίτλοι for the κεφάλαια in 1913, liv. Bruce Metzger discusses the divisions in 1968, 22–23 where he also briefly discusses the titles and refers to a complete list of them. Victor of Antioch (Cramer 1844 [*Catenae*]) and Theophylact (Theophylact, *Opera*) use κεφάλαια in their commentaries, and they also compose thematic titles for each text sequence. The disagreement about the number of κεφάλαια shows that there is no absolute agreement here either.

and in the characters provoke the agreement. The alleged larger units of the text do not function very much in most commentaries. The smaller units are stories that are held together by indications of space, time and characters. These "pearls on a string" still appear to be the focus of exegetical labor as a cursory glance at any twenty commentaries on Mark will show. Besides identifying the smaller pericopes, can research find any larger units that are open to intersubjective verification? One of the more "objective" attempts to structure the gospel involves using literature in the Greco-Roman world to find analogous structures to Mark. These "extra-textual models" illuminate the connections between Mark and other literature of the ancient world.

1.2.3. Extra-Textual Models

One can make a minor distinction between two ways of using extra-textual models to understand Mark. In one approach, a scholar finds a model in ancient literature and then applies the model to the text of Mark. The model, in this approach, guides the search for the Text Parts of Mark. The practical question to be asked is: Does the model help discover the structure (or a structure) of Mark, or does it force Mark onto a Procrustean bed? In the other approach, one searches Hellenistic texts to find another text that has some significant structural phenomenon in common with Mark. In this method, features of Mark are correlated with features in other ancient documents. Both of these approaches work on the level of *langue* (Hellenistic Greek) or *langage* (Greek, Hebrew, Latin, and so forth). First, I shall review approaches that operate by finding a model in ancient literature; then, I shall apply that model to the text of Mark.

J. Duncan M. Derrett interprets Mark as a sort of midrash on the OT texts describing the Exodus and the conquest of the promised land.[16] Here Exodus and Joshua provide the models

---

[16]Derrett 1985 (I), 23ff. on his OT model and 1985 (II), 315ff. for a summary of scriptural allusions. 1985 (I), xff.: Preparation for the trek (Mk 1:1–2:17); Exodus (Mk 2:18–3:12); the Crossing (Mk 3:20–5:20); Facing a

with which Derrett interprets the Markan structure. He finds ten sections in the gospel and attempts to draw close typological correspondences between individual OT texts (mostly Exodus and Joshua) and Markan stories. Derrett's attempt seems to be forced, as the following example illustrates: Mk 6:30–44 finds its model in Joshua 1 where Joshua has the people gather manna.[17] Jesus feeds and prepares his host to be a solid fighting force that will retake Canaan for God. Derrett's typological exegesis of the passage is a medley of more than thirty references to OT texts that illuminate the text.

Several scholars have attempted to see Mark as composed according to an ancient Jewish lectionary.[18] The lectionary is the extra-textual model with which they analyze Mark's structure. C. T. Ruddick claims that the gospel in its present form developed out of a "...cycle of preaching adapted to and influenced by the weekly readings which the church adopted from the synagogue."[19] Ruddick is able to correlate the individual stories of Mark (as divided by Codex Vaticanus) with the same lectionary beginning either in Nisan or Tishri. The ease with which he makes the correlations casts suspicion on the method itself. For example, depending on whether one starts the lectionary in Nisan or Tishri, Mk 6:30–44 has its basis in Gen 39, where Joseph is made overseer of the prison in Egypt, or the text has its basis in Gen 1:1–2:3/Ex 11:1–12:28 (first and second year readings)—the "passover meal."[20] Ruddick concentrates on the smaller Text Parts, i.e., the stories of Mark.

Rebellion (Mk 5:21–6:29); Invasion of the Land (Mk 6:30–9:1); Triumph (Mk 9:2–10:52); Provocation (Mk 11:1–12:44); Woe to Jerusalem (Mk 13); Martyrdom (Mk 14:1–15:47); Justification (Mk 16:1–8).

[17]Derrett 1985 (I), 120–124.

[18]Philip Carrington 1960. C. T. Ruddick 1969; and criticism based on the questionable existence of Jewish lectionaries in Mark's time in Derrett 1985 (I), 22.

[19]Ruddick 1969, 387.

Gottfried Schille uses several "homology" and catechesis texts (Heb 6:1ff., 1 Cor 13, Didache)[21] to identify a structure in Mark that comprises a number of different themes: the new teaching and spreading of the message (up to 3:6); boat motif and the faith content of the primitive Christian community (3:7–6:6a); legitimation of mission practice and looking back to the meal (6:6bf.; the meal in 6:31ff.); threatened life in the world (in word: the obligation of mission; in deed: "Haustafel") (8:27f); love commandment (10:32f.); apocalyptic hope (13:1f.).[22] The model is somewhat vague, but the catechesis texts provide the background for interpreting Mark in Schille's attempt to outline the text.

A more popular model has been that of Greek tragedy. Elias Bickerman referred to 8:27ff. as ἡ μετάβασις μετὰ ἀναγνωρισμοῦ (transition with recognition).[23] A number of other scholars have used categories from drama (from Aristotle, *Poet.*) to understand the text of Mark.[24] Gilbert G. Bilezikian does not claim that Mark

---

[20]Ruddick 1969, 417. And on Mk 6:30–44, see 1969, 392, 409.

[21]Schille 1957, 10 (on homology and catechesis) and 1957, 13 on the Gospel as following the foundational confession of the community.

[22]Schille 1957, 15, 16, 17, 19, 21. The last two sections of Schille's structure are extremely unclear—as are most of the section limits in his article. The emphasis on the audience of the text is good (1957, 12): mission proclamation for Gentiles, teaching for catechumens and reminders for community members such as the basis for baptism and eucharist. This is an example of pragmatics. See 1.4.

[23]Elias Bickermann [*sic*] 1923, 132 who also compares Mk 1:2–15 with the rhetorical prologue in Arist. *Rhet.* 3.14.

[24]Ernest Burch 1931, 349, 353: rising action to 8:30; 8:31, change of fortune with recognition— and Burch also discusses the problem of finding a tragic error in Jesus. Friedrich Lang 1977, 20. Martin Hengel 1985, 34–37: Mk 1:1–13, "salvation historical prologue"; 1:14–3:6, Jesus' activity in Galilee before the appointment of the twelve, first act; 3:7–8:26, climax of Jesus' activity, second act; 8:27–10:52, third act with the περιπέτεια and recognition; 11:1–13:37, fourth act with catastrophe; 14:1–15:39, pathos; 15:40–16:8, epilogue with *Deus ex machina* ([god from the machine] e.g., the angel).

is a Greek tragedy, but does find many points of comparison.[25] Mk 1:1–8:26 corresponds to the complication (from the beginning to the point before the hero's change in fortune), and Mk 8:31–16:8 corresponds to the dénouement (from the beginning of the change until the end). Mk 8:27–30 is the crisis and recognition scene.[26] It is combined with the reversal (περιπέτεια) that is signaled by Jesus' prediction of his suffering.[27] The theme of the first half of the Gospel is the unrecognized supernatural identity of Jesus, and the theme of the second half is the fulfillment of the Messianic mission.

Benoît Standaert has combined categories drawn from drama and the rhetoric of speech[28] to analyze Mark: 1:1–13 is the prologue; 1:14–6:13 is the narration; 6:14–10:52 is the argumentation, and; 11:1–15:47 is the dénouement (unwinding of the plot). Mk 16:1–16:8 is the epilogue. He divides the argumentation section into three parts: 6:14–8:26; 8:27–9:13; 9:14–10:52, with 8:22–26, 9:14–29 and 10:46–52 being transition texts. 8:27–9:13 is the pivot of the Gospel with the recognition. In the first section of the argument 6:14–16 introduces the proposition; 6:17–29 is a rhetorical digression; and 6:30–8:21 is the bread section with the incomprehension concerning Jesus. The third section (9:14–10:52) he entitles "the road of the disciples."[29]

The rhetorical chiasm (a, b, b', a') serves as a model for the structure of Mark which M. Philip Scott develops. He sees 9:7 as the center of the chiasm and uses Jesus' questions of people to help isolate different sub-sections of the text (3:33, 8:29, 10:18,

---

[25]Bilezikian 1977, 109.

[26]Bilezikian 1977, 58, 59, 77, 79 with reference to Aristotle's categories in *Poetics* 11, 18.

[27]Bilezikian 1977, 100, 101.

[28]Standaert 1978, 50ff. and see the summary in Standaert 1983, 23ff. In 1978, 107 Standaert calls 14:1ff. the catastrophe.

[29]On the argumentation section see 1983, 23ff. and 1978, 298. Hengel 1985, 141, n. 21 can see no decisive break at 6:13 because of its temporal relation to 6:30. Ferdinand Hahn 1985, 181 is also unable to see 6:14–10:52 as the argumentation over against 1:14–6:13 as the narration.

12:35 and the question to Jesus in 14:61).[30] Here it is quite obvious how the model is laid over the text of Mark.

Vernon K. Robbins and Mary Ann Tolbert are two scholars who use an extra-textual approach to correlate features of Mark with features in other ancient texts. They find structural phenomena in common between Mark and other ancient literature. First, they analyze the text of Mark, then they look outside for other ancient texts that illuminate structural features in Mark.

Robbins uses the rhetorical progression (a pattern of literary repetition) to find a structure for the text. In the course of an investigation of the portrayal of Jesus as teacher in the context of Greco-Roman culture, Robbins detects a three-fold progression. The elements are: Jesus goes to a new place with the disciples; he engages in a special situation of interaction; as a result of this interaction he summons his disciples anew.[31] The rhetorical progressions summarize old themes and introduce new ones. Robbins structures the entire text using his approach: 1:1–13,

---

[30]Scott 1985, 23 lists the questions he considers structurally important. The outline he proposes (Scott 1985, 25) is: 1:1–8, prologue; l:9–3:35, Prima Primae; 4:1–8:30, Secunda Primae; 8:31–10:31, Prima Secundae; 10:32–12:40, Secunda Secundae; 12:41–13:37, Supplementum; 14:1–14:64, Prima Tertiae; 14:65–15:47, Secunda Tertiae; 16:1–8, Epilogue. Standaert 1978, 37 notes that concentric composition played a role in ancient practice even though there was not ancient formal treatment. Standaert gives no examples of a type of ancient concentric structure that Scott proposes for Mark, although he does gives some examples of less baroque concentric structures in 1978, 379, n.1 (e.g., Lucian *Dem.* has monologues in 5–21 and 32–42 and Josephus *Bell.* 3.111–339 and 7.275–406 has battles sandwiching the book).

[31]Robbins 1992, 29 on rhetorical progression where he quotes *Ad Her.* 4.42.54 on *exergasia*: "...elaboration consists in dwelling on the same topic and yet seeming to say something ever new.... We shall not repeat the same thing precisely—for that, to be sure, would weary the hearer and not elaborate the idea—but with changes." 1992, 25ff. on the three-stage progression. The outline is summarized in 1992, 27 (See also Robbins 1981, 113 for a summary).

introduction; 1:14–3:6, Jesus and the gospel of God; 3:7–5:43, the healing Son of God; 6:1–8:26, the rejected prophet; 8:27–10:45, the suffering, dying, rising Son of Man; 10:45–12:44, the authoritative Son of David; 13:1–15:47, the future Son of Man and the dying Messiah-King; 16:1–8, conclusion. The above units are part of three phases of the relationship between Jesus and his disciples: 1:14–3:6, a phase which initiates discipleship; 3:7–12:44, a teaching/learning phase; 14:1–15:47, a phase of farewell and separation from the teacher.[32]

Robbins relates the phases to those found in Hellenistic literature, with particular reference to Xenophon's *Memorabilia* of Socrates. Xenophon's text provides a model with which Robbins correlates certain features in the text of Mark. The relations Robbins sees are as follows: Mark's introduction corresponds to *Mem.* 4.1.1–5; Mk 1:14–3:6 corresponds to *Mem.* 4.2.1–40; Mk 3:7–5:43 corresponds to *Mem.* 4.3.1–18; Mk 6:1–8:26 corresponds to *Mem.* 4.4.1–25; Mk 8:27–10:45 corresponds to *Mem.* 4.5.1–12; Mk 10:46–12:44 corresponds to *Mem.* 4.6.1–15, and; Mk 14:1–15:47 corresponds to *Mem.* 4.7.1–10.[33] In 3.4 we will compare the structure of Mark offered in this book with Robbins's approach.

A reference to Demetrius (*On Style*, 202) begins the discussion of structure in Tolbert's work:[34] Demetrius states that long sentences need "to be broken up into clearly defined groups 'on the analogy of roads with many signposts and resting-places' so that the reader may be guided through the thought." Tolbert looks for aural signposts for the text of Mark such as "repetitions of words, sentences, and episodes...lexical indicators to remind audiences of similar events or indicate the presence of something special (e.g., Mark's use of πάλιν, "again"), notations of time...shifts in geography or location," and so forth.[35] In Tolbert's approach, rhetoric is the "amplification of positions,

---

[32]Robbins 1992, 82–3.
[33]Robbins 1992, 60, 87–94, 126–28, 172–73.
[34]Tolbert 1989, 107ff.
[35]Tolbert 1989, 107.

theses or ideas, required by the aural orientation of communication in the ancient world...."[36] Her rhetorical structure divides the text into the prologue (Mk 1:1–13); the preaching tour in Galilee (1:14–10:52), and; the Jerusalem section (11:1–16:8). Chapters 1–10 contain Jesus' mission of sowing the word and responses to it, and 11–16 comprise an account of Jesus' true identity and the result of its publication.[37]

Tolbert finds correlations between ancient Greek novels and the structure of Mark. The novels serve as the model that illuminates various features of Mark's text. Novels such as Xenophon of Ephesus's *Ephesian Tale* and Chariton's *Chaereas and Callirhoe* have minimal introductions, begin *in medias res*, have episodic plots and journey motifs, have central turning points, and final recognition scenes. Xenophon, the least skillful of the novelists, supplies little detail about characters and places. He surrounds short dialogue scenes with narrative, and there is considerable repetition.[38] The oracle in Xenophon's novel (1.6.2), which outlines the events that will follow, corresponds to the programmatic parable of the sower in Mark 4.[39] Chariton's trial scene before the Persian king depicts a central turning point in the narrative where Chaereas sees Callirhoe after a long separation. This central scene corresponds to Mark 8:27–30. Xenophon's final recognition sequence (5.11.2–5.15.1) corresponds to Mark's final recognition sequence (14:60–63, 14:66–72, 15:39).[40] Tolbert does not seek to impose a structure drawn from ancient texts onto Mark, but uses the ancient texts to illuminate aspects of the Markan narrative.

All of the extra-textual approaches share the virtue of giving the scholarly community some idea of the way in which a structure of Mark can be found. The models provide a check or guideline against which one can evaluate the results of the

---

[36]Ibid.
[37]Tolbert 1989, 107ff., 231.
[38]Tolbert 1989, 65, 67.
[39]Tolbert 1989, 104–105, 121–122.
[40]Tolbert 1989, 74, 75.

scholarly research. If the model illuminates features in the text of Mark, then one can consider the model to be useful.

The other approaches to Mark's outline to be considered below concentrate on the text of Mark itself (the level of *parole*) without attempting to find similarities with other ancient texts. They are synchronic because they do not use the redaction/tradition distinction to structure text sequences.

1.2.4. Text-Internal Approaches

The rest of the scholars in this survey have methods that use internal features in the text to determine a Markan structure. For the sake of clarity we are going to impose some distinctions on these outlines of Mark. They can be distinguished accordingly: thematically oriented methods; literary methods; and methods that concentrate on changes in space, time, or characters to structure the text.[41] The majority of scholars use some approaches from all three different methods, but they tend to emphasize one over the other.

1.2.4.1. Thematic Methods

"Themes" in Mark are subjects or topics of the Markan language. Any attempt to structure Mark based on the content of the text can come under the rubric "thematic method." Ernst Lohmeyer uses the term "inner and outer aspects" in discussing the method of delimiting the larger units of Mark.[42] Thematic methods are "inner criteria." The themes are supposed to find longer sections of the text. Consequently, the themes should in some sense organize or dominate sections of the text. A hidden presupposition in this method (as in other outlines) is that the text is divisible into subtexts that are roughly equivalent in length. Therefore, scholars tend to look for themes that reflect

---

[41]See the discussion of markers in 2.4.2. Compare Lang's reference to changes in place, time and people in Mark (Lang 1977, 2) as the scenic elements of the story which are decisive for finding breaks in the text.

[42]See Lohmeyer in note 9, above.

this divisibility. Organizing structures that make use of changes in space, time, and characters will be discussed below (1.2.4.3). This latter method involves what Lohmeyer calls "outer aspects." A continuum exists between those who use the thematic methods ("inner aspects"), and those who use indications such as space and time changes. Very few scholars choose to use only thematic changes to structure the text. They usually combine themes with other features of the text to find an outline. One theme that has been very prevalent in outlines is Jesus' relationship with his disciples.

1.2.4.1.1. Stories about the Disciples

Stories about Jesus and his disciples provide the focus for these outlines. Redaction and tradition play little role in these outlines; they are synchronic. They do not appeal to other ancient literature as a model for the structure of Mark; they work on the level of *parole*. Sometimes the stories of discipleship appear in the midst of other patterns.

Robert Butterworth sees this pattern in the text of Mk 1–10:52: a story about Jesus' status or authority; a call to discipleship; various reactions to Jesus, and; a healing episode.[43] He admits that 11:1–12:44 does not fit this pattern and does not deal with the rest of the text. Various forms of repetitions concerning Jesus' relationship with his disciples have interested many scholars. According to Gustav Wohlenberg, three stories about the twelve apostles delimit new sections—3:7ff.; 6:6bff.; and 8:27. Wohlenberg also uses themes to structure the text, and the stories about the disciples play a large role.[44] Jean Delorme

---

[43]Butterworth 1972, 67ff.: 1:14–45 (with, e.g., 1:14–15, status of Jesus; 1:16–20, call of the disciples; 1:21–39, reactions to Jesus, 1:40–45, healing); 2:1–3:6; 3:7–5:43; 6:1–8:26; 8:27–10:52; 11:1–12:44.

[44]Wohlenberg 1910, VIIff., 30: 1:14–3:6, preparatory overview of Jesus' activity in Galilee; 3:7–6:6a, from the choosing of the disciples to rejection in Nazareth; 6:6b–8:26, sending out of the disciples to the healing of the blind man in Bethsaida; 8:27–10:45, messianic confession to the Jerusalem entry;

and Joachim Gnilka also use stories about the disciples to establish textual sections.[45] Scholars often combine the summaries and disciple stories to structure the text (see 1.2.4.2.1).

According to Alfred Kuby, Jesus' relationship with his disciples is the chief theme of Mark. The major break is 8:21, where the incomprehension of the disciples ends, and their misunderstanding that the messiah must suffer begins. Kuby's rubric for 1:1–8:21 is "...how Satan's loss of power becomes open and how the disciples nevertheless do not recognize their rabbi as the Messiah." In 8:22ff., the disciples do not understand that the Messiah must suffer.[46]

In forming their outlines of the text, Hugh Anderson and David Blatherwick also concentrate on Jesus' relationship with his followers.[47] Anderson divides several sections, using Jesus'

10:46–13:36, Jesus as Son of David in Jerusalem; 14:1–16:8, Jesus' departure: passion, death, and resurrection.

[45]Delorme 1972, 31ff.: 1:16–6:6a, the call of the disciples (1:16–3:12, call of the four to the institution of the twelve, 3:13–6:6a, from the institution to their sending on mission); 6:6b–8:26, from the formation of the disciples' mission until Peter's profession of faith; 8:27–10:52, from the profession to the passion predictions; 11–16, revelation in Jerusalem (11:1–13:37, Jerusalem confrontation; 14:1–16:8, accomplishment of passion and resurrection predictions). Gnilka 1978, 31, 32: 1:1–15, Initium; 1:16–3:12, Jesus works authoritatively before the people; 3:13–6:6a, Jesus' teaching and miracles; 6:6b–8:26, restless wandering; 8:27–10:45, call to follow the cross; 10:46–13:37, Jesus' work in Jerusalem; 14:1–16:8 passion and victory. Key disciple stories are 1:16–20, 3:13–19; 6:6b–13; 8:27–30 and 10:46–52.

[46]Kuby 1958, 56, n. 11, for the break at 8:22 (and see also 1958, 58). Kuby 1958, 54ff. gives this outline: 1:1–8:21 (1:16–3:19, call of the disciples and healing of the sick; 3:20–6:29, "no unifying concept"; 6:30–8:21, bread miracles); 8:22ff. (8:22–10:45, eye opening and passion announcement; 10:46–13:37, entry into Jerusalem and claim of Lordship; 14:1–14:72 [or 15:47], passion and the disciples' failure).

[47]Anderson 1976, 58ff.: 1:1–15, Preface: ground of the gospel; 1:16–3:12, Jesus' work in Galilee and its consequences; 3:13–6:6, the family of Jesus and "outsiders"; 6:7–8:26, missionary outreach and the disciples' lack of

relationship with his family and disciples as guide. Blatherwick also uses Jesus' relationship with his family and "church" to structure Mark.

Étienne Trocmé outlines Mark, using themes describing Jesus' relationship with his disciples: 1:1–3:12, call to the disciples and people, and rupture with leaders; 3:13–6:13, Jesus gives privileges to the disciples; 6:14–8:29, role of the disciples; 8:22[sic]–10:52, the disciples have a long apprenticeship of faith and of renunciation before the mission can be fulfilled; 11:1–13:37, the disciples portrayed from the perspective of their participating in the eschatological triumph of the Messiah over the bad shepherds of Israel; 14:1–16:8, the passion. Trocmé finds "sandwich" texts at the beginning and end of his sections (the similar stories in 3:13–19 and 6:7–13; the repetitions in 6:14–16 and 8:27–30; and the healings in 8:22–26 and 10:46–52).[48]

1.2.4.1.2. Themes Concerning Jesus and the Other Dramatis Personae

Rather than concentrating primarily on Jesus and his disciples, some researchers look for themes which include Jesus' relationship with the main characters in the story. Bernhard

---

understanding; 8:27–10:52, the will of God for Jesus and his disciples: the way of suffering; 11:1–16:8, the passion and resurrection. Blatherwick 1970, 192: 1:1–3:6, the unexpected appearance of Jesus in Galilee and the consequences that flowed from it; 3:7–6:6a, the family of Jesus in the situation created by the Jews' rejection of him; 6:6b–9:29, the mission of the church in the situation created by the death of "Elijah" and the Messiah (the last two sections correspond respectively with ἵνα ὦσιν μετ' αὐτοῦ and ἵνα ἀποστέλλῃ αὐτοὺς κηρύσσειν (Mk 3:14)); 9:30–10:52, the Christian way of life in the period between Jesus' death and the coming of God's kingdom; 11:1–16:8, the impending destruction of the temple and full eschatological drama in light of Jesus' death and resurrection. See 1970, 187 on the "theological framework" of Mark.

[48]Trocmé 1963, 66, 67 and on the "sandwich" texts, see 1963, 65, 66. Trocmé 1963, 178 believes 14–16 was absent from the original text of Mark.

Weiss divides the text into ten sections which include the following references to other *dramatis personae* in the text: 1:14–45, Jesus' public appearance in Galilee; 2:1–3:6, opposition; 3:7–6:6, separation of the receptive and unreceptive; 6:14–8:26, Jesus in heightened activity among the people; 8:27–10:45, Jesus instructing the disciples.[49] Ferdinand Hahn divides the text into three major sections: 1:14–8:26, Jesus' activity among his people; 8:27–10:45, Jesus teaching his disciples; 10:46–16:8, last encounters with opponents and the death and resurrection of Jesus.[50] Karl L. Schmidt, Paul Feine, Henry B. Carré, Chalmer E. Faw, and Walter Grundmann also developed outlines that include many references to Jesus and the other *dramatis personae*.[51]

---

[49]Weiss 1889, 509–513: 1:2–8, the Baptist's appearance as fulfillment of OT prophecies; 1:9–13, Jesus' baptism and anointing with the Spirit—he is proclaimed Messiah; 1. 1:14–45; 2. 2:1–3:6; 3. 3:7–6:6 (3:13–19 and 6:7–13 are brackets); 4. 6:14–8:26; 5. 8:27–10:45; 6. 10:46–13:37; 7. 14–15, passion; 16:1–8, resurrection.

[50]Hahn 1963, 96.

[51]Schmidt 1919, XIff.: 1:1–13, John the Baptist and Jesus; 1:14–45, Jesus' work in Galilee; 2:1–3:6, Jesus' conflicts with the leaders; 3:7–6:13, Jesus and the people; 6:14–8:26, Jesus outside Galilee in Gentile lands; 8:27–10:45, Jesus and his disciples, the passion draws near; 10:46–13:37, Jesus' last activity near and in Jerusalem; 14ff., Jesus' suffering and death. Feine 1923, 24: 1:1–13; 1:14–45, Jesus' appearance in Capernaum; 2:1–3:6, opposition of the Pharisees; 3:7–4:34, incomprehension of the Pharisees, of his family, and some of the people; 4:35–6:6, Jesus' activity from the point of view of faith and unfaith; 6:7–8:26, height of Galilee activity; 8:27–10:52, teaching, revelation of Jesus as Messiah, transfiguration, and passion predictions; 11–16, Jerusalem period (11–12, arguments with leaders; 13, teaching of parousia; 14–16, passion). Carré (1928, 105ff.) gives an outline of Mark based on two conflicting political and religious forces (1928, 126): popularity and opposition. 1:1–20, introduction; 1:21–45, popularity; 2:1–3:6, opposition; 3:7–8:26, Jesus' vain endeavors to avoid the consequences of the two forces he has set going; 8:27–16:8, Jesus withdraws from the territory (Galilee) where popularity and opposition are out of control and abandons the public ministry—the ministry to the twelve in preparation for the end and

30   *The Structure and Persuasive Power of Mark*

All the scholars in this section use themes about Jesus and his relationship with the disciples or other characters in the story to outline Mark. Researchers who use themes about the identity of Jesus to structure the text are also numerous. Their outlines can therefore be called "christological."

1.2.4.1.3. Christological Themes

Various characteristics of Jesus' identity correspond to different text sequences in the Markan narrative in the christological outlines. Each text sequence is identified by a different nuance in the text's picture of Jesus.

Rudolf Grob uses themes that concentrate on the "Messianic Secret" in Mark. He divides the text at 8:27 and describes the first unit as the "Secret of the hidden Messiah openly revealed." The second unit (8:27–16:20) is the "Messiah openly revealed." He further divides the text, using similar christological themes.[52]

---

culminating tragedy of the cross. Faw 1957, 23: 1, Jesus begins a popular ministry; 2:1–3:6, opposition; 3:7–35, Jesus appoints the disciples—the true family of God; 4:1–34, he teaches in parables; 4:35–7:37, (8:1–26) vigorous wonder working with amazed response; 8:27–10:45, way of cross and resurrection for master and disciples; 10:46–12:44, In Jerusalem: popularity and opposition as he teaches with a parable; 13, he teaches alertness for end signs; 14:1–15:41, he is arrested, tried and killed; 15:42–16:8, burial and resurrection. Grundmann 1959, vff.: 1:1–13, antecedents; 1:14–45, beginnings of Jesus' activity; 2:1–3:6, Jesus' encounter with opponents; 3:7–4:34, Jesus, the disciples, and the people; 4:35–5:43, The Lord who is over all; 6:1–44, end of the Galilee activity; 6:45–8:26, loyalty to incomprehending disciples, break with leaders, and turn to the Gentiles; 8:27–10:52, passion announcement and instruction in discipleship; 11:1–13:35, last activity in Jerusalem; 14:1–16:8, passion.

[52]Grob 1965, 353ff. 1:1–8:26 (1:1–4:34, revelation of the Son of God and Son of Man, Jesus' giving of self and word in salvific deed; 4:35–8:26, Jesus, Lord of the cosmic powers of the sea, demons and death, reveals himself in his giving of self in bread and table fellowship); 8:27–16:20, (8:27–13:34, revelation of Christ in the prediction of his way to the passion, death, and the

M. J. Lagrange sees changes in themes concerning the Gospel as providing the delimitations for the units of Mark.[53] The introduction is 1:1-13, with the rest of the outline as follows: 1:14-8:26, gospel of the Kingdom; 8:27-13:37, preparation for the future gospel; 14-16, passion and resurrection (the grand act and the main theme of the future gospel). Lagrange believes 8:27 is a *peripeteia* that divides the text into two main sections: in the first section Jesus preaches the gospel; in the second, Jesus becomes the object of the gospel.[54]

Changes in textual themes concerning Jesus' identity also form the nucleus of Dieter Lührmann's outline of the text. He looks for "seams" in the text, such as the geographical break at 11:1.[55] Lührmann sees no clear break in the textual material beginning with 1:16 and extending to 11:1.[56] Nevertheless, he delimits the text into the following units: 1:1-15, introduction; 1:16-4:34, Jesus' authority in word and deed (in Galilee); 4:35-8:26, a unit dominated by the christological question ("who is he?") with a spatial center in the sea and boat motifs; 8:27-10:52, an answer to 4:41 with christology as the theme—the "way" is a dominant spatial motif; 11:1-12:44, encounters with Jewish groups; 13, the end time is the theme; 14:1-16:8, the passion story.[57] Although they delimit the text in different ways, Léonard Ramaroson, David J. Hawkin, Gottfried Rau (Jesus' mission), and Petr Pokorný use christological themes to outline Mark.[58] Maurice Goguel gives a variation on the christological

---

completion of his kingdom; 14:1-16:20, the fulfillment of the revelation of Christ; betrayal, trial, passion, death, and resurrection of the Lord).

[53]Lagrange 1947, lxivff.

[54]Lagrange 1947, lxiv.

[55]Lührmann 1987, 23. (For his skeptical comments concerning Markan structure see above, note 3.)

[56]Lührmann 1987, 45.

[57]Lührmann 1987, 23, 32, 45, 93, 141, 185, 229.

[58]Ramaroson 1975, 233: 1:1-13, introduction; 1:14-20, introduction to part 1; 1. 1:21-8:26, Jesus appears as the powerful and resisted Messiah (1:21-3:6, when he begins in Capernaum; 3:7-4:34, when he commissions the twelve;

approach by dividing the text using the concept "gospel," with 1:14–8:26 being the "gospel of the kingdom;" and 8:27–10:52 comprising the "gospel of the Messiah."[59]

4:35–6:6a, when he does miracles on the sea and environs; 6:6b–7:23, when he sends his disciples on mission; 7:24–8:26, when he withdraws to Gentile territory); 2. 8:27–15:47, Jesus is the Messiah who accepts death (8:27–9:29, he must be put to death—he reveals it first in a pagan area: Caesarea; 9:30–50, he reveals the same thing in the holy land; 10:1–11:25, from Galilee to Jerusalem he seeks the predestined violent death; 11:27–12:46, he provokes his enemies; 13, speaking with friends; 14–15, Jesus put to death); 16:1–20, epilogue. Hawkin 1977, 108ff.: 1:1–13, introduction; 1:14–8:21, the mysterious person of Jesus revealed to "the many" (1:14–3:12, Galilee preaching; 3:13–6:34, widening of ministry and Jesus' rejection foreshadowed; 6:35–8:21, Jesus the bread of life for Jews and Gentiles); 8:22–16:8, the mysterious person of Jesus revealed to the disciples in esoteric teaching and action (8:22–10:52, the way of the cross; 11:1–13:44, ministry in Jerusalem; 13, apocalyptic discourse; 14:1–16:8, passion and resurrection). Hawkin (1977, 11) notes the motif of disciple incomprehension in 6:34–8:21 and 8:22–10:52. Rau 1985, 2036, 2075ff.: 1:1, superscript; 1:2–15, prologue; 1:16–3:6, beginning of Jesus' mission in Galilee; 3:7–6:6a, the new community of salvation as *familia Dei* (family of God) and the secret of God's kingdom; 6:7–8:26, the continuation and expansion of the mission to Israel; 8:27–10:52, mission in signs of the coming kingdom of God; 11:1–13:37, the coming of the Lord to his temple; 14:1–16:8, the martyrdom of the king of Israel at Passover. Pokorný 1985, 2004–6: 1:1, superscript: beginning of the gospel; 1:2–13, prologue— after me comes one who is stronger: the Baptist, baptism and temptation of Jesus; 1:14–3:6, new teaching with authority in Galilee; 3:7–6:29, "who is this" (in Galilee and the first journey among the Gentiles); 6:30–8:26, And all became full (in Galilee and on the second journey among the Gentiles); 8:27–10:52, "This is my beloved Son"—Christology and community instruction (in Caesarea Philippi and on the way to Jerusalem); 11:1–13:37, my house shall be a house of prayer for all peoples (Jerusalem); 14:1–15:47, Truly this man was God's Son (Jerusalem); 16:1–8, epilogue.

[59]Goguel 1909, 23ff.: 1:1–13, introduction; 1:14–8:26, (1:14–45, first success of Jesus' preaching; 2:1–3:6, conflicts with the Pharisees; 3:7–19, healings; 3:20–35, conflicts with the Pharisees; 4:1–34, parables; 4:35–6:6a, Jesus leaving

Mark: Structure, Messianic Secret, and Genre

These approaches correspond to what Lohmeyer would call the "inner" aspect of the text of Mark. They illuminate the complex relationships between Jesus, the disciples, and the other characters in the text. The christological outlines all illuminate the power and richness of the portrait of Jesus' identity in Mark. Given the depth of Mark's portrait of Jesus and the other *dramatis personae*, one would not expect such outlines to isolate the same features in the text as being structurally significant. The outlines "justify themselves" by pointing to important characteristics of the Markan narrative. Outlines that do not concentrate primarily upon themes but upon patterns and repetitions in the text can, for want of a better term, be called "literary."

1.2.4.2. Literary Methods

"Literary outlines" look for features internal to the text of Mark that correspond to the structure of the text. These outlines use characteristics of the text such as summaries of Jesus' activities, groups of identical kinds of stories, and other various kinds of repetitions. Literary methods are synchronic because they do not attempt to distinguish different historical levels in the text for the purposes of making the outline. They also concentrate on the text of Mark, and so remain on the level of *parole*.

1.2.4.2.1. Summaries

Some of the summaries of Jesus' activity have often been considered structural features of the text, that is, features that mark breaks in the text. Scholars combine the summaries with other features of Mark to build an outline. To use summaries as structural indicators one has to claim, as does Friedrich G. Lang,

---

Galilee to act in Gadara— a pagan land...; 6:6b–30, John the Baptist; 6:31–8:26, stories...); 8:27–10:52 (only with his disciples); 11:1–13:37, Entry in Jerusalem until the plot against Jesus; 14:1–16:8, From the plot of the Jews to the empty tomb.

that they establish breaks in the text.⁶⁰ C. H. Dodd originally used a few of the summaries to establish an ancient itinerary of Jesus using Acts 10:37–41 and 13:23–31; but his attempt is at least questionable, given the fact that he considers so few of the summaries in Mark.⁶¹ I. de la Potterie saw a summary statement followed by a story about the disciples as a literary feature that provides breaks in the text and indicates progressions of action. After defining the first major unit as 1:14–8:26 (the mystery of Jesus as Messiah progressively revealed), he isolates three crucial summaries (1:14–15; 3:7–12; 6:6b), each of which is followed by disciple stories (1:16–20; 3:13–19; 6:7–13). This results in the following divisions: 1:14–3:6; 3:7–6:6a; and 6:6b–8:26. His major divisions (1:14–8:26 and 8:27–16:8 [mystery of the Son of Man]) are thematic. He divides the second large division using different criteria (8:27–10:52 is a unit because of the three passion

---

⁶⁰Lang 1977, 7: 1:14ff. and 3:7–12 are "zäsurbildende Summarien" (because of prior scholars' opinions). Lang's (1977, 12) structure is: 1:1–13, Prologue; 1:14–3:6 Jesus' first appearance in Galilee; 3:7–8:21, the sea of Galilee as the center of Jesus' salvific activity (3:13–6:6a, the sea as the center of action; 6:6b–8:21, widened radius of action); 8:22–10:45, revelation of Jesus' being and way during the journey; 10:46–13:37, the Jerusalem temple as center of the conflict; 14:1–16:8, Jesus' passion during Passover. Lang also uses stichometry (1977, 11ff.) in an unconvincing way (see Koch 1983, 160, n. 18: his scenic units such as 2:13–28 are arbitrary, and he (occasionally) does not include such scenes as 3:7–12 in his enumeration of scenic units). He (1977, 10, 11) uses the enumeration to establish the most emphasized scene (5 or 7 scenes in each Text Part). Lang primarily uses scenic markers to do this outline, but he fails to include 11:1–16:8 as a unit in his outline even though he recognizes the Jerusalem marker (1977, 3), and he fails to include 1:14–8:21 as a section of his outline even though he recognizes the "Galilee" marker (1977, 7).

⁶¹C. H. Dodd 1932, 398: 1:14–16, 1:21–22, 1:39, 2:13, 3:7b–19, 4:32–34, 6:7, 12–13, 6:30 appealing to K. L. Schmidt. Charles W. Hedrick (1984, 291) notes the discrepancy between the lists in Dodd and Schmidt.

predictions, and so forth).⁶² X. Leon-Dufour, J. Radermakers, and Eduard Schweizer all use the summaries in a similar fashion.⁶³ Norman Perrin argues that summaries combined with a

---

⁶²De la Potterie 1966, 137ff.: 8:27–16:8, mystery of the Son of Man (8:27–10:52, way of the Son of Man [which he divides by the three passion predictions, disciple misunderstanding, and Jesus' teaching of the disciples]; 11:1–13:37, revelation in Jerusalem and definitive rupture with the Jews; 14:1–16:8, completion of the mystery— passion and resurrection of the Son of Man).

⁶³Leon-Dufour 1959, 210ff.: 1:1–13, introduction; 1:14–8:30, mystery of the Messiah (1:14–3:6, Jesus and the people, 3:7–6:6, Jesus and his own, 6:6–8:30, Jesus and his disciples); 8:31–16:8, the mystery of the Son of Man (8:31–10:52, the way of the Son of Man, 11:1–13:37, judgment of Jerusalem, 14:1–16:8, the passion and the resurrection, 16:9–20, appendix). Schweizer 1964, 342ff. and 1983, 214–15 (where Schweizer notes that his first three sections allegedly end with a rejection of Jesus): 1:1–13, beginning; 1:14–3:6, Jesus' authority and the Pharisees' blindness; 3:7–6:6a, Jesus' activity in parables and signs and the world's blindness; 6:6b–8:21, Jesus' activity including the Gentiles and the disciples' blindness; 8:22–10:52, Jesus' revelation in unhidden speech and the disciples' following; 11:1–16:8, passion and resurrection of the Son of Man. Radermakers 1974, 235ff. uses the following criteria: six double summaries of Jesus and his disciples (1:14–20, 3:7–19, 6:6b–13, 8:31–9:1, 10:32–45, 14:1–11); six sections each with an inclusio (e.g., 1:21 and 3:1–6 are two synagogue stories on the Sabbath; 3:20ff. and 6:1–6a are two stories about Jesus' family); and geographical references (e.g., 3:7–6:6a, the sea of Galilee and the boat). His outline: 1:1, beginning of the gospel; 1:2–13, John the Baptist, etc.; 1. 1:14–3:6, the kingdom of God that approaches, powerful teaching and controversies; 2. 3:7–6:6a, Jesus' family, the kingdom in parables and opposition to the forces of evil; 3. 6:6b–8:30, the question about Jesus and the bread section; 4. 8:31–10:31, the way of the Son of Man and the disciples to enter the kingdom; 5. 10:32–12:44, the judgment of Jerusalem by the Son of David; (13 is not included as a major section— Jesus' discourse on vigilance); 6. 14:1–15:47, the judgment of Jesus, blasphemy of the Son of Man, and recognition of the Son of God. 16:1–8, the empty tomb; 16:9–20, supplements.

geographical change are the major structural indicator in Mark.[64] In a variation on this argument, Leander Keck claims that a disciple story begins each section. The sections end with a summary of Jesus' activity.[65]

Rudolf Pesch uses a number of criteria (collections of material, spatial and temporal changes, standardizing composition, different story types, leading concepts, "Jesus" in the introductory sentence of a story) to structure the text. He also uses the summary at 3:7–12 to claim that 3:7 "clearly" begins a new section.[66] Interestingly enough, stichometry (estimating the number of letters in a line and the number of lines on a page of manuscript) plays little role in his commentary, compared to the major role it played in his earlier book when he tried to prove

---

[64]Perrin 1974c, 147 notes geographical shifts and summaries at 1:14, 3:7, and 6:6b: 1:1–13, introduction; 1:16–3:6, Jesus' authority in word and deed; 3:13–6:6a, Jesus as Son of God and rejected by his people; 6:7–8:21, Jesus as Son of God and misunderstood by his own disciples; 8:27–10:45, Christology and Christian discipleship in light of the passion; 11:1–12:44, the days in Jerusalem prior to the passion; 13:5b–37, apocalyptic discourse; 14:13–16:8, passion narrative— the texts inbetween are transitional summaries, stories, or introductions. Hedrick 1984, 310 cites four other summaries and geographical shifts (e.g., 4:33–34 and the shift in 4:35–36, 5:21, 9:30, and 10:1).

[65]Keck 1966, 355, 362ff.: 1:1–15, Introduction; 1:16–3:12, the work of Jesus and diverse responses to it; 3:13–6:7a; 6:7b–8:26, the failure of the disciples to understand. Heinrich Baarlink (Baarlink 1977, 75) erroneously depicts Keck as outlining all of Mark. Baarlink's outline (same method) is: (Baarlink 1977, 88ff.) 1:1–8:26 (sections beginning at 1:12–20; 3:6–19; 6:1–6:13); 8:27–10:52; 11:1–16:8.

[66]Pesch 1976, 32ff.: 1:1, superscript, 1:1–15, prologue; 1:1–3:6, Jesus' powerful entrance; 3:7–6:29, Jesus' teaching and miracles and their decisive effect; 6:30–8:26, Jesus' turning to the Jews and Gentiles; 8:27 (2nd half of the Gospel), 8:27–10:52, passion destiny of the Son of Man and the conditions of discipleship; 11:1–12:44; (13); 14:1–16:8. Pesch does not integrate his admission that 1:1–8:26 is the first half of the Gospel into his outline (1976, 39). He also does not include thematic titles for each major section.

by stichometry that Mark 13 was not part of the original text of Mark.[67]

Charles W. Hedrick wrote a searching analysis of the claim that certain summaries delimit sections of the Markan text. Hedrick attempts to prove that, with the exception of 10:1, the summaries have no evident contact with pericopes that precede and follow the summary in question. He concedes that 10:1 provides a broader literary structure for the unit in question. Hedrick compares the Markan summaries with those in Philostratus's *Vita Apollonii* to reach his results. The summaries give the story an expanded setting and lengthened time frame, but do not structure literary units.[68] To my knowledge, this is one of the few contributions in the literature that actually attempts to evaluate the methodology of using summaries to build an outline of Mark. Scholars (such as Pesch above) simply assume that a given summary provides a clear "break" in the text without giving a clear analysis of the concept "break."[69] Other features in the text of Mark have been taken to be indicative of the structure.

1.2.4.2.2. Literary Forms and Types of Stories

According to a number of scholars, combinations of identical kinds of stories constitute a structural principle in Mark. Pesch includes "collections of material" and "different story types" as important criteria for delimiting the text.[70] Ernest Best makes liberal use of these criteria in his attempt to structure Mark. For example, 2:1–3:6 is "the hostility of Jewish leaders." In other

---

[67]Pesch 1968, 55ff. using Nestle[25]. See criticism of his attempt to expunge Mk 13 using stichometry in Koch 1983, 166, n. 18.

[68]Hedrick 1984, 298, 309–311. For a discussion of the issue of summaries in structuring the Gospel of Matthew, see Hellholm's forthcoming article on Mt, section 3.2.2.2.

[69]See Pesch and Lang in this section.

[70]See the description of Pesch's approach in 1.2.4.2.1.

words, this is a group of stories that express hostility.[71] Mark 4 is a unit because it contains parables. 4:35–5:43 comprises four works and so is a unit (miracle stories).[72]

Austin Farrer looks for repetitions of various sorts of stories in Mark to structure the text. He delimits five cycles, with three formal elements in each.[73] Farrer makes comparisons of such repetitions as the call of the four (1:16–20), the call of the four extended (1:36–39), and the call of Levi (2:13–14).[74] Each of his cycles contains similar claims about repetitions in Mark.

On the continuum between "inner" and "outer" criteria, there are methods that rely on indications in the text that signal changes in scene (time, place, and characters). Thematic methods rely on "inner" criteria. Methods that use literary features such as "summaries" or "story types" are less content-oriented than thematic approaches because they rely on literary form, and not just the ideas that the text expresses. Methods that use changes in scene are even less oriented to content than literary approaches.

---

[71]Best 1965, 116–117.

[72]Best 1965, 118. Best delimits these Text Parts (1965, 112–125): 1:16–39, the new community; 1:40–45; 2:1–3:6; 3:13–19; 3:20–35; 4:1–34; 4:35–5:43; 6:14–10:52, Jesus on the move (6:14–29; 6:30–7:37; 8:1–26; 8:27–10:52, the journey to Jerusalem); 12:13–40; 14–15, passion narrative.

[73]Farrer 1954, 222: 1:1–15 exordium; A) first cycle with first handful of healings, 1:16–34, 1:35–2:12, 2:13–3:12; B) second cycle with second handful of healings, 3:13–6:6, 6:7–7:37; 8:1–26; C) third cycle with "two healings over," 8:27–9:29; 9:30–10:31, 10:32–10:52; D) fourth cycle with Jerusalem ministry, 11:1–19, 11:20–13:2, 13:3–14:11; E) fifth cycle with Passion, 14:12 (14:12–14:31, 14:32–15:21, 15:22) 16:8. In spite of all the scholarly critique of Farrer (e.g., Trocmé 1963, 62; Keck 1966, 353), he does find many interrelationships within the text—which is precisely Keck's own method in establishing an introduction to Mark (see below, n. 79). For a sympathetic treatment, see Harry Sawyerr 1961, 285ff.

[74]Farrer 1954, 201.

1.2.4.3. Markers

Scholars who use the geographical and temporal indications in the text to build an outline are numerous. The fundamental spatial movement of the narrative begins with the introduction, proceeds to Galilee, then to Judea, and finally to Jerusalem. The details of the geographical approach to the problems of a Markan outline are disputed, but the general approach is clear. It relies on a synchronic interpretation of the text on the level of *parole* (other texts are not used). This approach makes almost no use of thematic considerations for delineating the structure of the text. It uses indications of scene changes or "markers" to delimit the sections of their outlines. A "marker" is a signal that enables a hearer or receiver to structure a communication into its parts during the reception of the communication. "Markers" in this section include indicators in the text that signal the presence of a change in the narrative. Markers identify "outer" or "surface level" characteristics of the text. They include words in the text that indicate changes in the *dramatis personae*, narrative geography (or space), and narrative time (to be further discussed below in 2.4.2). A change in geography, for example, is a marker because it indicates that the narrative changes focus. "Themes" are, on the other hand, oriented more to the content of the narrative (such as christology). Gerhard Hartmann first used the word "marker" (*Merkmal*) to refer to the appearance of Jesus' name.[75]

Hartmann argues that when Jesus' name appears in the beginning of a new story (1:1; 1:9; 1:14; 3:7; 6:30; 8:27; 9:2; 10:32; 12:41; 14:53; and 15:1), it marks divisions in the text.[76] He admits 5:41 is an exception and does not get into the textual criticism of 12:41. Several occurrences of Jesus' name serve as proems

---

[75] Hartmann 1936, 97.
[76] Hartmann 1936, 55.

(prologues) to one of the seven major sections into which he divides the text.[77]

The "introduction" of the text usually comprises the first thirteen or fifteen verses in the text.[78] The category "introduction" remains fuzzy, and the delimitation of this section of the text is usually more intuitive than that of the other Text Parts.[79] Karl A. Credner finds three sections in the first thirteen

---

[77]Hartmann 1936, 61ff., 88–90. 1:1–8, introduction; 1:9–3:6, the appearance of Jesus of Nazareth; 3:7–6:29, Jesus and his disciples; 6:30–8:26, insufficient success; 8:27–10:32, [sic] the messiah comes to the fore—with the teaching of suffering and service; 10:32–12:40, successes of the "serving;" 12:41–14:52, Jesus—teacher of the necessity of giving up everything for people; 14:53–16:8, the destruction of Jesus' person and the beginning of the triumph. He divides each section into two smaller Text Parts (e.g., 6:30–7:23, the behavior of Jesus; 7:24–8:26, Jesus withdraws) using "conceptual brackets" (1936, 77). For example, 6:30 begins with outer good works and ends with inner evil works (7:23). In 7:24 Jesus removes himself temporarily from his people and in 8:23, 26 he removes himself from his people.

[78]Johann Bengel 1855, 166 and most of the scholars to be discussed below who use geography opt for 1:1–13. Wellhausen (1911, 38) is a rare exception (of those using the geographical method) who opts for 1:1–15.

[79]Keck 1966, 359–62 and Lührmann 1987, 32 (who do not primarily use the spatial markers to structure Mk) argue for their delimitation of the introduction (1:1–15). Lührmann argues 1) that only by binding Jesus' proclamation with the Baptist does it become clear that the beginning of the Gospel is not simply a picture of John who via Jesus' baptism is bound up with the gospel. 2) If the weight of this beginning switches to 1:14ff., then the beginning is not a mere prologue to Jesus' own gospel, but an interpretation of the entire history of Jesus—a key to the gospel. Keck argues 1) that the first fifteen verses are a genuine prologue to the entire text because 1:14ff. complements the title (1:1) and rounds out the whole introduction. 2) The relationship of Jesus and the Baptist establishes the introduction: a) παραδοθῆναι is a "theological word" and not primarily "biographical" and puts Jesus' preaching in a relationship with John's "divinely willed deathward work"; b) Jesus is stronger than John because of his exorcisms and so forth; Mark sees Jesus' healing and exorcism as identical with his

verses: 1:1–3, apologetic remark; 1:4–11, baptism; 1:12–13, temptation. Here markers indicating changes in the characters are presupposed (John and Jesus in baptism; Jesus' temptation). Credner is an exception to the general tendency to see the first thirteen or fifteen verses as a unified beginning.[80] Hedrick sees 1:1 as the *incipit* (initial sentence), and 1:2–14a as "John and Jesus at the Jordan in the wilderness." He uses a spatial and a character marker.[81]

The Galilee episode that follows has provoked wide divergence of opinion as regards its delimitation. Hedrick has tried to be most precise about the spatial markers: 1:14b–3:36, after John, Jesus preaches in Galilee; 4:1–34, parables; 4:35–5:25, other side of Galilee; 5:21–7:23, Jesus returns to Galilee; 7:24–31, Tyre and Sidon; 7:31–8:12, return to Galilee; 8:13–9:29, trip to the tetrarchy of Philip; 9:30–52, return to Galilee.[82] Others choose to see the text as more unified. One of the crucial points of debate is whether 8:27 constitutes a break in the geography (a new spatial marker). Among those who use spatial markers in their outlines and who see 8:27 as a major break is Dietrich-Alex Koch. He argues that 1:14–8:26 comprises a Text Part: Jesus' activity in Galilee.[83] Koch sees no basic change in place in 7:24ff.,

---

preaching (1:27, 8:11–13); Mark emphasizes Jesus as teacher and preacher (1:14ff.); therefore, Jesus is stronger than John because of his preaching. Consequently 1:14ff. should be tied to 1:1–13 since it fulfills John's word "stronger" which he utters about Jesus; c) εὐαγγέλιον is used in victory contexts in Hellenistic literature (5th century BCE–3rd century CE); Jesus' encounter with Satan is a text in which Jesus is victorious; therefore the εὐαγγέλιον in 1:14ff. is bound to 1:12ff. and should be considered part of the introduction.

[80]Credner 1836, 109.

[81]Hedrick 1983, 257.

[82]Hedrick 1983, 257ff. 267, 268. (He could have entitled, using a spatial marker, 4:1–34 as "by the sea: parables.")

[83]Koch 1983, 148–153. Koch 1983, 154ff. uses themes and not spatial markers to divide his 1:14–8:26 section: 1:14–3:6, Jesus' authority in word and deed; 3:7–6:6a, lack of understanding and unfaith concerning Jesus'

42   *The Structure and Persuasive Power of Mark*

and claims that Mark did not fundamentally distinguish between the different banks of Galilee.[84] 3:7 gives the clearest picture of Mark's geographical concepts, where, for example, the Decapolis is not mentioned as being separate from Galilee. 5:1 does not

---

miracles and teaching; 6:6b–8:26, further deeds (miracles) and words of Jesus. Arguments for 1:14–3:6: a) 3:6 is a climax from 2:1ff.; b) the above compositional balance of miracles (1:21–45) and teaching (2:1–3:6); c) 1:22 and 1:28 are redactional and point to the theme (the above title of 1:14–3:6) which binds the unit, and; d) 1:14ff. and 1:16ff. are a summary and disciple scene as are 3:7–12 and 3:13–19. Arguments for 3:7–6:6a: a) argument "d," above; b) Jesus' rejection in Nazareth (6:1–6a) is a break; c) there is a binding theme with Jesus' kin, home town, and disciples rejecting him (3:20, 30ff., 6:1–6:a, 4:13, 4:40) (this theme is the title of the Text Part); d) compositional balance: 3:20ff.–4:34 include teaching and 4:35–5:43 includes miracles; 6:1–6a binds the teaching and miracle sections together (6:2 σοφία and δυνάμεις). Arguments for 6:6b–8:26: 6:6b is a summary followed by a disciples' scene. Koch finds no break or new theme in this section. Due to the compositional balance of 1:14ff. and 3:7ff., Mark had to put extra miracle stories and so forth here (since he could not put them after 8:27). Rudolf Knopf, Hans Lietzmann, and Heinrich Wienel 1949, 121, 122: 1, first appearance in Capernaum; 2–7, Jesus' activity in Galilee; 7:24–8:26, Leaving Galilee; northern journey, etc.; 8:27–9:50, second northern journey to Caesarea Philippi, confession of Peter, etc.; 10, journey to Jerusalem, etc.; 11–13, Jerusalem days including the little apocalypse; 14–16, passion; 16:1–8, empty tomb (K/L/W use a content approach to divide their Mk 2–7: 2:1–3:6, controversies with the Pharisees; 3:7–32, call of disciples, etc.; 4, parables; 5, big miracles; 6, Jesus in Nazareth, etc.; 7, controversy with the Pharisees). Cranfield 1959, 14, 15: 1:1–13, beginning; 1:14–3:6, beginning of the Galilean ministry; 3:7–6:13, later stages of the Galilee ministry; 6:14–8:26, Jesus goes outside of Galilee. Bas van Iersel 1982, 120, 124, 125 and 1983, 45ff. sees a major break at 8:27, as does Augustine Stock 1985, 295 who summarizes some recent work. William L. Lane 1974, 23, 30: 1:14–3:6, initial phase of the Galilee ministry; 3:7–6:13, later phases of the ministry in Galilee; 6:14–8:30, withdrawal beyond Galilee.

[84]Koch 1983, 150, 151.

inform the reader that Jesus is no longer in Galilee.⁸⁵ The ὁδός in 8:27, Koch then argues, delimits the second major section of the text: 8:27–10:52—Jesus' way to Jerusalem.⁸⁶ The word ὁδός is a spatial marker that appears for the first time in conjunction with a mention of Jesus (a character marker).

Most of the others who work with the spatial markers to structure the text do not see 8:27 as a major break in the text.⁸⁷ They approach the "Galilee" period in diverse ways. At one end of the spectrum, they depict the Galilee activity as a unit (which they may divide into further Text Parts).⁸⁸ At the other end of the spectrum, they divide the Galilee period into different Text Parts.⁸⁹ Johann Bengel, for example, sees 1:14–9:50 as the Galilee

---

⁸⁵Koch 1983, 152ff. on the Decapolis and Mark's lack of information on it. See further 1983, 151 on 3:7ff.

⁸⁶Koch 1983, 147–149 argues for 8:27–10:52 as a unit, but includes it in a larger section 8:27–16:8 (Jesus in Jerusalem) in 1983, 158. He does not show how the markers establish the larger section. Cranfield 1959, 14 also has 8:27–10:52 as the "way to Jerusalem" as does van Iersel 1982, 124, 125, 134 and Stock 1985, 295. Lane 1974, 30 has 8:31–10:52 as the "journey to Jerusalem."

⁸⁷See the following notes for their structures.

⁸⁸Credner 1836, 109: 1:14–9:50, Jesus appears in Galilee as the messiah. Swete 1913, lviii: 1:14–9:50, ministry in Galilee. Robert H. Lightfoot 1950, 9: Mk 1–9, the Lord's work in northern Palestine. F. C. Grant 1951, 645, 646: 1:14–9:50, Jesus in Galilee (1:14–5:45, about the sea of Galilee; 6:1–9:50, wider journeys). Everett F. Harrison 1964, 177: 1:14–9:50, the Galilee ministry. Willi Marxsen 1969, 56: 1–9, Galilee. Eduard Lohse 1972, 83: 1–10, Jesus' activity in Galilee (Lohse then divides this unit into fourteen sections including 8:27–10:52 by using form and content). Ludger Schenke 1986, 64, 67: 1:14–10:52 (A-1. 1:14–3:6; A-2. 3:7–6:13; looking back—6:14–29; B-1. 6:30–8:26; B-2. 8:27–10:52).

⁸⁹C. G. Montefiore 1909, xiii: 1:14–7:23, ministry in Galilee and the territory of Philip; 7:24–9:50, Jesus' journeys into Tyrian territory and then through the Decapolis and Philip's territory, back to Galilee. Wellhausen 1911, 38: 1–5, Jesus teaches and heals in Capernaum and the surrounding area; 6–10, restless wandering in the territory of Philip and the Decapolis

section.⁹⁰ Erich Klostermann outlines 1:14–5:43 as "Jesus' work in Galilee," and 6:1–10:52 as "Jesus traveling." He subdivides the latter Text Part into 6:1–8:26 ("Jesus traveling around Galilee") and 8:27–10:52 ("Jesus on the way to Jerusalem").⁹¹ Mk 8:27 does not serve for either scholar as a major text break (at least on the first level of their outlines).

Mk 10:1 constitutes a break for a number of scholars who generally see Mark 10 as "Jesus in Judea." Rudolf Knopf, Hans Lietzmann, and Heinrich Wienel entitle Mk 10 as "travel to Jerusalem."⁹² The others who do not think that Mk 10 is a

---

and Jesus' journeying through Galilee and Perea to Jerusalem. Friedrich Hauck 1931, 6: 1:14–6:6a, Jesus' activity in Galilee; 6:6b–10:45, Jesus travels outside Galilee. Joseph Huby 1948, 469, 470: 1:14–7:23, Jesus' ministry in Galilee; 7:24–10:52, Jesus' journeys outside Galilee. Günther Dehn 1953, 9, 10: 1:14–6:13, Jesus in Galilee; 6:14–10:52, Jesus traveling (6:14–8:26, in Galilee and the northern border regions; 8:27–10:52, on the way to Jerusalem). Josef Schmid 1958, 7, 8: 1:14–6:6a, Jesus' activity in Galilee; 6:6b–10:52, Jesus' restless journeying. Alfred Wikenhauser 1959, 114, 115: 1:14–6:6a, Jesus' activity in Galilee; 6:6b–10:52, Jesus' restless journeying. Werner G. Kümmel 1966, 61, 62: 1:14–5:43, Jesus in Galilee; 6:1–9:50, Jesus' journeys inside and outside Galilee. Helmut Merkel 1978, 16: 1:14–5:43, Jesus in Galilee; 6:1–9:50, Jesus traveling inside and outside Galilee.

⁹⁰Bengel 1855, 166, 167: 1:14–9:50, In Galilee (he uses temporal markers to divide the unit—1:14–6:13, John arrested; 6:14–8:26, John murdered; 8:27–9:50, Jesus, Son of God, recognized).

⁹¹Klostermann 1971, 1. Klostermann (1971, 54 on 6:1–8:26) says that 6:6 is not the climax of 3:7ff. Klostermann notes that 1:41–5:43 with its four content groups (1:14–41, Capernaum, 2:1–3:35, conflicts; 4:1–34, parables; 4:35–5:43, big miracles) and 11:1–15:39 are clear Text Parts with 6:1–10:52 not being so clear.

⁹²Knopf, Lietzmann, and Wienel 1949, 121, 122. Credner 1936, 109: 10:1–52, Jesus travels to the Passover feast in Jerusalem. Montefiore 1909, xiv: 10:1–52, Jesus on the way to Jerusalem. Swete 1913, lvii: 10:1–52, period between Jerusalem and Galilee. Lightfoot 1950, 9: Mk 10, incidents between the departure from Galilee and arrival in Jerusalem, the capital. Kümmel 1966, 62: 10:1–52, Jesus' journey to Jerusalem. Marxsen 1969, 56: Mk 10, transition

separate unit usually combine it with the Galilee period.[93] Those who detect a major break at 8:27 often delimit 8:27–10:52 as a journey to Jerusalem.[94] As an exception to the rule, Bengel, F. C. Grant, and Everett F. Harrison combine Mk 10 with the Jerusalem period. Grant claims that 10:1–15:47 is "Jesus in Jerusalem," and Harrison argues that 10:1–16:8 is devoted to "ministry in Judea and Jerusalem."[95]

With the exception of Bengel, Grant, and Harrison, all the researchers discussed in this section believe that 11:1 is a break in the text (on the first level of their outlines).[96] The structure of the Jerusalem period provokes some disagreement. Those who concentrate on spatial markers tend to see one major Text Part for the Jerusalem period. Bengel, for example, puts under 11:1–16:20 the rubric "Jerusalem."[97] Those who are willing to use

---

(from Galilee to Jerusalem). Merkel 1978, 16: 10:1–52, Jesus' journey to Jerusalem. Hedrick 1983, 268: 10:1–11:10, Journey to Jerusalem.

[93] Those combining 10 with the Galilee period include: Lohse 1972, 83; Schenke 1986, 64, 67; and Huby, Dehn, Hauck, Schmid, Wellhausen and Wikenhauser in n. 89, above.

[94] Scholars claiming that 8:27 is a major break and delimit a section "Jesus on the way to Jerusalem" (8:27–10:52) include Koch (1983, 147–48), Cranfield (1954, 14), van Iersel (1982, 120), Lane (8:31–10:52, 1974, 30), and Stock (1985, 295). Some others who do not place 8:27 as a break on the first level of their outlines do use it as a Text Part (8:27–10:52) on the second or third level: Lohse 1972, 83; Schenke 1986, 64, 67; Dehn 1953, 9, 10; and Klostermann 1971, 1.

[95] Bengel 1855, 167: 10:1–16:20, In Judea (10:1–33, in the border area; 10:32–42, journey to the city; 10:46–52, in Jericho; 11:1–16:20, In Jerusalem). Grant 1951, 646 divides 10:1–15:47 as: 10:1–52, on the way to Jerusalem; 11:1–12:44, in Jerusalem; 13:1–37, apocalyptic discourse; 14:1–15:47, passion narrative. Harrison 1964, 177.

[96] Hauck (1931, 6) begins his Jerusalem section (10:46–16:8) with 10:46. Hedrick (1983, 268) sees the break at 11:11.

[97] Bengel (1855, 167) sees the Jerusalem section as part of a greater section "In Judea" (10:1–16:20), thus putting the Jerusalem section on the second level of his outline. He divides the Jerusalem Text Part as follows: 11:2–11,

thematic changes in outlines that are almost entirely geographical tend to see two periods in Jesus' Jerusalem ministry. Credner has 11:1–13:37 as "Jesus' solemn entry into Jerusalem and his stay there," and 14:1–15:47 as "Jesus arrested, crucified, and buried."[98] C. G. Montefiore and others who use spatial markers also believe that a new section on the passion begins at 14:1.[99] Koch isolates

---

royal entry; 11:12–19, the next day; 11:20–13:37, the next day (11:20–26; 11:27–12:44, in the temple; 13:1–37, temple and Olivet); 14:1–11, two days before passover; 14:12–72, first day of unleavened bread; 15:1–47, the festival. Wellhausen 1911, 38: 11–16, Jesus in conflict with Jewish authorities and judged and crucified by Roman authorities. Swete 1913, lviii: 11:1–16:8, the last week at Jerusalem. Hauck 1931, 6: 10:46–16:8, Jesus' departure in Jerusalem (10:46–13:37, Jesus' last activity in and around Jerusalem (including 11:27–12:37 and 13:1–37); 14:1–16:8, passion, death, and resurrection). Lightfoot 1950, 9: 11–16, Jesus' work in and near Jerusalem. Grant 1951, 646: see above, n. 95. Dehn 1953, 11–13: 11:1–16:20, Jerusalem (11:1–13:37, the struggle in Jerusalem; 14:1–15:47, passion; 16:1–20, victory). Schmid 1958, 8: Mk 11–15, Jesus' last days in Jerusalem. Wikenhauser 1959, 116: 11:1–16:20, Jesus' activity, passion, death, and resurrection in Jerusalem (11:1–26, Jesus' messianic activity; 11:27–12:44, Jesus' messianic teaching; 13:1–37, Jesus' speech about the end and his return; 14:1–16:20, Jesus' passion, death, and resurrection). Marxsen 1969, 56: 11–16, Jerusalem. Klostermann 1971, 1: 11:1–15:39, Jesus in Jerusalem (11:1–13:37, Jesus' appearance in Jerusalem; 14:1–15:39, the passion). Lohse 1972, 83: 11–16, way of suffering in Jerusalem (11–13, last days of Jesus in Jerusalem; 14:1–16:8, passion and resurrection.). Merkel 1978, 16, 17: 11:1–16:8, Jesus in Jerusalem: last activity, passion, and resurrection (Merkel remarks that 14:1–16:8 is a thematically unified complex [the passion]). Van Iersel 1982, 134: 11:1–15:39, Jerusalem. Stock 1985, 295: 11:1–15:41, Jerusalem. Schenke 1986, 67: 11:1–16:8 (A-1. 11:1–13:2; A-2. 13:3–37; 14:1–11 look forward; B-1. 14:12–25; B-2. 14:26–16:8).

[98]Credner 1836, 109.

[99]Montefiore 1909, xiv: 14:1–16:20 the passion and the resurrection. Huby 1948, 472: 14:1–16:20, passion and resurrection of Jesus. Knopf, Lietzmann, and Wienel 1949, 122: 14:1–15:47, passion story. Cranfield 1959, 14: 14:1–15:47, the passion. Kümmel 1966, 62: 14:1–16:8, the passion and resurrection narrative. Lane 1974, 31: 14:1–15:47, the passion narrative.

three periods: 11:1–12:44, arguments in Jerusalem; 13:1–37, eschatological speech facing the temple; and 14:1–16:8, passion and resurrection.[100] Hedrick finds four Text Parts in the Jerusalem period beginning at 11:11: 11:11–11:26, two preliminary entries into Jerusalem; 11:27–12:44, sayings and disputes with Jewish authorities in the temple; 13:1–37, sayings to the disciples outside the temple; and 14:1–16:8, passion narrative.[101]

Several scholars see a break in the text (on the first level of their outlines) at the point where Jesus' body is taken (or preparations are made for it to be taken) to the tomb. Most of these begin the last division of their outline at 16:1; a few, as Klostermann (15:40) does, begin it before that point.[102]

There are scholars who use thematic and geographical considerations to arrive at their outlines of the text. The geographical or spatial indications are one kind of marker.

1.2.4.4. Methods Combining Thematic and Spatial Changes

Most attempts to structure Mark using thematic changes to some extent also use the geography of the text. The assumption in the use of geography is that a given spatial change (such as the entry into Jerusalem) governs a segment of the text. In other words, the scholar assumes that Jesus remains in and around Jerusalem for a given portion of the text (e.g., without going unannounced by Mark to other places in which the stories in

---

[100]Koch 1983, 149, 150, 158. Koch notes that the section beginning with 14:1 clearly differentiates itself from what precedes it.

[101]Hedrick 1983, 268.

[102]Credner 1836, 109: 16:1–8, Jesus rises from the dead. Knopf, Lietzmann, and Wienel 1949, 122: 16:1–8, the empty tomb. Grant 1951, 646: 16:1–8, the empty tomb. Schmid 1958, 8: 16:1–8, triumph and epilogue of the gospel— the Easter message. Cranfield 1959, 14: 16:1–8 (9–20), the resurrection. Klostermann 1971, 1: 15:40–16:8, burial and Easter message. Lane 1974, 32: 16:1–8, the resurrection of Jesus. Van Iersel 1982, 128, 130: 15:40–16:8, grave. Stock 1985, 295: 15:42–16:8, the tomb.

11:1ff. would then take place). This assumption about the geographical coherence of the text needs to be specified because it can be challenged.[103] The assumption in the use of themes is that a given theme "governs" or delimits a section of the text. When the theme changes, according to this assumption, there is a new section in the structure of the text. The following outlines of Mark all include some reference to geography in their thematic approach to the text.

Carl F. Keil makes his two major divisions using spatial changes (1:14–9:50, Galilee; 10–16, Judea and Jerusalem), but uses spatial and thematic changes to structure the smaller Text Parts (1:14–3:6, Jesus' first appearance in Capernaum and environs; 3:7–6:13, the choosing of the twelve and their training; 6:14–9:50, northern Galilee until the transfiguration; 10, teaching the disciples and events on the way to Jerusalem; 11–13, messianic entry into Jerusalem and messianic testimony; 14–16, suffering, death and resurrection).[104] In varying ways Adolf Hilgenfeld, Johannes Weiss, Rudolf Knopf, Ernst Lohmeyer, Vincent Taylor, Sherman Johnson, and B. Harvie Branscomb follow the same method of focusing primarily on the geography of the text,

---

[103]Paul J. Achtemeier has claimed, for example, that the sign εἰς τὸ πέραν (to the other side) must refer to a west-east movement (Achtemeier 1975, 13). If this is true, then Mark lacks geographical coherence because he forgets to tell about the return journey between 5:1 and 5:21 (both being west to east trips). Against the kind of position represented by Achtemeier see Koch 1983, 161 n. 33. BAG ad loc. does not have "to the other side (in a west-east movement)" as a possible meaning of the phrase. 1 Mac 9:48 gives a use that may be east-west, based on the context. John 6:17 has a use of πέραν that is clearly east-west. More importantly the geography flows better looking at the sign as referring to an east-west movement in this context (5:21) since in Mk 6:1 Jesus goes to his home area which is in the Nazareth (1:9) region. Therefore, the sign does not have to have a reference which involves going in a west-east direction in the text of Mark. The sense "go to the other side" is not in question here—only the reference of the sign is being argued about. Our argument above is carried out on the level of *langue* (Greek).

[104]Keil 1879, 5, 6.

while making some use of thematic changes to build an outline of Mark.[105] The catechetical point of view that Lohmeyer includes

---

[105]Hilgenfeld 1875, 510–513: 1:1–13, beginning of the gospel; 1:14–9:50, open activity in Galilee: 10–13, Travel to Jerusalem—Jesus' appearances there; 14–15, passion; 16:1–8, resurrection. Weiss 1907, 68: Mk 1, introduction, Jesus' powerful entrance in Galilee; 2:1–8:26, Jesus' unsuccessful work in Israel; (2nd part) 8:27–15:47 (8:27–10:45, preparation of the disciples for Jesus' suffering; 11–13, Jerusalem; 14–15, passion); 16:1–8, end: empty tomb. Knopf 1919, 105: Mk 1, Jesus' powerful appearance in Galilee; 2:1–8:26, unsuccessful work in Israel; 8:27–16:8, second half (8:27–10:45, preparation of disciples for the suffering of the master; 10:46–13:37, time in Jerusalem; 14ff., passion; 16:1–8, resurrection). Branscomb 1937, ix–xii: 1:1–13, beginning of the gospel; 1:14–8:26, ministry in Galilee; 8:27–13:37, messiah in secret (11–13, ministry in Jerusalem); 14–16, death and resurrection of Jesus. Johnson 1960, 24–26: 1:1–8:26, earlier ministry (1:1–13, beginning of the Good News; 1:14–7:23, Galilean ministry; 7:24–8:26, Jesus among the Gentiles); 8:27–16:8, the cross and its foreshadowing (8:27–9:29, turning point; 9:30–50, return to Galilee; 10:1–52, on the way to Jerusalem; 11:1–12:44, Jerusalem ministry; 13, apocalypse; 14:1–15:47, passion; 16:1–8, empty tomb). Taylor 1966, 106–111: 1:1–13, introduction; 1:14–3:6, Galilean ministry; 3:7–6:13, height of the Galilee ministry; 6:14–8:26, ministry beyond Galilee; 8:27–10:52, Caesarea Philippi: journey to Jerusalem; 11:1–13:37, ministry in Jerusalem; 14:1–16:8, passion and resurrection. Lohmeyer 1967, 7, 8, 70, 121, 122, 160, 227, 287: 1:1–3:6, beginnings: healing and teaching; 3:7–6:16, on the sea of Genessaret (oriented to the disciples); (6:17–29 is an interlude); 6:30–8:26, bread miracles; 8:27–10:52, the way to the passion (oriented to the disciples); 11:1–13:37, (oriented to the disciples) Jesus' message in Jerusalem (for and against the holy city); 14:1–16:8, (oriented to the disciples) passion fulfillment of prophecies about suffering. Lohmeyer notes that (1967, 8) the first three sections take place in Galilee and surrounding pagan lands. Geography and theme are included in the above outline. He finds a catechetical point of view (1967, 8) in 1:1 and 1:14–20, message and disciples; 1:20–45, ἐπιφάνεια τοῦ σωτῆρος ἡμῶν; Mk 2, forgiveness of sins, fasting and Sabbath keeping. 1967, 70: 3:7–6:16, the faith content of the primitive Christian community entrusted to the disciples—what was once secret (teaching and work) is now revealed plainly to the

50   *The Structure and Persuasive Power of Mark*

in his outline involves the users of the text and is thus a pragmatic approach.

A question that becomes obvious is: Does Mark have a structure that can be recognized by the community of scholars? If not, is there more than one structure? Or is there any structure at all?

1.2.4.5. Multiple Structures

Each of the structures above assumes that there is one "correct" structure of the text. Only a few individuals do not feel a need to assert one absolute structure. Hengel doubts there is an absolute structure, though he himself offers one proposal.[106] Elizabeth Struthers Malbon writes that "no one overall 'outline' of Mark can do justice to its overlapping narrative patterns...."[107] Harald Riesenfeld, Jean Delorme, Hans Conzelmann/Andreas Lindemann, and Philipp Vielhauer each propose several structures of the text. Vielhauer looks at the text from the point of view of spatial and chronological markers and sees 11–16 as a geographically and chronologically closed complex. He then delimits 1–10 as "Jesus' travels" (and claims that it has three or four parts). He also asserts a deep break in the text at 8:27, if one does not ask where Jesus goes, but what he does in the text. From this thematic point of view, Vielhauer outlines Mark as follows:

---

community. 1967, 122: 6:30–8:26, after the word and work of the Lord, meals which Jesus celebrates and then the community after him (no distinction between Jews and Gentiles in the community); 1967, 160: 8:27–10:52, the necessity of suffering. Haenchen (1966, 34) adopts Lohmeyer's scheme without using the thematic titles.

[106]Hengel 1985, 141, n. 14: "Of course there is no 'absolutely valid' solution here. We cannot reconstruct exactly the plan which Mark made for himself before writing the Gospel. Therefore discussion of details will be endless." See above, n. 24 for Hengel's outline.

[107]Malbon 1993, 214, n. 11.

1–8:26, Jesus in and around Galilee; 8:27–10:52, Jesus' way to the passion; and 11–16, Jesus in Jerusalem.[108]

Perhaps the text of Mark, given its nature as a narrative, resists attempts to find one "absolute" structure. Each outline surveyed above points to interesting characteristics of the Markan narrative. In this work I shall use text linguistics to present an outline (Chapter Three) that is based on narrative markers (2.4.2), including scene changes (space, time, and

---

[108]Vielhauer 1975, 331. Riesenfeld 1954, 159: 1–9, baptism, activity and travels in Galilee; 10, journey to Jerusalem; 11–13, entrance in Jerusalem and proclamation shortly before the passion; 14:1–16:8, passion and resurrection report. (1954, 160): The above structure based on the real or stylized course of Jesus' life accompanies the following systematic or Christological structure based on the "clear break" at 8:27: 1:1–13, introduction; 1:14–8:26, the Son of Man and Israel with Jesus' activity and opposition to him; 8:27–13:37, the Messiah as teacher and judge (8:27–10:52, the teaching of the disciples by the Messiah; 11:1–13:37, the messianic entry and teaching about authority and the end [as preparation of the passion]). Delorme finds three structures in the text including the structure based on Jesus' relationship with his disciples and others described in n. 45. The geographical structure is (1972, 13, 33): 1:1–13, Judea; preparation for Jesus' ministry; 1:14–9:50, ministry in Galilee and the frontier territories; 10:1–52 ascent to Jerusalem; 11–16, Jerusalem. Delorme also finds a "dramatic" structure (1972, 17ff., 33): 1:1, Jesus Christ Son of God; 1:1–13, God proclaims Jesus "Son of God;" 1:14–8:26, "Who is Jesus?" 8:27–16:8, Jesus reveals himself. Delorme's summary in 1972, 33ff. does not cohere well with his depiction of the structure in 1972, 13–31. Conzelmann and Lindemann 1977, 242ff. find a geographical structure: 1–9, Jesus' activity in Galilee (1:1–15, prologue; 1:16–5:43, Jesus' appearance in Galilee; 6–9, Jesus' activity in Galilee and the surrounding region); 10, Jesus' journey to Jerusalem; 11–15, Jesus' passion in Jerusalem; 16:1–8, tomb story. They also find a Christological structure: 1:1–8:26, where Jesus' Messiahship is hidden; 8:27ff., the confession of Jesus as Messiah is open (in the disciples' journey, travel, and under the cross). 8:27–10:52 emphasizes the passion in Peter's confession, the transfiguration, and the passion predictions (8:31, 9:31, 10:33ff.).

characters). But there is no need to assert that all other outlines are incorrect. It may be that outlines identify structural features in a text that has no "one" structure. From a semiotic point of view, outlines tend to combine syntax (the relation of signs to each other), semantics (the relation of signs to their meaning), and sometimes pragmatics (the relation of signs, meanings, and users). The delineation of texts into different sequences is a syntactic activity. But semantics plays a role because researchers are able to give each text sequence a thematic title that summarizes the content or main thrust of the given section of the text. Occasionally, outlines mention the "reader" or some kind of function of the narrative (such as catechesis). These questions are pragmatic in nature because they involve the users of the text of Mark. One of the very important aspects of Mark is the theme or motif of Jesus' hidden identity, which has come to be called the "Messianic Secret." This theme is openly referred to in various (although not all) outlines of the text. The next section of this chapter will examine this theme or motif. Then several scholars' beliefs about the effect of Mark on his audience will be reviewed. In the final section I shall examine various proposals for understanding Mark as a genre. The structure of the text, the thematic content of the text, and the role of the users of the text will all play a role in the generic analysis of Mark that I propose in Chapter Four.

1.3. The Messianic Secret

Motifs are an example of a sign larger than a word. The working definition used in this work of a narrative motif is "a proposition about the characters that is true of a number of the text's parts and therefore can be inferred from those Text Parts" (see 4.2.7.1 below; the definition is the author's). The most famous motif found in Mark is the "Messianic Secret."

1.3.1. William Wrede and Rudolf Bultmann

Toward the end of the nineteenth century Mark was gradually losing the historical confidence that interest in the liberal "lives of Jesus" had ardently bestowed on it. William Wrede dealt a further crushing blow to the trust in Markan historicity. As is well known in New Testament studies, Wrede argued that the theme of the secret Messiah dominated the Markan material. According to Wrede, in "...Mark's account Jesus strictly and of set purpose kept his Messianic dignity secret even after the disciples' confession, into his very last period."[109] This is reflected in the injunctions to the demons to be silent, the prohibitions after the healings, the prohibitions after Peter's confession and the transfiguration (9:9), and the preservation of the incognito in 7:24 and 9:30.[110] The parable theory is another example of the secret (4:10–13, 33).[111] However, as Wrede notes, if Jesus' ministry had no Messianic attributes, it would not have been worth recounting.[112] Mark forgets his presuppositions sometimes and allows traditions to shine through that are contradictory to the secret messiah.[113] These include the occasional understanding of the parables (3:23ff., 12:12), the spreading fame of Jesus (1:45, 7:36ff., 7:24),[114] the Jerusalem entry in Mark 11,[115] and Jesus' confession before the high priest.[116] Peter's confession in 8:27ff. gives Wrede trouble, and he resolves the problem by distinguishing two groups of material in Mark. One group includes stories based on supernatural knowledge of Jesus, and it includes the divine statements in the baptism and transfiguration, the confession of demons, Jesus' own teachings, and Peter's confession.[117] This group is "attuned" to the idea of the Messianic Secret. Peter's confession fits in because of the μυστήριον in 4:11. The other group comprises the entry, the

---

[109]Wrede 1901/1971, 24.
[110]Wrede 1901/1971, 25, 34, 35, 36.
[111]Wrede 1901/1971, 56.
[112]Wrede 1901/1971, 125–126.
[113]Wrede 1901/1971, 25.
[114]Wrede 1901/1971, 125–126.
[115]Wrede 1901/1971, 125, 238.
[116]Wrede 1901/1971, 238.
[117]Wrede 1901/1971, 239.

confession before the High Priest, and the address "Son of David" in the blind man's mouth. Here ordinary people perceive the Messiah and consequently the secret is simply excluded. This is partly explained because the Messianic Secret comes from the tradition and not Mark.[118] Wherever the solution to the contradictions lies, Wrede has remained a force to be reckoned with in all subsequent Markan scholarship. Wrede works with a diachronic semantics on the level of *parole* (the text of Mark) because he uses the tradition/redaction distinction. Bultmann took over Wrede's thesis that there is a Messianic Secret in Mark, but he modified it slightly because he primarily located the motif on the level of the Markan redaction.[119]

Mark is, for Bultmann, a book of secret epiphanies (Dibelius's phrase) combined with a Messianic Secret that includes the parable discourse, the prohibitions to demons, the prohibitions after miracles, and the disciples' silence until the resurrection. The Messianic Secret is present to show that faith in Jesus as the Messiah began at the resurrection.[120] Bultmann connects Mark with the Pauline circle of Hellenistic Christianity, although Mark is not a product of Pauline theology.[121] This is true because of the presence of the union of the Hellenistic kerygma about Christ—including the Christ myth of Phil 2:6ff. and Rom 3:24—with the traditions about Jesus. So the fundamental presupposition of the composition of Mark is that the Jesus who speaks is the "one recognized in faith and worship as the risen Lord," and who is present in the church.[122] The incognito is a characteristic of the Messiah. The Christ myth is apparent in Mark for Bultmann, with the exception of the pre-existence motif which Mark has not taken over. Bultmann works with a

---

[118]Wrede 1901/1971, 145, 227.

[119]Bultmann 1963, 346, and see the index for editorial judgments on passages such as Mk 8:30 (Ibid., 258).

[120]Bultmann 1963, 346.

[121]Bultmann 1963, 346–47.

[122]Bultmann 1963, 348.

diachronic semantics on the level of *langue* (since he uses other NT texts).

1.3.2. The Determination of the Evidence

Closely aligned to the problem of defining the motif is the question of what Text Parts are to be taken into consideration in the investigation of the Messianic Secret. G. Minette de Tillesse,[123] Heikki Räisänen, and William Robinson have been particularly good in clarifying this issue. Since the Messianic Secret motif has been used by so many scholars to unify the Gospel of Mark, all scholars must define the set of Text Parts being used. Most do, as a matter of fact, make this exegetical step. Robinson summarizes well the texts usually drawn on since Wrede: 1. Prohibitions to demons (1:25, 34; 3:12); 2. prohibitions after other miracles (1:43–45; 5:43; 7:36; 8:26); 3. prohibitions after Peter's confession and the transfiguration (8:30; 9:9); 4. Jesus' intention to preserve his incognito (7:24; 9:30ff); 5. a prohibition not by Jesus himself (10:47ff).[124] Wrede also appealed to three other groups: the parable theory in 4:10–12; the section in 4:21ff.; and the texts in which disciples misunderstand. Wrede believed that certain texts in Mark, such as Jesus' entry into Jerusalem and his confession before the High Priest, contradicted the Messianic Secret (see 1.3.1 above). These contradictions should also include miracles without commands to silence and Messianic addresses to Jesus without rebuke.[125] Robinson also gives a useful summary of the exorcisms and miracles in Mark:

Exorcisms	Miracles	
1. 1:21–28	1. 1:29–31	8. 6:32–44
2. 5:1–20	*2. 1:40–45	9. 6:45–52
3. 9:14–20	3. 2:1–12	*10. 7:31–37
	4. 3:1–6	11. 8:1–10
	5. 4:35–41	12. 8:22–26

---

[123]Minette de Tillesse 1968.
[124]Robinson 1973, 14.
[125]Wrede 1901/1971, 36, 70.

*6. 5:21–24, 35–43   13. 10:46–52
7. 5:25–34

Only the exorcism in 1:25 contains a command to silence. The only miracles that include such a command are the three marked with asterisks.[126] Considering the manifold nature of the above evidence, it is easy to see why interpreters have been hard pressed to find a consistent Messianic Secret in Mark. There is little agreement on what constitutes the Messianic Secret, as a quick glance at the work of Räisänen and Minette de Tillesse will show.

1.3.3. The Explanation of the Motif

In addition to the question of the level of the text being investigated, the linguistic derivation of the motif, and the definition of the set of Text Parts is the following issue: Once a scholar has answered the above questions, what is the "explanation" for the motif? Here one can approach the problem from two points of view which have been discussed above in the introduction: semantics, or the relation of signs and their meanings; and pragmatics, which includes signs, their meanings, and a consideration of the users of the signs. In the case of Mark, the users of the signs are the author with the author's mental intentions or goals and the audience with their beliefs. The "user" of a text includes the sender (or author) of the text and the receiver (or audience). Both semantic and pragmatic approaches to Mark are taken by many scholars, and it seems apparent that an attempt to distinguish exegetical methods using the linguistic abstractions mentioned above could be of some help to the exegetical enterprise.

1.3.4. The Diachronic Issue and the Motif's Definition

The Messianic secret motif clearly stands in the forefront of those motifs that have been used to unify the Gospel of Mark.

---

[126]Robinson 1973, 19.

Mark: Structure, Messianic Secret, and Genre   57

The controversy over Wrede's work has remained great, and the methodological issues behind the debate need to be clarified. The debate has been carried out on three different historical levels.[127] There is the level of Mark as a literary composition, the level of the early Christian community's stories about Jesus, and the level of Markan redactional contributions to the old tradition. The level of Mark as a literary composition is the text as it stands and does not include attempts to distinguish tradition from redaction. One examines the literary composition using synchronic analysis. None of the German NT interpreters under discussion in this section considered it appropriate to investigate Mark as a "literary composition." The reluctance of these scholars to approach Mark on the level of its literary composition explains their unwillingness to look at Mark in a fully synchronic manner. One examines the early tradition (the community's stories) by doing diachronic analysis, and one does redaction criticism using a combination of synchronic and diachronic analysis. Wrede, using diachronic analysis on the level of *parole* (the text of Mark), located the origin of the Messianic Secret at the stage of the early Christian traditions about Jesus.[128] Bultmann, using synchronic and diachronic analysis, located the motif on the level of the Markan redaction.[129] Bultmann also went beyond the text of Mark and compared it to the other synoptic gospels and to the Pauline kerygma, and so worked on the level of *langue*. Most contemporary debate presupposes a combination of synchronic and diachronic analysis.

An option beyond Wrede and Bultmann has surfaced, however, which involves looking at Mark as a literary composition and de-emphasizing the distinction between tradition and redaction in Mark.[130] As long as a scholar does not

---

[127]For the linguistics behind this, see Frankemölle 1982.
[128]Wrede 1901/1971, 228, 236.
[129]Bultmann 1963, see 346 and index.
[130]On this point and against composition criticism see Räisänen 1976, 16, n. 31. In his 1990 translation and revision, Räisänen presents a less critical

clearly distinguish between these three levels from which Mark can be considered, one reaches no verifiable and clear results. Since the issue is historical, what may appear to be a solution on one level may not be a solution on the other two levels. The diachronic approach dominates this discussion because the scholars attempt to locate the temporal origin of the motif.

The next obvious issue is how the "Messianic Secret" motif is to be described linguistically, and what the semantic rules are for deriving the motif (or proposition) from a given sequence of text. This problem has been seldom discussed, and its solution has been implicitly but uncritically assumed by nearly all scholars writing in the area. An exception is the work of Robinson and Räisänen, who have asked themselves the question, "What exegetical principles justify the postulation of a Messianic Secret in Mark?"[131]

1.3.5. Two Attempts to Evaluate the Facts: Heikki Räisänen and Jack Dean Kingsbury

Räisänen[132] attempts to disassociate all of Wrede's evidence from the Messianic Secret motif, with the exception of the commands to the demons and the commands to the disciples.[133] His solution to the problem of the Messianic Secret is that Mark uses it as a "revelational historical" motif in which the Messianic Secret is revealed during the time of the passion (e.g., 15:39). In this (history of revelation) interpretation of the motif, Mark's thought is that: "the death and resurrection of Jesus *together* would constitute the decisive watershed between hiddenness and openness. A valid christological confession is only possible in

---

view of literary interpretations that approach Mark as a narrative (1990, 14, 15).

[131]Robinson 1973, Räisänen, 1976/1990.
[132]Räisänen 1990, 242–243.
[133]Räisänen 1990, 242.

the new, post-Easter situation."[134] But Räisänen admits that there is also a striking "*Öffentlichkeitsmotiv*" in Mark that does not square with the Messianic Secret, and Räisänen admits that he (Räisänen) does not much care whether his explanation is accepted.[135] He argues instead that Mark must not be viewed as merely a collector or as a great theological thinker but as someone with his own theological accents. This is a mediating position between the form and the redaction critics' views of Mark. One can thus find no unified picture of Mark's theology. This approach works primarily on a semantic level. Räisänen does work diachronically with the redaction/tradition distinction, but he assumes no more about Mark than can be learned on the basis of the alleged redactions. The readers of Mark do not figure in the Finnish scholar's exegesis. In other words, Räisänen attempts to solve the Messianic Secret problem on the basis of text semantics and the redaction/tradition distinction alone.

Jack Dean Kingsbury has made a strong response to Räisänen's contention that Mark has many traditions that are contradictory to a "Messianic secret." Kingsbury associates the secret identity motif with "Son of God" more than with "Messiah" (except in 8:29–30).[136] Kingsbury uses Räisänen's basic texts[137] (1:24–25, 34; 3:11–12; 8:29–30; 9:2–9) to argue this position. He also adds 1:1; 1:11; 5:7; 12:1, 6; 14:61–64; and 15:39 to argue cogently for a "Son of God" secrecy motif instead of a "messianic secret."[138] In Kingsbury's view, the "openness" motif

---

[134]Räisänen 1990, 249. In the original edition (1976, 166) he noted that "something essential about Jesus first came to be apparent after his earthly activity."

[135]Räisänen 1976, 167–168 ("Es liegt mir auch nicht viel daran, ob sie [the history of revelation interpretation] angenommen werden wird oder nicht"). This statement is not included in the 1990 translation.

[136]Kingsbury 1983, 14–15.

[137]Räisänen 1990, 242. Kingsbury 1983, 12, 14, 22.

[138]Kingsbury 1983, 47–155 gives an extended analysis of this "Son of God" christology.

that Räisänen[139] finds in Mark does not really contradict the secrecy motif. For example: 15:39 does not contradict 9:9, because the injunction to the disciples concerning the transfiguration events in 9:9 is not broken by the centurion or by the disciples themselves; the parable in 12:1–12 does not break the secret, because the Jewish leaders do not become "insiders" (4:10–12) and accept Jesus' truth-claim about the beloved son and so forth; 14:61–62 does not contradict the secret because the high priest's question expects a negative answer, and he charges Jesus with blasphemy; the "Son of David" passages (10:46–52; 11:1–11; 12:35–37) do not reveal Jesus' identity as Son of God; the "Son of Man" passages (before the public), such as 2:10, 2:28, and 8:38, do not contradict the secret because "Son of Man," even though it is a title of majesty, used in public as a circumlocution for "this man" or something similar, does not function to explain the identity of Jesus.[140] The title in Jesus' own mouth points to himself as "this man" (earthly, suffering, and vindicated) and expresses his "divine authority in the face of opposition."[141] It is "without content as far as the identity of Jesus as such is concerned for it does not inform the reader 'who Jesus is.'"[142]

---

[139]Räisänen 1990, 224–241.

[140]Kingsbury 1983, 16–21, 159–170.

[141]Kingsbury 1983, 168.

[142]Kingsbury 1983, 174. Some of Kingsbury's arguments (1983, 159ff.): 1. "Son of Man" is not conjoined with the name "Jesus." "Son of God" and "Son of David" are occasionally paired with "Jesus" (1:1, 24 [3:11 shows this to be a variant form of "Son of God"], 5:7, 10:47). 2. "Christ" (as a title or name) also appears with other titles in 1:1 (as a name), 9:41 (as a name), 12:35, 14:61, and 15:32; 3. the High Priest does not use "Son of Man" to designate Jesus even though Jesus had publicly used the title earlier (2:10, 2:28, 8:38); God calls Jesus "Son" in 1:11 and 9:7 as does the narrator in 1:1 (if the text is correct); the predication formulas do not use "Son of Man" (1:24, 3:12, 6:50, 8:29, 9:7, 13:21, 14:61, 62; 15:39); 4. "Son of Man" does not reveal who Jesus is for the disciples (2:28 and 4:41) or for the Jewish public (compare 2:10, 28 with 6:14–16 and 8:28 where the title does not function in the public rumors).

Räisänen works with a diachronic method (on the level of *parole*) by emphasizing the distinction between redaction and tradition. He finds striking contradictions to the secrecy motif. Kingsbury gives a synchronic reading of Mark on the level of *parole* and sees more unity in the text's secrecy motif. He works with Mark as a literary unity.

1.3.6. The Reader

A number of scholars use the concept of the "reader" of Mark to approach the problem of the Messianic secret. This crosses over from semantics to pragmatics, since the "reader" may be understood to be an original user of the text. In the case of the scholars discussed below, there is little attempt to analyze just who the "reader" is that they are referring to in their analyses.

1.3.6.1. Martin Dibelius

Martin Dibelius was one of the first to address the Messianic secret from the perspective of the reader, and for him the readers correspond to the disciples of Jesus. Dibelius uses a salvation history motif, the Messianic Secret, and the concept of Mark as a book of secret epiphanies to analyze the text's coherence. The Messianic Secret is a common denominator of the text. In Markan additions such as 5:43a, 7:36 and 8:26, Jesus does not will to be celebrated as a wonder worker. The Messianic Secret ties the paradigms and "Novellen" together.[143] Dibelius claims that the intention of the Gospel is that Jesus be identified as the Messiah, yet be hidden until the resurrection. This is reflected in the new epoch that Peter's confession introduces with its passion predictions and transfiguration.[144] In the baptism and temptation Jesus is revealed to the reader who is initiated into the secret of Jesus' worth.[145] Mark composes chapter four with his parable theory and shows that the divine

---

[143]Dibelius 1961, 225, 226.
[144]Dibelius 1961, 232.
[145]Dibelius 1961, 233–234.

in the parables can only be understood by those with open eyes.[146] Mark helps his readers to a correct understanding of Jesus. In the episode about the leaven in 8:14ff., Mark also shows the reader that Jesus gives the true bread (approaching a Johannine sense).[147] This composition (8:14ff.) of Mark interprets the tradition in a salvation historical sense. For Dibelius, these particularities show Mark's point of view.[148] The stories about Jesus are secret epiphanies. This standpoint (epiphanies) orders the collection of the traditions and their reworking.[149]

From a linguistic point of view Dibelius's concerns are very wide ranging. Dibelius's use of the categories of Messianic Secret, secret epiphanies, and salvation history to describe the content of the text is an example of semantic research that aims to discover what makes the text coherent (semantic coherence). His approach to semantic coherence is diachronic because it notes Mark's contributions to drawing the traditions of the text together. He works on the level of *langue* because he examines all three synoptic gospels. In addition to semantics, Dibelius also treats questions of pragmatics (audience/readers). His remarks about the text initiating the reader into the secret of Jesus' worth are a concern of pragmatics. The precise nature of "reader" in his terminology is a little unclear. It may approach a phenomenologically implied reader (briefly discussed in 2.3.3). Or Dibelius may simply mean the original readers of the Gospel.

1.3.6.2. G. Minette de Tillesse

G. Minette de Tillesse works primarily on the level of the literary composition of Mark, although he also uses the redaction/tradition distinction. He does not want the motif of the Messianic Secret fragmented in the way that scholars such as Räisänen fragment it, and he presupposes a unity in Mark that

---

[146] Dibelius 1961, 229–230.
[147] Dibelius 1961, 230.
[148] Dibelius 1961, 231.
[149] Dibelius 1961, 234.

justifies him in rejecting any "partial explanation" of the text (e.g., not including all the usual motifs under the rubric "Messianic Secret").[150] Minette de Tillesse's conclusion is that the reader is gradually prepared for the revelation of the Messianic status of Jesus by a narrative in which Jesus' Messianic status slowly becomes more apparent until its culmination in the passion and resurrection.[151]

1.3.6.3. Elias Bickerman

The "reader" of the text has also played a role in Elias Bickerman's treatment of the Messianic Secret. Bickerman appeals to Origen and Augustine to understand the motif. Origen claims that it is "vain to preach Christ and silence the cross." Bickerman notes that one understands the paradoxical economy of the good news only by understanding the cross.[152] In the myopic eyes of the ancient crowds, if Jesus had not been crucified he would have had the appearance of one of the Messianic pretenders.[153] Other inspired figures in that era pretended to be the Messiah or a Son of God, but were not themselves crucified. Bickerman recognizes the fact that the disciples are initiates into the secret, but only the readers really know what is going on.[154]

1.3.6.4. Hans J. Ebeling and Nils Dahl

Hans J. Ebeling[155] dropped all consideration of the Messianic Secret as a unifying factor of the text of Mark and understood it solely in its role of making readers think of themselves as the elect who are called to faith and a response to God's grace. The reader experiences a trembling joy over the conscience of

---

[150] Minette de Tillesse 1968, 19ff.
[151] Minette de Tillesse 1968, 236, 251, 280, 281, 304, 318.
[152] Bikerman [sic] 1946, 187.
[153] Ibid.
[154] Bickermann [sic] 1923, 137; Bikerman [sic] 1946, 181, 184.
[155] Ebeling 1939, 145, 187, 224.

election and an uneasy sense of the obligation to which the elect are called.[156] Nils Dahl, while not accepting Ebeling entirely, sees the Messianic Secret as paraenetic with an emphasis on the call to awake in light of the resurrection mystery that elicits awe.[157] There is also an emphasis on the call to the community to conform itself to the pattern of the salvation given it. The audience consists of the Christian community, and the text does not have a missionary orientation. The readers know the secret of Christ from the beginning.[158] The evangelist sees a community (perhaps the Roman church) in danger of taking the Gospel for granted and wants it to wake up. Mark uses the hidden and rejected Christ to do this.[159]

1.3.6.5. Kingsbury

Kingsbury sees the Gospel as inviting the reader to join the centurion (15:39) and the post-Easter disciples (14:28, 16:7) in confessing Jesus to be the Royal Son of God. The reader follows the text (which discloses Jesus in stages) as Peter confesses Jesus (8:29), then as Bartimaeus appeals to him to be Son of David, until the declaration by the centurion (15:39).[160] The Son of Man aspect of Mark holds out a promise to the reader to be included in the elect at Jesus' parousia (9:1, 13:27). A warning for the reader is implied in the statements (8:38, 13:24–26, 14:62) that prophesy the fate of those who are ashamed of Jesus.[161]

1.3.6.6 Summary

The solutions that appeal to readers and to the author's intentions use a method that takes pragmatics (signs and users) into account, whereas the approach of Räisänen tends to ignore

---

[156]Ebeling 1939, 187.
[157]Dahl 1976, 55, 60.
[158]Dahl 1976, 56.
[159]Dahl 1976, 63ff.
[160]Kingsbury 1983, 90–91.
[161]Kingsbury 1983, 176.

Mark: Structure, Messianic Secret, and Genre 65

the readers and does not make any crucial statements about the author's intention. It should also be apparent that Ebeling uses a sort of "implied reader," while Dahl appeals to the actual first readers (for references see 1.3.6.4 above).

1.3.7. Messianic Secret and Salvation History

Relating the Messianic Secret to other aspects of the theology of the Gospel of Mark is a good way to draw the text together. Hans Conzelmann and Georg Strecker are two scholars who have used the Messianic Secret motif to unify the text.

1.3.7.1. Hans Conzelmann

Hans Conzelmann has raised an important issue in reference to Mark and the Messianic Secret. He wants to make statements about Mark and the theology of salvation history. For Conzelmann the Messianic Secret is a Markan theologoumenon that holds the key to Mark, who is understood to have used it as a theology of the cross that stamped the work of Jesus.[162] The Messianic material then makes trouble for Mark.[163] The present understanding of Jesus through the resurrection bridges the historical distance between Jesus' life and the post-resurrection period. Revelation exists in Jesus' time, but is disclosed through Easter. The continuity of the two epochs is guaranteed by the theory of the Messianic Secret, which is the hermeneutical presupposition of the Gattung (form) "gospel" that unites separate material. Since the Messianic Secret is a hermeneutical theory and not an historical one, Mark has no salvation historical outlook as such in distinction from Luke.[164] These remarks by Conzelmann are somewhat vague and difficult to understand. His method is primarily that of text-internal semantics of the diachronic kind because he works with the redaction/tradition

---

[162]Conzelmann 1957, 294. Conzelmann 1968, 39–40.
[163]Conzelmann 1957, 294.
[164]Conzelmann 1957, 295.

distinction in Mark. He attempts to define the semantic coherence of the entire text.

1.3.7.2. Georg Strecker

A salvation historical perspective is present in Mark, according to Georg Strecker, if one may assume that he and Conzelmann mean similar things by the difficult terms. The two scholars may not be in profound disagreement, but Strecker does see Mark as conscious of a difference between past and present, given the presence of chronological and geographical references in the Gospel.[165] Mark is trying to give a picture of the life of Jesus as a self-contained event in which the salvation event is salvation history. The Messianic Secret implies the christological knowledge that the history of the earthly Jesus does not rest in itself, but is directed to the enthronement of the eschatological kyrios. The community practices the once hidden proclamation and brings the Messianic Secret theory to expression.[166] Strecker concludes that the kerygmatic goal is not so different from the historical goal (*Botschaft als Bericht*). The message or kerygma is report (which has a historical goal).[167] Here Strecker is attempting to determine the semantic coherence of Mark, and he is working with pragmatics. This is so because his categories of "*Botschaft*" and "*Bericht*" seek to determine the function of the entire text for author and original audience.

1.3.8 Conclusion

There are many other variations on which texts constitute the Messianic Secret and what the explanations for the phenomenon are. We shall deal with the problem again (4.4). References to much of the relevant literature with histories of interpretation and classifications of the many kinds of solutions can be found in Minette de Tillesse and Räisänen and will not be

---

[165]Strecker 1964, 103.
[166]Strecker 1964 103, 104.
[167]Ibid.

repeated here.[168] Scholars who use a synchronic approach are more likely to argue that the motif helps establish the coherence of the text (e.g., Kingsbury, Ebeling). Scholars such as Räisänen who work with a diachronic approach tend to fragment the motif and are not as likely to argue that it contributes to the coherence of Mark. The only scholar willing to work on the level of *langage* (several languages) has been Bickerman. He was willing to see parallels to the motif in other literature by using a more abstract formulation concerning the temporarily hidden identity of a religious figure or god. Most of the other scholars work on the level of *parole* (the text of Mark only), while some compare the motif in Mark to that of the other gospels (*langue*).

Tied to both of these methodological issues is the level of the text of Mark that the scholars envision—Mark as a literary composition; or Mark as a text comprising community tradition and Markan redaction. Kingsbury's work concentrates on the text as a literary composition, and consequently Mark appears to have more coherence than in those approaches that are primarily interested in isolating Mark's contribution to the secrecy motif. Another fundamental difference in work on the secret depends on the distinction between semantics and pragmatics. If one emphasizes the meaning of the secret in the text by defining the motif and interpreting the texts that the motif comprises, one works semantically (signs and their meaning). But if one emphasizes the effect of the secret on an implied or real reader, then one works with pragmatics (signs, meanings, and users). In Chapter Four I shall argue that the reader-oriented function of the Messianic Secret contributes to the understanding of Mark as a written speech act.

Closely related to the problem of the effect of the Messianic Secret on the reader is the effect of the entire text of Mark on a reader. This is a question of pragmatics because it involves the users of the text (namely the author, who is using the language to communicate, and the audience as the receiver of the author's communication).

---

[168]See also James Blevins 1981.

1.4. The Text's Effect on the Audience

Outlines have elements of syntax, semantics, and pragmatics, but they concentrate on the limits of the sequences that make up the text and so are mainly syntactic. When scholars summarize the content of the Text Parts, they are using semantics. The Messianic Secret is one of the fundamental building blocks of the content of the Mark, and often appears in outlines of the text. Researchers usually approach it from the point of view of semantics (signs and their meanings), but when the reader is included, they are using a pragmatic approach. One can extend their concern for the effect of the Messianic secret on the reader to the effect of the entire text on the reader. The scholars surveyed next are interested in this question of Mark's function.

1.4.1. Norman Perrin and the Function of Mark

Norman Perrin dedicated much of his scholarly life to Mark and the attempt to understand the way Jesus is portrayed in the Gospel. As can be seen from his later work, which draws on the philosophy of language and other methods, his scholarship flowered in many directions, including the question of what was Mark's function.[169] To understand Mark, Perrin appealed to historical criticism, literary criticism, the philosophy of language, the insights of the historians of religion, and those of the history of Christian hermeneutics.[170] By literary criticism Perrin meant the "form of the text and the way such forms function, the language of the text, and what can be known about the way such language functions." Under historical criticism Perrin included the intent of the author and the meaning the text had for its intended readers.[171] Perrin's work on Mark concentrated on the use of the christological titles in the Gospel with an emphasis on the tradition/redaction distinction. In this aspect of his work Perrin used a diachronic approach because of his attempt to

---

[169]Perrin 1976.

[170]Perrin 1974a, 47 and passim.

[171]Perrin 1974a, 43.

isolate editorial additions. One of his prime conclusions on Markan christology is that with "Christ" and "Son of God" Mark establishes rapport with his readers who have a false divine man christology.[172] This is a concern of pragmatics: what did the audience believe, and how does the Gospel affect them? Mark corrects the false christology and interprets the important titles "Christ" and "Son of God" using the "Son of Man" title to express an apocalyptic emphasis, Jesus' authority in the present, and Jesus' suffering with its culmination in the passion.[173]

Perrin moved toward what he called literary criticism in his later years.[174] By this Perrin meant that one should look for the function of a passage in its gospel context. One of his insights into narrative is that it is "mimetic" and tends to draw the reader into it.[175] The emphasis on "readers" that we have frequently referred to above is not new in biblical criticism and may prove to be a fruitful category for exegesis. His remarks on the "mimetic" function of narrative is a concern of pragmatics in linguistics and may help determine the function of a gospel such as Mark.

1.4.2. William Beardslee

William Beardslee[176] has done much work in analyzing the nature of narrative texts, using an adaptation of Alfred North Whitehead's philosophy of process. One concept of the many-faceted approach Beardslee uses is that of the way in which readers appropriate narrative texts for their own life experience and world view. One does not just read a narrative text; instead, one is drawn into a narrative text that can challenge the reader's expectations and view of reality by using surprising or even shocking language. Beardslee's emphasis on myths as complexes

---

[172] Perrin 1974b, 112–115.
[173] Perrin 1974b, 121.
[174] Perrin 1974a, 43.
[175] Perrin 1974a, 37.
[176] Beardslee 1975.

of symbols that organize, shape, and enlarge our experience and views of the world departs from the existentialist emphasis on the "moment of decision."[177] Beardslee's remarks are also a concern of pragmatics, since they are aimed at determining the function of narrative texts (how they affect audiences). His approach may also help in determining the function of an entire narrative text such as Mark.

1.4.3. Hendrikus W. Boers

Hendrikus W. Boers has written an essay in which he analyzes Mk 8:27–33 as a macro-sentence.[178] Boers seeks to determine how the text can be viewed as a unit. To do this, the tradition-historical analysis of the text as a product of disparate, contradictory units is put aside in an attempt to understand the coherence of the text. Boers does not deny the validity of the tradition-historical analysis; he does want to understand the pericope on the level of the text as a coherent unit. The reader is drawn into the narrative. The process of drawing the reader into the Christ mystery (as the Centurion is drawn in) is one of the fundamental purposes of the Markan narrative. If this is true, it will affect the scholar's judgment on the question of the pragmatics of Mark: is it a biography, or report, or a kerygmatic document in its intended function (intended by the author)?

1.4.4. Other Scholars on Mark's Effect on the Audience

Strecker (1.3.7.2) emphasizes Mark as *Botschaft* and as *Bericht*, as we have discussed above. Strecker's position involves pragmatics and consequently presupposes a knowledge of what Mark was trying to do to his audience with the text.

Heinz-Dieter Knigge raises the issue of kerygma or history very well in relation to Willi Marxsen's completely kerygmatic understanding of Mark.[179] The Markan language is clearly that of

---

[177]Beardslee 1975, 302, 305, 308, 309, 314.
[178]Boers 1981, 2.
[179]Knigge 1968, 63–64.

report. Any other function of the text must be argued for as Bultmann did with his theory of the cultic Christ myth and cultic legend.

The scholars who discuss the Messianic Secret and its effect on the reader belong in this section on pragmatics, but for clarity's sake we have kept them in the discussion of the Messianic Secret motif (1.3.6). They describe or hypothesize the text's intended effect on its audience by pointing to Mark's desire to draw the reader into the secret of Jesus' identity. This serious linguistic and theological issue will reappear often in the course of this work.

For Mary Ann Tolbert, Mark is a rhetorical text. A reader is drawn to ask the question: what kind of earth am I (in response to the parable in 4:2ff. and in response to the entire text). The purpose of the text is to persuade hearers to have faith in the gospel of Jesus Christ and to follow in his way. The Gospel exhorts Christians (probably suffering persecution) and proselytizes those on the edge of the community.[180] She writes: "All the characters, their words, and their actions have been molded as they are to communicate to or have an effect upon an audience. They are not copies of the world; they are, instead, a world of their own, created especially to persuade."[181] Tolbert's concern for the reader is a pragmatics issue.

From a semiotic point of view the question of the genre of Mark includes considerations of the syntax, semantics, and pragmatics of the language. The outlines usually include aspects of syntax, semantics, and occasionally pragmatics when they mention the effect of the text upon the audience. Work on the Messianic Secret focuses on the semantics or meaning of the text. Scholars concerned about the reader are moving into the area of pragmatics. Genre questions also involve the scholar in research on the level of *langue* or *langage*, since texts in other languages are often used to make comparisons with Mark. Usually, genre

---

[180]Tolbert 1989, 288, 299, 302, 304.
[181]Tolbert 1989, 223.

discussions are synchronic, since the tradition/redaction distinction does not play much of a role.

1.5. The Question of Genre

The issue of what genre of literature Mark belongs to includes structure, semantics, and pragmatics.[182] The scholar has to have a global view of the text including the outline, content (semantics), and the effect on the audience (pragmatics). Genre research has to be on the level of *langue* or *langage*, since other texts are compared with Mark. Most of the discussion is synchronic. In a succinct overview of the issue of genre, Tolbert writes: "The agreements between authors and readers, their shared expectations that compose genres, arise from familiarity with previous similar texts."[183] Scholars who discuss genre have to give an account of Mark's relationship to ancient literature.

1.5.1. Pearls on a String: Karl L. Schmidt

Schmidt carries on his investigation of the gospels in his famous essay on the position of the gospels in the general history of literature ("Die Stellung der Evangelien in der allgemeinen Literaturgeschichte").[184] In this essay he gives his image of the gospel stories as loosely connected pearls.[185] The gospel stories come out of a *Sitz im Leben* of a religious movement and are cultic legends.[186] This concern for the users of the text is an example of an approach to genre that uses pragmatics. In his essay Schmidt never finds an exact parallel to the gospel genre from pagan literature or Jewish literature. The approach in this essay is *langage* internal, because it looks at a number of texts in many languages to help understand the nature of the Gospel of Mark.

---

[182] See Hellholm's work referred to in 2.4.
[183] Tolbert 1989, 55.
[184] Schmidt 1923.
[185] Schmidt 1923, 127, 128.
[186] Schmidt 1923, 127, 76.

Schmidt's works, especially his earlier one, provided a firm foundation for the form critical work of Bultmann and Dibelius.

1.5.2. Kerygmatic Literature: Bultmann and Dibelius

The development of NT form criticism in the works of Bultmann and Dibelius concentrated on the nature of the synoptic gospels. They analyzed the literary forms on two levels: the level of the separate traditions (forms that are the root of the gospels) and the level of the form of the entire gospel itself. They also were both interested in the history of the traditions and wanted to use form criticism to differentiate secondary material from dominical sayings, and so forth. Bultmann, however, did more work on the level of the gospels as a genre than did Dibelius, and did not presuppose a theory of the nature of early Christian preaching.

Martin Dibelius did some synchronic work in his research on Mark and the nature of "gospel." Dibelius is not willing to call Mark a "gospel." Matthew earns that distinction first. For Dibelius "gospel" means the salvation preaching of and about Jesus. But "gospel" in this sense lies primarily outside Mark, who only occasionally points to the gospel. Mark grounds the preaching with stories, as opposed to presenting the preaching itself. The first words of the book do not describe the book, but instead describe the Christian value of the Baptist as the "beginning of the Salvation preaching." Matthew contains part of the preaching in a historical context and also orders it in a systematic didactic style. Matthew contains more of the "gospel" than Mark.[187] Dibelius's assumption that the gospel "is equivalent to the preaching itself" orders this line of reasoning. In so far as Mark gives paraenetic Christian teaching by recounting words of Jesus, the book contains Christian proclamation and not just illustrative (or narrative) examples of the proclamation.[188] Dibelius here implicitly identifies teaching with proclamation.

---

[187]Dibelius 1961 262, 264.
[188]Dibelius 1961, 262.

Matthew does not have narrative as the chief matter, but has the systematic didactic presentation noted above. As exegetical proof,[189] Dibelius appeals to Mt 24:14 par. and 26:13 par. τοῦτο τὸ εὐαγγέλιον (this gospel) versus Mark's τὸ εὐαγγέλιον (gospel) and claims that Matthew's use of "gospel" related the word more closely to his book than Mark's use of the word did. Therefore, for Mark, "gospel" (which means preaching) is a reality standing outside the book. Matthew offers the "gospel" in his book. Dibelius does not seem to succeed in making this distinction since he has not proved what the original uses of "gospel" were. In questions this complex, the scholar should not assume a definition of "gospel" and judge Mark on that basis. Dibelius does semantics on the level of *langue* when he discusses the meaning of the term "gospel." He appeals to Matthew's use of the word to determine its meaning in Mark. Avoiding tradition history, this is a synchronic approach to the question about what constitutes the genre "gospel"; it looks at other complete texts to answer the question.

Bultmann makes a number of remarks on the structure of Mark that concern the issue of genre. He describes ways in which Mark links stories such as succession, place connection, and temporal joints.[190] Mark wants to give "his collection the appearance of a story coherent geographically, chronologically, and in part also materially. He further sometimes betrays a feeling of the inadequacy of putting stories one after another or joining them together, and of the need for proper descriptions."[191] The geographical picture is roughly coherent. This concern of Bultmann is primarily syntactic, since it deals with the linear arrangement of the text sequences. Bultmann also gives examples of several schematic motifs, such as Jesus teaching (1:21, 2:2, etc.) with the crowds surrounding him.[192] These comments on motifs are a concern of semantics. He comments on

---

[189]Dibelius 1961, 264.
[190]Bultmann 1963, 338ff.
[191]Bultmann 1963, 340, 341.
[192]Bultmann 1963, 342, 343.

various sequences in Mark that existed prior to the Gospel. The conflicts in 2:1–3:6 or 3:35 contain no "pragmatism" and so are accidental in their location in Mark. "Pragmatism" here presumably means an intention on the part of the author in the construction of the text—what we call a concern of pragmatics (the author as a user of the signs). Bultmann believes there is no particular intentionality here because conflicts appear later in chapter 11 and 12. Such conflicts are historicizing and appear as appropriate preparations for the coming disaster. If one claims that 3:7–6:13 contains the theme of "Jesus ministering among the people and their rejection of him," one must say the theme applies to Jesus' whole life. Putting Mk 6:14–8:26 under the rubric "Jesus ministering among the Gentiles" is forced because it is based on insignificant geography. Consequently, a point of view does not order Mark's composition. This judgment about theme is an example of text semantics. One exception is 8:27, where the esoteric instruction about the Messiah begins.[193] Christian dogma is responsible for this teaching. This scene, however, is not depicted as a natural outcome of the disciples' relation to Jesus, nor as a recognition just won from them by him. According to Bultmann, the scene is "a new epoch for the 'reader' only and not for the life of Jesus."[194] The role of the disciples in 8–10 represents the "reader or church."[195] None of this shows historical interest in the disciples as historical personalities. Bultmann gets into issues of pragmatics here by asking about the users of the Markan language (readers as users of the signs). He wants to know what the sender's (Mark's) intentions were and whether we can find any intentions at all in the text. He also touches on a problem of semantics by questioning the appropriateness of various thematic titles to summarize the content of the text. Consequently, Bultmann has built a picture of the structure, semantics, and pragmatics of the text. He then can make statements about genre.

---

[193]Bultmann 1963, 349–350.
[194]Bultmann 1963, 350.
[195]Ibid.

As a type of literature, Mark is unique because of the Gospel's relationship to the kyrios, who is the cultic deity of the Hellenistic church.[196] The evangelists include stories about Jesus to give the kerygma a definite place and task.[197] It is natural, Bultmann holds, that the "tradition which had an historical person at its centre should have been conceived in the form of a coherent, historical, biographical story." But the unique nature of the gospels can only be understood from the character of the Christian kerygma which the gospels serve to expand and illustrate.[198] Acts 10:37ff. and 13:24ff. help explain the expansion of the kerygma with the story of the Baptist, and Acts 2:22 along with 10:38 show Jesus' earthly life being included in the same process.[199] Mark thus serves the Christian kerygma, and the death and resurrection stand in the foreground as saving acts that are known by faith and become effective for the believer in the baptism and the Lord's Supper.[200] These reasons give rise to Bultmann's view that the gospels are expanded cult legends. The Christ myth gives Mark, the book of secret epiphanies, not a biographical unity, but a unity based on the myth of the kerygma. Bultmann does not like comparing the genre of the gospels to that of *Vita Apollonii* and *The Lives of the Philosophers* because those works do not assume a similar cultic myth. This interest in kerygma and cult are concerns of pragmatics since the users of the language are in question. He does not accept an analogy with Hellenistic biographies because the gospels say nothing about "...Jesus' human personality, his appearance and character, his origin, education and development...."[201] Therefore the gospels are an original creation of the church. Since they did not spawn a distinct genre, Bultmann prefers not

---

[196]Bultmann 1963, 369.
[197]Bultmann 1963, 338.
[198]Bultmann 1963, 370.
[199]Bultmann 1963, 341.
[200]Bultmann 1963, 370.
[201]Bultmann 1963, 372.

to use the term "genre" to describe the gospel type.[202] This is a *langue* internal semantics of a diachronic variety because Bultmann is attempting to determine the nature of Mark as a genre by looking at Greek texts from Mark's time and from other times. In addition, Bultmann uses this method to help determine the function (pragmatics) of the text for its author and original audience through his use of the "cult legend" category.

1.5.3. The Gospel as Aretalogy

Does the gospel genre of the gospel of Mark have literary analogies in Hellenistic culture? Howard C. Kee has dealt with this question in this specific form: Is there a genre called "aretalogy" in Hellenistic culture and is Mark an example of this genre?[203] Kee answers both parts of his question with a resounding negation. The genre "aretalogy" has the following definition (quoted by Kee) in the work of Morton Smith and Moses Hadas:

> ...a formal account of the remarkable career of an impressive teacher that was used as the basis for moral instruction. The preternatural gifts of the teacher often included power to work wonders; often his teaching brought him the hostility of a tyrant, whom he confronted with courage and at whose hands he suffered martyrdom. Often the circumstances of his birth or death involve elements of the miraculous.[204]

This definition of genre is semantic because it focuses only on content and not on function or structure. In denying the existence of a genre "aretalogy," which includes extended narratives, Kee appeals to texts such as Strabo, *Geog.* 17.1.17, where Strabo speaks of temple texts describing the ἀρεταί

---

[202]Bultmann 1963, 372, 374. The apocryphal gospels are simply legendary adaptations and expansions of the canonical gospels. The canon cut off new gospel works (1963, 374).
[203]Kee 1973, 402ff.
[204]Kee 1973, 404, quoting M. Hadas/M. Smith 1965, 3.

(divine acts) of Serapis at his temple at Canopus.[205] Klaus Berger, in his extensive study of New Testament literary genres, lists a number of examples of similar texts that describe the acts of gods in inscriptions, papyri, and in literary texts.[206] Kee and Berger are both skeptical of the existence of a genre of "narrative aretalogy." Kee rejects parallels such as the *Vita Apollonii* because the short "aretalogical" texts are just tales of the mighty acts of a god or goddess, whereas the *Vita Ap.* contains much non-miraculous material (and so is not analogous to the aretalogies referred to above), and ends with no martyrdom at the hands of a tyrant.[207] Berger notes the futility of expanding the concept of aretalogy (from the bare list of miracles) to an "aretalogical" life of philosophers that includes martyrdom, because the actual texts such as *Vita Ap.* do not end in martyrdoms.[208] In an interesting (but *ad hominem* and therefore questionable) argument, Berger traces a view of the whole thesis about gospels and aretalogy. He finds the ideologically colored concept of the θεῖος ἀνήρ (divine man) in the background where the concept of θεῖος ἀνήρ comprises the sum of all unorthodox christology. The modern theologian can, in reference to the background miracle-aretalogies of Mark and John, "...establish, when reading the miracle stories, that already the New Testament authors opposed miracles as critically as he does."[209] This discussion of

---

[205]Kee 1973, 403.

[206]Berger 1984, 1219, 1220.

[207]Kee 1973, 409, 410.

[208]Berger 1984, 1227, 1228.

[209]Berger 1984, 1229, 1230. And on the question see Kingsbury 1983, 28–37 who has a concise overview of the issue and concludes that the debate has not yet run its course. His entire work argues against the presence in Mark of a negative christology of Jesus a θεῖος ἀνήρ (divine man) miracle worker. Sharyn Dowd 1988, 7ff., 23ff. argues that the days of the usefulness of the θεῖος ἀνήρ concept are over. See Carl Holladay 1977, 1, who gives a history of research concerning the use of the concept. In his work Holladay finds no coherent unified sense of the term in Hellenistic Judaism. Hans-Dieter

aretalogy is concerned about the content of such an alleged genre. The question of content is a concern of semantics. Since it is also concerned about the question of the outline (namely the texts' ending) of such a genre, syntax is also involved. Since these scholars primarily use other texts in Hellenistic Greek, the discussion is on the level of *langue*. It is synchronic, since redaction and tradition do not play a role in the discussion.

1.5.4. The Gospel as Biography and Other Options

One of the most popular recent views of Mark is that it is an example of Hellenistic biography. Charles Talbert argues that the gospels are similar to biographies that comprise texts that argue against a false interpretation of a philosopher or ruler.[210] He deals with Bultmann's objections to this position by attempting to show that ancient lives occasionally contained mythical elements and had cultic functions.[211] This is an issue of semantics (mythical elements in the ancient biographies) and pragmatics, due to the interest in the audience's context (a cult). He rejects Bultmann's argument that the gospels are eschatological and therefore can have nothing to do with ancient literature (as a genre).[212] This question of content is a concern of semantics. Talbert argues that both ancient biographies and the gospels have an attitude of inclusive reinterpretation of traditions, and that it "...is not a world negating one which prohibits Christian self-expression in the literary forms of the profane world."[213] Berger approves of Talbert's thesis and notes that the gospels are to be explained by reference to the genre "biography," which in turn is indebted to the genre "encomium."[214] Talbert's concern

---

Betz 1982, 235 is more open to the concept's usefulness in NT research and defines it as meaning "übermenschlich," or "coming from God."

[210]Talbert 1977, 94, 127. Talbert calls such biographies "Type B."
[211]Talbert 1977, 25ff., 92ff.
[212]Cited in Talbert 1977, 4ff.
[213]Talbert 1977, 127.
[214]Berger 1984, 1243–1245.

with "cultic function" is one of pragmatics, because it involves the users of the language. Clearly a concern for the genre of Mark needs to deal with questions of pragmatics. Most of the texts used for comparison are in Greek, so the investigation takes place on the level of *langue*. It is synchronic without much concern for diachronic development.

Robbins describes the genre of Mark as "eschatological *memorabilia* in the tragic mode."[215] Robbins notes that Justin and other patristic writers referred to the gospels as "*memorabilia*."[216] He uses the term "eschatological" because the "dynamics of plot time within story time are likely to be most prominent in prophetic, eschatological and apocalyptic texts."[217] The plot and point of view reflect the general dynamics of tragedy. The *memorabilia* literature in Greece featured people of wisdom who transmitted that wisdom to disciples. The person is described as an adult, a disciple-gathering teacher, who transmits his wisdom to disciples. The death of the philosopher/teacher is also recounted.[218] There is a general movement from the introduction to the teacher through a series of sections in a teacher/disciple cycle that ends with the death of the teacher.[219] The reader is challenged to respond to the value system of the teacher and to imitate the protagonist's thought and action.[220] Robbins uses semantic and pragmatic features to analyze the genre of Mark. The teacher/disciple cycle also is a syntactic feature. He analyzes the texts of Xenophon and Mark on a literary level using a synchronic method.

---

[215]Robbins 1994, 115–117. See also 1.2.3 for his outline of the text.
[216]Robbins 1992, 66, 67.
[217]Robbins 1994, 115. "Plot time" is the narrator's arrangement of events in Mark. "Story time" is the period from the promise of Isaiah until the Son of Man's return (1994, 113).
[218]Robbins 1992, 62, 63.
[219]See 1.2.3 for the teacher/disciple cycle in Mark and Xenophon.
[220]Robbins 1994, 115–116.

Hengel views "John Mark" as being responsible for a "revolutionary innovation" in the writing of the first gospel.[221] Nevertheless, according to Hengel, the text can "well be compared with a biography".[222] The gospels are of a special

---

[221] Hengel 1985, 52.
[222] Hengel 1985, 32. See 139, n. 8 for references to the literature and to Hellenistic texts (such as Plutarch's biographies and the biographies of Pythagoras and Alexander). Guelich (1983, 190) responds to Talbert's work with the argument that refuting Bultmann's arguments about myth, cult, and attitude (eschatology) of the gospels may say more about the weakness of Bultmann's arguments than about the thesis that the gospels are biographies. Talbert's arguments about the ancient biographies being mythical and cultic do not define the genre of biography. Albrecht Dihle, the classical philologist, argues that there is no distinct genre "biography" in Greek literature (Dihle 1983, 396), although he does believe one can speak of a literary *Gattung* "biography" in the first and second centuries CE (1983, 398). Plutarch (*Alex.* 1) is an exception to the lack of discussion of a genre "biography" in ancient literary theory (1983, 397):

οὔτε γὰρ ἱστορίας γράφομεν, ἀλλὰ βίους, οὔτε ταῖς ἐπιφανεστάταις πράξεσι πάντως ἔνεστι δήλωσις ἀρετῆς ἢ κακίας, ἀλλὰ πρᾶγμα βραχὺ πολλάκις καὶ ῥῆμα καὶ παιδιά τις ἔμφασιν ἤθους ἐποίησε μᾶλλον ἢ μάχαι μυριόνεκροι καὶ παρατάξεις αἱ μέγισται καὶ πολιορκίαι πόλεων.

(We are not writing histories but lives; the expression of virtue or vice is not above all in the most conspicuous acts, but often a small act, a word or a joke made an impression of character rather than battles with ten thousand deaths, the greatest lines of battle, and sieges of cities).

The descriptions of people's lives come in many different kinds of literature such a encomium that are not biographies (1983, 399). Dihle finds no specific similarities between ancient biographical writing and the canonical gospels (1983, 402). His main argument is anthropological (and based on the assumption that Aristotle and peripatetic philosophy (1983, 393) influenced the development of biography): "Die Vorstellung, daß sich die eigentlich

character in that they are "narratives of a 'biographical' saving event in Jesus of Nazareth the Son of God, culminating in his death, which is unique and valid for all."[223] Very important for this work is Hengel's approval of the statement (by S. Schulz) that the constitutive elements of a gospel include "geographical connections, chronological sequences and biographical details."[224] These are concerns of syntax (the connections and sequences) and semantics (the details). Hengel then remarks:

> ...his derivation of this "consecutive, integrated *historia Jesu*" from the popular tradition of the θεῖος ἀνήρ (divine man) lives, as for example those of Apollonius of Tyana, Alexander of Abonuteichos and Peregrinus Proteus, is unfortunate. Popular θεῖος ἀνήρ lives of this kind cannot be demonstrated as a specific genre, and the gospels have little to do with the later high-literary and partly polemical works of Lucian and Philostratus about these "heroes".[225]

Berger is more open to the analogy of lives such as the *Vita Ap.* He approves of Jonathan Z. Smith's work on the hiddenness of Jesus and the disciples' misunderstanding in Mark and

---

wichtigen, weil moralisch bewertbaren Wesenzüge eines Menschen erst im Laufe seines Lebens durch das eigene Handeln herausbilden, konnte auf das Erdenleben des menschgewordenen Gottes schwerlich angewendet werden" (Dihle 1983, 402, compare 406). Biographies are interested in character development with a moral purpose (as in Plutarch) and are realizations of timeless moral values. The gospels assume an already perfect man. The *Vita Ap.* is not a biography because the religiously motivated miracles and travel stories determine the structure (1983, 401). The plethora of different genres contained in that text make it unfruitful for solving the question of the origin of the gospel genre. If one does not think of the specific genre of Greek biography (as in Plutarch), one can call the gospels biographies of Jesus because their biographical framework determines their literary form (1983, 406).

[223]Hengel 1985, 140 n. 8.
[224]Hengel 1985, 158, n. 80.
[225]Ibid.

compares gospels to Hellenistic lives of religious figures. The definition of "gospel" that Berger concludes with comes from Smith: "A 'gospel' is a narrative of a son of god who appears among men as a riddle inviting misunderstanding."[226] Smith's emphasis on the content of the narrative is semantics. His comment about the effect of a gospel on an audience (misunderstanding) is an example of pragmatic analysis. Hubert Cancik believes that Hellenistic and Roman readers would have taken Mark as a biography.[227] This also is pragmatics because of its claim about the cultural response of the audience. Christopher Bryan agrees that educated Gentile readers would have perceived Mark to be a "life."[228]

---

[226]Berger 1984, 1265. See the definition in Jonathan Z. Smith 1975, 36. Smith (1975, 22) quotes a fascinating account of a nineteenth century French magician who summons Apollonius's spirit. The magician's

> ... 'experience' of Apollonius did not accord with his expectation. This drove Lévi to a reexamination of the *Vita* in the light of his experience and to a new understanding of his experience in the light of his reconsideration of the *Vita.*

Smith compares the gospels with the *Vita Ap.* and the Iamblichus's *Vita Pyth.* David L. Tiede 1984, 1728 doubts whether the motif of misunderstanding is adequate for evaluating the centrality of the passion of Jesus in Mark.

[227]Cancik 1984b, 96. Cancik does not claim there was a specific genre "biography" in antiquity. He goes on to compare the text to biographical material in the OT prophetic books and to the Roman historiographical texts concerning the death of Nero (Cancik 1984b, 95ff., 104ff.) such as Suet., *Nero* 46ff.). In another essay Cancik (1984a, 121ff., 127ff.) compares Mark to Lucian's *Demonax* and includes the following characteristics: there are no descriptions of Demonax's appearance; chronology is not important for Lucian; there are no childhood stories; there is nothing on Demonax's inner development, etc.

[228]Bryan 1993, 25. Bryan (using a set of features adapted from Richard A. Burridge 1992) compares Mark with texts from 100 BCE to 185 CE by looking at characteristics such as title, opening, subject, geographic setting, arrangement of material, characterization, units of composition, common

The most comprehensive comparison of the gospels and ancient Greco-Roman biographical literature has been done by Richard A. Burridge. After an extensive discussion of the literary theory of "genre," Burridge adopts this approach: "Genre is a major literary convention, forming a 'contract' between author and reader; it provides a set of expectations for the reader about the author's intentions, which helps in the construction of the meaning on the page and the reconstruction of the author's original meaning, as well as in the interpretation and evaluation of the communication contained within the work itself."[229] He uses a set of characteristics including opening features (title, opening words), subject (including the verbs' subjects), internal features, and external features to analyze the "family resemblances" between the gospels and the ancient biographies. External features include mode of representation (e.g., drama or narrative), size, structure or sequence, literary units, use of sources, and methods of characterization. Internal features include setting, topics, style, attitude or values, quality of characterization, and authorial intention and purpose.[230] For the synoptic gospels, Burridge lists proposals for authorial intention that include the following functions: encomium, example, information, entertainment, the preservation of memory, teaching, apologetics, and polemics.[231] He concludes that there are similarities between the gospels and the "subgenre of religious or philosophical βίοι. Below this level they are βίοι Ἰησοῦ, and below that is the level of the individual meaning of

---

motifs (e.g., birth, deeds and death of the hero), written style, length, and function (Bryan 1993, 27–64).

[229] Burridge 1992, 255, and see 26–54.

[230] Burridge 1992, 109–127. "Family resemblances" are discussed in 1992, 39, 44, 242. In a supplement to Burridge's history of interpretation (Burridge 1992, 4), Martin Buss has found a number of late nineteenth century and early twentieth century scholars (such as Georg Heinrici 1913, 6–9) who considered the similarities between the gospels and ancient biography even though they did not identify the two (Buss, forthcoming).

[231] Burridge 1992, 214–217.

each gospel."[232] The characteristics Burridge uses include syntactic, semantic, and pragmatic features. He works with texts as they stand in a synchronic fashion. His use of Greco-Roman material is an analysis on the level of *langage*.

Robert Guelich's work suggests that the debate is far from over. Guelich defines gospel as a "...literary genre whose form and content consist of 'the gospel of Jesus Messiah, Son of God.'"[233] His definition takes syntax (form) and semantics into consideration. His is a development of Bultmann's and Dodd's positions.[234] On the opposite extreme Marius Reiser claims that Ps. Callisthenes' *Vita Alex.* is the nearest analogy to Mark in Hellenistic literature.[235] Tolbert argues that Greek novels are the best analogy to Mark with reference to authors such as Xenophon of Ephesus (*An Ephesian Tale*). While admitting that Mark is not an erotic novel of the ancient type, she focuses on the novels' brief scenes, dialogue with narrative summaries, central turning points, and final recognition scenes. She finds these characteristics of popular literature present in Mark.[236] If a

---

[232]Burridge 1992, 247.

[233]Guelich 1984, 219. Guelich rejects all ancient literary analogies and argues that the gospels' structure arose from a common outline of the kerygma found in Acts 10:34–43 (1984, 209ff., 217) which is at the base of Mark and possibly John.

[234]See Dodd in 1.2.4.2.1 and Bultmann above in 1.5.2.

[235]Reiser 1984, 160. Reiser arrives at this position by comparing grammatical (1984, 135ff) and narrative (1984, 143ff) similarities between Mark and Ps. Callisthenes.

[236]Tolbert 1989, 65. Tolbert also compares the simple Greek and paratactic style of Xenophon of Ephesus and Mark (1989, 68). Her objections to biography, aretalogy and memorabilia as analogies to Mark are interesting: "aretalogy" does not appear to be a consistent designation for a group of texts which contain miracle catalogues; ancient biographies usually chart a life from birth to death and biography's main focus on the life of a central figure misses Mark's interest in the responses to Jesus of disciples and so forth; "memorabilia," which focuses on the relationship of the teacher and disciples (see Robbins 1992, 60–69), undervalues other parts of the story of

"historical/biographical type of ancient novel existed (with Philostratus's *Vita Ap.* as its heir) it would clearly be the generic home of the Gospels...."[237] Clearly, no major agreement has been reached on the question of Mark's genre. Syntax (form and sequences of the text's units), semantics (content), and pragmatics (function or cultural context) will need to be taken into account. Diachrony (tradition and redaction) do not appear to play much of a role in genre analysis, and it must be on the level of *langue* (Hellenistic Greek) or *langage* (Greek, Latin, Hebrew, Coptic, and so forth).

1.6. Interpretation and Linguistics

The linguistic method I shall develop in the next chapter is designed to clarify and help solve some of the problems confronted in this survey of several issues in Markan scholarship. It will focus particularly on the problem of structure, including the pragmatic side of the structure. Diachronic issues concerning redaction and tradition will be left aside (although they are necessary for a complete interpretation of the text).

By no means am I making the claim that this linguistic method flows naturally out of the history of Markan scholarship. It comes, rather, from a "secular field" (text linguistics).

Mark (such as miracles and Jesus' character). Xenophon's *Memorabilia* is completely unlike Mark in rhetorical and stylistic polish (Tolbert 1989, 58, 59). Robbins (1992, 63ff.) argues that there could be wide varieties of literary skill in the memorabilia genre.

[237]Ibid.

CHAPTER 2

A TEXT LINGUISTIC METHOD: SEMANTICS, PRAGMATICS, AND STRUCTURE

2.1. The General Approach

A distinction that will be fundamental in this work is the difference between semantics and pragmatics. Semantics, as we mentioned in the introduction, is the relationship between a sign and its meaning; pragmatics is the relationship between a sign, its meaning, and its users. Syntax is the relationship between signs.[1] Below I shall present a theory of semantics that I believe can be useful for biblical studies. Then I shall discuss the issue of pragmatics from two points of view: the presuppositions that an author and audience share in order for communication to take place; and the use of language to do certain things—a phenomenon that has come to be known as "speech acts." With the discussion of speech acts I shall review some of the criteria that have been developed to understand the nature of an entire text as a speech act.

After the treatment of semantics and pragmatics I shall discuss a semiotic approach to outlining a text that uses syntax, semantics, and pragmatics. The outline (or structure) to be

---

[1] See the Introduction, above.

presented in Chapter Three will use two basic techniques. The first technique involves ordering the text into its different narrative levels or frames of communication. A frame is the context in which a communication takes place. An author and audience are in one frame of communication, for example, and the characters who are communicating with each other are in a frame that is embedded within the author and audience frame. If a character tells a story in which other characters communicate with each other, then the narrated characters are in a still more deeply embedded frame of communication. In Mk 12:1-12, for example, the narrator describes the context of Jesus' parable. Jesus' words take place in a frame that is embedded within the narrator's frame. When the tenants in the parable speak (Mk 12:7), their words are in a frame that is itself embedded in the frame of Jesus' speech to his audience. One can imagine a series of picture frames beginning with a large frame that contains a smaller frame which in turn contains a still smaller frame, and so forth. The second technique used to make the linguistic outline will be a series of narrative markers. Markers are indicators that help an audience structure a communication. They mark or indicate such things as changes in scene (time, place, and characters). If an author includes titles or chapter headings, the titles or chapter headings would be another kind of marker.

The linguistic method discussed in this chapter will be used in Chapters Three and Four. The communication frames and the markers will be used in Chapter Three to give an outline of Mark. In Chapter Four I shall discuss several texts in Mark from the point of view of the speech act that governs the entire text of Mark. Insights drawn from understanding Mark as a speech act will also illuminate the discussion regarding the literary genre of the Gospel of Mark. This governing speech act guides the interpretation of the narrative world that Mark creates, including the Messianic Secret.

The semiotic concepts (syntax, semantics, pragmatics) given in the introduction are analytical tools designed to clarify the way language works. They do not appear as pure realities in human linguistic experience. For example, two signs never have a purely syntactic relationship. They also have some meaning (semantics). And semantics cannot appear without pragmatics. There must be some users of the meaningful signs.

There are any number of theories of how one should go about analyzing the meaning of language. One concept I adopt from the outset is that of a pragmatic communicative approach to meaning.[2] Here one looks at the meaning which the users of a language ascribe to it by their use of the language. The linguist does not create an aggressive world view such as materialism and then claim that all language not reducible to the philosophical metaphysics is meaningless. A linguist can understand the use of an ancient language's words without believing that the objects talked about exist (e.g., angels or demons).[3] Semantics is the area of linguistics that investigates meaning.

2.2. Semantics

One of the basic concepts of semantics that has not yet been fully adopted by NT scholars is the distinction between sense and reference. The distinction goes back to the ancient world. A given word (a noun in this case) has a conceptual meaning and can refer to an element in reality. The concept is not the same as the reference. Sextus Empiricus speaks of the Stoics' distinguishing the word, the concept in our understanding, and the reality referred to by the word:

> They (the Stoics) say three things correspond to one another: what is signified, what signifies and what is the reality (happening—object or event). Of these, on the one hand, the signifier is the sound such as "Dion." The signified, on the other hand, is the thing itself made known by the sound which (i.e., the thing) we

---

[2]Hellholm 1980, 38; Arthur Gibson 1981, 102 (for meaning as use). Compare Jacques Derrida 1976, 70: "If words and concepts receive meaning only in sequences of differences, one can justify one's language, and one's choice of terms, only within a topic (an orientation in space) and an historical strategy."

[3]For more discussion of this issue, see 2.2.2.

perceive as corresponding to our understanding. But the barbarians do not understand even though they hear the sound. The reality is that which exists outside—e.g., Dion himself.[4]

In other words there is a signifier, "Dion," a concept in our understanding that corresponds to the word "Dion," and the actual Dion (the reference of the word).

2.2.1. The Triangle

To visualize this distinction between a word, its sense, and its reference one can use the triangle developed by Stephen Ullmann using the work of C. K. Ogden and I. A. Richards (see figure 1):[5]

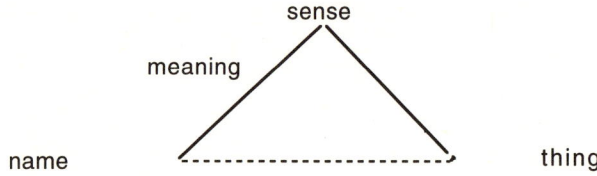

Fig. 1. The triangle

The triangle is simply a pictorial representation of the insights about language that the Stoics had already developed. The "name" position on the triangle corresponds to the Stoics' "signifier." The "sense" position corresponds to the Stoics'

---

[4]τρία φάμενοι συζυγεῖν ἀλλήλοις, τό τε σημαινόμενον καὶ τὸ σημαῖνον καὶ τὸ τυγχάνον, ὧν σημαῖνον μὲν εἶναι τὴν φωνήν, οἷον τὴν Δίων, σημαινόμενον δὲ αὐτὸ τὸ πρᾶγμα τὸ ὑπ' αὐτῆς δηλούμενον καὶ οὗ ἡμεῖς μὲν ἀντιλαμβανόμεθα τῇ ἡμετέρᾳ παρυφισταμένου διανοίᾳ, οἱ δὲ βάρβαροι οὐκ ἐπαίουσι καίπερ τῆς φωνῆς ἀκούοντες, τυγχάνον δὲ τὸ ἐκτὸς ὑποκείμενον, ὥσπερ αὐτὸς ὁ Δίων (Adv. Log. 2.11; Greek text from ed. LCL, translation is the author's).

[5]Ullmann 1957, 69ff.

"signified."⁶ And the "thing" position on the triangle corresponds to the Stoics' "reality."

2.2.2. The Trapezium

Kurt Baldinger and his student Klaus Heger have recently developed a useful approach to semantics⁷ in which they have attempted to go beyond the triangle to more adequately deal with the complexity of language. Their model uses a number of technical terms. The *signifiant* is the material substance of the sign (such as the sound or the ink marks on the page). *Signifiant* corresponds to the triangle's "name." *Signeme* means a unit of any rank that is used as a sign (a word, sentence, or dialogue, etc.). A *signeme* is a sign viewed from both its material aspect and its content. The *signifié* is the content level of the sign. *Signifié* corresponds to the triangle's "sense." A *sememe* is one of the signeme's meanings. The sum total of the *sememes* corresponding to a given *signeme* constitute the *signifié* or total content of a *signeme*. If a word (one kind of *signeme*) has three meanings, then

---

⁶The idea of language expressing thoughts or concepts or experiences is old. Porphyr. *De Abst.* 3.3. connects language with thought in the following way: εἰ δὴ προφορικός ἐστι λόγος φωνὴ διὰ γλώττης σημαντικὴ τῶν ἔνδον καὶ κατὰ ψυχὴν παθῶν...(If then an uttered discourse is a sound made by the tongue indicative of inner experiences [impressions] and experiences in the soul...). Aristotle *De Interp.* 1(16a) has a similar statement: Ἔστι μὲν οὖν τὰ ἐν τῇ φωνῇ τῶν ἐν τῇ ψυχῇ παθημάτων σύμβολα, καὶ τὰ γραφόμενα τῶν ἐν τῇ φωνῇ (Words in speech are signs of experiences [impressions] in the soul, and those [words] that are written are signs of those in speech). Even behaviorist-oriented linguists (or logicians) such as Willard van Orman Quine are sometimes willing to admit a connection between language and inner experience, as in Quine 1961, 16 (speakers articulate the world into elements, spirits, etc.—the way a speaker conceptualizes the world poses a problem for the translator). The distinction between sense and reference is also as old as the Stoics, as Franz von Kutschera argues in Kutschera 1975, 54, n. 32. J. P. Louw has a clear discussion of the entire issue in Louw 1982, 50.

⁷Heger 1976, 33; Baldinger 1980, xx.

it would have three *sememes*. Together the *sememes* would constitute the word's *signifié*. A *sememe* comprises *semes*. A *seme* is an abstract entity of one language and means a "minimal unit of meaning." The *seme* theoretically means one thing alone and is only meant to be an analytical tool. There is no claim that *semes* exist in the human mind as infinitesimally small bits of meaning. A *noeme* is a *seme* that exists in two or more languages or in different stages of one language.[8] The argument for their existence is based on the attempt to prove that several concepts such as kinship relations can be linked into a logical system (e.g., brother, sister), which can be shown to cross some language barriers.[9] "Class" connotes a group of elements that exist in a logical class or set.[10] A class corresponds to the triangle's "reference." A word such as "angel," for example, can refer to a large "class" or set of beings. Heger developed a trapezium using the above plethora of terms (see figure 2 below).[11]

---

[8]On *noemes* see Baldinger 1980, 267; Heger 1976, 5, 43, 338. Wolfgang Lorenz and Gerd Wotjak 1977 have done a very profound analysis of the relationship between language and thought. They also have tried to enumerate a number of *noemes* that they feel are common to many languages in Lorenz and Wotjak 1977, 310ff. See the review by Raible in Raible 1981. Raible (in Raible 1983, 3, 8) discusses another option for understanding the ability of speakers of different languages to understand each other. He speaks of a "representation" of an object that includes many intersubjectively agreeing markers (such as the many markers involved in a representation of the class of dogs). From this set of markers a language chooses certain relevant ones to be the meaning of the word that refers to the given object (such as "dog").

[9]Baldinger 1980, 99, 100ff. In this way one can convincingly argue that systems of concepts are not limited to one language. This position does not commit the linguist to the claim that concepts are completely extra linguistic. Instead, the linguist must claim only that systems of concepts are not limited to one language. The concepts "living"/"non-living" can, for example, be assumed to exist in at least several European languages.

[10]Baldinger 1980, 269; Heger 1976, 35, 47ff., 60, 337.

[11]Heger 1976, 51; Baldinger 1980, 155, 260.

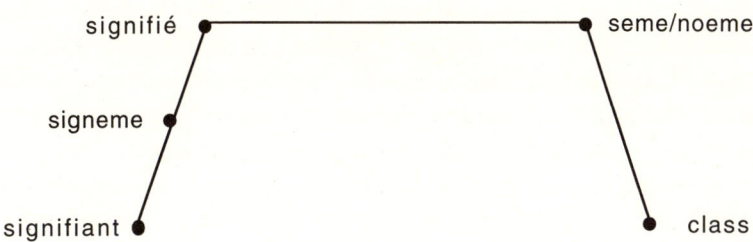

Fig. 2. The trapezium

An example of *signeme* (a word in this case) is ἄγγελος (angel). Ἄγγελος can mean a supernatural being known as an "angel" in English. This would be one *sememe* of the word. One of the *semes* of "ἄγγελος" in ἀπεστάλη ὁ αγγελος Γαβριήλ (the angel Gabriel was sent) in Lk 1:26 would be "supernatural." The otherworldly messenger *sememe* of "ἄγγελος" in the NT contains a number of *semes* such as "supernatural," "messenger," and so forth. Another *sememe* of "ἄγγελος" is a "human messenger." This *sememe* would have different semes including "human" and so forth. The *noemes* for the sign in question are concepts that are not limited to NT Greek but which are also present, for example, in English. "Living," "supernatural," and "human" would be *noemes* if the English concepts can be expressed in NT Greek. Consequently, *noemes* can be viewed as *semes* which appear in several languages. If translation is viable, then the linguist needs to assume the existence of *noemes* as entities not bound to one language. The "angel" *sememe* of "ἄγγελος" in the NT refers to the elements of a class of angels in this semantic theory. The individual angels are elements of the class that corresponds to the word "angel." In this way the linguist can speak of the extension or reference of a sign such as "angel" without committing himself or herself to the ontological reality of the class. The person who decides on the existence or non-existence of the class of "angels" does it as a philosopher, theologian, or a person who has had a vision of an angel after being stranded on a mountain cliff for twelve hours, and so forth.

When one considers a *signeme* such as a word as it is actually used in a real context, one can find the Ullman/Ogden/Richards triangle as a specific instance of the semantic trapezium. On the level of *parole*, one examines signs as they are used in actual contexts; on the level of *langue*, one examines signs as they are used in the entire system of a language. On the level of *parole*, the linguist considers the sign in its actual use (a token) and not the sign in its potential use (type) on the level of *langue* or even *langage* (which includes all *langue* systems). Heger and Baldinger use another technical term to describe the phenomenon in which an interpreter chooses one meaning from among the multiple possible senses of a word or sign. They call this phenomenon "monosemization." If a term such as "angel" can have several meanings or "sememes," then the context usually allows one to pick out the correct meaning—to "monosemize" the word. The same context also allows one to decide which angel(s) of the class of angels is being referred to in the larger context. The angel(s) being referred to in an actual context are a "sub-class" or sub-set of the class of all the possible angels to which the word can refer.

The diagram of the triangle as an analysis of a signeme on the *parole* level of abstraction is figure 3 below.[12]

---

[12]Heger 1976, 58; Baldinger 1980, 260.

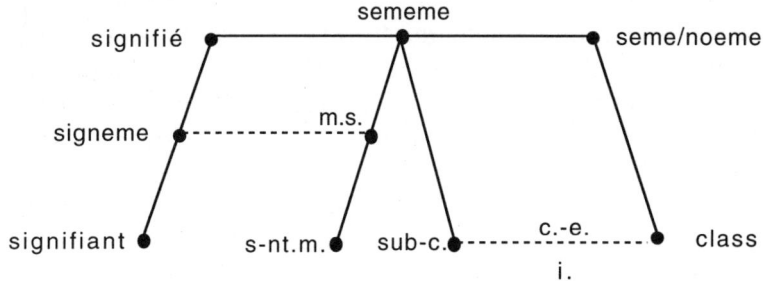

Abbreviations: m. = monosemization; m.s. = monosemized signeme; s-nt. m. = signifiant of the monosemized signeme; c.-e. = relation of class to elements; i. = inclusion; sub-c. = subclass.

Fig. 3. The triangle as an analysis of a *signeme* on the *parole* level of abstraction.

A word or *signifiant* that appears on the level of *parole* has been "monosemized" by the context. It has (if it is not ambiguous) one meaning or *sememe* and only refers to one thing or group of things. If the word "angel" appears in a context that identifies it as "Gabriel," for example, then there would be one element (i.e., Gabriel) in the "sub-class" position of the triangle. These facts are depicted in the triangle that appears in the middle of the trapezium. The *signifié* position of the trapezium usually consists of a multiple group of *sememes* (the intension of a word). A word when considered on the level of *langue* (as a type) has multiple meanings or *sememes*. But when one considers a word on the level of *parole* (as a token) it usually has one *sememe* only unless it is ambiguous. The context (sentence and text) helps a receiver pick out the correct *sememe* from among those *sememes* present in the *signifié*. A reader of the NT, for example, is usually able to tell whether the text is speaking of a "supernatural being" kind of angel or a "human messenger" kind of angel. The context therefore enables the reader to "monosemize" the *signeme*. This is a technical term used to describe the way context points to one *sememe* in a *signifié* with several *sememes*. A (m.-s.) monosemized *signeme* such as the supernatural kind of angel then refers to the elements of a sub-class[13] of the *signeme* ἄγγελος. ῎Αγγελος on the level of *langue* refers to the elements of a class composed of supernatural and human beings, for example, but on the level of *parole* the word only refers to some element of a sub-class of the larger class (e.g., an element of the sub-class of heavenly angels). The "otherworldly being" *sememe* of "angel" thus, on the level of *langue*, has a class composed of all possible angels. The word "angel" can be used in a sentence such as "Mary asked the angel...." Only from the larger context of the expression does one know that the particular element of the sub-class of "angel" is an angel called Gabriel (Lk 1:26).[14] Similarly, a word such as "serve" in "she served them" (Mk 1:31) can have a *sememe* such as "act in the capacity of a servant." The class of the word "serve" in this case could include an almost infinite variety of actions. Nevertheless, the context of the expression may precisely identify the sub-class as serving food and so forth. It is important

---

[13]Lizzie S. Stebbing (1952, 104) has a discussion of "class" in her work on logic:

> Accordingly, we shall distinguish in meaning between "extension" and "denotation". The extension of a term signifying a class-property of a given class is all the subclasses collectively. For example, "Man" is a term signifying a certain class; it denotes each individual man; the extension of "man" is the collective membership of all subclasses of the superclass *man*, e.g., it comprises *white men, black men, brown men, yellow men, red men.* Another way of saying the same thing is: the extension of a term signifying a class-property is all the varieties distinguished as subclasses. The extension, therefore, are *classes*, not individuals; the denotation is the *membership of the classes*, not the classes.

See Hellholm (forthcoming), p. 15. At the risk of unclarity, I shall use "extension" and "denotation" as synonyms in this work.

[14]See Roland Harweg in 2.4.2.2 for treatment of the phenomenon of substitution. Heger's *"Signemrang* 5" treats the nature of reference to specific objects (see Heger 1976, 330ff., and 226ff.).

not to confuse sub-class and *sememe*. The characteristics of an angel such as "greeting a woman" or "carrying a sword" (as in Gen 2) should not be identified with *semes* of the word "angel."[15]

2.2.3. Lexicography

This semantic theory has some repercussions for writing NT wordbooks. A given word cannot be taken on the level of its general use in an entire language (*langue*) and be correlated with one and only one *sememe* (or concept), as Arthur Gibson has shown.[16] A word can have many possible meanings (*sememes*). But in its use in a text a word should be considered to have one meaning (*sememe*) unless the word is ambiguous. There is no need to try to formulate some super-concept to encompass all possible *sememes* of a word and then find the "super-concept" in a given text. Semasiology is a term that is used to describe semantic analysis when one starts with a given word (on the level of *langue*) and attempts to find all of its possible *sememes*. This is the approach of a lexicographer. Onomasiology is a term that is used to describe semantic analysis when one starts with a concept (or *noeme*) and attempts to find all the words that can correspond to the concept. Theological wordbooks often take this kind of approach. This semantics can deal with signs that are larger than words—the domain of the lexicographer.

The trapezium is designed to cope with signs that are larger than the rank of a word.[17] If we substitute a text like Mark

---

[15] Gibson discusses the referential fallacy in Gibson 1981, 205, 206. In this fallacy, one confuses reference with sense (sub-class with *sememe*).

[16] Gibson 1981, 194, 195 argues well against a simple one word/one concept correlation. Barr 1961, 232, 233 gives an example of an attempt to find a unified concept in two *sememes* of παραμυθέομαι (comfort). See Cook 1988 for an example of *sememe* analysis of the phrase "without your father" in Mt 10:29.

[17] In addition to the trapezium, Heger has developed a system of analyzing language by beginning with the simplest *signemes* (such as *morphemes*) and moving up to more complex *signemes* (such as specifications of narrative

(something on the level of *parole*) for *signeme*, then the *sememes* would include all the elements of the narrative world of Mark (stories about Jesus, etc.).[18] The sub-class part of the trapezium would be the elements of the sub-classes that are referred to by the concepts of the text. Whether these sub-classes exist in reality or not would be a question for the historian and theologian. For example, is the element in the sub-class of the word "demon" in Mk 1:23ff. real?[19] The *sememe* of the Greek word is "demon" in

---

worlds like that of a fable). On this example (narrative world or possible world), see Elisabeth Gülich, Klaus Heger, and Wolfgang Raible 1979, 25, 26, 108. "Specification" is a technical term used by Heger for a text that specifies or constructs a narrative world like a fable. See also Heger 1976, 325. He calls the different *signeme* levels "*Signemränge*." See Heger 1976, 70ff. and 330ff. for a summary of the different levels of *signemes*. The hierarchy of *signeme* levels is intended to be applicable to all languages. Heger distinguishes each level from the next by giving specific differences. The same *signeme* can belong to different levels depending on how it is analyzed. Heger's system is an analytical tool used to show how complex the semantics of a text is. He, for example, defines *signeme* levels that include abstract concepts or phrases, phrases with information about speakers, and phrases that make assertions about the world. Due to the complexity of the system I will not attempt to sketch it in full in this chapter.

[18]Hellholm 1980, 40, 89; van Dijk 1977, 29 ("possible world"); see also Norman Petersen's discussion of narrative worlds (Petersen 1978b, 23, 40, 52ff.). Rhoads and Mitchie 1982 discuss things that make up narrative world of Mark, such as the plot, narrative point of view.

[19]Hartmut Kubczak has examined the referential dimension of language carefully (Kubczak 1975, 1978). In a discussion of the issue of ontological neutrality, Kubczak says that it is not the linguist's task to decide whether or not a text is "fictive" or "real." But he notes that the last two categories may be *semes* in a text. In this case the linguist needs to analyze them (e.g., a fable with a fable title). Kubczak writes that a "world" may be specified or constructed through a *langue* sign (Kubczak 1978, 47). A set of examples is Kubczak's following statement: "Allerdings ist in diesem Zusammenhang wieder zu berücksichtigen, daß in einem Text durch sprachliche Mittel eine 'Welt' gewissermassen spezifiziert sein kann (z.B. durch die Angaben

English. The sub-class of the word contains one element in Mk 1:23ff., namely the demon referred to in the text. But whether this demon existed in the real world (or exists) is a question that the linguist does not need to answer in order to understand the text. Ultimately, of course, the exegete must grapple with this question as a human being, but not in her or his role as linguist. Besides dealing with the meaning of signs, semantics can also analyze what other signs the given signs in a text presuppose.

2.2.4. Semantic Presuppositions

Semantic presuppositions are an aspect of semantics that deals with signs that are not included in the text, but that are presupposed by the text. If one speaks of a semantic presupposition[20] in a Text Part, then one must be able to show that the TP's meaning presupposes another word or larger *signeme*. If παραβολαῖς (parables) in Mk 3:23 appeared without a parable following, then one could claim that by semantic presupposition Mk 3:23 assumes some kind of parables spoken by Jesus. The subject of the parable would remain obscure. A

Märchen, Fabel, Tatsachenbericht usw.). Dies hat natürlich Auswirkungen auf die möglichen Deutungen von *Der Baum flüsterte etwas*" (Kubczak 1978, 79). In the "tree whispered a bit" example one would interpret the text differently according to the world (or possible world) that is specified. The author may be using a metaphor (real world) or discussing talking trees (in a story world such as the *Cologne Mani Codex*). Kubczak (1978, 34, and see further 1975, 69ff.) gives a diagram of extension in which relations such as processes (e.g., "all gods are becoming free") and conditions (e.g., "all gods are free") are included along with things (e.g., masses ["water"], qualities ["blue"], objects ["human"], and comparisons ["bigger"]). Teun van Dijk 1985, 105ff., in a similar vein, speaks of facts as the extension (or reference) of meaningful sentences. Sequences of sentences on the extensional level are linked with "...configurations of facts, such as states of affairs, events, actions, or complex episodes of these."

[20]For a brief remark on the presupposition problem see Hellholm 1980, 41; Wolfgang Dressler 1973, 98ff., and the index there under "präsupposition."

semantic presupposition as used here is a proposition or group of propositions that can be inferred from the meaning of a Text Part. It can be asserted that the semantic presuppositions of a statement provide the necessary conditions for the truth or falsity of that statement.[21] An example of a semantic presupposition is Mk 4:33. The crowds are presupposed in Mk 4:33 to again be in Jesus' audience, even though Mark does not specify when the crowds returned after the disciples and Jesus are alone in Mk 4:10.

---

[21]Ruth Kempson 1975, 49 uses a set of truth tables to distinguish logical entailment from a presupposition. A truth table assigns truth or falsehood values to two statements to describe the relationship between the two statements. She uses the following symbols in her truth tables: "S" = a statement; "T"="True"; "F"="False"; "v"="or"; "$\rightarrow$" = "if one statement is true (e.g., S1), then another statement is true (e.g., S2)" (in the direction of the arrow); and "~"="not." She distinguishes semantic presupposition from entailment thusly: An entailment relation between two statements S1 and S2 (S1 entails S2) is as the truth table defines it:

S1	S2
T $\rightarrow$	T
F $\leftarrow$	F
F $\rightarrow$	T v F

(Respectively: if S1 is true then S2 is true, if S2 is false then S1 is false, if S1 is false then S2 is true or false).

A semantic presupposition with S1 presupposing S2 is:

S1	S2
T $\rightarrow$	T
~(TvF) $\leftarrow$	F
F $\rightarrow$	T

(Respectively: if S1 is true then S2 is true; if S2 is false then S1 is not true or false, if S1 is false then S2 is true). A historical statement such as "Herod killed John (S1)" presupposes "Herod exists (S2)". If Herod does not exist, then on this analysis S1 and its negation do not have a truth value. If, for example, there are no crowds (S2) to hear all the parables in Mk 4:33, then the statement in 4:33 (S1) is neither true nor false.

Semantics in text linguistics can offer biblical studies the very important tools of sense and reference, *sememe* and *seme,* and other analytical categories. The above discussion of semantics brackets out the users of the language. Pragmatics investigates the users of language along with signs and their meanings. Below I shall review pragmatics from the perspective of the common presuppositions that a sender (e.g., an author) and receiver (e.g., an audience) share in order for communication to happen. I shall also review pragmatics from the perspective of the use of language to do things—the phenomenon called "speech acts." One can also use "speech acts" to understand the function of an entire text as a textual speech act.

2.3. Pragmatics

Pragmatics includes any consideration of the users in understanding language. Below I shall treat two areas of pragmatics: the presuppositions an author expects an audience to share, and the use of speech acts in a text. An interpreter is often called upon to supply cultural information that does not appear in the text. This is one of the most difficult parts of exegesis. But without such information, the modern reader (as well as the ancient audience) cannot successfully understand what the author intends to communicate.

2.3.1. Pragmatic Presuppositions

A pragmatic presupposition is a proposition or group of propositions that are necessarily shared by a speaker and hearer if a text is to be understood.[22] This group of propositions may be

---

[22] Heinrich Plett grounds the pragmatic coherence of a text in the person(s) of the sender and receiver of the communication (Plett 1979, 91; Hellholm 1980, 46–52). Receivers add information to a text on the basis of their knowledge (presuppositions about reality) and thereby create a better understood or more coherent TP. Ernst Grosse (1976, 13) notes that even in a monologue an author (or sender) takes the needs, expectations, and knowledge of the intended receiver into account. Emanuel Vasiliu treats the

referred to as a universe of discourse that the speaker (or author) and hearer (or audience) share. One can also say that without this shared universe of discourse there can be no successful communication.[23] We are not trying to establish an absolutely precise distinction between the two sorts (semantic and pragmatic) of presuppositions, because the borders between semantics and pragmatics are fluid anyway.[24] If the distinction is useful for text exegesis I shall regard it as provisionally justified.

Siegfried Schmidt has remarked that the more pragmatic presuppositions a speaker assumes, the more difficult it is for the communication partner to understand.[25] A group of these presuppositions can be called a "pragmatic universe of discourse." Ruth M. Kempson has developed a picture of a pragmatic universe of discourse that is shared by author and audience (or speaker and hearer) in which "S" is the speaker, "H" is the hearer and "Pi" is a given proposition:

1. S believes Pi.
2. S believes H knows Pi.
3. S believes H knows S believes Pi.
4. S believes H knows S believes H knows Pi.[26]

---

same phenomenon from language users' expectations about what will be said (Vasiliu 1979, 459, 460, 461).

[23]One would be foolish to claim that all linguists agree on any major point, and the problem of presuppositions (both semantic and pragmatic) is no exception. The concepts I develop here are due to Hellholm 1980, 41, 47, 48; Plett 1979, 79–91; Markus Wörner 1978, 46–48; Robert Stalnaker 1973, 395–397, 399; Siegfried Schmidt 1973, 101–105; Kempson 1975, 49, 160, 167, 189; and van Dijk 1977, 68 , 112, 207, 229, 230.

[24]Klaus Hempfer (1981, 322, 337) distinguishes between contextually invariant (i.e., presuppositions that are indicated by the language alone) and contextually variant presuppositions. That is close to the distinction between semantic and pragmatic presuppositions.

[25]Schmidt 1973, 105.

[26]Kempson 1975, 167.

In the case of Mark one obviously cannot check whether these statements (#1–4 above) are true. But in making the assertion that something may be a pragmatic presupposition of a given text, one needs to be conscious that one is asserting that Mark believes his audience is aware of some proposition (#2). In addition, Mark believes that the hearer knows that Mark believes some proposition (#3). In other words, in Mark's perception, the audience knows that Mark shares the pragmatic presupposition. Mark must also believe that his audience knows that he expects them to share the pragmatic presupposition (#4).

These presuppositions can include anything that the author expects the audience to know. Examples of things that can condition the partners of a communication (according to Schmidt) include socio-economic presuppositions that comprise social roles, status and economic situation. Socio-cultural and cognitive-intellectual presuppositions comprise knowledge of the world, experience, education, and knowledge of a text. Biographical-psychic presuppositions comprise personal competencies, disposition, present biographical situation, intentions, and goals.[27]

In reference to Mark, interpreters are faced with the problem of ignorance of the author and original audience. The problem is further complicated by the fact that the original readers may not have known things that Mark believed they did. Thus, one can distinguish between the audience Mark presupposed and the actual original audience. Scholars can make hypotheses, however, that often include speculations about the pragmatic presuppositions of Mark (biographical-psychic). Examples are: the "audience was in Rome"; "the audience had a divine man Christology"; "Mark wanted to develop a theology of the cross because of the plethora of charismatic miracle workers"; "Mark's audience believed Jesus would return soon to their location in Galilee," and so forth. It is obvious that the more such presuppositions Mark assumes, the more difficult interpretation

---

[27]Schmidt 1973, 104 gives these possible descriptions of the presuppositions in a communication.

will be for the original audience. Audiences from a later time will face an even harder task in establishing what the pragmatic presuppositions of a given TP are (i.e., those between the original author and audience).

An example of a possible socio-cultural (cognitive-intellectual) pragmatic presupposition is the fever in Mk 1:29-31. Could Mark have believed it to be demonic? If he did, and if he expected his audience to be aware of this, then the healing is actually an exorcism. On the other hand, the text clearly does not force the ancient reader to believe that Mark views the fever as demonic. The evidence is quite ambiguous and this is a pragmatic presupposition that one can easily do without.[28]

---

[28]Bickermann [sic] 1923, 132, n. 3 suggests that fever is a demon possession. But his texts from Luc. *Philops.* 9 and Richard Reitzenstein 1904, 18-19 do not prove this for all cases of fever. Lucian's narrator first mentions drawing off fevers, snakes and also mentions healings. The narrator, in an ironic personifying comment, asks if fevers are afraid of holy names. Reitzenstein presents a Christian amulet that pictures an angel who controls fever. In Pradel 1907, 20.20 (medieval) a demon brings fever. *Conf. Cypr.* 8 (ed. Baluzius) has a woman demoniac who suffers a καῦμα (fever). Karl Preisendanz 1974 (209ff., section on Christian magic), P. 10, P. 5a, and P. 5b has certain amulets in which Christ is asked to protect from demons and sickness including fever, but the two do not seem related as cause and effect in 5a (although the demon may cause the fever in P. 10). Preisendanz 1974 P 13 has a list of powers from which the suppliant wants to be protected. Fevers and hurts from people are also in the last. *b. Ber.* 34b, a fever miracle of Hanina ben Dosa, makes no mention of a demon and the "fever leaves (חלצתו חמה)" the sick boy because "he asked mercy for him." Compare John 4:52. I am indebted to William Brashear for the following references: W. E. Crum 1922, 543 gives a Coptic text of a Christian amulet with the story of Peter's mother-in-law in which the fever is due to the devil (ⲃⲓ ⲙⲉⲩ ⲡⲉⲍⲉⲙⲁⲙ ⲡⲁⲛⲧⲓⲕⲓⲙⲉⲛⲟⲥ: take from her this fever of the adversary). In this development of the tradition the sickness is clearly devilish, but one does not need to draw conclusions about Mark. Crum gives references to similar amulets with the same narrative (no date). Brashear 1975, 28 published a magic amulet with a prayer to various deities and angels (3-4th

2.3.2. Pragmatics and the Trapezium

One can consider this aspect of pragmatics from the point of view of the trapezium theory. Baldinger[29] considers what the users add to the semantic meaning of words to be "semes of symptom" (of the author) and "signal" (reader). For example if πυρετός (fever)[30] in Mk 1:31 had a specific meaning for the audience of Mark, the analysis would construct a *seme* of symptom/signal to account for this fact. When Mark used the word πυρετός he would have included the *seme* "demon," and his audience would have the same *seme* when they read the word. The *seme* would not be present in the normal semantic analysis of the word. Besides examining the presuppositions that a sender and receiver share, pragmatics also considers a sender's use of language as an instrument or tool. This ability of language to "do things" has come to be called "speech acts."

---

c. CE): φυλάξαται Τουθούν, ὧν ἔτεκεν Σάρα, ἀπὸ πάντος ῥίγους καὶ πυρετὸς [sic] τριτέου...(Various gods) will keep Tuthos whom Sarah bore from every shivering illness and fever, tertian.... Brashear edited another Greek papyrus (an amulet in *Papyri Greek and Egyptian* 1981, 49 [p. 193]), which gives the history of Jesus healing Peter's mother-in-law: θεράπευσον καὶ νῦν τὴν δούλην σου τὴν φοροῦντα τὸ ἅγ[ιον] ὄνομά σου ἀπὸ πάσης νόσου καὶ...π]υρετους...καὶ ἀπὸ πάσης βασκοσύνης καὶ ἀπὸ πάντος πν[ευμ]α[τος] πονηροῦ (Heal now your slave, who bears your holy name, from every disease and fever and from every enchantment and from every evil spirit). Here sickness, witchcraft, and evil spirits appear in the same list, but are not clearly related. For another fever amulet and bibliography, see Franco Maltomini 1981, 111ff. These texts do not establish the thesis that in Mark fever is seen as devil-caused, but they do show that fever could be seen as devil-caused among certain groups in the ancient world. In Lk 4:39 the fever may be personified.

[29]Baldinger 1980, 232ff., 254ff.
[30]See 2.3.1.

2.3.3. Speech Acts

Speech act theory considers our ability to do things with language such as make assertions about the world, make promises, baptize, celebrate the eucharist, and so forth. The use of language in speech acts is an ancient insight. Plato already noted that speaking is a kind of act (ἆρ' οὖν οὐ καὶ τὸ λέγειν μία τις τῶν πράξεών ἐστιν; is not therefore speaking also one of the acts?). Aristotle included, among the types of speech: command; prayer; narrative; warning; and question and answer. Apuleius listed the following speech acts: commanding, demanding, being enraged, desiring, vowing, being angry, hating, being envious, being favorable to, lamenting, admiring, despising, reproving, regretting, and bewailing.[31] There are many ways moderns have used to classify speech acts.

---

[31]Hellholm 1980, 532 quoting Plato's Cratylus 387b. See also Aristotle *Poetics* 19.7 (1456b) for the σχήματα τῆς λέξεως ...ἐντολὴ καὶ τί εὐχὴ καὶ διήγησις καὶ ἀπειλὴ καὶ ἐρώτησις καὶ ἀπόκρισις καὶ εἴ τι ἄλλο τοιοῦτον. Apuleius, the second century orator, wrote a philosophical work entitled *Peri Ermeneias* in which he made use of Peripatetic and Stoic logic. M. S. Sullivan (1967, 18 quoting Apuleius, *Peri Ermeneias* I, p. 146, 4–14 (265) ed. P. Thomas) refers to Apuleius's remark that there are many forms of speech. To these forms of speech Apuleius opposes a kind that he calls "declarative" (*pronuntiabilis*), which is alone subject to truth or falsity:

> sed cum disseramus oratione, cuius variae species sunt, ut imperandi mandandi succensendi optandi vovendi irascendi odiendi invidiendi favendi miserandi admirandi contemnendi obiurgandi paenitendi deplorandi...est una inter has ad propositum potissima, quae pronuntiabilis appellatur, absolutam sententiam comprehendens, sola ex omnibus veritati aut falsitati obnoxia....

Martin Buss summarizes ancient speech act theory and relates it to medieval exegesis and modern speech act analysis (Buss 1988, 132, n. 6, and Buss, forthcoming).

Klaus Brinker[32] offers the following typology for speech acts according to their function: 1. information function (e.g., report, explanation, claim); 2. directive ("Appell") function (e.g., command, request, counsel with textual examples such as a legal text, sermon, propaganda); 3. obligation function (e.g., promise, warning with textual examples such as a contract, guarantee, vows); 4. contact function (e.g., thanks, condolence, greetings with textual examples such as condolence letters and love letters); 5. declaration function (e.g., baptism, definition, nomination with textual examples such as a will, a declaration of guilt, and an authorization). This last class (declaration) has been called "performative" and is usually bound to a specific social institution.[33] Brinker's typology is closely tied to that of John R. Searle,[34] who (along with J. L. Austin) is a modern pioneer of the theory of speech acts. Searle gives the following typology (which Brinker follows closely): representatives (or assertives), directives, commissives, expressives, and declarations. "Assertives" corresponds to Brinker's "information function." "Directives" corresponds to Brinker's identical category. "Commissives" commit the speaker to a certain course of action and correspond to Brinker's "obligation function." "Expressives" express a psychological state and correspond to Brinker's "contact function." Searle's "declarations" correspond to Brinker's identical category. Searle notes that "the successful performance of one of its members [a declaration] brings about the correspondence between the propositional content and reality, successful performance guarantees that the propositional content corresponds to the world: if I successfully perform the act of appointing you chairman, then you are chairman...."[35] He mentions a supernatural kind of declaration as when God says "let there be light."[36] Here one can compare the declarative

---

[32]Brinker 1981, 139, 140.
[33]See 2.3.5.
[34]See Searle 1976, 10ff.
[35]Searle 1976, 13.
[36]Searle 1976, 15, n. 3.

speech acts (declarations) in Mark, as in the case where Jesus says to the little girl, "rise." In this case, where one uses speech acts to understand the language of an ancient text such as Mark, one is doing linguistic ethnography.[37]

Every utterance in Mark can be viewed as a speech act. For example, it is rare in Mark that Jesus is the object of an imperative (what Brinker calls a directive). The disciples' imperative ἀπόλυσον (dismiss) in 6:36 is unique. Closely related are the requests for help from Bartimaeus (ἐλέησον, have mercy) in 10:47/48 and the father in 9:22, 24 (βοήθησον, help), and the request for a position in glory by the two disciples in 10:37 (δός, give, permit). The only other imperatives directed to Jesus are from revilers as in 14:65 Προφήτευσον (prophesy),[38] 15:30 σῶσον (save), and 15:32 καταβάτω (come down). The greeting in 15:18, χαῖρε, does not seem to function as a command. Jesus often addresses other *dramatis personae* with imperatives as in 5:41 and 6:50. Without getting too deeply into the wide range of problems in speech act theory, I shall consider some categories relevant for this question about Mark: What was the Gospel meant to do to the audience? Was it meant to make a report or to do something else like convert the readers or comfort or direct the life of a community?

The author of a speech act such as ταλιθα κουμ (little girl arise, 5:41) creates a communicative instruction (an "illocution"). The intended consequence of the instruction on the part of the receiver ("perlocution") is "the little girl rises from the dead." Austin notes that: "Saying something will often, or even normally, produce certain consequential effects upon the feelings, thoughts, or actions of the audience, or of the speaker, or of other persons."[39] The perlocution is the act which the speaker causes to be performed. Martin Buss distinguishes

---

[37]The editor of Searle's article comments on the possibility of such ethnographic work (Searle 1976, 23).

[38]In manuscript notes of his lectures, Austin classified the noun "prophecy" as a"constative" or assertion (Wörner 1978, 54).

[39]Austin 1975, 101.

illocution and perlocution in this way: an illocution is what is done "in" a speech act; and a perlocution is "what is done 'by' a speech act, with a focus on what comes after the utterance has ceased."[40]

Wolfgang Iser has applied the theory of speech acts to fictional literature and works with a concept of an implied reader of a text and the ways in which novels alter the implied reader's perception of the world.[41] Sections of *Tom Jones*, for example, are analyzed by Iser as altering the implied reader's perception of perfection in which the author, Henry Fielding, raises the problem of self deception. The similarity of Iser's and Beardslee's approach in respect to the effects of texts on readers is evident, although both approaches were developed independently.[42] Robert Fowler distinguishes between the real reader, the implied reader, and the narratee.[43] The real reader corresponds to the real author. The implied reader corresponds to the implied author. Fowler writes that "...a text implies a role or persona for both the author and reader." The role is an image of the author and reader which the real author creates. In addition, some texts include a narrator and narratee who are persons who are supposed to be telling and listening to the story (as in the *Thousand and One Nights*, where Scheherazade is the

---

[40]Buss 1988, 130.

[41]Iser 1976, 50ff. (the implied reader) and 107ff. on *Tom Jones*. Rhoads and Mitchie 1982, 137ff., and 158, n. 1 have an extended discussion of the concept of an implied reader and give various approaches to using the concept on the Gospel of Mark. They suggest that "the overall narrative leads the reader to see the hidden rule of God in Christ Jesus and to follow him" in 1982, 137. An implied reader is imaginary. J. E. Botha has made extensive use of speech acts in his interpretation of NT texts. See his bibliography in Botha 1991, 219, and see the bibliography in J. G. du Plessis 1991, 140–42. Buss relates speech act theory to the concerns of form criticism in Buss 1988. Hugh C. White reviews the use of speech acts in literary criticism in White 1988.

[42]See Beardslee in 1.4.2.

[43]Fowler 1985, 10, 11.

narrator and the sultan the narratee). In this work we will retain the term "implied reader," although it is anachronistic, and in historical terms one should probably speak of an "implied hearer," or "implied receiver." "Implied reader" is anachronistic because literature was probably heard or read aloud in Mark's time.[44] It is not completely anachronistic because the lector who read the text aloud to an audience was a reader.

2.3.4. Individual Gospel Stories as Speech Acts

One particularly important question in this field—what kind of speech act are Markan narratives? For the analysis of the speech act involved in a work of fiction, Susan Lanser adds an additional type of speech act to the schema mentioned above (2.3.3.)—hypotheticals. Hypotheticals look like assertions but involve a speaker who "...brings a hypothetical or alternative world into existence *and* commits him- or herself to representing that world consistently." This speech act (with the novel as her example) "...has the important role as a medium of cultural communication, the communication of values and norms, ways of seeing the world."[45] Should one call the Markan narratives "reports" or "stories"? A report as a speech act can be defined as being a sequence of sentences with the illocutionary role as a whole of assertion. This role involves imparting information. The sentences of a report could be tied together with "and," and the large sentence would have the same illocutionary role as the entire text. Franz von Kutschera,[46] who notes this criterion of

---

[44]See Achtemeier 1990, 15ff. for many references. Compare Stephen Moore's similar position in Moore 1989, 84ff. Bryan examines the oral characteristics of Mark's composition and concludes that Mark was meant for public performance (1993, 67–151, 167–170).

[45]Lanser 1981, 290 and 293, respectively. Mary L. Pratt (Pratt 1977, 143, 152) also includes literary texts in a class of speech acts that describes a world that is hypothetical or fictive and that overlaps in some way with the real world. Literary speech displays experience and relates the unexpected.

[46]Kutschera 1975, 140–141.

reports, also claims that one could not do this with the different sentences of a discussion. This is the case because in a discussion, sentences have roles such as thesis, counter-thesis, and argument, which differ from the illocutionary role which the entire text has as a whole. Stories, however, can contain imperatives and questions which appear in speech that the author narrates. Reports can also have such illocutions (imperatives and questions). A story however does not usually have the illocutionary role of report because stories are often fictional. Reports make assertions about the real world. Stories (fictional) can also communicate things about the world.[47] Susan Suleiman writes about the function of fictional narrative:

> To tell a story in order to communicate "something else"—an insight, a conviction, even some sort of precept—this has been for centuries the ambition not only of preachers and moralists of all sorts, but also, in a more or less clearly formulated way, of novelists. There is no need to cite names; from Richardson to Zola, from Rousseau to D. H. Lawrence, one of the constant elements of the "realist" impulse is the didactic element, the desire to *say* (even if only indirectly) *something*.[48]

The Markan narrative (as an illocution) resembles fiction because it creates a narrative world. As an illocution the narratives in Mark are also like reports in that they make an assertion about the figure Jesus Christ and are clearly not meant to be understood as fiction.[49] The resurrection narrative asserts that Jesus is still alive, for example, and the apocalyptic section asserts that Jesus will return. The title of the Gospel in 1:1 indicates that the narrative is to be taken as "good news."[50] The

---

[47]As in Lanser's "hypothetical" illocutionary act, n. 60.
[48]Translated in Lanser 1981, 293.
[49]See Strecker's "Botschaft als Bericht" in 1.3.7.2.
[50]Bryan 1993, 35 notes that the opening of the Gospel is an "assertion." Mark wishes his hearers to "believe or go on believing that Jesus is the anointed, the Son of God," and "to lead lives that accord with this" (1993, 60–

title is probably an illocution which encourages the reader not to view the work as a narrative interested only in the past facts of history. The discussion of Mark as kerygma in Chapter One[51] supports this view of Mark as illocution. The perlocution would be the reader's (or hearer's) actual acceptance of the text as "good news." Reports usually do not make this kind of claim on the reader. History books and other kinds of reports may have political or moral purposes underlying them, but this is not a necessary characteristic of reports. Since the Markan narrative makes assertions about Jesus as a report makes assertions, and since the Markan narrative claims the allegiance of the reader, we shall call the speech act "gospel narrative." Religious narratives can be non-fiction as can other kinds of stories. Charles Talbert compares such stories (gospels) to "cultic biographies,"[52] such as the *Vita Apollonii*. The speech act "gospel narrative" has its own peculiar illocutionary force in that it makes assertions about the world and encourages the allegiance of the reader. This illocutionary force is similar to that possessed by other narratives such as that of Apollonius, whether or not Talbert is right in his identification of the literary genre "cultic biography."[53]

The persuasive force of the gospels is also indicated by the strong responses of their pagan critics who attempted to "refute" the claims in the gospels. The truth claim expressed in Mk 1:1 can be illuminated by one Hellenistic critic's attack on narratives in Mark and Matthew. This anonymous philosopher of the third

---

61, see also 131 and 166). See the discussion in 3.2.2, 3.3.2 and Appendix One.

[51]See 1.3.7.2 and 1.5.2.

[52]Talbert 1977.

[53]Ira A. Greenberg, a psychologist, has done research on the changes in audience attitudes brought about by psychodrama (Greenberg 1968, 151ff., 201ff.). Such research could conceivably be carried out using the text of Mark. Moore 1989, 105 refers to some recent psychoanalytic studies of how readers actually read. Edgar McKnight (1985, 104–110) discusses the psychoanalytic approach of N. Holland to actual readers' experience of literature.

century objected to the story in which Jesus walks on the sea (Mk 6:45–52 par.) because Galilee is a lake (and not a sea) where storms do not happen, and where it only takes two hours to cross (and not nine as in the disciples' case). Mark abandons truth completely when he tells this extremely laughable story (ἔξω τοίνυν τῆς ἀληθείας πολὺ βαίνων ὁ Μάρκος σφόδρα γελοίως τοῦτο συγγράφει τὸ μύθευμα...). The critic's conclusion from these "childish histories" is that the gospel is a sophisticated theatrical trick (ἐκ τοιούτων παιδισκῶν ἱστοριῶν ἐγνώκαμεν σκηνὴν σεσοφισμένην εἶναι τὸ εὐαγγέλιον).[54] After naming Mark and quoting (with reasonable accuracy) Mk 5:8–14, the philosopher concludes that the story is a piece of sad theater, or more probably a fiction. If it has some kinship with truth, then it is truly an occasion for a great deal of laughter for gapers (πενθικὸν...θέατρον...ὅθεν, ὡς ἐγὼ κρίνω, πλάσμα τῆς ἱστορίας ταύτης ἡ ἀφήγησις. εἰ δ' οὐ πλάσμα τυγχάνει, τῆς δ' ἀληθείας συγγενές, γέλως ὄντως ἱκανὸς τῶν χασμωμένων ἐστί).[55] The critic's extremely skeptical response to the truth claims of the gospel illustrates the illocutionary force of the text (and in particular Mark's claim in 1:1 to be telling "good news"). The extended critique of the gospels by certain pagan authors shows that a reader (or hearer) cannot simply read the text, decide that it is true, and then ignore it. In the struggle between competing philosophies in late antiquity the Hellenists needed to refute decisively the gospels in order to empty them of persuasive force.[56] (Skeptical responses to proclamations [non-Christian] of "good news" in Hellenistic culture are referred to in Appendix One.) The gospels did succeed in persuading many people.

---

[54]The philosopher's response is reviewed in Cook 1993, 240–43. The text is in Harnack 1911, 3.6 (42–45).

[55]Harnack 1911, 3.4 (34–39).

[56]The "pagan" responses to the gospels are discussed with bibliography in Cook 1993.

According to ancient Christian authors, early Christian language (such as the Gospel of John) was very persuasive.[57] In response to those who attacked the narrative truth of the gospels, Augustine wrote, for example, that: "through these texts the Christian religion has been disseminated through the whole world."[58] Origen emphasized the hearer's response to the gospel in his definition:

> A gospel then is a discourse containing an announcement of matters that with good reason make the hearer rejoice (because they help the hearer) when he/she accepts what is announced. Such a discourse is not any less a "gospel" if it is examined in relation to the hearer. Either a gospel is a discourse comprising the arrival of a good for the believer or a discourse that announces the arrival of an expected good.[59]

Augustine's and Origen's statements indicate that one should consider the effect of gospels on hearers and readers when analyzing their function. The persuasive power of the gospels can be approached by describing them as written speech acts. To understand an entire text as a written speech act, scholars have developed a series of criteria.

2.3.5. Textual Written Acts

In dealing with an entire text such as Mark, we can describe it as a textual written act in analogy to an oral speech act. David Hellholm, in drawing on the work of Ernst U. Grosse,[60] has made a useful list of possible criteria for determining what kind of

---

[57]The persuasive force of early Christian language (with reference to the Gospel of John, Origen's discussion of the persuasive force of Jesus' language and other Christian preaching, and some other patristic figures who discussed the role of Biblical language in conversion) is the theme of Cook 1994.

[58]Aug. *De Cons. Evang.* 1.7.10 (CSEL 43.10).

[59]The reference is in Appendix One.

[60]Grosse 1976.

written act a text is. Some preliminary groundwork for understanding these criteria is necessary. In speech act theory a distinction has been drawn by Markus Wörner between performatives and other speech acts.[61] A performative act is only present in language when a convention for an institutional act exists. An institutional (as opposed to everyday) situation presupposes that only a person in a specific social role can perform the performative act (e.g., baptism, eucharist). Anyone without any specific social role can make a speech act (e.g., a promise). Not just anyone can carry out a baptism, which is a performative act. In Roman religion when the Pontifex Maximus declared a young woman to be a vestal virgin, a performative speech act took place. The priest's words were as follows: "I take you, Amata, to be a Vestal priestess, who will carry out sacred rites which it is the law for a Vestal priestess to perform on behalf of the Roman people, on the same terms as her who was a Vestal on the best terms."[62] With those words the Pontifex made the young woman a priestess. Because of the institutional guidelines, one may speak of a "performative" speech act. In Searle's terms, performative speech acts are a kind of declaration.[63] Declarations (declarative speech acts) such as definition ("I define this word to mean . . .") do not require the extra-linguistic institutional guidelines that performatives have.

Another analytical tool for speech act theory is a distinction Grosse[64] draws between a proposition and its meta-propositional basis. Often one can describe a speech act using a meta-propositional main clause and a propositional subordinate clause, such as "I command you (the meta-propositional basis) to come out (the proposition)." "The demon comes out" would be the proposition in its full form. Grosse shows that much of modern language can be analyzed in this way. The meta-

---

[61]Hellholm 1980, 55, 58; Wörner 1978, 86ff., 244.

[62]Mary R. Lefkowitz and Maureen J. Fant 1992, 290. The text is from Aulus Gellus, *Attic Nights* 1.12.

[63]Searle, 1976, 14, 15.

[64]Hellholm 1980, 57; Grosse 1976, 15, 16, 44–94.

propositional basis shows the receiver how he/she should understand the proposition (e.g., as demand, promise, surmise, or factual claim).

Hellholm's basic criteria for determining the nature of a textual written act here cast in terms of Mark are:[65]

1) *The distinction between performatives and other speech acts.*

The distinction between performatives and other speech acts can be made if institutional or official factors are present. There may be a performative act present, since all the stories are traced back to Jesus, the Son of Man and Son of God figure, who gives the stories authority. The εὐαγγέλιον (gospel) is grounded in this powerful figure. Jesus' role in the Christian community can be presupposed as a probable ground for considering the text of Mark to be a performative written act. Jesus himself guarantees the text, if our point of view is correct. The voice from heaven in 1:9 and 9:7 defines Jesus as being "Son of God" who should be heard and is itself (as the voice of God) the ultimate source of authority in the text. This results in two performative acts: on the one hand, the voice of God guarantees the authority of Jesus, and on the other hand, Jesus' authority guarantees the authority of the text.

2) *Pre-signals.*[66]

Pre-signals include the author's name, titles,[67] or Gattung names at the beginning of a text that instruct the receiver in the function and sometimes the kind of text he/she is confronting. In Mark, the εὐαγγέλιον of 1:1 may have this precise role. The verse may be a title that describes the way in which one is to take the content of the text. The "Good News" of Jesus Christ probably does not mean the "Book of Jesus Christ," but may describe the function of the text that would be an announcement of good

---

[65]For the following criteria see Hellholm 1980, 60ff.

[66]Pre-signals such as meta-communicative expressions and substitions on a meta-frame are defined in the section below on narrative markers (2.4.2).

[67]See Peter Hellwig's work on titles (Hellwig 1984). He notes that titles verbalize themes (Hellwig 1984, 14).

tidings to the receiver. This could be the case even though εὐαγγέλιον in 1:1 has not yet come to be a genre designation.

3) *The order of the Text Parts.*

Next to pre-signals, the order of the Text Parts is the most important textual illocution indicator. The sequence of the Text Parts tells one whether a text is story, report, discussion, and so forth. In the chapter on the outline of Mark I shall present certain textual markers or indicators (discussed in 2.4.2) that structure the sequence of the Text Parts of Mark. The order of the Text Parts should help reveal aspects of the written act that we call Mark.

4) *Text beginnings and text endings.*

A text's beginning and end is often important in analyzing it as a written act. Mark's beginning in 1:1 should be crucial in searching for the nature of the text. The end is more controversial.

5) *The Appeal factor.*

The "appeal factor" is another important element in written acts. The frequency of value words and expressions, and rhetorical figures[68] help make a text appealing and prevent a reader from thinking that the author intends only to rehearse a set of facts. In Mark, for example, Jesus is never presented in a negative light or as having evil thoughts.

6) *Meta-propositional bases.*

The meta-propositional bases are also important for instructing the receiver about the correct understanding of the propositions of Mark. When Jesus gives a command, such as "Sell all that you have," the reader is able to understand the proposition embedded in the command.[69]

---

[68]For an excellent survey of rhetorical figures in Mark, see Tolbert 1989 in the index.

[69]For an extended treatment of speech acts along these lines, see Jerry M. Sadock 1974 and Gisa Rauh 1978.

7) *Proposition types.*

The proposition types of a text are important in determining what kind of written act it is. In Mark we have third person type propositions (He, she, it, they, etc.), second person type propositions (you) and first person propositions (I, we). The narrator speaks in third person proposition types.

This topic (Mark as a written act) will be treated further in Chapter Four (4.2). Syntax, semantics, and pragmatics can all be used to understand the structure or outline of a text. In the following treatment I shall make use of all those categories and especially of speech acts to develop an approach to the outline of Mark.

2.4. *The Outline or Structure of a Text*

Text linguistics cannot bracket out all subjectivity in the attempt to find an intersubjectively checkable structure of the text of Mark, but it can encourage the scholar to look for empirical signs in the text that help the scholar to divide the text and describe the function and interrelation of the TP's. In genre analysis, Hellholm has shown that more work of this sort must be done in order to establish syntagmatic (linear) criteria for analyzing genres.[70]

The structure is another way of approaching form criticism's analysis of the genre of a text (or class of texts) as content, *Sitz im Leben,* and form.[71] An interpreter has to be concerned about a text's genre, because it aids the reader in understanding the text, in so far as a genre creates a set of expectations in the reader.[72] Our interest is in the analysis of the historical meaning of Mark, and the structural analysis should guide the analysis of the text's

---

[70] Hellholm, 1982.

[71] See Hellholm 1983, 3 for reference to Gunkel and his program for analyzing genre and a comparison with text linguistics (compare the table in Hellholm 1980, 74). Lars Hartmann discusses the content and illocution (speech act) of apocalyptic in Hartmann 1983, 333, 334.

[72] Hartmann 1983, 331.

meaning. The structure (sometimes called "macro-structure") of a text in our approach is something that is recognizable on the surface level (as opposed to those methods working with deep structures) of a text. The concept of structure used in this work has three elements: a syntactic element, a semantic element, and a pragmatic element. Hellholm notes that the "...central phenomenon in recognizing the macro-structure is the delimitation of texts into 'functional text sequences' of different ranks."[73] A text sequence is a section of the text that includes smaller sections of text within it. In an outline, the largest text sequence has the highest rank. Mk 1:1–8:26, for example, includes the introduction within it. The introduction is a "text sequence" of a smaller rank. Each section of text has a function. Finding an outline involves three processes that comprise syntactic, semantic, and pragmatic approaches to the structure of a text.[74] For Hellholm the syntactic element of the macrostructure is the delimitation of the text into sequences of different ranks.[75] The semantic element in his view discloses the different thematic text sequences. One can thus see a text as a sequence of sub-themes (that correspond to and delimit Text Parts) and themes that organize the sub-themes in a hierarchical fashion.[76] Hellholm sees

---

[73]See Hellholm 1982, 171.

[74]See Hellholm 1982, n. 75 who defines "functional textsequences" as: (a) text "delimitation" into textsequences of different ranks (syntactical macro-structure); (b) "semantic macro-structures" disclosing thematic text-sequences; (c) "pragmatic macro-structures," i.e., "macro-speech acts" accomplishing a certain sequence of speech acts...."

[75]See Hellholm 1982, ibid. Text delimitation will be discussed at length in section 2.4.2 of this chapter.

[76]See Hellholm 1982, ibid., Hellholm 1980, 36, and Plett, 1979, 102ff., who uses changes in themes for the concepts of text semantic extension (how long a subject lasts in the text) and text semantic delimitation (where a subject stops). Plett notes that themes (or sub-themes) often correspond to headings (Plett 1979, 103); he also comments that actual headings given in a text can be text thematically irrelevant. The elements of the Text Part are subsumed under a sub-theme or theme. A sub-text lasts as long as a sub-

the pragmatic element of the structure as speech acts that accomplish a certain sequence of speech acts.[77] Van Dijk gives a terse formulation that summarizes the issue of semantic and pragmatic structures: "Semantic and pragmatic macrostructures are also systematically related. The semantic structure is the propositional content of the macro-speech act, and conversely, the macro-speech act is the pragmatic function of the theme or the topic of the text."[78] The "macro-speech act" is the speech act that governs the entire text.[79]

---

theme does. A change in theme or sub-theme results in a change in the semantic delimitation (segmentation) of a text (Plett 1979, 103, 104 discusses text semantic extension and text semantic delimitation). I propose to use "theme" in text linguistic work as a useful tool to describe the propositions in a given unit or TP without burdening the linguist or exegete with the task of showing how all of a text's propositions could be logically deduced from a more abstract proposition. Hellholm 1980, 36 argues that all the expressions of a text should be deducible from a theme, in agreement with Plett 1979, 103, 112. Their word "deducible" is more like deriving the sentences of the recipe from such a theme as "Puréed Chestnuts" (as in Plett 1979, 108ff.).

[77]Hellholm 1982, n. 75.

[78]Van Dijk 1979, 519ff. Van Dijk further discusses the pragmatic aspect of macrostructure in van Dijk 1977, 238–245.

[79]Inger Rosengren, in a discussion of van Dijk, also gives a brief statement of the relation of pragmatic and semantic macrostructures. Rosengren first writes that the semantic macrostructure is the theme of the text, and that macrostructures are given back (for analysis) by propositions. Rosengren then writes:

> Außer auf der semantischen Ebene gibt es Makrostrukturen auch auf der pragmatischen Ebene. Ein Makro-Sprechakt wird durch eine bestimmte Sequenz von Sprechakten ausgeführt. Die semantischen und pragmatischen Makrostrukturen sind schließlich systematisch aufeinander bezogen.

Then she follows with a statement very similar to that of van Dijk above (Rosengren 1980, 278). See Rosengren 1987 for a study of the hierarchic and sequential structure of illocutions (speech acts) in a text.

Heinrich F. Plett considers what we call the pragmatic aspect of the structure under the rubric "text pragmatic extension." This he defines as a Text Part determined by the functional unity of a text. A text strategy or illocution creates a functional unity by subordinating the other illocutions of a text to the main text strategy.[80] In other words, if the illocution (what is done in the speech act) is "to show that certain people reject God's commands," then the various parts of that text (Mk 7:1–13) are subordinated to that main text strategy. A. Ferrara calls this main text strategy a macro-speech act. This macro-speech act in a text is itself implemented by the linear chain of speech acts in the text.[81] Ferrara notes that the relation of the macro-speech acts to the micro ones is hierarchic. For example, the macro-speech act of a text could be "to prove the innocence of my client." This speech act is realized through the use of a chain of subordinate speech acts, such as proving that the client was thousands of miles away. When a speech act controls other speech acts, N. Fotion uses the term "Master speech act" to describe the phenomenon. One of his examples is "let us pray." The master speech act "let us pray" requests prayer, and also expresses the force of all the other speech acts which are to follow.[82] Fotion writes about such acts: "[they] have the function of supervising, controlling, directing, guiding (however one wishes to refer to it) other speech acts." In this work I shall use the term "governing" speech act. Under the name "voluntary (linguistic) offerings," Fotion includes examples such as "let me tell you a story," or "You know what happened to me yesterday?" Also included are "book titles and tables of contents, announcements by the speaker about the nature and content of his talk, newspaper headlines and program announcements (as at philosophy association meetings)."[83] This category is extremely important in understanding Mark as a governing speech act. The text in Mark

---

[80]See Plett 1979, 82–84.
[81]A. Ferrara 1985, 141. Speech acts are discussed in 2.3.3.
[82]N. Fotion 1971, 233, 234, 237, 238.
[83]Fotion 1979, 617–18.

1:1 is, I shall argue, a key to understanding the force of the entire text of Mark. As applied to Mark, the question raised under the pragmatic aspect of the structure is what the function of the Markan narrative was in the first century.

As an approach to the structure of Mark I shall divide the text into its frames of communication, viz. the context, such as author and audience in which a communication takes place. I shall also make use of a set of narrative markers that help the receiver to structure a communication such as changes in the scene (time, place, and *dramatis personae*). The frames and markers will delimit the text into sequences (syntactic aspect of the structure). Summaries of the texts in Mark will give an indication of the semantic structure. I shall also include certain references to the function of the Text Parts by naming the speech acts in the text (pragmatic aspect of the structure).

2.4.1. Communication Frames

The analysis of the structure of Mark presupposes the scholar's ability to order the text into different frames or levels of communication. Borrowing a term from Erving Goffman, I shall use "frame" to describe the context in which a communication takes place.[84] An author communicates with an

---

[84] "Frames" in Goffman's analysis mean "principles of organization which govern events (1974, 10, 11)." His use of the term is much broader than in this work. For Goffman, frameworks of understanding make sense out of events and help structure the "experience individuals have at any moment of their social lives" (1974, 13). An actor, who, for example, leaves his role and speaks to the audience (instead of speaking to fellow performers), breaks the frame and mixes levels of being (1974, 395). The author's characters are supposed to communicate with other characters. The author communicates with the audience. The "fool" actor in Goffman's example dissolves the "reality" of the play. Mk 13:14, "let the reader understand" comes to mind as a parallel! Text linguists such as Gülich, Heger, and Raible (1979, 81; and compare Hellholm 1980, 77, 78) use the

audience. The characters an author describes communicate with each other. The frame of communication of the author includes author and audience (Frame 1). Within that frame of communication is the frame that includes characters speaking to characters (Frame 2). If a character tells a story in which the members of the story communicate with each other, then there is a still deeper embedded frame (Frame 3). One can use the image of a larger picture frame that includes a smaller frame which itself includes a still smaller frame, and so forth.

The literary theorist Susan Lanser has developed a theory of narrative frames for fiction that correspond closely to the frames of communication described above.[85] She begins with an example (like a set of Chinese boxes) from a children's book in which a public narrator tells a story. A character in the story tells a story which itself contains a character who tells a story. The shift from one frame of narration to another is "...marked by phrases like 'he said,' divisions of discourse, quotation marks, etc."[86] She distinguishes discourse from narrators who tell stories and characters who are simply interacting with each other as actors.[87] When a character who is included in the public narrator's communication tells a story, he or she becomes a private narrator. Mary Ann Tolbert, discussing Mark, notes that when a character such as Jesus tells a story with its own independent agents, he becomes a private narrator. When he predicts the future or tells about the past he also functions as a private narrator.[88] The different narrative frames can each have

---

term "communication level" to describe the different contexts in which communications in a text take place.

[85]Lanser 1981, 133ff.
[86]Lanser 1981, 141, n. 36.
[87]Lanser 1981, 137.
[88]Tolbert 1989, 92, 93. Tolbert prefers to locate Jesus' private narration in narrative frame three. Since Jesus' speech is indicated in Frame one by the public narrator, I shall leave his private narrations in Frame 2 and mark it with a "PN." Characters speaking to each other in the frame of normal discourse are in Frame 2, and characters speaking as private narrators will

characters who communicate with each other.[89] The public narrator (who tells the story to the implied audience) has the "...strongest *diegetic authority*—authority attached to an authorial voice."[90] The characters have *mimetic authority*.[91] The communication frames contain important indicators about the illocutionary force of the text. Lanser notes that texts such as novels contain "...*evaluative illocutions*, either direct or embedded,

---

be marked as speaking in Frame 2 PN. Lanser makes it clear that she locates characters' normal discourse in the same narrative frame as characters' private narrations in 1981, 134, n. 33.

[89]Lanser 1981, 135.
[90]Lanser 1981, 142.
[91]Lanser 1981, 142. In Lanser 1981, 19ff., she traces this distinction back to Plato's distinction (*Rep.* 3) between authorial discourse (*diegesis*) and character's speech (*mimesis*). This distinction creates a spectrum with an author's discourse on one end, indirect speech in the middle, and direct discourse and quoted documents on the other end (*mimesis*) where the narrator is least involved (1981, 187ff.). Plato writes (*Rep.* 3.392d–393a):

> ἆρ' οὐ πάντα ὅσα ὑπὸ μυθολόγων ἢ ποιητῶν λέγεται διήγησις οὖσα τυγχάνει ἢ γεγονότων ἢ ὄντων ἢ μελλόντων; λέγει τε αὐτὸς ὁ ποιητὴς καὶ οὐδὲ ἐπιχειρεῖ ἡμῶν τὴν διάνοιαν ἄλλοσε τρέπειν ὡς ἄλλος τις ὁ λέγων ἢ αὐτός

> (Are not therefore all things which are spoken by mythographers or poets a narrative of things which have happened or which exist or which will come to pass?...The poet himself speaks and does not attempt to convince us that anyone other than he is speaking).

The next example from Homer illustrates Plato's use of the term μίμησις (*mimesis*) where the author speaks in the words of a character (Chryses in the example) and not as a narrator. For rhetoricians' practice of composing "in character" (ἠθοποιία, προσωποποιία) (delineation of character, putting speeches in the mouths of characters), see Mack/Robbins 1989, 44. "Delineation of character" involves composing a speech in keeping with the

spoken by the authorial voice and/or created personae: commentary and assertions about events, states, beings, values, problems, and ideas that have meaning in the historical world."[92]

For example, the title of Mark according to an ancient editor, ΕΥΑΓΓΕΛΙΟΝ ΚΑΤΑ ΜΑΡΚΟΝ (Gospel According to Mark), is on a higher frame of communication than the title given by the author of Mark that we take to be verse 1:1. The editor indicates the text's author for a group of readers. The author describes his text for his readers. The editor's title serves as a meta-frame for the author's title, which in turn serves as a meta-frame for the narrator's depiction of the events of Jesus' ministry. The narrator's communication is the meta-frame for the speech of the characters in the text. The characters' speech can serve as a meta-frame for a still deeper frame of communication. The parable told by Jesus in Mark 12:1–12, for example, contains the speech of other characters. Once the text is ordered into its frames (as will be done in chapter 3), a set of markers or signals will be used to structure the text in each frame.

2.4.2. Narrative Markers

Elisabeth Gülich and Wolfgang Raible[93] have done extensive work with signals that organize narrative texts. They assume, as a hypothesis, that a hearer or reader of a communication can recognize the structure of the text on the "surface level." "Surface level" implies that one can recognize the signals in the text as the text develops in a linear manner.[94] They define a "marker" (*Merkmal*) to mean a signal that enables a hearer or receiver to structure a communication into its parts during the

---

character, and the second type involves creating a character by means of the kind of speech attributed to it (Mack/Robbins 1989, 44).

[92]Lanser 1981, 292.

[93]Gülich, Heger, and Raible 1979, 76–99. See also Hellholm 1980, 78ff. and 1982, 177ff.

[94]Gülich, Heger, and Raible 1979, 74, 75.

reception of the communication.[95] Instead of "marker," one could use any term such as "indicator" or "identifier." Markers give a reader the ability to structure the text that she or he is reading. The chapter titles in a book, or the titles of the acts in a play, are two examples of important textual signals that "mark" parts of the text. Since a chapter title "stands for" an entire section of a text, I shall call it a "substitution" marker. As a pronoun "stands for" a noun, so a title can "substitute" or stand for a part of a text. In the beginning of this chapter, the title "Chapter Two" substitutes for the entire text of the chapter. If Mark 1:1 is a title, then it "substitutes" or "stands for" the entire text of Mark, or possibly just the section of the text that concerns John the Baptist.[96] Another kind of marker is present when a narrator gives an indication that speech is to follow. In a phrase such as "Jesus said, 'little girl arise,'" the narrator frames the command by identifying the speaker (Jesus) and by indicating that speech will follow by using the verb "said." The content of the speech activity, "little girl arise," takes place within the frame of communication that includes the characters of Mark's text speaking to one another. But the phrase "Jesus said" takes place on the frame of communication between the author of Mark (the narrator) and Mark's audience. Consequently these markers will be called "meta-communicative" markers below. They stand on a higher frame of communication than what is actually spoken (or written).[97] The superscription to Mark,

---

[95]Gülich, Heger, and Raible 1979, 75, 76. D. Schifferin (1987) analyzes discourse markers including the following: "Oh," "Well," "and," "but," "or," "so," "because," "now," "then," "y'know," and "I mean." Gülich and Raible include many other types of markers in their approach.

[96]This issue will be addressed at the beginning of Chapter Three.

[97]Goffman quotes Gregory Bateson's analysis of "metacommunication" among animals where the latter use signals to do the following: acknowledge a signal emitted by another; ask for a signal to be repeated; indicate a failure to receive a signal, and so forth (Goffman 1974, 210, n. 15). These signals are close to our use of the term to describe a narrator's indication that speech activity follows (or precedes). Goffman (1974, 211)

"Gospel according to Mark" or "According to Mark," is an indication of the author of a text and so is a kind of "metacommunicative" noun phrase. It is probably an editor's attempted identification, and alerts the reader to expect a communication from an author. It is on a higher "frame" of communication than the text of Mark's gospel, since it describes the author of the text that will follow. Speech acts (2.3.3) provide another indication of slices of a text. In Mk 12:34 the narrator notes that no one dares to question Jesus further. Questioning (and answering) is a kind of speech act. The questions had begun in the episode beginning in 11:27. Consequently, 11:27–12:34 constitutes a part of Mark's text because of the speech act marker.[98] Goffman discusses another type of marker that marks off an activity from the "ongoing flow of surrounding events." It is a temporal or spatial bracket and is like the wooden frame of a picture.[99] He gives the example in Western dramaturgy when, "at the beginning, the lights dim, the bell rings, and the curtain rises; at the other end, the curtain falls and the lights go on.... And in the interim, the acted world is restricted to the physical arena bracketed by the boundaries of the stage."[100] Goffman quotes Mary Douglas, who makes a reference to the framing function of "once upon a time." That phrase creates a mood in the hearer who is ready for a story.[101] To cite another example, if an episode took place in Galilee, "Galilee" would be the spatial marker. These spatial and temporal markers will be called "episode" markers below. When a narrator identifies a character by name, another kind of "bracket" or "marker" appears in the text. While that character

---

uses the term "connectives" to describe tags such as "he said" and "he answered."

[98]See the analysis in Chapter 3.

[99]Goffman 1974, 251. Lang 1977 uses such "scenic" markers in his outline. Rhoads and Mitchie note that these "settings" provide the overall framework for the movement of the plot (1982, 63).

[100]Goffman 1974, 252.

[101]Goffman 1974, 252, n. 5.

appears in an episode, a "slice of life" or "strip"[102] is created in which that character is present. In Mark 11:27, for example, high priests, scribes and elders appear to question Jesus. The pronoun "them" in 12:1 indicates that they are still part of the audience of the parable that follows. They respond with force in 12:12. The "slice of life" indicated by these characters, therefore, lasts from Mark 11:27 to 12:12. These markers will be called "character" markers below. Syntactic connectives such as "therefore" constitute the last class of markers to be used in the following investigation.[103]

Gülich and Raible have applied their theory to a fable of James Thurber's, "The Lover and His Lass," and reached results similar to those of another linguist (Heger) who used a different approach. The *Visions of Hermas* serve as the focus of Hellholm's investigation, in which he applied a similar set of markers to Hermas's text.[104] The markers I shall use in the analysis of Mark include the following: meta-communicative markers, substitution markers, speech act markers, episode markers, character markers, and syntactic markers. As the markers are extensively discussed elsewhere (see the above note), I shall give only a short account here.

2.4.2.1. Meta-Communicative Markers

On the highest order (one), by hypothesis, stand the meta-communicative markers. They function as markers that signal the beginning or end of a communication situation. In other words, they indicate that a communication is going to take place or

---

[102]"Strip" is a term Goffman uses to "refer to an arbitrary slice or cut from the stream of ongoing activity" (Goffman 1974, 10).

[103]Gülich and Raible do not include "speech acts" in their list of markers (Gülich, Heger, and Raible 1979, 87ff.), but Heger (1976, 280ff.) includes speech acts as one of his "Signemränge" or "sign ranks." If Heger is correct, no analysis of a text can avoid dealing with the issue of speech acts.

[104]Gülich, Heger, and Raible 1979, 76–99. See also Hellholm 1980, 78ff., and 1982, 177ff.

stop. They are a form of speech referring to speech. A narrator signals that a character will speak. In a sentence, the meta-communicative verbs signal the emission or reception of a written or spoken message. In Mark, some of the verbs that signal the emission of a message are: εἰπεῖν, λαλεῖν, διδάσκειν, ἀποκρίνεσθαι, συζητεῖν, κράζειν, ἐπερωτᾶν, διαστέλλειν, προσεύχεσθαι, and διαλογίζεσθαι (say, speak, teach, answer, argue, cry, question, command, pray, and discuss). Meta-communicative verbs in Mark that signal the reception of a message include ἀκούειν (hear) and συνίεναι (understand). In "Jesus said, 'p'" where p is a proposition, the "said" functions as a meta-communicative verb. The "Jesus said" stands on a higher frame of communication than the content of the saying because it is the narrator's introduction to the message. A noun such as εὐαγγέλιον (gospel) might also be a meta-communicative marker if it indicated a communication situation by giving some indication of the time, place, and participants. As a matter of fact, in Mark it gives no indication of the author. But the editor's addition, "The Gospel according to Mark," does indicate the sender of a communication (Mark) and so it is a meta-communicative marker.

Several different kinds of communication have been classified by K. Heger,[105] who distinguished between a monologue, a dialogue, and a polyoration structure. In a monologue, one person speaks. In a dialogue, two people or groups speak; and in a polyorational structure, three or more people or groups speak to one another. In the analysis of Mark these kinds of structures will be distinguished.

A specific type of meta-communicative marker is the call to attention. Here a speaker demands that his or her audience pay special attention to what is said. Examples in Mark are βλέπετε (see, 4:24) and ἀκούετε (hear, 4:3) placed before a speech.[106]

---

[105] Heger 1976, 302–308.
[106] For further discussion of this marker, see Hellholm 1980, 83, and the references there.

2.4.2.2. Substitution Markers

The substitution markers follow in importance, by hypothesis, the meta-communicative markers. A "substitution" is the replacement of one linguistic expression (*substituendum*) by another (*substituens*).[107] In a substitution, one sign (*substituens*) stands or substitutes for another (*substituendum*). In relation to large segments of texts, Gülich/Raible and Hellholm have used a term called "substitution on a meta-frame."[108] This is the case because such a meta-frame substitution as "The Lover and His Lass" (title for a fable of Thurber) replaces a whole text and stands on a frame different from the narrative language of the fable. This different frame is called a meta-frame, since it comments on the frame of the narrative (or object) language. By use of these markers the text speaks about itself without there necessarily being any allusion to the sender or receiver who participates in the communication situation. Ἀρχή ...θεοῦ (Beginning ...of God) in Mark 1:1 is an example of a substitution on a meta-frame. The text of Mark itself is in the frame of the "object language." The words Ἀρχή ...θεοῦ are an example of

---

[107]Raible 1972, 194ff.; Harweg 1979, 20 and passim. Roland Harweg developed the theory of syntagmatic substitution, which concentrates on phenomena that bind sentences together as in a case when the pronoun like "they" substitues for "scribes and Pharisees" (Gülich and Raible 1977, 115–126; Harweg 1979; Plett 1979, 60–70). Harweg also developed a macro-syntactic element which considers how texts combine groups of sentences and then refer to these groups of sentences. An example of this phenomenon would be the title of part of a play, "Act I." Elisabeth Gülich and Wolfgang Raible have continued this approach to understand how the sentences of a text can be organized into hierarchically arranged Text Parts (Gülich and Raible 1977, 120; Hellholm 1980, 75–76; see both for the two dimensional model of a text involving syntagmatic substitution and the macro-syntactic element).

[108]See Gülich, Heger, and Raible 1979, 87ff., and Hellholm 1980, 84ff. A more literal translation of "Metaebene" would be "meta-level," but given my use of "frames of communication," I shall use the other translation.

the text speaking about itself, so linguists speak of a meta-frame or meta language where an analytical language is devised to speak about daily or object language. The word "gospel" in the editor's title is a reference to the entire text of Mark and so it is a substitution marker. Consequently the editor's title is both a meta-communicative marker (because of Mark's name) and a substitution marker.

Another substitution marker is the substitution in a narrative frame. This marker includes those words of a text (*substituens*) which have a larger range of meaning than that for which they substitute (*substituendum*).[109] This marker does not, therefore, stand on a meta-frame in relation to the portion of a text for which the marker substitutes. In Mark there are many examples of this kind of marker such as a noun like λόγον (the *substituens*) in 8:32, which substitutes for the passion teaching in 8:31 (the *substituendum*). The term λόγον (word) is an abstraction for the passion teaching but does not stand on a meta-frame in relation to the passion teaching. This is so because λόγον is integrated into the narrative. But a title of a book, such as Ἀρχή ...θεοῦ, is a substitution which stands on a meta-frame in relation to the language of the text. Since substitution-on-a-narrative frame markers do not stand on a meta-frame, they will not be placed on Order Two of the marker hierarchy but will be used in conjunction with other markers. Order One comprises the meta-communicative markers. For the use of both kinds of substitution markers, see the analysis of the structure of Mark.

---

[109] Raible develops the concept of an abstraction frame of a text in distinction from the text's object language and meta language frames. Consequently, he calls these markers "substitutions on an abstraction frame." See Raible 1972, 13, 150, and the other references and discussion in Hellholm 1980, 86–87. For the sake of clarity, I shall call this marker a substition in a narrative frame.

2.4.2.3. Speech Act Markers

Speech acts constitute a marker which is closely related to meta-communicative expressions. Since speech acts presume the existence of a communication I shall place them on Order Three of the marker analysis. They do not stand in a meta-frame in relation to a text. Commands, warnings, questions, answers, and so forth are all examples of speech acts.[110]

The structural role of the speech act markers in Mark will be, by hypothesis, consigned to the third order of the hierarchy. Only occasionally will speech acts be appealed to as the primary marker for the structuring of a Text Part.

2.4.2.4. Episode Markers

By hypothesis, episode markers come next in importance. They include changes in time and place that appear in the text. Since an episode marker such as Ἱεροσόλυμα (Jerusalem, 11:1) can encompass other episode markers such as ἱερῷ (temple; 11:27) and so forth, Hellholm uses the name *Nachfolgemerkmale* for the markers that divide sections of text delimited by one episode marker into smaller sections.[111] I shall call an episode marker that governs others an "absolute marker"; the markers such as "temple" in the above example will be called "relative markers." In the analysis of Mark, as in 11:1–16:8, the largest episode marker (an absolute episode marker) such as "Jerusalem" will be used to structure episodes of smaller range, such as the teaching in the temple (the relative episode marker) in 11:27–12:44.

---

[110]See Heger 1976, 280ff., and Plett 1979, 82, 83 for examples. Also see Wörner 1978, passim. See also Austin 1975, Searle 1969, and Sadock 1974. See 2.3.3.

[111]Hellholm 1980, 91–92. Hellholm 1982, 179 uses the term "relative episode marker" for this phenomenon and opposes it to "absolute episode" markers. Spatial, temporal, and character markers were discussed as being important in narratives in Theon's *Progymnasmata* 5.1ff. (ed. Butts 1987=ed. Spengel 4, p. 78).

2.4.2.5. Character Markers

Since episode markers will appear on the Order Four of our analysis, the next markers will be on Order Five. These are character markers that include those words that describe changes in the group of characters in a given Text Part. In the Jerusalem section in 11:1–16:8, for example, many characters appear but the location remains the same. Character markers, therefore, appear on Order Five of the marker hierarchy. When a character is the object of a verb or the subject of a passive verb I shall call it a CM(P) (passive character marker).

2.4.2.6. Syntactic Markers

The markers to be considered last are sentence and text connectors. Adverbs and conjunctions that relate sentences or groups of sentences fall under this rubric. Καθώς, οὖν, καί, and ἀλλά are elements in this set of markers that also help structure texts. They will be placed on Order Six of the marker hierarchy.

2.4.3. Establishing a Structure

After the text of Mark is ordered into the various communication frames, the markers can be applied to organize the Text Parts, beginning with the meta-communicative markers (Order One) and proceeding in the order described above to the syntactic markers (Order Six). The markers on the highest communication frame (that of the editor) are investigated; then one can proceed to the next communication frame, and so on. This process allows the scholar to arrange the text into different frames for the purpose of hierarchically outlining the text.

I shall place the number indicating the level of the outline on the left of the symbol for text part (TP). In our analysis level 00 (^{00}TP) describes the communication frame of the editor with its meta-communicative marker. Level 0 (^{0}TP) describes the communication frame of the author's title with the title as a substitution marker. Level 1 (^{1}TP) then describes the communication frame of the narrator. The markers are applied to the analysis of this level of the text and enable the scholar to develop further levels of the text in the same way that one organizes an outline. Every outline uses some form of embedded levels. For example, "II.C.1" in an outline using Roman numerals would be on the third level of the outline. In an outline using the "legal" style (such as the one used in this work), "II.C.1" in the Roman outline would correspond to "2.3.1."

In our analysis of Mark, Level One is structured by episode markers that describe the largest geographical portions of Jesus' ministry. Level Two is then comprised of further divisions of those geographical episodes. After the markers that structure the narrator's communication frame are exhausted, I continue to structure the text by moving to the next communication frame (the characters' speech) and applying the markers to it. In this way a tentative structure of Mark is developed that will guide interpretation of the text. The structure will be based on empirically checkable surface level markers.

Each level, such as for example ^{1}TP, should be divided into sections using the same kind of markers. In the case of ^{1}TP, the episode markers divide it into sections. ^{00}TP and ^{0}TP contain the only markers that stand on a meta-frame to ^{1}TP (namely meta-communicative and substitution on a meta-frame markers). If Mark had included chapter titles or something similar, they would stand on a meta-frame to level ^{1}TP (namely ^{0}TP). When working with a TP such as ^{3}TP$^{1.1.1}$(1:2–8), the "3" indicates the level of the given TP. The third number to the right of "TP" (1.1. "1") indicates that the TP (1:2–8) is the first section of ^{2}TP$^{1.1}$(2–11). The second "1" to the right in ^{2}TP$^{1.1}$ indicates that this TP is the first section in ^{1}TP^1(1:2–13).

(The writer apologizes for the profusion of numbers and symbols included in the next chapter, but they are necessary for communicating the intention of this work in a succinct fashion. The next chapter will use the markers and communication frames to present an approach to the structure of Mark. A reader who finds herself or himself frustrated by the profusion of symbols in the following chapter could perhaps skip over it, look at the summary in Appendix Two, read the discussion in Chapter Four and then later return to Chapter Three later.)

CHAPTER 3

A LINGUISTIC OUTLINE OF MARK

3.1. Introduction

In this section I shall discuss the outline to be given later in this chapter in more detail. The concept of outline used in this work is discussed in 2.4. It has a syntactic, semantic, and pragmatic element. This chapter's outline of Mark contains elements of all three aspects. The syntactic element comprises the communication frames and the delimitation of the text into Text Parts. The semantic aspect comprises the abstracts that describe the content of Mark. The indications of the kinds of speech acts in Mark are a concern of pragmatics. In the following introduction to the outline of Mark there will be a discussion of the frames of communication (2.4.1) and the markers (2.4.2) that are used to structure the text. The frames are the context in which the communication takes place and include the frame of the editor's title, the frame of the author's title for his work, the frame of the narrator and the narrator's audience, and the frame of the characters who speak to each other. There are still more deeply embedded frames of communication. After placing the text in its different frames of communication, the markers (discussed in 2.4.2) are used to divide the text into text sequences. The markers allow the hearer to structure a communication and include titles and scenic indicators such as changes in space, time, and characters. I shall describe the major episodes found using the frames and markers. To do the outline, a number of abbreviations for the frames and markers will need to be used; they are included at the end of the introduction along with a brief description of the process of using the frames and markers to produce an outline.

3.2. The Frames of Communication

The outline gives a picture of the structure of Mark that is based on ordering the text into its different frames of communication and using an organized set of markers to divide the text into units of meaning (Text Parts).[1] The text must first be divided into its communication frames before the ordered set of markers for finding the Text Parts can be applied.[2]

3.2.1. Frame 00

The 00 frame of communication contains an editor's title (or "name label")[3] for the text—ΕΥΑΓΓΕΛΙΟΝ ΚΑΤΑ ΜΑΡΚΟΝ

---

[1]See Gülich, Heger and Raible 1979, 127ff., for the insight that Heger's *Signemränge* (units of meaning) correspond to the TPs that Gülich and Raible delimit using narrative markers.

[2]See the discussion of the method in 2.4.

[3]Hellholm 1990, 112ff. prefers to call the secondary *inscriptiones* such as Ἀποκάλυψις Ἰωάννου and Διδαχὴ τῶν δώδεκα ἀποστόλων "name labels" instead of "titles," and to use the term "title" for the *incipit*s (Rev. 1:1–3 and Διδαχὴ κυρίου διὰ τῶν δώδεκα ἀποστόλων τοῖς ἔθνεσιν). There is a clear difference as Hellholm notes: "In both instances there is a change in the adnominal genetive constructions from John or the Twelve Apostles as revealer or originator to Jesus Christ or the Lord respectively." He argues that a "name label" may be arbitrary (like a name) without making much difference, whereas a title is not. The "name label" is merely for identification purposes and differentiates the text from other productions by the same author or by different authors (and was first used by the Greeks in library cataloging in contrast to the eastern practice of using a work's title for

(Gospel According to Mark)—according to the text that is given in this chapter and arranged into its frames of communication.⁴ On this frame an editor (scribe?) informs the readers of the nature of the text by identifying the editor's opinion of the author.⁵ Since some kind of title such as this stands in all important manuscripts, it is included in the text analysis even though the historical reliability of the title's claim about the author can be doubted.⁶ The point here is that an editor is

---

a book's entry—see Ruth French-Strout 1956, 256–257). Labels were often put on the outside of scrolls, at the start of a text, and at the end in a colophon (Burridge 1992, 112). The labels included the author's name and a brief title. The name labels are not completely arbitrary because of the genre-designations in the *inscriptiones* (Hellholm 1990, 114). Since the *inscriptio* in Mark does primarily serve to differentiate the text from other gospels, "name label" would be an apposite term for it. The editor makes the important step of using ΕΥΑΓΓΕΛΙΟΝ for a genre-designation.

⁴Based on Nestle-Aland 1979.

⁵Hengel 1985,73, 83 considers the possibility that the first copyist of the Gospel included the title. Since the title seems to assume the existence of other gospels, Lührmann (1987, 4) argues that it cannot have been originally with the text of Mark. See also Vielhauer 1975, 255 and Burridge 1992, 192–93. If the editor was considering gospels such as Thomas and so forth, then Lührmann's argument loses force. Helmut Koester objects to Hengel's thesis (1989, 373, n. 2, 376, n. 2) because of the late second century evidence Hengel uses and because Papias and other sources show there was no uniformity in the designation of the gospels. Marcion first used the term "gospel" for a writing, according to Koester (1989, 376).

⁶See the major introductions and commentaries for the development of this point. The title shows an awareness of the other gospels. Hengel 1985, 66ff. gives some good reasons for accepting the longer title (instead of ΚΑΤΑ ΜΑΡΚΟΝ) as being original. The important MSS other than ℵ and B have the longer form. Of twenty papyri of the gospels from the 2nd and 3rd c. only 3 have *inscriptiones* or *subscriptiones*. 𝔓66 has (*inscriptio*) ΕΥΑΓΓΕΛΙΟΝ ΚΑΤΑ ΙΩΑΝΝΗΝ. 𝔓75 has the *subscriptio* ΕΥΑΓΓΕΛΙΟΝ ΚΑΤΑ ΛΟΥΚΑΝ and the *inscriptio* ΕΥΑΓΓΕΛΙΟΝ ΚΑΤΑ ΙΩΑΝΝΗΝ. 𝔓4,64,67 (which belong together) have a page with ΕΥΑΓΓΕΛΙΟΝ ΚΑΤΑ ΜΑΘΘΑΙΟΝ. The originals of these

communicating something he/she feels is important about the text to an audience that probably has knowledge of some of the other gospels. Which gospels in particular an editor is thinking of is an open question. It could be the other canonical gospels or it could be Thomas or other apocryphal texts. As such, it stands in the highest frame of communication. At this stage, ΕΥΑΓΓΕΛΙΟΝ ΚΑΤΑ ΜΑΡΚΟΝ has come to mean "gospel" as a literary genre.

3.2.2. Frame 0

The 0 frame of communication contains what is probably the author's (whom we shall call Mark) title for his work which he aims at his intended audience. This audience was likely different from that audience which the editors of the gospels envisioned. Mk 1:1 is probably a title regardless of the exact temporal reference of ἀρχή (beginning viz. of John's ministry or of the entire ministry of Jesus) and regardless of the grammatical nature of the genitive εὐαγγέλιον ’Ιησοῦ (gospel about/of Jesus— objective or subjective). To understand the title, such decisions need to be made, but it still remains a title as a unit. The title stands in a higher frame of communication than that of the work itself, since it describes the work as a text containing the "gospel." This issue—and objections to taking 1:1 as a title—is discussed further in 3.3.2 below.

3.2.3. Frame 1

Mark's description of characters and events appears as Frame 1 in the analysis.[7] Here the author as narrator describes for the audience the background of events and characters. Mark also

---

MSS probably go back into the 2nd c. The longer form also has support in the Old Latin, Coptic versions, Irenaeus, Clement of Alexandria, the Muratorian canon and Tertullian. This wide and early attestation rules out a late origin for the titles.

[7]See Petersen's remarks on the narrator and his point of view, in Petersen 1978a. See other interesting remarks on the narrator, in Rhoads and Mitchie 1982, 35ff.

describes and explains the words of characters of the OT and the words of the characters that include Jesus and his generation. The narrator is of the omniscient variety.[8]

3.2.4. Frames 2–4

The author also describes words found in the mouths of characters in the narrative. These characters' conversations and monologues are presented in Frame 2. Since the author describes the characters who speak, the author stands in a higher Frame (1) in relation to what is communicated by the characters. Characters speaking in Frame 2 sometimes quote words of other characters. The words of those figures are in Frame 3. When speech in Frame 3 itself indicates a communication, that communication will appear in Frame 4.

The words of OT figures can be found in Frame 2 OT. These figures are described (in Frame 1) by the author and are explicitly identified as coming from the holy writings of Israel. The author applies the ancient words to the events of the Gospel. The speech of figures who are described by characters in Frame 2 appears on communication Frame 3. David, for example, is described by Jesus in 12:36. Jesus speaks in Frame 2 of the analysis. The speech of David, since he is a figure identified as speaking in the OT, appears in Frame 3 OT. When Jesus, speaking in Frame 2, narrates the speech of the evil vineyard workers in 12:7, their speech appears in Frame 3. A character in Frame 2 can also narrate its own speech by indicating it with λέγω ὑμῖν (I say unto you). The speech referred to in this way appears in Frame 3 of the analysis (e.g., 11:23) and is marked with an "HS" (his or her own speech). When Frame 2 OT indicates speech, that speech is in Frame 3 SOT (speech of characters in Old Testament quotation). An example of this is Mk 1:3b, where the voice in the wilderness speaks in Frame 3 SOT. Scripture (the words of Isaiah in Frame 2 OT) describes this voice. The narrator (Frame 1) has informed the reader that the

---

[8]On point of view, see also Tolbert 1989, 51.

scripture to follow comes from Isaiah. Likewise when Frame 3 OT describes a communication, that communication appears in Frame 4 SOT of the analysis (speech of characters in Old Testament quotation). An example of this is Mk 12:36 where David's speech (scripture) in Frame 3 OT, "the Lord said to my Lord," indicates a communication in Frame 4 SOT, "Sit...." The "Sit at my right hand until I put your enemies under your feet" is one of most deeply embedded communications in the Gospel of Mark. Jesus obviously approves of this communication which he quotes from Scripture, as coming directly from the mouth of the Lord.

When a character speaks as a private narrator (discussing past, present, or future),[9] it is marked with a "PN" in the analysis, as in Jesus' parables of chapter four and in Jesus' description of coming events in 14:13b–15. When an otherworldy character or narrator speaks without the mediation of any thisworldly character, it is marked with an "ON," as in 1:11b where the voice from heaven speaks. The heavenly voice appears on the same communication frame (2) as that of other *dramatis personae*, but it seems useful to mark them, given the unusual nature of the source. If the narrator included Satan's words in 1:13, for example, they would also be marked with an "ON."

3.2.5. *The Dynamic Interaction of the Frames*

Each communication frame in the analysis therefore includes the next frame within itself (e.g., Frame 1 includes Frame 2 within its purview). The image of a large picture frame containing a smaller frame which itself contains a smaller frame helps to make this phenomenon understandable. This analysis of Mark is, on the one hand, vulnerable because it does not isolate redactional additions. On the other hand, the analysis of the text into communication frames enables the scholar to perceive

---

[9]See Plato's definition of "narrative" (*Rep.* 3) and the use of "private narrator" in Lanser's and Tolbert's work in 2.4.1.

editor, author entitling his work, author as narrator, characters, and characters whose speech is narrated by other characters. These identifications, though they may be questioned, are based on text-internal evidence and not on decisions about tradition history and redaction that are so easily subject to skepticism.[10] By doing such an analysis of the text as a unit of communication, the scholar can see the material as internally coherent and can use the information to seek the ancient meaning of the text as it stands and was probably meant by the author to be understood. As a next step the scholar can do tradition history and redactional analysis. The analysis of the text into communication frames also helps to isolate the text-internal and text-external communications of Mark.[11] Frames 00, 0 and 1 involve direct communication between editor or author (or author as implied narrator) and an audience. All these figures unfortunately remain obscure, even though the editor's opinion of the author's name is clear. The audience of the editor's title may well have been the entire church. For exegesis a central problem is what Mark expected his audience to know. The text-internal communication comprises all the remaining frames where characters communicate with one another. Ultimately, all the communication frames are directed to the audience, but the communication frames distinguish direct from indirect communications. The frames also aid the scholar in using the markers to divide the text into TPs.

The significance of the communication frames appears clearly in the work of one recent commentator on Mark. Although her approach is different from that of this work with regard to Frame 3, Tolbert makes good use of communication frames in her commentary on Mark.[12] Outside the world of the text (which she calls the fictional world) are the author and

---

[10]Gülich and Raible 1977, 46, 47.

[11]For reference to this distinction and further bibliography, see Hellholm 1980, 43, 83, 84.

[12]Tolbert 1989, 90ff.

authorial audience (the audience imagined by the author).[13] On Frame 1 is the implied author/narrator and implied reader/narratee. In Mark's text there is no character as narrator (as in Conrad's *Lord Jim*). Therefore, the implied author is identical to the narrator.[14] Similarly, there is no character as narratee; so the implied audience is identical to the narratee. The communications between characters in the text are in Frame 2. And Frame 3 contains any narratives with independent agents that characters in the text might narrate.[15] The model helps Tolbert understand the different amounts of knowledge and perception available in the different frames.[16] The narrator, for example, is omniscient: he knows internal thoughts (2:6–7); he knows decisions made away from the main scene (3:6); he knows Jesus' private words (14:35–36), and so forth. The characters hear only what is given in Frame 2, so their knowledge is limited. The reader knows who Jesus is from the first verse and thus can evaluate the characters' response to Jesus. Although Jesus is a character in the narrative, he shares in the omniscience of the narrator. He knows the thoughts of others (2:8), and he predicts the future (8:31). He heals (6:12–13), and has power over nature (4:39–41). In this way Jesus bridges the divine-human divide by having some of the power of the omniscient narrator. Mark blends the perspective of the narrator and Jesus and gives the text one single dominant point of view, with the result that the story has no moral or ideological ambiguity (unlike some modern

---

[13] Tolbert 1989, 92, 53.

[14] Tolbert 1989, 93. Tolbert (1989, 52) defines the implied author as the "ideal version of the writer created by the sum of choices in making the text." This includes the narrator's point of view, and the selection and arrangement of material. The implied reader (1989, 53) is "the role of the reader implied in the text."

[15] Tolbert 1989, 92. Frame 3 in this work's approach is different (see 2.4.1 and 3.2.4). Since the character is still speaking to the same audience (other characters) we keep these texts in Frame 2—but they are distinguished from other texts in Frame Two (as frame 2 PN).

[16] Tolbert 1989, 93ff.

novels where the narrator's evaluation of the characters does not cohere with their actions).[17] The result of this union of the narrator's and Jesus' point of view is that the implied reader identifies with Jesus' point of view, and only as the disciples identify with Jesus' point of view does a reader identify with them.[18]

The frames also clarify the use of irony in the text. The narrator and implied reader share knowledge that enables the reader to recognize when the story appears to say something that is not intended. Gail O'Day notes that "there is always some kind of opposition between the two levels of meaning in irony—either contradiction, incongruity, or incompatibility."[19] For instance, in 15:18–32 "King of the Jews" and "Christ" are used to ridicule Jesus. However, the reader knows that the titles are correct from the narrator's point of view. Kingsbury notes the irony in the High Priest's question to Jesus in 14:61. The question can only be answered in the negative according to the High Priest's point of view (14:63–64). But the secret of who Jesus is glimmers through the question anyway.[20] This verbal irony builds connection between the author and readers. Situational irony, arising from situations and not word plays, also appears in the interplay of the frames. The disciples, for example, receive private teaching (4:12–12, 4:34), but have no insight about Jesus (4:41). The disciples watch Jesus feed the 5,000 in 6:35–44, but cannot imagine how he can feed the 4,000 in 8:1–9.[21]

The frames do not identify implicit references to the Old Testament, but they do provide an indication of the OT texts that the narrator marks explicitly. 1:2–3 gives an example of the use the narrator/implied author makes of different frames of

---

[17]Tolbert 1989, 94ff.
[18]Tolbert 1989, 97, n. 13.
[19]O'Day 1986, 23.
[20]Kingsbury 1988, 18.
[21]Tolbert discusses irony in 1989, 98ff. She also discusses the parables of 4:3–8, 14–20, 12:1–11 as an example of third degree narrative. They function as typological guides to Mark in her analysis of the text (1989, 103ff.).

communication. 1:2a gives the narrator's identity of the Scriptural author in Frame 1, even though part of what follows is not from Isaiah. The language in 1:2b–1:3 appears in Frame 2 of the analysis and is used by the narrator to illuminate the events surrounding the appearance of John the Baptist. The same speaker (in Frame 2 OT) who sends "my messenger" also describes the "voice of one crying in the wilderness." That voice in turn speaks in Frame 3 SOT of the communication to a number of unidentified people (ἑτοιμάσατε, prepare). By combining what were originally verses in Malachi and Isaiah the author as narrator identifies the sender and the one who observes the voice in the wilderness. Thus, one naturally assumes that the sender identifies the messenger and the voice. The narrator uses this subtle interplay of Frame 2 OT (the sender) and Frame 3 SOT (the messenger's voice) to explain John's identity. The different frames (narrator in one, sender in 2 OT, and the voice's communication in 3 SOT) are carefully interwoven and interpret each other.

The same dynamic process is evident in Jesus' use of scripture in 11:17. The narrator (in Frame 1) describes Jesus' teaching. Jesus (in Frame 2) quotes scripture to those listening in the temple. The actual quotation (in Frame 3 OT) depicts a speaker describing "my house of prayer." Since the description seems to be a statement about the future ("shall be called"), it is also a private narration (PN-type of speech).[22] Jesus continues (in Frame 2 again) with a description of his audience's actions, which are opposed to what God (the speaker) wants the house of prayer to be. The different communication frames of the narrator, Jesus, and the Scripture are interwoven in the one verse to give the reader a clear picture of Jesus' motivation in cleansing the temple.

The public narrator weaves the different frames together and can do so with different scriptural voices. The narrator also

---

[22] If one takes it as a gnomic future then it is not a private narration about the future. Compare Lührmann 1987, 193, who emphasizes what the temple is "supposed to be" in his interpretation.

weaves together the work of the private narrators. When characters in the text become narrators in their own right (telling a story, speaking of past or future), we have marked their speech with a "PN" in the analysis of the communication frames. Jesus' parables (e.g., 2:19ff., 4:1–34, 7:18ff., 12:2ff.) and teachings about his passion (e.g., 8:31) qualify as narratives, as does the question of the Sadducees in 12:19ff. Narration of the future (as in 13:1ff.) is usually Jesus' domain, but the woman who touches Jesus' garment narrates the future in an interior monologue (5:28).[23] The leaders in 11:31–32 narrate the future in a sense by posing a logical dilemma to themselves about their possible responses to Jesus. The text obviously pictures Jesus with the power to narrate the future. Only the woman with the flow of blood shares in this power (5:28), as do John in 1:8 and the young man in 16:7. Private narrations about the past also are important in the text as in Jesus' remarks about Elijah in 9:13, and other characters' references to Moses' teachings in 10:4 and 12:19ff.[24] Tolbert has shown that the parable of the sower (4:3–9) can be taken as a typological guide to the responses to Jesus in the text.[25] In this case the public narrator uses Jesus' own story to help the audience understand people's reactions to Jesus. The private narrators' accounts of the past and the future are woven into the story which the narrator constructs for the audience and extend the temporal limits of the story world.

Otherworldly characters speak without human mediation in frame 2 ON in 1:11, 9:7 and 16:6–7. The message of the voice from heaven in 1:11 and 9:7 (discussed above in 2.3.5) serves to undergird the authority of Jesus who in turns gives the Markan narratives authority. God's assertion about Jesus can be interpreted as a performative speech act.[26] The narrator uses the

---

[23] Private narrations by Jesus about the future also include: 8:34ff., 9:1, 9:9, 9:31ff., 9:42ff. (also about the present), 10:29ff., 10:33ff., 11:23ff., 12:40, 13:2–37, 14:9, 14:13ff., 14:18, 14:25, and 14:62.

[24] The witnesses also narrate the past in 14:58.

[25] See Tolbert in note 21, above.

[26] This type of speech act is discussed in 2.3.5.

assertion of God to reveal Jesus' identity, and the narratives in turn make a claim on the allegiance of the reader. The angel's (young man's) imperative and assertion in 16:6–7 also reveal Jesus' identity by claiming that he has risen from the dead and that the women should make this known. The narrator also uses this assertion to encourage the reader to follow Jesus. The otherworldly figures discussed above reinforce the narrator's (1:1) own point of view.

When a character indicates his or her own speech (e.g., "I say to you," "I command you") I have marked it with an "HS." The speech act involved is that of a "solemn assertion." The emphasis by the speaker on who is speaking underscores the authority of what is said. The narrator portrays Jesus as one who uses this kind of communication. Jesus underscores in this fashion his healing and exorcism commands in 2:11, 5:41, and 9:25. He also underscores his statements about the future using this type of speech in 3:28, 8:12, and so forth.[27] Once Jesus uses solemn assertion to speak about the past in 9:13 (re: John and Elijah), and once he uses it to speak about the present in 12:43–44. Jesus uses solemn assertion one time to give a command to all people (13:37). Usually Jesus' speech appears in Frame 2 with that of the other characters described by the narrator. But when Jesus describes his own speech it shifts to Frame 3. That subtle change, however, emphasizes the importance of his words and ought not be be overlooked.

Exegesis can, of course, be carried out without being aware of the communication frames and the types of communication that have been identified here. But surely knowing about the frames helps the reader of Mark to better understand the working of the text. Each frame governs and interprets the frame below it. Being aware of the communication frames enables a reader to understand how Mark weaves together speech from different times and places to construct a coherent narrative.

---

[27]Compare 9:1, 9:41, 10:15, 10:29, 11:23, 11:24–25, 13:30–31, 14:9, 18, 25.

3.3. The Markers

The markers also contribute to the understanding of the inter-relationships in Mark. Once the communication frames are clear, the markers enable the scholar to divide the text as in an outline and thereby establish the largest units (or TPs) and the smaller units that are governed by the former.

3.3.1. The Inscriptio (^{00}TP)

The title "Gospel According to Mark," since it appears in frame 00, stands out clearly from the body of the text. The editor's title is a meta-communicative expression that refers to the entire text, including the author's title (1:1). Because it contains the author's name it is a meta-communicative expression, and because it refers to the entire text it is a substitution in a meta-frame.[28] The editor wants the text to be taken as the creation of Mark. This marker indicates the communication situation by telling the editor's audience who wrote the book. The title seems to be an attempt also to ground the reliability of the text.[29]

Further, the editor's title apparently also compares the work with the other gospels in the NT corpus by using a title similar to that of the other gospels. All four gospels (or the ones the editor knows) are thus identified as belonging to the same genre. The editor (or editors) of the NT wants Mark to be considered as a genre in the context of the other three gospels (and their inscriptions). Philipp Vielhauer (see Appendix 1) notes that the ΚΑΤΑ ΜΑΡΚΟΝ (According to Mark) is probably an abbreviation for ΕΥΑΓΓΕΛΙΟΝ ΚΑΤΑ ΜΑΡΚΟΝ (Gospel According to Mark—actually in MSS A, D, L, etc. and see note 6). This hypothesis is represented by Irenaeus and Athanasius.

---

[28] Hellholm 1980, 86 discusses expressions that have characteristics of both markers. Compare the analysis of an author's name in a superscript in Gülich and Raible 1979, 103.

[29] The story about Peter and Mark grows until Peter confirms the Gospel, see Kalin 1975.

Irenaeus refers to a four-fold gospel and Athanasius refers to a gospel set with only four elements. (See Appendix 1 for this evidence and for some remarks on the lexicographical background of εὐαγγέλιον.)

Origen's remarks on the meaning of the word "gospel" (see the appendix) suggest that a message is good news only if accepted. This is a hermeneutical remark, since it is concerned about the pragmatics of author and audience. Nevertheless, the editor (if Vielhauer and the above remarks are correct) and Mark both claim that the work is true and "good news."[30] Most likely, εὐαγγέλιον (gospel) contains a *seme* "good news" when used in context in Mark. Such a *seme* could not be claimed for all uses of the word, but does seem appropriate for the word's use in Mark. If this *seme* is correct, the reader is engaged in a decision process from the very beginning of the text. One must decide if the text is good news or not. When the reader of Mark (any reader) considers the text as an example of the genre which includes the other three gospels (in the NT at least), she or he follows the editor's guiding inscription. We assume (a diachronic judgment) that an editor who was aware of some of the other three gospels added the inscription, although no manuscripts lack some form of the inscription. Somebody named Mark may have written the Gospel, and although this is an interesting diachronic matter, it does not affect the synchronic interpretation of the text. The inscription uses ΚΑΤΑ ΜΑΡΚΟΝ (according to Mark), instead of ΤΟΥ ΜΑΡΚΟΥ (of Mark), to emphasize that the gospel is according to Mark's presentation and not just Mark's Gospel (*genitivus auctoris*).[31]

---

[30] On the truth claim issue see 2.3.4 (re 1:1). Appendix One also contains references to skeptical attitudes toward εὐαγγέλιον. See also Homer, *Od.* 14.152ff., 166ff. for a skeptical response, discussed in Schniewind 1931, 117.

[31] Blass, Debrunner, and Funk (1961) secs. 163, 224.2. Lührmann 1987, 4 "κατά verweist vielmehr auf das *eine* Evangelium, als dessen spezielle Gestalt das jeweilige Evangelium erscheint." Hengel 1985, 65 takes a similar position. Compare the title in *Corpus Medicorum Graecorum IV* (ed. J. Ilberg) 1927, 175 ΙΠΠΟΚΡΑΤΟΥΣ ΓΕΝΟΣ ΚΑΙ ΒΙΟΣ ΚΑΤΑ ΣΩΡΑΝΟΝ (The

3.3.2. The Title: Mk 1:1 (⁰TP)

The substitution in a meta-frame (1:1) is more controversial because of the exegetical ambiguities. But most of the possible translations, such as "Beginning [or foundation] of the Gospel about Jesus Christ [or the Gospel of Jesus] Son of God," can be taken to be a comment on the entire text from 1:2 to the end. This is the case whether or not there is a specific temporal reference to John's ministry. For example, if John is the beginning, then the rest of the text is the continuation of the gospel. The title would then refer primarily to John, but would assume that the rest of the text is a continuation of the gospel. If the whole text is the beginning or foundation of the gospel, the

---

Birth and Life of Hippocrates According to Soranus). The ΚΑΤΑ probably distinguishes Soranus's work from other lives of Hippocrates. Eus. *Eccl. Hist.* 5.8.10 has ... τῆς κατὰ τοὺς ἑβδομήκοντα ἑρμηνείας τῶν θεοπνεύστων γραφῶν (the translation of the divinely inspired Scriptures according to the seventy). Here the scriptures are referred to in their Septuagint form or presentation. So the κατὰ phrase is not simply a periphrasis for the genitive (*pace* BAG "κατά 7c"). Jos. *c. Apionem* 1.3.18 writes concerning Thucydides: πολλὰ δὲ καὶ Θουκυδίδης ὡς ψευδόμενος ὑπό τινων κατηγορεῖται, καίτοι δοκῶν ἀκριβέστατα τὴν καθ' αὑτὸν ἱστορίαν συγγράφειν (Thucydides is often accused of lying by certain people—even though his version of history is reputed to be the most accurate). There the κατά (according to) phrase indicates that Thucydides' version of history is in question as opposed to that of others, and so in this case it is not merely another way of expressing the genitive. An index search of ΚΑΤΑ on the *TLG* (capital letters with no accents) revealed 283 uses, most of which were in titles or sub-titles. Philo, *de opificio mundi* t has ΠΕΡΙ ΤΗΣ ΚΑΤΑ ΜΩΥΣΕΑ ΚΟΣΜΟΠΟΙΙΑΣ (Concerning the Creation of the Cosmos According to Moses). This is similar to Eus. *Prep. Ev.* 8.7.1.t ΠΕΡΙ ΤΗΣ ΚΑΤΑ ΜΩΣΕΑ ΘΕΟΣΕΒΟΥΣ ΠΟΛΙΤΕΙΑΣ (Concerning the God-fearing Polity According to Moses). Similar uses are also in *Prep. Ev.* 8.1.1.t and 8.8.1.t. Eus. *Prep. Ev.* 11.1.1.t has ΩΣ Η ΚΑΤΑ ΠΛΑΤΩΝΑ ΦΙΛΟΣΟΦΙΑ...(The Philosophy Acording to Plato). These uses of the preposition also show that it is not merely a periphrasis for the genitive, but refers to Moses' or Plato's versions of the topics in question.

expression in 1:1 is clearly a descriptive title.[32] Mk 1:1 and the inscription indicate that the text is to be taken as "gospel." Genre designation is a very important function of substitutions in a meta-frame, as Hellholm notes:[33]

> ...this type of substitution also "informs the receiver of the function of the text." This function is particularly important, when the substitution is a manifestation of a generic concept such as "Gospel" or "Apocalypse," since a genre designation "rules the—nevertheless very many—possibilities of interpretation and curtails them: one laughs...at the death of an innocent man in a burlesque but one grieves therefore in a tragedy."

The exegetical problems of the verse are manifold.[34] Helmut Koester argues that 1:1 is either a phrase a scribe added to indicate the point in his manuscript where a new writing began, or that the phrase is a reference to a message introduced by John's preaching and begun by Jesus' preaching of the kingdom. "Nothing in the text indicates that this phrase should be understood as a designation of Mark's entire work," Koester

---

[32]In Peter Hellwig's terms (1984, 8ff.) the title is a description and not a headline or indirect title (such as a moral used as a title). Hellwig (1984, 19) also notes that titles often verbalize themes. Descriptive titles (1984, 9ff) can give information about the co-text's theme, illocution, genre, author, and so forth. A "co-text" is the actual segment of communication that is associated with a title (1984, 5).

[33]Hellholm 1982, 177, where he quotes Ernst Grosse and Wolfgang Raible. And compare Hellholm 1980, 85 and see Hellholm (forthcoming) 3.2.2.3 on Mt 1:1.

[34]For a position against 1:1 as title see Strecker 1979, 215, n.134. Wolfgang Feneberg (1974, 186–188) would disagree with the opinion that 1:1 is a title and refers 1:1 to 1:4–8. In that case 1:1 would be a substitution for a very small segment of text. But Feneberg and Strecker are probably incorrect because "gospel" would still be a substitution (by semantic implication: a beginning assumes a middle and end) for the continuation of the text after the story of John.

writes. Ancient writings do not have "cryptic phrases which mysteriously suggest their true genre to the modern interpreter," but instead begin with formal dedications or with sentences describing the first subject treated.³⁵ Koester's claim about ancient literature is not true in certain cases, as Hellholm has shown concerning the incipits (introductory lines) of Revelation and Didache.³⁶ Under either interpretation that Koester offers for 1:1, the phrase refers to part of the content of Mark. But the gospel "begun" by Jesus' preaching continues in the rest of the text. So even under Koester's interpretation, 1:1 can be seen to refer to the entire text. This is not to say that εὐαγγέλιον is a word meaning a literary document at this stage; but it does refer to the words in the text of Mark, since they are the proclamation of and by Jesus.³⁷ Consequently, we do not need to claim that 1:1 is a "cryptic" indication of the genre of the text.

---

³⁵Koester 1989, 370.

³⁶Rev. 1:1–3 and Διδαχὴ κυρίου διὰ τῶν δώδεκα ἀποστόλων τοῖς ἔθνεσιν (The teaching of the Lord through the twelve apostles to the nations). See Hellholm 1990, 112. See further note 3, above. Hellholm 1990, 122, n. 60 quotes W. D. Davies and D. C. Allison: "The question of whether 1.1 [Mt] is a general title should take into account this consideration: it was a custom in the prophetic, didactic, and apocalyptic writings of Judaism to open with an independent titular sentence announcing the content of the work. Compare (references from Hellholm 1990, 119) titles such as Hos 1:1, Amos 1:1, Isa 1:1, 1 Enoch 1:1–2, Lk 1:1–4, Gospel of Thomas CG II, 32, 10–12, and Apocryphon of John CG II, 1, 1–4.

³⁷Compare the distinction between *suppositio materialis* and *suppositio formalis*. Hellholm 1990, 119 notes that the distinction is between text-external and text-internal references. In *suppositio formalis* the reference is to objects or states of affairs. In *suppositio materialis* the reference is to texts or sub-texts within the text itself. For example, in *suppositio formalis* εὐαγγέλιον (gospel) refers to the content of John's and Jesus' proclamation and the rest of the message of Mark. In *suppositio materialis*, εὐαγγέλιον would refer to the words of the text of Mark. A simpler example: in *suppositio formalis* "Jesus" refers to the individual. In *suppositio materialis*, "Jesus" refers to the six letters in the word. Hellholm notes that Ἀποκάλυψις Ἰησοῦ Χριστοῦ (The

If we are correct in seeing it as a title,³⁸ the author, as the editor does with the inscription, uses the substitution in 1:1 to define the central figure of the text and to claim that the text should be accepted as εὐαγγέλιον or "good news." The claim that the text is "gospel" is a speech act whose illocution to the audience is "accept this text as good news," and whose perlocution is the actual acceptance of the text as good news on the part of the audience.³⁹ The perlocution is obviously not automatic and would involve a reader's entire life. The title encourages the reader's decision. Mark asks the reader to see the following materials as a joyous proclamation by or about Jesus Christ (the Son of God).⁴⁰ We call this speech act a "governing"

Revelation of Jesus Christ) stands in *suppositio materialis* to the Apocalyptic Letter that follows (Hellholm 1990, 122, n. 60).

³⁸Scholars who see 1:1 as a title (a substition on a meta-frame in the text grammatical terminology) for the contents of the entire book include: Wellhausen 1903, ad loc. (a substitution for the whole text that begins here); Wohlenburg 1910, ad loc. (1:1 is a title and description of the entire book); Klostermann 1971, ad loc. (sees it as a title of the book); Lohmeyer 1967, ad loc. (sees God as beginning the process in John, and yet 1:1 describes the content of the whole book); Cranfield 1959, ad loc. (1:1 is a title referring to 1:2–13); Taylor 1966, ad loc. (takes it as a reference to the entire Gospel); Gnilka 1978, 42 (takes 1:1 not as a title [*Überschrift*] but as the name of the content of the book with John as the beginning); Keck 1965/66, 359 (takes it as a title since ἀρχή refers to the whole book which is the Christian gospel about Jesus); Feneberg 1974, 186–188 (does not see 1:1 as a title but understands the genitive as appositive, subjective, and objective and refers it to 1:4–8); Zehrer 1969, 103 (sees the verse as a substitution for the gospel events); Pesch 1976, 75, 76 (sees ἀρχή as meaning "foundation" and "beginning" and refers 1:1 to the entire text). Lührmann 1987, 33 sees 1:1 as a title of 1:1–15 with an objective genitive (εὐ. Ἰ.).

³⁹Gospel as speech act is discussed in 2.3.4.

⁴⁰I have so far avoided the text critical question by enclosing [υἱοῦ θεοῦ] in brackets. The witness for the expression is so good that one could probably explain the omission as a mistake if it was only absent in MSS dependent on one another. The evidence at least leaves one in doubt. Peter M. Head (1991,

speech act, since it guides the interpretation of all the speech acts that follow (see 2.4 above).

It seems possible to leave aside some of the logical or grammatical possibilities.[41] The problem of the meaning of ἀρχή is an example. To take ἀρχή as "basis" or "element" with no chronological reference goes against the usual *sememe* "beginning" in the rest of Mark (10:6, 13:8, 19), where the word is clearly chronological. It is of course possible that the word has several *sememes* in Mark, but if possible one should try to interpret the word with the usual Markan *sememe*. BAG gives only one possibility in the NT for the *sememe* "first cause" in Rev 3:14. Heb 5:12 and 6:1 contain an adjectival use of the word in the genitive where it means something like "elemental," which is not similar to the use in Mk 1:1. The overwhelming evidence ("beginning" and other *sememes* not relevant for the context such as "ruler") linguistically blocks out other possibilities. The word can have a *sememe* such as "foundational beginning," which may indicate a slightly different sense of "beginning" than the English word often has (e.g., Sir 29:21; Plat. *Ep.* 326e; Pindar, *Nem.* 1.8; and Demosthenes, *Olynthiaka* 3.2 [29]). One should probably not choose a *sememe* foreign to NT Greek for a word in Mark that otherwise can be interpreted perfectly well.

The problem of the genitive is much more complex. To take, for example, εὐαγγελίου Ἰησοῦ Χριστοῦ (Gospel of Jesus Christ) as a subjective genitive (Jesus' proclamation), and to then refer ἀρχή to John's ministry, is inadequate. John preaches about Jesus, and this implies an objective genitive interpretation of 1:1 (the gospel about Jesus...). Opinions on whether to take the genitive

---

627–629) argues that the shorter text is the more difficult reading (given the important Markan usage of "Son of God"). There is a scribal tendency to add "Son of God" to other gospel texts. The shorter reading explains the longer readings. Finally, it is difficult to see why a scribe beginning the first verse of a work would make a mistake. These arguments of Head's justify the brackets.

[41] See Allen Wikgren 1942 and Cranfield 1959, ad loc. and the other commentaries for the many possibilities.

in 1:1 as objective, subjective or appositive are extremely diverse.[42] Gerhard Friedrich argues[43] that the distinction is not that important, since Jesus' proclamation includes himself, his cross, and his resurrection in the Gospel of Mark (e.g., 8:31ff.). One does not need to be quite as unconcerned as Friedrich is, but it may be correct to say that the Greek genitive does not always aim at the kind of precision of modern grammarians. A *signeme* such as 1:1 may include both relationships described by the concepts "subjective" and "objective genitive." So in my opinion, the above discussion leaves two major possibilities: "the beginning of Jesus' gospel," and "the beginning of the gospel about Jesus." Only the second possibility allows a reader to see 1:1 merely as a substitution for John's proclamation. But even here, the "gospel about Jesus" will also refer to the rest of the text. John would be the beginning and the rest of the text would be the continuation of the gospel about Jesus (by semantic implication of the word ἀρχή). Compare Hos 1:2 (LXX), Ἀρχὴ λόγου...(Beginning of the word), where the whole work is the word of the Lord to Hosea by semantic implication. The reader is asked to look at the text, on either major interpretation, as a good piece of news that claims his/her allegiance. In my opinion neither exegetical possibility can be excluded by philological or linguistic analysis.

---

[42]The genitive: Paul in Rom 1:9 may take εὐαγγέλιον 'Ι. as an objective gen., since Rom 1:1 has εὐαγγέλιον θ. (gospel of God) as a subjective gen. and refers to the proclamation of Christ in 1:2ff. Therefore Wikgren 1942, 14, 15 is probably wrong when he says such an objective genitive is not present in Paul. Rom 15:19 is also an obj. gen. For Feneberg see n. 10. Gnilka 1978, 43 opts for a subjective and objective genitive. Wellhausen 1909, ad loc.— obj. genitive. Pesch 1976, ad loc.— obj. genitive. Lagrange 1947, ad loc. takes it as an obj. genitive with John being the beginning. Pesch 1976, ad loc. refers to 13:10 and 14:9 and sees 1:1 as an objective genitive. Cranfield 1959, 35,36 takes the sub. gen. as primary with an objective gen. as an implicit undertone based on Mt 11:5par and LXX uses of the translation of מבשר (proclaimer of good news).

[43]Friedrich discusses Mk 1:1 in 1935, 726.

3.3.3. The Major Episodes (^1TP)

The structure of the text that the markers establish shows that Mark is not a completely inept text, from a narrative point of view.[44] Though there is no tight chronological or geographical scheme, there is a rough picture of a story line.[45] Rhoads and Mitchie note that the settings (my "episode markers") "provide the overall framework for the movement and for the development of plot."[46] The major episodes or Text Parts isolated by the episode markers in our analysis are: $^1TP^1$ or 1:2–13 (the wilderness area around the Jordan where John and Jesus are active); $^1TP^2$ or 1:14–8:26 (Jesus' activity in Galilee and environs); $^1TP^3$ or 8:27–10:52 (Jesus' journey to Jerusalem); $^1TP^4$ or 11:1–16:8 (Jesus in Jerusalem and environs). All these Text Parts are marked by the episode markers, as can be seen by checking the analysis.[47] The "1" to the left of TP (Text Part) in the above example indicates the level of the outline. The number to the right of "TP" indicates the division of the Text Part. In $^1TP^1$ the "1" to the right of "TP" means the first section of the Text Part. The "2" in $^1TP^2$ means the second section of the Text Part.

The section from 1:14–8:26 is the most amorphous Text Part because there is no statement in 1:14 that "Jesus went into Galilee and the *surrounding area...*" Nevertheless, the division seems justified because of the surrounding sections (1:2–13 and 8:27ff.) and because of the lack of any clear geographical marker dividing 1:14–8:26 into two or more large subsections. The

---

[44]Contrast the work of Tolbert (1989, 11, and passim), who sees uncovering coherence in the text as being a mark of persuasive interpretation, with the work of deconstructionists who see little coherence (see Moore 1989, 165ff. for an example).

[45]Kee 1977, 64 correctly argues that there is no one outline of Mark. See also Achtemeier (1975, 13) who argues against any attempt to give a sequentially accurate account of Jesus' ministry using Mark.

[46]Rhoads and Mitchie 1982, 63.

[47]Bengel 1855, 166, 167 gives a similar but not identical analysis of Mark.

remark in 15:41 about Jesus' time in Galilee may support ^{1}TP^2, as may the remark about the region around Galilee in 1:28. Mark may indicate with the last remark that he sees Jesus' activity in and around Galilee as a unit. In addition, with one exception, there are no words for Jesus' travels in a region other than the episode marker "Galilee" in ^{1}TP^2. There are many references to cities such as Tyre and Bethsaida that lie outside Galilee, but Mark uses no episode markers such as Gaulanitis, etc. The exception is "Decapolis" in 7:31, but there the sea of Galilee is identified as being in its midst.

Werner Kümmel's[48] division of the section at 6:1 is not justified by any episode marker at that point. Because of Jesus' journey to Gerasa (or Gadara) in 5:1, Kümmel's titles "Jesus in Galilee" and "Jesus in Galilee and Outside" do not reflect the text's geography. We do not know what Mark's concept of Galilee was; and Koch's attempt to carefully identify it is unconvincing.[49]

Koch's position that the geographical markers justify a major division in the text at 8:27 is better grounded.[50] This coheres nicely with the plot change at 8:27. Koch bases his position on

---

[48]Kümmel 1966, 61, 62 has 1:14–5:43 under "Jesus in Galilee" and 6:1–9:50 under "Jesus in Galilee and neighboring areas."

[49]Koch 1983, 151ff. Koch wants to keep 5:1–20 and 7:32ff. inside Galilee or Jesus' usual area of activity. Koch's argument for the first TP is that Mark does not say Jesus left Galilee. His argument for the second TP is that Jesus is back in his area of activity at the sea of Galilee. But Koch says that Mark sees 8:27–9:29 (1983, 148) as taking place outside of Galilee, because of the marker in 9:30. But 9:30 does not say that Jesus "returned" to Galilee. Only because Mark mentions "Caesarea Philippi" can one claim that 8:27–9:29 is a TP with a unified geography. Where Mark sees Galilee's limits is ambiguous. Mark may have seen the east bank as part of Galilee or he may not have. Consequently, Koch alters the EMs mentioned above to conform to his division at 8:27 (TPs on the east side of the sea are either "inside" or "outside" Galilee because of his thematic hypothesis about 8:27.).

[50]See Koch 1983, 149ff. See also the discussion in 1.2.4.3. For a discussion (brief) of overlapping structures in Mark, see Riesenfeld 1954, 160.

the travel notices in 8:27; 9:30; 10:1; and 10:32. He also argues that ὁδός (way) does not appear in 1:14–8:26 in reference to a journey of Jesus, but does so appear in 8:27; 9:33, 34; 10:17, 32, 46, 52. Nevertheless, Mark does not say in 8:27 that Jesus begins a journey to Jerusalem, and there is no indication that Mark identifies one road with all the occurrences of ὁδός. Lk 9:51, on the other hand, gives an episode marker that would justify even better the kind of division Koch wants to make. 10:32 and 33 indicate that the journey is to Jerusalem, where the events described in 8:31 will take place. The argument about ὁδός and the events in 8:31 and 10:32ff. justify Koch's division at 8:27, using the episode markers. 10:32ff. makes the episode markers even clearer.

The Text Parts in Frame 1 contain the following large TPs on level 2 that seem to be concentrated in the second half of the Gospel. $^1TP^3$ (Mk 8:27–10:52) contains a large TP governing 8:27–9:29 ($^2TP^{3.1}$) where Jesus is in the Caesarea Philippi region. Then in $^2TP^{3.2}$ (9:30–50) Jesus journeys through Galilee. 10:1–52 ($^2TP^{3.3}$) depicts the journey through Judea and Perea. $^1TP^4$ (11:1–16:8) comprises Jesus in Jerusalem and environs. Jesus' first day in Jerusalem is $^2TP^{4.1}$ (11:1–11). His second day is $^2TP^{4.2}$ (11:12–19). The third day begins (with an unclear end) in $^2TP^{4.3}$ (11:20–25). Mark drops chronology markers and locates Jesus in the temple for controversies and teaching in $^2TP^{4.4}$ (11:27–12:44). Jesus gives the apocalyptic discourse in view of the temple in $^2TP^{4.5}$ (13:1–37). Mark then returns to chronology (now using the Passover) in $^2TP^{4.6}$ (14:1–11) in a TP that describes the events two days before the Passover. The first day of unleavened bread and the following events, including the Lord's Supper and the trial of Jesus, are described in $^2TP^{4.7}$ (14:12–72). Then the crucifixion events, beginning the morning before the Sabbath, are narrated in $^2TP^{4.8}$ (15:1–47). The resurrection story happens on the day after the Sabbath in $^2TP^{4.9}$ (16:1–7).

The episode markers are not divorced from the thematic structure of the Gospel. Such major changes in the narrative as the dawning understanding of Jesus' real nature in 8:27ff. can be identified with a major episode marker change that encompasses

8:27–10:52.⁵¹ Yet the geographical markers probably cannot be forced to correspond to a major theological division based on geography, such as "Galilee vs. Jerusalem."⁵² There simply is not enough evidence to establish such a geographical theology using text-internal semantics alone. For example, people from Jerusalem support Jesus (3:8), and Pharisees and Herodians located in Galilee (no mention of Jerusalem) plot to kill Jesus (3:6).

As suggested above, at 8:27 a large section begins ($^1TP^3$ [8:27–10:52]) that leads up to Jesus' last days in Jerusalem ($^1TP^4$ [11:1–16:8]). It probably is not a chance occurrence, then, that the TPs in the second half of the Gospel are oriented to a series of journeys after which Jesus ends up in the city to be crucified. From a chronological point of view the last few days of Jesus' life occupy far more text space ($^2TP^{4.1}$ff. [11:1ff.]) than any other time. The most activity in the smallest spatio-temporal region occurs in Jerusalem ($^1TP^4$). So the narrative markers help show the narrative's focus. The fact that 8:27 begins the teaching about the events of Jesus' last days indicates a thematic unity of the TPs following 8:27.

---

⁵¹See in particular Koch 1983, 147ff.

⁵²See Malbon 1982, 242ff. for a good survey of the opinions of Lohmeyer, Lightfoot, et al. about the Jerusalem vs. Galilee motif in the Gospel. Malbon (1982, 251ff.) opts for a structuralist approach that sees the following relationship in the Gospel:

chaos:order::sea:land::foreign lands:Jewish homeland::Galilee:Judah.

See also Malbon 1986, 154–60.

> "On the way" is the key mediator between these oppositions (Malbon 1986, 166–67): "Thus, to be on the way to Galilee is not to escape the challenges of life but to risk involvement in the paradox of power and suffering. It is no wonder those who stand at the beginning of this way, whether the markan women at the empty tomb or the markan readers, are amazed and afraid. Mediation of ORDER and CHAOS is not made easy by Jesus who was crucified and is on the way to Galilee—just possible."

A Linguistic Outline of Mark 161

The earlier TPs also give an indication of narrative meaning. ^{1}TP^1 (1:2–13) introduces John (his baptism and baptism of Jesus) and Jesus in the wilderness away from the Galilee area of most of Jesus' public ministry. The baptism and voice help define Jesus' identity, as does Jesus' solitary encounter with Satan and the angels in the wilderness area where he was led by the Spirit to be tempted. As a matter of fact, ^{1}TP^1 contains the only TP where Jesus confronts otherworldly figures alone (1:12–13 [^{2}TP$^{1.2}$]). Mark then uses this wilderness episode to give a preliminary picture of who Jesus is. The voice from heaven identifies Jesus as "My beloved Son." If the text is correct, the narrator in 1:1 identifies him in the same way ("Jesus Christ, Son of God"). The public narrator thus accepts the point of view of the most authoritative voice in the Gospel—that of God. Mk 1:2–3 shows that God's point of view determines the values of the story—God sends the messenger to prepare the way of the Son.[53]

^{1}TP^2 (1:14–8:26) comprises the great majority of Jesus' public teaching and miracle working. The other large segment of public teaching in 11:27–12:44 (^{2}TP$^{4.4}$) is oriented to Jesus' controversies with the Jewish leaders, even though the crowds are present. Mark pictures Jesus' public activity as concentrated outside of Jerusalem. Perhaps, ^{1}TP^2 indicates that Mark had a more positive attitude toward Galilee than Jerusalem (a possible pragmatic presupposition). It also gives a strong geographical focus of Jesus' activity; it was not in India or Egypt. The large number of towns and villages mentioned in ^{1}TP^2 may also indicate that Mark's readers had some familiarity with, and interest in, the places of Jesus' activity (a possible pragmatic presupposition). In this section Jesus is with the crowds for about two thirds of the verses. In one third of the verses Jesus is alone with the disciples or heals people without the crowds being present.[54] Most of the

---

[53] Kingsbury 1983, 57.

[54] Jesus is alone with the disciples in: 1:16–20; 3:13–19; 4:10–20 (circa); 6:6b–13, 30–33, 45–52; 7:17–23; and 8:10, 13–21. He is alone with people he heals

outlines mentioned in 1.2 above have thematic titles for the various sections—whatever method they use—that contain references to Jesus' identity. Jesus' activities provoke four questions about his identity (or the nature of his teaching and authority) in 1:27; 2:7; 4:41; and 6:3.[55] The demons answer this question (Jesus is God's Son or God's Holy One) several times in 1:24–25, 34 (the narrator establishes the demons' correct point of view), in 3:11–12 (Jesus establishes the correctness of their name for him), and in 5:7.[56] The reader is aware of these answers even if no one else understands. The text does not give a psychological explanation for Peter's confession in 8:27ff., but the narrative in 1:14–8:26 pictures Peter's experience of Jesus as teacher (who also calls disciples with authority), exorcist, healer, worker of nature miracles, and as a powerful figure who can impart his power to his disciples (6:7, 12, 13). The reader (who is the obvious focus of the implied author's art) also experiences this picture of Jesus.

$^1TP^3$ (8:27–10:52) contains public teaching and one exorcism along with private teaching about the passion among other topics. But, because of the episode markers, it is primarily oriented to Jesus' journey in the direction of Jerusalem. The journey to Jerusalem is explicated by the passion teaching contained in $^1TP^3$. In two thirds of the verses, Jesus is alone with the disciples or with other individuals (the children and those who bring them in 10:13–16, and the rich man in 10:17–22).[57] That is a marked change from the focus of the narrative in the previous Text Part, where in two thirds of the verses Jesus appears along with the crowds. The disciples begin to understand Jesus as Messiah, although misunderstanding still plagues them (8:30, 33), and some hear the heavenly voice

---

(with disciples sometimes present) in: 1:29–31; 5:1–13, 18–20, 42–43; 7:24–30, 33–35; and 8:23–26.

[55] Kingsbury 1983, 88.

[56] Kingsbury 1983, 89.

[57] Jesus is with the crowds (with the disciples being present) in: 8:34–9:1; 9:14–27; and 10:1–9, 10:46–52.

identify Jesus as his beloved Son (9:7). Thomas Söding notes that this way of suffering, which calls the disciples to follow the cross, may have already been spoken of in 1:2.[58]

1TP4 has the largest amount of material in the smallest spatio-temporal region. It probably presents the focus of the entire Gospel (crucifixion and resurrection). Jesus and his followers, without the public playing a role, are the focus of the action in about half of the verses of this section.[59] If the approach to the Messianic Secret in 4.4.3 is correct (compare 1.3.5 above), then there is a progressive revelation of the identity of Jesus as the Son of God in Mark, including the episode of 11:1–16:7. Again the focus of this narrative picture of Jesus is the reader. The text draws the reader into its world and challenges the reader to accept its picture of Jesus' identity and take up the challenge of discipleship. In the entire narrative, the spatial markers show that Jesus constitutes the theme of the action: in only a few verses do *dramatis personae* act in a different location from that of Jesus (before his death on the cross).[60] Most of these verses are connected in one way or another with Jesus' passion.[61]

---

[58]Söding 1987, 120, n. 107.

[59]Jesus and the followers (without the public playing a role) appear in: 11:1–4, 7–8, 11–14, 19–25; 13:1–37; 14:3–9, 12–42; 15:40–41 (the women), 42–47 (Pilate is present); and 16:1–8.

[60]1:45 (the proclamation of the leper); 3:6 (the plot of the Pharisees and Herodians to kill Jesus); 6:12–13 (the twelve on mission); 6:14–29 (Herod and John's death); 7:30 (the Syrophoenecian woman finds her daughter exorcized); 11:4–6 (the disciples and the colt); 14:1–2 (the plan to kill Jesus); 14:16 (the disciples prepare the passover); and 14:66–72 (Peter's denial of Jesus).

[61]3:6 and 14:1–2 are clearly related to his death. 6:14–29 depicts the death of John with Herod's and others' opinions of Jesus as the setting. 11:4–6, 14:16, and 14:66–72 are all loosely tied to Jesus' death. The Jerusalem entry inaugurates his last days in Jerusalem. The passover (prepared for in 14:16) contains Jesus' theological depiction of his death (14:22ff.). And Peter denies Jesus (14:66ff.) during the trial where Jesus' death is sealed.

Each of the Text Parts delimited in the analysis is a *signeme* in Heger's terminology.[62] A given TP has a conceptual meaning (sense) and a reference (sub-class). The reference in the case of most of the Text Parts is an event in the Markan narrative world's depiction of the ministry of Jesus of Nazareth. The author presents stories that consist of features that have been abstracted from an event and narrates them for the reader.[63]

3.4. Comparison with Other Outlines

It will be immediately obvious that the Text Parts of the structure presented in Chapter Three are similar to those (pericopes) that can be found in any commentary. The structure presented in this chapter can be easily examined because the analysis is based on intersubjectively checkable surface markers. I would agree with Hengel and Malbon (see 1.2.4.5 above) that one should not claim to have an absolutely valid structure of Mark. The use to which one puts the structure can be more useful than structure for structure's sake. Surely, using a clear method is an improvement over outlines that proceed from intuition alone. But having a method such as the one in this work does not guarantee that an outline is correct. It would be foolhardy to try to argue "against" all the outlines presented in Chapter One and then attempt to argue for the one in this work. The outlines in the first chapter help uncover coherence in the text and the myriad themes and motifs present in Mark. Mk 8:27 and 11:1 have the best claim to be invariants in the various approaches to the Markan structure, but even they do not always function as such in each outline (see 1.2.2 above). Nevertheless they are both watershed texts and most outlines uncover that fact. The outline presented here is constructed using narrative markers and not motifs as the primary criterion for finding TPs. If it is useful in Markan scholarship, then it will have served its purpose.

---

[62]See Gülich, Heger, and Raible 1979, passim and especially 127ff.

[63]Raible 1980, 321 remarks that texts are abbreviations of what they denote or refer to (quoting Edmund Husserl 1970, 355).

A Linguistic Outline of Mark   165

Comparisons with other outlines are useful. Robbins's structure can be correlated with that of this chapter in the following way: his introduction (1:1–13) corresponds to the episode in the wilderness, 1:2–13; the Galilean ministry episode in 1:14–8:26 corresponds to Robbins's divisions of the text into 1:14–3:12; 3:13–6:6a; and 6:6b–8:26; the travel narrative, 8:27–10:52, corresponds to Robbins's 8:27–10:45; and the Jerusalem episode, 11:1–16:8, corresponds to Robbins's 10:45–12:44; 13:1–15:47; and 16:1–8. Robbins's method (see 1.2.3 above) breaks the larger units into smaller units. To incorporate the structure of Chapter Three into Robbins's socio-rhetorical approach, one could also compare the speech act analysis of the Markan text with the rhetorical units of argumentation that Burton Mack and Robbins find in the gospels.[64]

Chapter Four will use the analysis of Chapter Three to explore the relation of the governing speech act to several texts in Mark. I shall show how understanding Mark as a speech act can illuminate the understanding of Mark as an example of the genre "gospel." I shall also approach the Messianic Secret as an aspect of the larger governing speech act.

In order to produce an outline using text linguistic categories, many abbreviations will have to be used. These abbreviations follow. The nature of the markers is discussed in Chapter Two.

3.5. Abbreviations: Communication Frames

Frame 00: The frame of an editor (e.g., ΕΥΑΓΓΕΛΙΟΝ ΚΑΤΑ ΜΑΡΚΟΝ).
Frame 0: The frame of the author's title for the text (1:1).
Frame 1: The frame of the narrator's communication to the reader (e.g., 1:4).
Frame 2: The frame of the characters' speech with other characters (e.g., 1:7b).

---

[64] Mack and Robbins 1989.

Frame 2 OT: The frame of an explicit OT quotation containing characters speaking to other characters (e.g., 1:2b) whose meta-frame is Frame 1.

Frame 2 PN: The division of Frame 2 in which a character's speech is a narration and the character functions as a private narrator (telling a story, making a statement about the past or future), such as 4:3–9.

Frame 2 ON: The division of Frame 2 in which an otherworldly narrator or character speaks without mediation through a human character (e.g., 1:11b).

Frame 3: The frame whose meta-frame is Frame 2. This frame comprises speech which is narrated by characters in Frame 2 (e.g., 12:7b). In 12:7b the vineyard workers speak about the heir. Their speech is contained in Jesus' parable. The parable is itself speech (in Frame 2) which introduces the vineyard workers' statement with the meta-communicative verb "εἶπαν." The narrator (in Frame 1) describes Jesus and introduces his parable with the meta-communicative verb "λαλεῖν."

Frame 3 OT: The division of Frame 3 of an explicit OT quotation that is referred to in the speech of a character in Frame 2 (e.g., 12:10b).

Frame 3 SOT: Speech of characters in Old Testament quotation; the division of Frame 3 which contains speech quoted by Scripture in Frame 2 OT (e.g., 1:2 the voice's message).

Frame 3 ON: The division of Frame 3 in which an otherworldly character speaks without mediation through a human character (e.g., 12:26).

Frame 3 HS: The division of Frame 3 in which a character speaking in Frame 2 indicates his or her own speech (e.g., "I say to you"), such as 14:30b.

Frame 4: Speech of a character whose identity is given on meta-Frame 3 (e.g., 7:11).

Frame 4 SOT: Speech of characters in Old Testament quotation; the division of Frame 4 with speech quoted by Scripture in Frame 3 OT (e.g., 12:36).

Frame 4 ON: The division of Frame 4 in which an otherworldly narrator or character speaks without mediation through a human character (e.g., 12:36).
(1, 2) or (2, 3): Text that is in indirect speech will be marked as appearing between two communication frames (e.g., "(1, 2)" in 8:16).
* The asterisk marks text that is an interior monologue (e.g., 5:28).

3.5.1. Explanation of the Subdivisions: OT, SOT, PN, ON

For purposes of clarity I have given some indications of certain types of speech using the following abbreviations.
OT: An explicit OT quotation. It can serve as a meta-frame for other characters' speech as in David's speech in 12:36. Since the narrator/implied author speaks in Frame 1, explicit OT quotations of characters speaking to each other first appear in Frame 2. The narrator identifies which OT texts are in question in Frame 1.
SOT: The speech of characters in Old Testament quotation which is itself quoted by a character in scripture on a higher meta-frame (e.g., 3 OT is a higher meta-frame than 4 SOT in 12:36). In 12:36 Jesus, speaking in Frame 2, quotes David who speaks in Frame 3 OT. When David describes the speech of the Lord, the Lord's speech is in Frame 4 SOT. Speech in an OT-frame (such as 3 OT in this example) is the meta-frame for speech in an SOT-frame (such as 4 SOT in the example). The SOT-type could in turn be a meta-frame for deeper embedded speech. Since Frame 1 contains the narrator's voice, the words (as an OT-type of speech) of explicitly identified Scriptural authors first appear in Frame 2. Consequently, there is no 2 SOT-type. The SOT-type first appears in Frame 3.
PN: The language of a character who speaks as a private narrator (telling a story, making a statement about the past or future). The PN-type could be a meta-frame for speech in a deeper embedded frame as in 12:7, where Jesus as a private narrator gives the words of the tenants (who speak in Frame 3).

ON: The speech of an otherworldly narrator or character without mediation through a human character. The otherworldly character is introduced by the narrator in Frame 1 and so that character's speech appears first in Frame 2 as in 1:11b. An ON–type statement could be a meta-frame for another character's speech.

HS: When a character indicates his or her own speech. The narrator first gives characters' speech in Frame 2 so there is no 1 HS or 2 HS. In Jesus' words "truly I say to you" in Frame 2 in 3:28, he indicates his own speech which then appears in Frame 3 HS. As a matter of fact, there is no 4 HS type in Mark.

Occasionally there is overlap between the sub-types, as in 3:28 where Jesus' speech also functions as a private narration about the future.

3.6. Abbreviations: The Markers

AA: A call to attention (a kind of Meta-Communicative marker).
CM: A change in a character or a group of characters.
CM(P): A character that is or becomes passive.
CONJ: Conjunction marker.
EM: An episode marker change.
EMa: An absolute episode marker (governed by no higher EM).
EMr: A relative EM (governed by a higher EM).
EM(S): Change in a spatial marker.
EM(T): Change in a temporal marker.
MC: A meta-communicative marker.
MC(Dia): A dialogue.
MC(Mon): A monologue.
MC(Poly): A polyoration (more than two groups of speakers).
SM: A substitution on a meta-frame.
SN: A substitution in a narrative frame.
SmPr: A semantic presupposition.
SPAC: A speech act.
TP: A Text Part.
An ellipse (...) is used to indicate the inclusion of all the relevant markers between the two examples of the marker listed. For

example: $^4TP^{1.1.1.2}$ (1:4–6) CM: Ἰωάννης...Ἱεροσολυμῖται would also include Ἰουδαία (the people from Judea).
( ): After a TP is listed, parentheses include the chapter and verse identification of the given TP.

3.7. Using the Frames and Markers to Produce an Outline

These markers were discussed below in Chapter Two. Here I will give a brief summary of how they will be used in the following text. One first orders the text into the different frames of communication. In the case of Mark those frames are as follows: the editor (superscript in Frame 00); the author's title (1:1) in Frame 0; the author as narrator (Frame 1); the characters' communication with each other (Frame 2); the characters' quotation of other characters' speech (Frame 3); and so forth. The frames are found on the right hand side of the pages of the outline.

Then one uses the ordered series of markers first on communication Frame 00, then 0, then 1, then 2, and so on. The editor's superscript contains a meta-communicative marker (MC) that indicates the author. The author's comment in 1:1 is a substitution (SM, title) for all that follows, even if the title refers primarily to John as the beginning of the gospel. No other meta-communicative or substitution markers govern Frame 1. Any such markers would have to be on a meta-frame (00 or 0) and contain a remark such as "Chapter 1," which would be a substitution marker. Following the ordered series one then comes to the episode markers (EM). They describe the spatial and temporal coordinates of what goes on. The primary episode markers such as $^1TP^2$ "Galilee" and environs (Mk 1:14–8:26) in turn govern secondary (or relative) episode markers such as time in Capernaum and so forth. One then moves on to the character markers (CM) to structure the text in communication Frame 1. After one has ordered all the Text Parts in Frame 1, Frame 2 is then analyzed using the markers in the ordered series.

The use of the levels of the outline is reviewed in 2.4.3 above. They should not be identified with the communication frames, and for a given Text Part such as ^{1}TP, the next level (^{2}TP$^{1.1}$, ^{2}TP$^{1.2}$ etc.) is structured by use of a similar marker (such as relative episode markers). In the last mentioned example, the number to the left of "TP" indicates the level, and the second number to the right of "TP" indicates the section of Level 2 that is being considered. The fact that there are two columns of numbers to the right of "TP" in the example also indicates that the TP is on Level 2. The second number to the right of "TP" indicates that ^{2}TP$^{1.1}$ is the first section of all the text contained in ^{1}TP^1. ^{2}TP$^{1.2}$ is the second section of text contained in ^{1}TP^1. The layout of the following text is relatively simple. On the right hand side the text is ordered into the different frames of communication (see "Abbreviations. Communication Frames" above). These range from frames 00 to 4. They are indicated by the numbers (00...4) at the top of the page that correspond to the indented columns below. The phrase in Mk 1:2, for example, is in Frame 1. On the left hand side of the page the text is ordered into Levels ranging from 00 (such as 00 in ^{00}TP) to 7. One could continue dividing the text much further. The Levels do not correspond (one-to-one) exactly to the communication frames, but Levels 00, 0 and 1 do correspond with communication Frames 00, 0, and 1. Each Level in turn governs a lower Level (^{1}TP^1 organizes ^{2}TP$^{1.1}$ and ^{2}TP$^{1.2}$). This is similar to the way in which larger sections of an outline organize smaller sections.

As we already mentioned, the meta-communicative (^{00}TP) and Substitution (^{0}TP) markers govern the entire text. Absolute episode markers (EMa) then organize Level 1 (^{1}TP). In ^{1}TP^1 (1:2–13), Level 2 is governed by relative episode markers (EMr, such as the Jordan area in ^{2}TP$^{1.1}$ (1:2–11)). Level 3 in ^{2}TP$^{1.1}$ is marked by indications of time (EMr). Level 4 in ^{3}TP$^{1.1.1}$ (1:2–8) is marked by changes in the groups of character markers. Isaiah is in focus in ^{4}TP$^{1.1.1.1}$ (1:2–3), then John and the crowds (^{4}TP$^{1.1.1.2}$ (1:4–6)) and finally John alone (^{4}TP$^{1.1.1.3}$ (1:7–8)). These markers are used on the text in communication Frame 1 in the order established in 2.4.2 (MC, SM, EM, CM, etc.). A narrative in communication Frame 2 (such as Mk 13:5ff.) is in turn organized by using the markers in the given order. "Jesus says" (an MC) in 13:5 organizes the whole narrative. There are no substitution markers (such as "part one of my speech"), so the episode markers are used to structure the narrative. Then the character markers are used. Each different level corresponds to a different kind of narrative marker in a given Text Part. A summary of the analysis is given in Appendix 2 to aid the reader.

00TP MC and SM: ΕΥΑΓΓΕΛΙΟΝ ΚΑΤΑ ΜΑΡΚΟΝ An Editor's Title. SPAC: Text is one of several gospels.
0TP(1:1) SM: 'Αρχή...θεοῦ] Author's Title. SPAC: Text is true— an εὐαγγέλιον containing gospel narratives; perlocution— the receiver's acceptance of the text as "good news."
1TP[1](1:2–13) EMa: (S) ἐρήμῳ. John and Jesus in the wilderness.
2TP[1.1](2–11) Emr: (S) 'Ιορδάνῃ. John and Jesus at the Jordan.
3TP[1.1.1] (2–8) EMr: ἐγένετο the appearance of John before Jesus' in ἐκείναις ταῖς ἡμέραις (9). John's baptismal ministry in the wilderness.
4TP[1.1.1.1](2–3) CM: 'Ησαΐᾳ. MC: γέγραπται. SPAC: prophecy (an assertive). CONJ: καθώς. Isaiah's prophecy of God's word applied to John, Jesus, and the crowds.
4TP[1.1.1.2] (4–6) CM: 'Ιωάννης...'Ιεροσολυμῖται. John's baptism of the crowds and his lifestyle.
4TP[1.1.1.3](7–8) CM: ἐκήρυσσεν. MC.Mon: Ibid. SPAC: proclamation (an assertive). John's proclamation.
3TP[1.1.2](9–11) EMr: (T) ἐκείναις ταῖς ἡμέραις. CM: 'Ιησοῦς. The baptism of Jesus.
4TP[1.1.2.1](9) CM: 'Ιησοῦς... 'Ιωάννου. Jesus' baptism by John.
4TP[1.1.2.2](10) CM: πνεῦμα. Deutevision: Jesus sees the Spirit coming upon him.
4TP[1.1.2.3](11) CM: φωνή (otherworldly being). MC: Ibid. SPAC: assertion. The voice (God's) describes Jesus' relationship to God.

A Linguistic Outline of Mark 173

0 0 0 1 2 3 4

ΕΥΑΓΓΕΛΙΟΝ ΚΑΤΑ ΜΑΡΚΟΝ
1:1 Ἀρχὴ τοῦ εὐαγγελίου Ἰησοῦ Χριστοῦ [υἱοῦ θεοῦ].
1:2 Καθὼς γέγραπται ἐν τῷ Ἠσαΐᾳ τῷ προφήτῃ,
Ἰδοὺ ἀποστέλλω τὸν ἄγγελόν μου πρὸ προσώπου
σου, ὃς κατασκευάσει τὴν ὁδόν σου· 1:3 φωνὴ
βοῶντος ἐν τῇ ἐρήμῳ, (2 OT)
Ἑτοιμάσατε τὴν ὁδὸν κυρίου, εὐθείας ποιεῖτε
τὰς τρίβους αὐτοῦ, (3 SOT)
1:4 ἐγένετο Ἰωάννης [ὁ] βαπτίζων ἐν τῇ ἐρήμῳ καὶ
κηρύσσων βάπτισμα μετανοίας εἰς ἄφεσιν ἁμαρτιῶν.
1:5 καὶ ἐξεπορεύετο πρὸς αὐτὸν πᾶσα ἡ Ἰουδαία
χώρα καὶ οἱ Ἱεροσολυμῖται πάντες, καὶ ἐβαπτίζοντο
ὑπ' αὐτοῦ ἐν τῷ Ἰορδάνῃ ποταμῷ ἐξομολογούμενοι
τὰς ἁμαρτίας αὐτῶν. 1:6 καὶ ἦν ὁ Ἰωάννης
ἐνδεδυμένος τρίχας καμήλου καὶ ζώνην δερματίνην
περὶ τὴν ὀσφὺν αὐτοῦ, καὶ ἐσθίων ἀκρίδας καὶ μέλι
ἄγριον. 1:7 καὶ ἐκήρυσσεν λέγων,
Ἔρχεται ὁ ἰσχυρότερός μου ὀπίσω μου, οὗ οὐκ
εἰμὶ ἱκανὸς κύψας λῦσαι τὸν ἱμάντα τῶν
ὑποδημάτων αὐτοῦ. 1:8 ἐγὼ ἐβάπτισα ὑμᾶς ὕδατι,
αὐτὸς δὲ βαπτίσει ὑμᾶς ἐν πνεύματι ἁγίῳ. (2 PN)
1:9 Καὶ ἐγένετο ἐν ἐκείναις ταῖς ἡμέραις ἦλθεν
Ἰησοῦς ἀπὸ Ναζαρὲτ τῆς Γαλιλαίας καὶ ἐβαπτίσθη εἰς
τὸν Ἰορδάνην ὑπὸ Ἰωάννου. 1:10 καὶ εὐθὺς ἀναβαίνων
ἐκ τοῦ ὕδατος εἶδεν σχιζομένους τοὺς οὐρανοὺς καὶ
τὸ πνεῦμα ὡς περιστερὰν καταβαῖνον εἰς αὐτόν· 1:11
καὶ φωνὴ ἐγένετο ἐκ τῶν οὐρανῶν,
Σὺ εἶ ὁ υἱός μου ὁ ἀγαπητός, ἐν σοὶ εὐδόκησα. (2 ON)

²TP¹·²(12–13) EMr: (S) ἔρημον; (T) εὐθύς...τεσσεράκοντα. CM: πνεῦμα αὐτόν...σατανᾶ (Otherworldly beings and Jesus). Jesus' temptation in the wilderness away from John.

¹TP²(1:14–8:26) EMa: (S) Γαλιλαίαν; (T) μετά. Jesus' ministry in Galilee and environs.
   ²TP²·¹(14–15) CM: ' Ιησοῦς (thisworldly being). MC: λέγων. SPAC: κηρύσσων (an assertion and two directives). SN: τὸ εὐαγγέλιον τοῦ θεοῦ (for 1:15). Jesus' proclamation in Galilee.
   ²TP²·²(16–20) EMr: (S) θάλασσαν...Γαλιλαίας. CM: Jesus and the four disciples. Jesus' call of the first disciples.
      ³TP²·²·¹(16–18) CM: Σίμωνα... ' Ανδρέαν. MC: εἶπεν. SPAC: Δεῦτε...ποιήσω (directive and assertion). The first two disciples.
      ³TP²·²·²(19–20) EMr: (S) ὀλίγον. CM: ' Ιάκωβον... ' Ιωάννην. SPAC: ἐκάλεσεν (a directive). The next two disciples.

1 2 3 4

1:12 Καὶ εὐθὺς τὸ πνεῦμα αὐτὸν ἐκβάλλει εἰς τὴν ἔρημον. 1:13 καὶ ἦν ἐν τῇ ἐρήμῳ τεσσεράκοντα ἡμέρας πειραζόμενος ὑπὸ τοῦ Σατανᾶ, καὶ ἦν μετὰ τῶν θηρίων, καὶ οἱ ἄγγελοι διηκόνουν αὐτῷ.
1:14 Μετὰ δὲ τὸ παραδοθῆναι τὸν Ἰωάννην ἦλθεν ὁ Ἰησοῦς εἰς τὴν Γαλιλαίαν κηρύσσων τὸ εὐαγγέλιον τοῦ θεοῦ 1:15 καὶ λέγων ὅτι
Πεπλήρωται ὁ καιρὸς καὶ ἤγγικεν ἡ βασιλεία τοῦ θεοῦ· μετανοεῖτε καὶ πιστεύετε ἐν τῷ εὐαγγελίῳ.
1:16 Καὶ παράγων παρὰ τὴν θάλασσαν τῆς Γαλιλαίας εἶδεν Σίμωνα καὶ Ἀνδρέαν τὸν ἀδελφὸν Σίμωνος ἀμφιβάλλοντας ἐν τῇ θαλάσσῃ· ἦσαν γὰρ ἁλιεῖς. 1:17 καὶ εἶπεν αὐτοῖς ὁ Ἰησοῦς,
Δεῦτε ὀπίσω μου, καὶ ποιήσω ὑμᾶς γενέσθαι ἁλιεῖς ἀνθρώπων.
1:18 καὶ εὐθὺς ἀφέντες τὰ δίκτυα ἠκολούθησαν αὐτῷ. 1:19 Καὶ προβὰς ὀλίγον εἶδεν Ἰάκωβον τὸν τοῦ Ζεβεδαίου καὶ Ἰωάννην τὸν ἀδελφὸν αὐτοῦ καὶ αὐτοὺς ἐν τῷ πλοίῳ καταρτίζοντας τὰ δίκτυα, 1:20 καὶ εὐθὺς ἐκάλεσεν αὐτούς. καὶ ἀφέντες τὸν πατέρα αὐτῶν Ζεβεδαῖον ἐν τῷ πλοίῳ μετὰ τῶν μισθωτῶν ἀπῆλθον ὀπίσω αὐτοῦ.

2TP2.3(21–34) EMr: (S) Καφαρναούμ; (T) σάββασιν. Jesus in Capernaum on the Sabbath.
   3TP2.3.1(21–28) EMr: (S) συναγωγήν. Jesus teaching and exorcising in the synagogue.
      4TP2.3.1.1(21–22) CM: ἐξηπλήσσοντο. Jesus teaching the worshipers.
      4TP2.3.1.2(23–25) EMr: (T) εὐθύς. CM: ἄνθρωπος. MC(Dia): λέγων...λέγων. SPAC: (24) two questions, assertion (οἶδα) (25) ἐπετίμησεν (rebuke—a directive) ἔξελθε (a declarative). Encounter of the demoniac and Jesus: the exorcism.
         5TP2.3.1.2.1(23–24) MC: ἀνέκραξεν λέγων. SPAC: two questions and one assertion (οἶδα). The demoniac's remarks.
         5TP2.3.1.2.2(25) MC: ἐπετίμησεν...λέγων. SPAC: Ibid. & φιμώθητι, ἔξελθε (a "supernatural" declarative whose illocutionary force is to exorcise). Jesus rebukes and exorcises the demon.
      4TP2.3.1.3(26) CM: τὸ πνεῦμα. The spirit leaves.
      4TP2.3.1.4(27–28) CM: ἅπαντες. MC(Mon): συζητεῖν. SPAC: question and two assertions. The worshipers' response to the teaching and exorcism, and the consequent fame of Jesus.
   3TP2.3.2(29–34) EMr: (S) οἰκίαν, (T) εὐθύς. Healing in Peter's house.
      4TP2.3.2.1(29–31) CM: πενθερά. Jesus heals Peter's mother-in-law.

1 2 3 4

1:21 Καὶ εἰσπορεύονται εἰς Καφαρναούμ· καὶ εὐθὺς τοῖς σάββασιν εἰσελθὼν εἰς τὴν συναγωγὴν ἐδίδασκεν. 1:22 καὶ ἐξεπλήσσοντο ἐπὶ τῇ διδαχῇ αὐτοῦ· ἦν γὰρ διδάσκων αὐτοὺς ὡς ἐξουσίαν ἔχων καὶ οὐχ ὡς οἱ γραμματεῖς. 1:23 καὶ εὐθὺς ἦν ἐν τῇ συναγωγῇ αὐτῶν ἄνθρωπος ἐν πνεύματι ἀκαθάρτῳ καὶ ἀνέκραξεν 1:24 λέγων,
Τί ἡμῖν καὶ σοί, Ἰησοῦ Ναζαρηνέ; ἦλθες ἀπολέσαι ἡμᾶς; οἶδά σε τίς εἶ, ὁ ἅγιος τοῦ θεοῦ.
1:25 καὶ ἐπετίμησεν αὐτῷ ὁ Ἰησοῦς λέγων,
Φιμώθητι καὶ ἔξελθε ἐξ αὐτοῦ.
1:26 καὶ σπαράξαν αὐτὸν τὸ πνεῦμα τὸ ἀκάθαρτον καὶ φωνῆσαν φωνῇ μεγάλῃ ἐξῆλθεν ἐξ αὐτοῦ. 1:27 καὶ ἐθαμβήθησαν ἅπαντες ὥστε συζητεῖν πρὸς ἑαυτοὺς λέγοντας,
Τί ἐστιν τοῦτο; διδαχὴ καινὴ κατ' ἐξουσίαν· καὶ τοῖς πνεύμασι τοῖς ἀκαθάρτοις ἐπιτάσσει, καὶ ὑπακούουσιν αὐτῷ.
1:28 καὶ ἐξῆλθεν ἡ ἀκοὴ αὐτοῦ εὐθὺς πανταχοῦ εἰς ὅλην τὴν περίχωρον τῆς Γαλιλαίας.
1:29 Καὶ εὐθὺς ἐκ τῆς συναγωγῆς ἐξελθόντες ἦλθον εἰς τὴν οἰκίαν Σίμωνος καὶ Ἀνδρέου μετὰ Ἰακώβου καὶ Ἰωάννου. 1:30 ἡ δὲ πενθερὰ Σίμωνος κατέκειτο πυρέσσουσα, καὶ εὐθὺς λέγουσιν αὐτῷ περὶ αὐτῆς. 1:31 καὶ προσελθὼν ἤγειρεν αὐτὴν κρατήσας τῆς χειρός· καὶ ἀφῆκεν αὐτὴν ὁ πυρετός, καὶ διηκόνει αὐτοῖς.

4TP2.3.2(32–34) EMr:(T) 'Οψίας CM: ἔφερον...πάντας. Jesus heals during the evening.
2TP2.4(35–38) EMr:(S) ἔρημον τόπον; (T) πρωΐ...λίαν. Jesus and his disciples in a desolate place for prayer.
3TP2.4.1(35) CM: ἀναστάς. Jesus prays alone.
3TP2.4.2(36) CM: Σίμων καὶ οἱ μετ' αὐτοῦ. Simon and the others look for Jesus.
3TP2.4.3(37–38) CM: εὗρον αὐτόν. MC.Dia: λέγουσιν...λέγει. Jesus tells the disciples about his purpose of proclamation.
4TP2.4.3.1(37) MC: λέγουσιν. SPAC: assertion. They tell him about those searching for him.
4TP2.4.3.2(38) MC: λέγει. SPAC: ἄγωμεν (command) & γάρ (assertion in support of the command). Jesus' reason for his itinerating mission: to proclaim.
2TP2.5(39–44) EMr: (S) συναγωγὰς...Γαλιλαίαν. (compare 1:38 ἀλλαχοῦ...κωμοπόλεις...ἐκεῖ). Jesus preaching and exorcising in the synagogues and healing a leper.
3TP2.5.1(39) CM: ἦλθεν (Jesus); CM(P): δαιμόνια. Jesus' activity in the synagogues.
3TP2.5.2(40–44) CM: λεπρός. MC.Dia: λέγων...λέγει...λέγει. SPAC: παρακαλῶν...καθαρίσθητι...ὅρα. Jesus heals a leper.
4TP2.5.2.1(40) CM, MC: παρακαλῶν. SPAC: Ibid.—a request (a directive). The leper asks for cleansing.
4TP2.5.2.2(41) CM, MC: λέγει. SPAC: θέλω, καθαρίσθητι (an expressive and a declarative). Jesus commands him to be cleansed.
4TP2.5.2.3(42) CM: λέπρα. The leprosy leaves.
4TP2.5.2.4(43) CM: ἐμβριμησάμενος. Jesus sends the man away.
4TP2.5.2.5(44) CM, MC: λέγει. SPAC: ὅρα...ὕπαγε (commands, one intended perlocution fails [45]). Jesus' commands to the man.

1 2 3 4

1:32 Ὀψίας δὲ γενομένης, ὅτε ἔδυ ὁ ἥλιος, ἔφερον πρὸς αὐτὸν πάντας τοὺς κακῶς ἔχοντας καὶ τοὺς δαιμονιζομένους· 1:33 καὶ ἦν ὅλη ἡ πόλις ἐπισυνηγμένη πρὸς τὴν θύραν. 1:34 καὶ ἐθεράπευσεν πολλοὺς κακῶς ἔχοντας ποικίλαις νόσοις καὶ δαιμόνια πολλὰ ἐξέβαλεν καὶ οὐκ ἤφιεν λαλεῖν τὰ δαιμόνια, ὅτι ᾔδεισαν αὐτόν. 1:35 Καὶ πρωῒ ἔννυχα λίαν ἀναστὰς ἐξῆλθεν καὶ ἀπῆλθεν εἰς ἔρημον τόπον κἀκεῖ προσηύχετο. 1:36 καὶ κατεδίωξεν αὐτὸν Σίμων καὶ οἱ μετ' αὐτοῦ, 1:37 καὶ εὗρον αὐτὸν καὶ λέγουσιν αὐτῷ ὅτι
Πάντες ζητοῦσίν σε.
1:38 καὶ λέγει αὐτοῖς,
"Ἄγωμεν ἀλλαχοῦ εἰς τὰς ἐχομένας κωμοπόλεις, ἵνα καὶ ἐκεῖ κηρύξω· εἰς τοῦτο γὰρ ἐξῆλθον.
1:39 καὶ ἦλθεν κηρύσσων εἰς τὰς συναγωγὰς αὐτῶν εἰς ὅλην τὴν Γαλιλαίαν καὶ τὰ δαιμόνια ἐκβάλλων.
1:40 Καὶ ἔρχεται πρὸς αὐτὸν λεπρὸς παρακαλῶν αὐτὸν [καὶ γονυπετῶν] καὶ λέγων αὐτῷ ὅτι
Ἐὰν θέλῃς δύνασαί με καθαρίσαι.
1:41 καὶ σπλαγχνισθεὶς ἐκτείνας τὴν χεῖρα αὐτοῦ ἥψατο καὶ λέγει αὐτῷ,
Θέλω, καθαρίσθητι·
1:42 καὶ εὐθὺς ἀπῆλθεν ἀπ' αὐτοῦ ἡ λέπρα, καὶ ἐκαθαρίσθη.
1:43 καὶ ἐμβριμησάμενος αὐτῷ εὐθὺς ἐξέβαλεν αὐτόν 1:44 καὶ λέγει αὐτῷ,
Ὅρα μηδενὶ μηδὲν εἴπῃς, ἀλλὰ ὕπαγε σεαυτὸν δεῖξον τῷ ἱερεῖ καὶ προσένεγκε περὶ τοῦ καθαρισμοῦ σου ἃ προσέταξεν Μωϋσῆς, εἰς μαρτύριον αὐτοῖς.

²TP²·⁶(45) EMr:(S) ὁ δὲ ἐξελθών...ἐρήμοις τόποις. CM: Ibid. SPAC: κηρύσσειν. The leper proclaims the word and Jesus withdraws from the cities.
²TP²·⁷(2:1–12) EMr:(S) Καφαρναοὺμ...ἐν οἴκῳ. Jesus heals the paralytic.
  ³TP²·⁷·¹(1) CM: εἰσελθών. MC: ἠκούσθη. SPAC: ἐστίν (assertion). Jesus goes to a house.
  ³TP²·⁷·²(2) CM: πολλοί. A crowd gathers.
  ³TP²·⁷·³(3–4) CM: ἔρχονται...παραλυτικόν. The paralytic is brought by friends.
  ³TP²·⁷·⁴(5) CM: Ἰησοῦς. MC.Mon λέγει. SPAC: ἀφίενται (a declarative). Jesus forgives the paralytic.
  ³TP²·⁷·⁵(6–11) EMr:(S) ἐκεῖ. CM: γραμματέων. MC.Dia: διαλογιζόμενοι...λέγει. Narrator introduces the scribes and Jesus responds to their blasphemy charge by healing the paralytic.
    ⁴TP²·⁷·⁵·¹(6–7) MC: διαλογιζόμενοι (interior monologue). CM: τινες. SPAC: accusation (a declarative comprising two questions and an assertion). Report of the scribes' thoughts.
    ⁴TP²·⁷·⁵·²(8–11) CM: Ἰησοῦς. Jesus' argument against the scribes including the healing.
      ⁵TP²·⁷·⁵·²·¹(8–10a) MC.Mon: λέγει. SPAC: ἵνα δὲ εἰδῆτε (an argument comprising two questions and a conclusion (ἵνα) whose intended perlocution is the persuasion of the scribes). Jesus' argument.
      ⁵TP²·⁷·⁵·²·²(10b–11) MC.Mon: λέγει τῷ παραλυτικῷ. SPAC: ἔγειρε (a declarative that is also part of the conclusion in 10a). Jesus commands the paralytic to rise.
  ³TP²·⁷·⁶(12) CM: πάντων. MC.Mon: λέγοντας. SN: οὕτως. SPAC: δοξάζειν (praise—an expressive whose propositional content is the οὕτως phrase). The crowd's response to the incident.

1 2 3 4

1:45 ὁ δὲ ἐξελθὼν ἤρξατο κηρύσσειν πολλὰ καὶ
διαφημίζειν τὸν λόγον, ὥστε μηκέτι αὐτὸν δύνασθαι
φανερῶς εἰς πόλιν εἰσελθεῖν, ἀλλ' ἔξω ἐπ' ἐρήμοις
τόποις ἦν· καὶ ἤρχοντο πρὸς αὐτὸν πάντοθεν.
2:1 Καὶ εἰσελθὼν πάλιν εἰς Καφαρναοὺμ δι' ἡμερῶν
ἠκούσθη ὅτι
    ἐν οἴκῳ ἐστίν.
2:2 καὶ συνήχθησαν πολλοὶ ὥστε μηκέτι χωρεῖν μηδὲ τὰ
πρὸς τὴν θύραν, καὶ ἐλάλει αὐτοῖς τὸν λόγον. 2:3 καὶ
ἔρχονται φέροντες πρὸς αὐτὸν παραλυτικὸν αἰρόμενον
ὑπὸ τεσσάρων. 2:4 καὶ μὴ δυνάμενοι προσενέγκαι αὐτῷ
διὰ τὸν ὄχλον ἀπεστέγασαν τὴν στέγην ὅπου ἦν, καὶ
ἐξορύξαντες χαλῶσι τὸν κράβαττον ὅπου ὁ παραλυτικὸς
κατέκειτο. 2:5 καὶ ἰδὼν ὁ Ἰησοῦς τὴν πίστιν αὐτῶν
λέγει τῷ παραλυτικῷ,
    Τέκνον, ἀφίενταί σου αἱ ἁμαρτίαι.
2:6 ἦσαν δέ τινες τῶν γραμματέων ἐκεῖ καθήμενοι καὶ
διαλογιζόμενοι ἐν ταῖς καρδίαις αὐτῶν,
    2:7 Τί οὗτος οὕτως λαλεῖ; βλασφημεῖ· τίς δύναται
    ἀφιέναι ἁμαρτίας εἰ μὴ εἷς ὁ θεός;
2:8 καὶ εὐθὺς ἐπιγνοὺς ὁ Ἰησοῦς τῷ πνεύματι αὐτοῦ ὅτι
οὕτως διαλογίζονται ἐν ἑαυτοῖς λέγει αὐτοῖς,
    Τί ταῦτα διαλογίζεσθε ἐν ταῖς καρδίαις ὑμῶν; 2:9 τί
    ἐστιν εὐκοπώτερον, εἰπεῖν τῷ παραλυτικῷ,
        Ἀφίενταί σου αἱ ἁμαρτίαι,
    ἢ εἰπεῖν,
        Ἔγειρε καὶ ἆρον τὸν κράβαττόν σου καὶ
        περιπάτει;
    2:10 ἵνα δὲ εἰδῆτε ὅτι ἐξουσίαν ἔχει ὁ υἱὸς τοῦ
    ἀνθρώπου ἀφιέναι ἁμαρτίας ἐπὶ τῆς γῆς ⁻
λέγει τῷ παραλυτικῷ,
    2:11 Σοὶ λέγω,
    ἔγειρε ἆρον τὸν κράβαττόν σου καὶ ὕπαγε εἰς τὸν
    οἶκόν σου. 3 HS
2:12 καὶ ἠγέρθη καὶ εὐθὺς ἄρας τὸν κράβαττον ἐξῆλθεν
ἔμπροσθεν πάντων, ὥστε ἐξίστασθαι πάντας

²TP².⁸(13–14) EMr:(S) θάλασσαν (T) πάλιν. Jesus by the sea.
³TP².⁸.¹(13) CM: ὄχλος. Jesus teaches the crowd.
³TP².⁸.²(14) EMr:(S) παράγων...τελώνιον. CM: Λευίν. SPAC: 'Ακολούθει (directive). Jesus calls Levi.
²TP².⁹(15–22) EM:(S) οἰκίᾳ. Jesus in Levi's (?) house.
³TP².⁹.¹(15–17) CM: τελῶναι...ἁμαρτωλοὶ...γραμματεῖς. Jesus defends eating with sinners and tax collectors.
⁴TP².⁹.¹.¹(15) CM: τελῶναι...ἁμαρτωλοί. The sinners and tax collectors.
⁴TP².⁹.¹.²(16) CM: γραμματεῖς. MC.Mon: ἔλεγον. SPAC: Question. The scribes' challenge.
⁴TP².⁹.¹.³(17) CM: 'Ιησοῦς. MC.Mon: ἀκούσας...λέγει. SPAC: Answer. Jesus answers the scribes' question to the disciples.
³TP².⁹.²(18–22) CM: μαθηταὶ 'Ιωάννου...Φαρισαῖοι. Jesus defends his non-fasting disciples.
⁴TP².⁹.².¹(18) MC: λέγουσιν. SPAC: Question. Disciples of John and the Pharisees challenge Jesus.
⁴TP².⁹.².²(19–22) MC: εἶπεν. SPAC: Answer with an embedded question. Jesus responds.
⁵TP².⁹.².².¹(19–20) CM: οἱ υἱοί. SPAC: parabolic teaching. A parable and application.
⁵TP².⁹.².².²(21–22) CM: οὐδεῖς. SPAC: parabolic teaching. Two proverbial-parabolic sayings to support 19–20.

A Linguistic Outline of Mark 183

1 2 3 4

καὶ δοξάζειν τὸν θεὸν λέγοντας ὅτι
Οὕτως οὐδέποτε εἴδομεν.
2:13 Καὶ ἐξῆλθεν πάλιν παρὰ τὴν θάλασσαν· καὶ πᾶς ὁ
ὄχλος ἤρχετο πρὸς αὐτόν, καὶ ἐδίδασκεν αὐτούς. 2:14
καὶ παράγων εἶδεν Λευὶν τὸν τοῦ Ἀλφαίου καθήμενον
ἐπὶ τὸ τελώνιον, καὶ λέγει αὐτῷ,
Ἀκολούθει μοι.
καὶ ἀναστὰς ἠκολούθησεν αὐτῷ. 2:15 Καὶ γίνεται
κατακεῖσθαι αὐτὸν ἐν τῇ οἰκίᾳ αὐτοῦ, καὶ πολλοὶ τελῶναι
καὶ ἁμαρτωλοὶ συνανέκειντο τῷ Ἰησοῦ καὶ τοῖς μαθηταῖς
αὐτοῦ· ἦσαν γὰρ πολλοὶ καὶ ἠκολούθουν αὐτῷ. 2:16 καὶ
οἱ γραμματεῖς τῶν Φαρισαίων ἰδόντες ὅτι ἐσθίει μετὰ
τῶν ἁμαρτωλῶν καὶ τελωνῶν ἔλεγον τοῖς μαθηταῖς αὐτοῦ,
Ὅτι μετὰ τῶν τελωνῶν καὶ ἁμαρτωλῶν ἐσθίει;
2:17 καὶ ἀκούσας ὁ Ἰησοῦς λέγει αὐτοῖς [ὅτι]
Οὐ χρείαν ἔχουσιν οἱ ἰσχύοντες ἰατροῦ ἀλλ' οἱ κακῶς
ἔχοντες· οὐκ ἦλθον καλέσαι δικαίους ἀλλὰ
ἁμαρτωλούς.
2:18 Καὶ ἦσαν οἱ μαθηταὶ Ἰωάννου καὶ οἱ Φαρισαῖοι
νηστεύοντες. καὶ ἔρχονται καὶ λέγουσιν αὐτῷ,
Διὰ τί οἱ μαθηταὶ Ἰωάννου καὶ οἱ μαθηταὶ τῶν
Φαρισαίων νηστεύουσιν, οἱ δὲ σοὶ μαθηταὶ οὐ
νηστεύουσιν;
2:19 καὶ εἶπεν αὐτοῖς ὁ Ἰησοῦς,
Μὴ δύνανται οἱ υἱοὶ τοῦ νυμφῶνος ἐν ᾧ ὁ νυμφίος
μετ' αὐτῶν ἐστιν νηστεύειν; ὅσον χρόνον ἔχουσιν
τὸν νυμφίον μετ' αὐτῶν οὐ δύνανται νηστεύειν. 2:20
ἐλεύσονται δὲ ἡμέραι ὅταν ἀπαρθῇ ἀπ' αὐτῶν ὁ
νυμφίος, καὶ τότε νηστεύσουσιν ἐν ἐκείνῃ τῇ ἡμέρᾳ.
2:21 οὐδεὶς ἐπίβλημα ῥάκους ἀγνάφου ἐπιράπτει ἐπὶ
ἱμάτιον παλαιόν· εἰ δὲ μή, αἴρει τὸ πλήρωμα ἀπ'
αὐτοῦ τὸ καινὸν τοῦ παλαιοῦ καὶ χεῖρον σχίσμα
γίνεται. 2:22 καὶ οὐδεὶς βάλλει οἶνον νέον εἰς ἀσκοὺς
παλαιούς· εἰ δὲ μή, ῥήξει ὁ οἶνος τοὺς ἀσκούς καὶ ὁ
οἶνος ἀπόλλυται καὶ οἱ ἀσκοί· ἀλλὰ οἶνον νέον εἰς
ἀσκοὺς καινούς. (2 PN)

²TP²·¹⁰(2:23–3:6) EMr:(T) σάββασιν. Two Sabbath conflicts.
³TP²·¹⁰·¹(23–28) EMr:(S) σπορίμων. CM: μαθηταὶ...Φαρισαῖοι. Jesus defends his disciples' grain picking.
⁴TP²·¹⁰·¹·¹(23) CM: αὐτὸν...μαθηταί. The grain field setting of the debate.
⁴TP²·¹⁰·¹·²(24–28) CM: Φαρισαῖοι...αὐτῷ. MC:Dia: ἔλεγον...λέγει. The Pharisees question Jesus, and he responds.
⁵TP²·¹⁰·¹·²·¹(24) CM: Φαρισαῖοι. MC: ἔλεγον. SPAC: Question as accusation (a declarative). Their question about the disciples' activity.
⁵TP²·¹⁰·¹·²·²(25–28) CM: Jesus, CM(P): αὐτοῖς. SPAC: Response. Jesus answers.
⁶TP²·¹⁰·¹·²·²·¹(25–26) MC: ἔλεγεν. SPAC: argument. The David analogy.
⁶TP²·¹⁰·¹·²·²·²(27–28) MC: ἔλεγεν. SPAC: ὥστε (conclusion). The conclusion from analogy.
³TP²·¹⁰·²(1–6) EMr:(S) συναγωγήν. CM: ἄνθρωπος. Jesus defends his sabbath healing of the man's bad hand.
⁴TP²·¹⁰·²·¹(1–2) CM: εἰσῆλθεν...παρετήρουν. Jesus, the man, and the hostile observers.
⁴TP²·¹⁰·²·²(3–4a) CM: Jesus. Jesus speaks to the sick man and onlookers.
⁵TP²·¹⁰·²·²·¹(3) CM: λέγει. MC.Mon: Ibid. SPAC: command. Jesus commands the man to rise.
⁵TP²·¹⁰·²·²·²(4a) CM: λέγει. MC.Dia: Ibid. SPAC: Question. Jesus questions the onlookers about sabbath healing.
⁴TP²·¹⁰·²·³(4b) CM: οἱ. Their silence.

1 2 3 4

2:23 Καὶ ἐγένετο αὐτὸν ἐν τοῖς σάββασιν παραπορεύεσθαι διὰ τῶν σπορίμων, καὶ οἱ μαθηταὶ αὐτοῦ ἤρξαντο ὁδὸν ποιεῖν τίλλοντες τοὺς στάχυας.
2:24 καὶ οἱ Φαρισαῖοι ἔλεγον αὐτῷ,
Ἴδε τί ποιοῦσιν τοῖς σάββασιν ὃ οὐκ ἔξεστιν;
2:25 καὶ λέγει αὐτοῖς,
Οὐδέποτε ἀνέγνωτε τί ἐποίησεν Δαυίδ ὅτε χρείαν ἔσχεν καὶ ἐπείνασεν αὐτὸς καὶ οἱ μετ' αὐτοῦ, 2:26 πῶς εἰσῆλθεν εἰς τὸν οἶκον τοῦ θεοῦ ἐπὶ Ἀβιαθὰρ ἀρχιερέως καὶ τοὺς ἄρτους τῆς προθέσεως ἔφαγεν, οὓς οὐκ ἔξεστιν φαγεῖν εἰ μὴ τοὺς ἱερεῖς, καὶ ἔδωκεν καὶ τοῖς σὺν αὐτῷ οὖσιν;
2:27 καὶ ἔλεγεν αὐτοῖς,
Τὸ σάββατον διὰ τὸν ἄνθρωπον ἐγένετο καὶ οὐχ ὁ ἄνθρωπος διὰ τὸ σάββατον· 2:28 ὥστε κύριός ἐστιν ὁ υἱὸς τοῦ ἀνθρώπου καὶ τοῦ σαββάτου.
3:1 Καὶ εἰσῆλθεν πάλιν εἰς τὴν συναγωγήν.
καὶ ἦν ἐκεῖ ἄνθρωπος ἐξηραμμένην ἔχων τὴν χεῖρα· 3:2 καὶ παρετήρουν αὐτὸν εἰ τοῖς σάββασιν θεραπεύσει αὐτόν, ἵνα κατηγορήσωσιν αὐτοῦ. 3:3 καὶ λέγει τῷ ἀνθρώπῳ τῷ τὴν ξηρὰν χεῖρα ἔχοντι,
Ἔγειρε εἰς τὸ μέσον.
3:4 καὶ λέγει αὐτοῖς,
Ἔξεστιν τοῖς σάββασιν ἀγαθὸν ποιῆσαι ἢ κακοποιῆσαι, ψυχὴν σῶσαι ἢ ἀποκτεῖναι;
οἱ δὲ ἐσιώπων.

⁴TP².¹⁰.².⁴(5a) CM: λέγει. MC.Mon: Ibid. SPAC: ἔκτεινον (a healing command— a declarative). Jesus commands the sick man to be healed.
⁴TP².¹⁰.².⁵(5b) CM: αὐτοῦ. The sick man is healed.
⁴TP².¹⁰.².⁶(6) EMr: ἐξελθόντες. CM: Φαρισαῖοι...Ἡρῳδιανῶν. The Pharisees and Herodians plot his death.
²TP².¹¹(7–12) EMr:(S) θάλασσαν. Healings and exorcisms by the sea.
³TP².¹¹.¹(7a) CM: 'Ιησοῦς...μαθητῶν. Jesus and the disciples go to the sea.
³TP².¹¹.²(7b–8) CM: πλῆθος...Σιδῶνα. SN: ὅσα. The diverse crowd arrives after hearing about Jesus.
³TP².¹¹.³(9) C: εἶπεν...αὐτοῦ. MC: Ibid. SPAC: Ibid. (command). Jesus commands his disciples to keep a boat ready because of the crowd.
³TP².¹¹.⁴(10) CM: πόλλους...ὅσοι. Jesus heals the sick.
³TP².¹¹.⁵(11–12) CM: πνεύματα...αὐτόν. MC.Dia ἔκραζον...ἐπετίμα. The unclean spirits encounter Jesus.
⁴TP².¹¹.⁵.¹(11) CM: πνεύματα. MC: ἔκραζον. SPAC: Ibid.: assertion/confession. The spirits identify Jesus as Son of God.
⁴TP².¹¹.⁵.²(12) CM: ἐπετίμα. MC: Ibid. SPAC: Ibid. (rebuke: a directive). Jesus rebukes them in order that they be silent.

²TP².¹²(13–19) EMr:(S): ὄρος. CM: οὕς...αὐτός...δώδεκα. Jesus chooses the twelve.

A Linguistic Outline of Mark

1 2 3 4

3:5 καὶ περιβλεψάμενος αὐτοὺς μετ' ὀργῆς, συλλυπούμενος ἐπὶ τῇ πωρώσει τῆς καρδίας αὐτῶν λέγει τῷ ἀνθρώπῳ, Ἔκτεινον τὴν χεῖρα. καὶ ἐξέτεινεν καὶ ἀπεκατεστάθη ἡ χεὶρ αὐτοῦ. 3:6 καὶ ἐξελθόντες οἱ Φαρισαῖοι εὐθὺς μετὰ τῶν Ἡρῳδιανῶν συμβούλιον ἐδίδουν κατ' αὐτοῦ ὅπως αὐτὸν ἀπολέσωσιν. 3:7 Καὶ ὁ Ἰησοῦς μετὰ τῶν μαθητῶν αὐτοῦ ἀνεχώρησεν πρὸς τὴν θάλασσαν, καὶ πολὺ πλῆθος ἀπὸ τῆς Γαλιλαίας [ἠκολούθησεν]· καὶ ἀπὸ τῆς Ἰουδαίας 3:8 καὶ ἀπὸ Ἱεροσολύμων καὶ ἀπὸ τῆς Ἰδουμαίας καὶ πέραν τοῦ Ἰορδάνου καὶ περὶ Τύρον καὶ Σιδῶνα, πλῆθος πολύ ἀκούοντες ὅσα ἐποίει ἦλθον πρὸς αὐτόν. 3:9 καὶ εἶπεν τοῖς μαθηταῖς αὐτοῦ ἵνα
πλοιάριον προσκαρτερῇ αὐτῷ διὰ τὸν ὄχλον ἵνα μὴ θλίβωσιν αὐτόν· (1, 2)
3:10 πολλοὺς γὰρ ἐθεράπευσεν, ὥστε ἐπιπίπτειν αὐτῷ ἵνα αὐτοῦ ἅψωνται ὅσοι εἶχον μάστιγας. 3:11 καὶ τὰ πνεύματα τὰ ἀκάθαρτα, ὅταν αὐτὸν ἐθεώρουν, προσέπιπτον αὐτῷ καὶ ἔκραζον λέγοντες ὅτι
Σὺ εἶ ὁ υἱὸς τοῦ θεοῦ.
3:12 καὶ πολλὰ ἐπετίμα αὐτοῖς ἵνα
μὴ αὐτὸν φανερὸν ποιήσωσιν. (1, 2)
3:13 Καὶ ἀναβαίνει εἰς τὸ ὄρος καὶ προσκαλεῖται οὓς ἤθελεν αὐτός, καὶ ἀπῆλθον πρὸς αὐτόν. 3:14 καὶ ἐποίησεν δώδεκα [οὓς καὶ ἀποστόλους ὠνόμασεν] ἵνα ὦσιν μετ' αὐτοῦ καὶ ἵνα ἀποστέλλῃ αὐτοὺς κηρύσσειν 3:15 καὶ ἔχειν ἐξουσίαν ἐκβάλλειν τὰ δαιμόνια· 3:16 [καὶ ἐποίησεν τοὺς δώδεκα,] καὶ ἐπέθηκεν ὄνομα τῷ Σίμωνι Πέτρον, 3:17 καὶ Ἰάκωβον τὸν τοῦ Ζεβεδαίου καὶ Ἰωάννην τὸν ἀδελφὸν τοῦ Ἰακώβου καὶ ἐπέθηκεν αὐτοῖς ὀνόμα[τα] Βοανηργές ὅ ἐστιν Υἱοὶ Βροντῆς· 3:18 καὶ Ἀνδρέαν καὶ Φίλιππον καὶ Βαρθολομαῖον καὶ Μαθθαῖον καὶ Θωμᾶν καὶ Ἰάκωβον τὸν τοῦ Ἁλφαίου καὶ Θαδδαῖον καὶ Σίμωνα τὸν Καναναῖον 3:19 καὶ Ἰούδαν Ἰσκαριώθ, ὃς καὶ παρέδωκεν αὐτόν.

²TP²·¹³(20–35) EMr:(S) οἶκον. Jesus defends himself in the Beelzebul controversy and affirms his true family.
³TP²·¹³·¹(20) CM: ἔρχεται ὄχλος. Jesus and crowd. Episode introduction.
³TP²·¹³·²(21) CM: οἱ παρ' αὐτοῦ. SPAC: ἐξέστη (accusation). Jesus' family accuses him of insanity.
³TP²·¹³·³(22) CM: γραμματεῖς. MC: ἔλεγον. SPAC: Ibid. (accusation—a declarative). The scribes make the Beelzebul accusation.
³TP²·¹³·⁴(23–29) SN: παραβολαῖς. SPAC: Ibid., parabolic teaching. CM: προσκαλεσάμενος αὐτούς. Jesus responds to the scribes' argument with two parables.
⁴TP²·¹³·⁴·¹(23–27) MC: ἔλεγεν. The parabolic sayings about Satan and the strong man.
⁵TP²·¹³·⁴·¹·¹(23) SPAC: Question. CM: σατανᾶς. The question about Satan.
⁵TP²·¹³·⁴·¹·²(24–27) SPAC: Answer.
⁶TP²·¹³·⁴·¹·²·¹(24) CM: βασιλεία. CONJ: καί. The divided kingdom.
⁶TP²·¹³·⁴·¹·²·²(25) CM: οἰκία. CONJ: καί. The divided house.
⁶TP²·¹³·⁴·¹·²·³(26) CM: σατανᾶς. CONJ: καί. The divided Satan.
⁶TP²·¹³·⁴·¹·²·⁴(27) CM: οὐδείς...ἰσχυροῦ. CONJ: ἀλλ'. The intruder and strong man parable.
⁴TP²·¹³·⁴·²(28–29) MC: λέγω. SPAC: Ἀμήν (solemn assertion). Jesus comments about the scribes' blasphemy in an amen saying.
³TP²·¹³·⁵(30) CM: ἔλεγον. MC: Ibid. CONJ: ὅτι. SPAC: Ibid. (explanation—an assertive). The narrator's explanation of vv. 28–29.

1 2 3 4

3:20 Καὶ ἔρχεται εἰς οἶκον· καὶ συνέρχεται πάλιν [ὁ] ὄχλος, ὥστε μὴ δύνασθαι αὐτοὺς μηδὲ ἄρτον φαγεῖν. 3:21 καὶ ἀκούσαντες οἱ παρ' αὐτοῦ ἐξῆλθον κρατῆσαι αὐτόν· ἔλεγον γὰρ ὅτι
    ἐξέστη.
3:22 καὶ οἱ γραμματεῖς οἱ ἀπὸ Ἱεροσολύμων καταβάντες ἔλεγον ὅτι
    Βεελζεβοὺλ ἔχει καὶ ὅτι ἐν τῷ ἄρχοντι τῶν
    δαιμονίων ἐκβάλλει τὰ δαιμόνια.
3:23 καὶ προσκαλεσάμενος αὐτοὺς ἐν παραβολαῖς ἔλεγεν αὐτοῖς,
    Πῶς δύναται Σατανᾶς Σατανᾶν ἐκβάλλειν; 3:24 καὶ ἐὰν βασιλεία ἐφ' ἑαυτὴν μερισθῇ, οὐ δύναται σταθῆναι ἡ βασιλεία ἐκείνη· 3:25 καὶ ἐὰν οἰκία ἐφ' ἑαυτὴν μερισθῇ, οὐ δυνήσεται ἡ οἰκία ἐκείνη σταθῆναι. 3:26 καὶ εἰ ὁ Σατανᾶς ἀνέστη ἐφ' ἑαυτὸν καὶ ἐμερίσθη, οὐ δύναται στῆναι ἀλλὰ τέλος ἔχει. 3:27 ἀλλ' οὐ δύναται οὐδεὶς εἰς τὴν οἰκίαν τοῦ ἰσχυροῦ εἰσελθὼν τὰ σκεύη αὐτοῦ διαρπάσαι, ἐὰν μὴ πρῶτον τὸν ἰσχυρὸν δήσῃ, καὶ τότε τὴν οἰκίαν αὐτοῦ διαρπάσει. 3:28 Ἀμὴν λέγω ὑμῖν ὅτι (2 PN)
    πάντα ἀφεθήσεται τοῖς υἱοῖς τῶν ἀνθρώπων τὰ
    ἁμαρτήματα καὶ αἱ βλασφημίαι ὅσα ἐὰν
    βλασφημήσωσιν· 3:29 ὃς δ' ἂν βλασφημήσῃ εἰς τὸ
    πνεῦμα τὸ ἅγιον, οὐκ ἔχει ἄφεσιν εἰς τὸν αἰῶνα,
    ἀλλὰ ἔνοχός ἐστιν αἰωνίου ἁμαρτήματος· (3 PN, HS)
3:30 ὅτι ἔλεγον,
    Πνεῦμα ἀκάθαρτον ἔχει.

³TP².¹³.⁶(31) CM: μήτηρ αὐτοῦ...ἀδελφοί. Jesus' mother and brothers call him.
³TP².¹³.⁷(32–35) CM: ὄχλος. SPAC: assertion ('Ιδού). Jesus and the crowd respond to his mother and brothers.
    ⁴TP².¹³.⁷.¹(32) CM, MC: λέγουσιν. SPAC: assertion. The crowd notifies Jesus of his family's search.
    ⁴TP².¹³.⁷.²(33) CM, MC: λέγει. SPAC: τίς. Jesus questions them about the identity of his family.
    ⁴TP².¹³.⁷.³(34–35) CM, MC: λέγει. SPAC: assertions. Jesus reveals the nature of his true family.

²TP².¹⁴(4:1–34) EMr:(S) θάλασσαν. Jesus' parables of the word and kingdom by the sea.
  ³TP².¹⁴.¹(1–2a) CM: αὐτόν...ὄχλος. SN: παραβολαῖς. SPAC: παραβολαῖς...διδαχῇ. Introduction to the teaching in parables.
  ³TP².¹⁴.²(2b–8) CM: αὐτόν...ὄχλος, CM(P): αὐτοῖς. MC(AA):(3a) ἀκούετε. SPAC: Ibid. & parabolic teaching (a form of assertion). MC.Mon: ἔλεγεν. Jesus teaches the crowd with the sower parable and exhorts them to hear it.
    ⁴TP².¹⁴.².¹(3) CM: ὁ σπείρων. The sower.
    ⁴TP².¹⁴.².²(4) CM: ὁ μέν. The seed by the road.
    ⁴TP².¹⁴.².³(5–6) CM: ἄλλο. The seed on the rocky ground.
    ⁴TP².¹⁴.².⁴(7) CM: ἄλλο. The seed in the thorns.
    ⁴TP².¹⁴.².⁵(8) CM: ἄλλα. The seed in the good earth.
  ³TP².¹⁴.³(9) MC: ἔλεγεν, (AA) ἀκουέτω. SPAC: Ibid. (the intended perlocution is the actual hearing of the parable on the part of the receivers). The challenge to hear the parable.

1 2 3 4

3:31 Καὶ ἔρχεται ἡ μήτηρ αὐτοῦ καὶ οἱ ἀδελφοὶ αὐτοῦ καὶ ἔξω στήκοντες ἀπέστειλαν πρὸς αὐτὸν καλοῦντες αὐτόν. 3:32 καὶ ἐκάθητο περὶ αὐτὸν ὄχλος, καὶ λέγουσιν αὐτῷ, Ἰδοὺ ἡ μήτηρ σου καὶ οἱ ἀδελφοί σου [καὶ αἱ ἀδελφαι σου] ἔξω ζητοῦσίν σε. 3:33 καὶ ἀποκριθεὶς αὐτοῖς λέγει, Τίς ἐστιν ἡ μήτηρ μου καὶ οἱ ἀδελφοί [μου]; 3:34 καὶ περιβλεψάμενος τοὺς περὶ αὐτὸν κύκλῳ καθημένους λέγει, Ἴδε ἡ μήτηρ μου καὶ οἱ ἀδελφοί μου. 3:35 ὃς [γὰρ] ἂν ποιήσῃ τὸ θέλημα τοῦ θεοῦ, οὗτος ἀδελφός μου καὶ ἀδελφὴ καὶ μήτηρ ἐστίν.
4:1 Καὶ πάλιν ἤρξατο διδάσκειν παρὰ τὴν θάλασσαν· καὶ συνάγεται πρὸς αὐτὸν ὄχλος πλεῖστος, ὥστε αὐτὸν εἰς πλοῖον ἐμβάντα καθῆσθαι ἐν τῇ θαλάσσῃ, καὶ πᾶς ὁ ὄχλος πρὸς τὴν θάλασσαν ἐπὶ τῆς γῆς ἦσαν. 4:2 καὶ ἐδίδασκεν αὐτοὺς ἐν παραβολαῖς πολλά καὶ ἔλεγεν αὐτοῖς ἐν τῇ διδαχῇ αὐτοῦ,
4:3 Ἀκούετε. ἰδοὺ ἐξῆλθεν ὁ σπείρων σπεῖραι. 4:4 καὶ ἐγένετο ἐν τῷ σπείρειν ὃ μὲν ἔπεσεν παρὰ τὴν ὁδόν, καὶ ἦλθεν τὰ πετεινὰ καὶ κατέφαγεν αὐτό. 4:5 καὶ ἄλλο ἔπεσεν ἐπὶ τὸ πετρῶδες ὅπου οὐκ εἶχεν γῆν πολλήν, καὶ εὐθὺς ἐξανέτειλεν διὰ τὸ μὴ ἔχειν βάθος γῆς· 4:6 καὶ ὅτε ἀνέτειλεν ὁ ἥλιος ἐκαυματίσθη καὶ διὰ τὸ μὴ ἔχειν ῥίζαν ἐξηράνθη. 4:7 καὶ ἄλλο ἔπεσεν εἰς τὰς ἀκάνθας, καὶ ἀνέβησαν αἱ ἄκανθαι καὶ συνέπνιξαν αὐτό, καὶ καρπὸν οὐκ ἔδωκεν. 4:8 καὶ ἄλλα ἔπεσεν εἰς τὴν γῆν τὴν καλήν καὶ ἐδίδου καρπὸν ἀναβαίνοντα καὶ αὐξανόμενα καὶ ἔφερεν ἐν τριάκοντα καὶ ἐν ἑξήκοντα καὶ ἐν ἑκατόν. (2 PN)
4:9 καὶ ἔλεγεν,
Ὃς ἔχει ὦτα ἀκούειν ἀκουέτω.

³TP².¹⁴.⁴(10–20) SN: παραβολάς. EMr:(T) ὅτε (S) κατὰ μόνας. CM: οἱ περὶ αὐτόν, δώδεκα. MC.Dia: ἠρώτων...ἔλεγεν, etc. Jesus alone with the disciples in dialogue about parables.
⁴TP².¹⁴.⁴.¹(10) CM: ἠρώτων. SPAC: Ibid. The question about the parables.
⁴TP².¹⁴.⁴.²(11–20) CM: Jesus. CM:(P) αὐτοῖς. SPAC: Answer. Jesus' answer.
⁵TP².¹⁴.⁴.².¹(11–12) MC: ἔλεγεν. SN: μυστήριον (for 14–20). SPAC: assertion. The first part of Jesus' answer about the kingdom mystery.
⁵TP².¹⁴.⁴.².²(13–20) MC: λέγει. The second part of Jesus' answer: the sower.
⁶TP².¹⁴.⁴.².².¹(13b) CM: οἴδατε. SPAC: question. Jesus questions the disciples' misunderstanding.
⁶TP².¹⁴.⁴.².².²(14–20) CM: sower, etc. SPAC: interpretation of a text (an assertive). Jesus interprets the parable.
⁷TP².¹⁴.⁴.².².².¹(14) CM: ὁ σπείρων. Meaning of the sower and his seed.
⁷TP².¹⁴.⁴.².².².²(15) CM: οὗτοι. Interpretation of the seeds by the road.
⁷TP².¹⁴.⁴.².².².³(16–17) CM: οὗτοι. Interpretation of the seeds on rocky soil.
⁷TP².¹⁴.⁴.².².².⁴(18–19) CM: οὗτοι. Interpretation of the seeds in the thorns.

1 2 3 4

4:10 Καὶ ὅτε ἐγένετο κατὰ μόνας, ἠρώτων αὐτὸν οἱ περὶ αὐτὸν σὺν τοῖς δώδεκα τὰς παραβολάς. 4:11 καὶ ἔλεγεν αὐτοῖς, Ὑμῖν τὸ μυστήριον δέδοται τῆς βασιλείας τοῦ θεοῦ· ἐκείνοις δὲ τοῖς ἔξω ἐν παραβολαῖς τὰ πάντα γίνεται, 4:12 ἵνα βλέποντες βλέπωσιν καὶ μὴ ἴδωσιν, καὶ ἀκούοντες ἀκούωσιν καὶ μὴ συνιῶσιν, μήποτε ἐπιστρέψωσιν καὶ ἀφεθῇ αὐτοῖς. (2 PN)
4:13 Καὶ λέγει αὐτοῖς, Οὐκ οἴδατε τὴν παραβολὴν ταύτην, καὶ πῶς πάσας τὰς παραβολὰς γνώσεσθε; 4:14 ὁ σπείρων τὸν λόγον σπείρει. 4:15 οὗτοι δέ εἰσιν οἱ παρὰ τὴν ὁδόν· ὅπου σπείρεται ὁ λόγος, καὶ ὅταν ἀκούσωσιν, εὐθὺς ἔρχεται ὁ Σατανᾶς καὶ αἴρει τὸν λόγον τὸν ἐσπαρμένον εἰς αὐτούς. 4:16 καὶ οὗτοί εἰσιν οἱ ἐπὶ τὰ πετρώδη σπειρόμενοι, οἳ ὅταν ἀκούσωσιν τὸν λόγον εὐθὺς μετὰ χαρᾶς λαμβάνουσιν αὐτόν, 4:17 καὶ οὐκ ἔχουσιν ῥίζαν ἐν ἑαυτοῖς ἀλλὰ πρόσκαιροί εἰσιν, εἶτα γενομένης θλίψεως ἢ διωγμοῦ διὰ τὸν λόγον εὐθὺς σκανδαλίζονται 4:18 καὶ ἄλλοι εἰσὶν οἱ εἰς τὰς ἀκάνθας σπειρόμενοι· οὗτοί εἰσιν οἱ τὸν λόγον ἀκούσαντες, 4:19 καὶ αἱ μέριμναι τοῦ αἰῶνος καὶ ἡ ἀπάτη τοῦ πλούτου καὶ αἱ περὶ τὰ λοιπὰ ἐπιθυμίαι εἰσπορευόμεναι συμπνίγουσιν τὸν λόγον καὶ ἄκαρπος γίνεται. (2 PN)

⁷TP².¹⁴.⁴.².².².⁵(20) CM: ἐκεῖνοι. Interpretation of the seeds in the good earth.
³TP².¹⁴.⁵(21-34) CM: crowd (αὐτοῖς) SmPr based on 4:33-34. Jesus teaches the crowd again.
⁴TP².¹⁴.⁵.¹(21-23) MC: ἔλεγεν. AA: βλέπετε, ἀκούετε. CM: αὐτοῖς. SPAC: parable-teaching. Parable of the lamp with explanation.
⁵TP².¹⁴.⁵.¹.¹(21) CM: λύχνος. The lamp parable.
⁵TP².¹⁴.⁵.¹.²(22) CM: κρυπτόν...ἀπόκρυφον. CONJ: γάρ. Reason for the parabolic saying.
⁵TP².¹⁴.⁵.¹.³(23) CM: ὅς. AA, SPAC: ἀκουέτω. Warning to hear.
⁴TP².¹⁴.⁵.²(24-25) MC: ἔλεγεν. CM: Ibid. SPAC: βλέπετε (warning—a directive). Warning about hearing based on the metaphor of measuring.
⁵TP².¹⁴.⁵.².¹(24) CM: βλέπετε, ἀκούετε. AA: Ibid. The warning to listen carefully with the measure saying.
⁵TP².¹⁴.⁵.².²(25) CM: ὅς CONJ: γάρ. SPAC: Ibid. (a supporting assertion). Reason for the warning.
⁴TP².¹⁴.⁵.³(26-29) MC: ἔλεγεν. SN: οὕτως (for 26b-29). SPAC: parable. Parable of the self growing seed and the kingdom of God.
⁴TP².¹⁴.⁵.⁴(30-32) MC: ἔλεγεν. SPAC: parable. Parable of the mustard seed and the kingdom of God.
⁵TP².¹⁴.⁵.⁴.¹(30) SPAC: Question. Jesus' question about the kingdom.
⁵TP².¹⁴.⁵.⁴.²(31-32) SPAC: Answer using a parable. SN: ὡς (for 31b ὅς...32). The parable of the mustard seed.
⁴TP².¹⁴.⁵.⁵(33-34) MC: ἐλάλει...ἀκούειν. SN: παραβολαῖς (for all the parables in 4:2ff.). CM: αὐτοῖς...ἰδίοις. SmPr: At some point after 4:20 the crowds have returned: probably at 21 where the parables begin again. Jesus interprets the parables to his disciples (which he taught the crowds with).

1 2 3 4

4:20 καὶ ἐκεῖνοί εἰσιν οἱ ἐπὶ τὴν γῆν τὴν καλὴν σπαρέντες, οἵτινες ἀκούουσιν τὸν λόγον καὶ παραδέχονται καὶ καρποφοροῦσιν ἓν τριάκοντα καὶ ἓν ἑξήκοντα καὶ ἓν ἑκατόν. (2 PN)
4:21 Καὶ ἔλεγεν αὐτοῖς,
Μήτι ἔρχεται ὁ λύχνος ἵνα ὑπὸ τὸν μόδιον τεθῇ ἢ ὑπὸ τὴν κλίνην; οὐχ ἵνα ἐπὶ τὴν λυχνίαν τεθῇ; 4:22 οὐ γάρ ἐστιν κρυπτὸν ἐὰν μὴ ἵνα φανερωθῇ, οὐδὲ ἐγένετο ἀπόκρυφον ἀλλ' ἵνα ἔλθῃ εἰς φανερόν. 4:23 εἴ τις ἔχει ὦτα ἀκούειν ἀκουέτω. (2 PN)
4:24 Καὶ ἔλεγεν αὐτοῖς,
Βλέπετε τί ἀκούετε. ἐν ᾧ μέτρῳ μετρεῖτε μετρηθήσεται ὑμῖν καὶ προστεθήσεται ὑμῖν. 4:25 ὃς γὰρ ἔχει, δοθήσεται αὐτῷ· καὶ ὃς οὐκ ἔχει, καὶ ὃ ἔχει ἀρθήσεται ἀπ' αὐτοῦ. (2 PN)
4:26 Καὶ ἔλεγεν,
Οὕτως ἐστὶν ἡ βασιλεία τοῦ θεοῦ ὡς ἄνθρωπος βάλῃ τὸν σπόρον ἐπὶ τῆς γῆς 4:27 καὶ καθεύδῃ καὶ ἐγείρηται νύκτα καὶ ἡμέραν, καὶ ὁ σπόρος βλαστᾷ καὶ μηκύνηται ὡς οὐκ οἶδεν αὐτός. 4:28 αὐτομάτη ἡ γῆ καρποφορεῖ, πρῶτον χόρτον εἶτα στάχυν εἶτα πλήρη[s] σῖτον ἐν τῷ στάχυϊ. 4:29 ὅταν δὲ παραδοῖ ὁ καρπός, εὐθὺς ἀποστέλλει τὸ δρέπανον, ὅτι παρέστηκεν ὁ θερισμός. (2 PN)
4:30 Καὶ ἔλεγεν,
Πῶς ὁμοιώσωμεν τὴν βασιλείαν τοῦ θεοῦ ἢ ἐν τίνι αὐτὴν παραβολῇ θῶμεν; 4:31 ὡς κόκκῳ σινάπεως, ὃς ὅταν σπαρῇ ἐπὶ τῆς γῆς, μικρότερον ὂν πάντων τῶν σπερμάτων τῶν ἐπὶ τῆς γῆς, 4:32 καὶ ὅταν σπαρῇ, ἀναβαίνει καὶ γίνεται μεῖζον πάντων τῶν λαχάνων καὶ ποιεῖ κλάδους μεγάλους, ὥστε δύνασθαι ὑπὸ τὴν σκιὰν αὐτοῦ τὰ πετεινὰ τοῦ οὐρανοῦ κατασκηνοῦν. (2 PN)
4:33 Καὶ τοιαύταις παραβολαῖς πολλαῖς ἐλάλει αὐτοῖς τὸν λόγον καθὼς ἠδύναντο ἀκούειν·

²TP²·¹⁵(35–41) EMr:(T) ἐκείνῃ...ὀψίας (S) εἰς τὸ πέραν.
MC.Poly: λέγει...λέγουσιν, etc. CM: Ibid. Jesus stills the storm.
   ³TP²·¹⁵·¹(35–38a) CM: λέγει...ἀφέντες. MC: λέγει. SPAC: διέλθωμεν (a directive). Jesus and the disciples leave the crowd.
   ³TP²·¹⁵·²(38b) CM: ἐγείρουσι...λέγουσιν CM(P): αὐτόν. MC: Ibid. SPAC: question. The disciples awaken Jesus.
   ³TP²·¹⁵·³(39) CM: διεγερθείς...εἶπεν. MC: Ibid. SPAC: σιώπα, πεφίμωσο (two declaratives). Jesus awakens to rebuke the wind and to silence the sea.
   ³TP²·¹⁵·⁴(40) MC: εἶπεν. SPAC: τί (two questions). Jesus asks the disciples why they have no faith.
   ³TP²·¹⁵·⁵(41) CM: ἐφοβήθησαν. MC: ἔλεγεν. SPAC: τίς. The disciples respond to the miracle by questioning Jesus' identity.

²TP²·¹⁶(1–20) EMr: (S) εἰς τὸ πέραν...Γηρασηνῶν. Jesus exorcises in the Gerasa region.
   ³TP²·¹⁶·¹(1) EMr, CM: ἦλθον. They arrive on the other side of the sea.
   ³TP²·¹⁶·²(2–5) EMr, CM: ὑπήντησεν. The narrator's description of the possessed man.

A Linguistic Outline of Mark

1 2 3 4

4:34 χωρὶς δὲ παραβολῆς οὐκ ἐλάλει αὐτοῖς, κατ' ἰδίαν δὲ τοῖς ἰδίοις μαθηταῖς ἐπέλυεν πάντα 4:35 Καὶ λέγει αὐτοῖς ἐν ἐκείνῃ τῇ ἡμέρᾳ ὀψίας γενομένης, Διέλθωμεν εἰς τὸ πέραν. 4:36 καὶ ἀφέντες τὸν ὄχλον παραλαμβάνουσιν αὐτὸν ὡς ἦν ἐν τῷ πλοίῳ, καὶ ἄλλα πλοῖα ἦν μετ' αὐτοῦ. 4:37 καὶ γίνεται λαῖλαψ μεγάλη ἀνέμου καὶ τὰ κύματα ἐπέβαλλεν εἰς τὸ πλοῖον, ὥστε ἤδη γεμίζεσθαι τὸ πλοῖον. 4:38 καὶ αὐτὸς ἦν ἐν τῇ πρύμνῃ ἐπὶ τὸ προσκεφάλαιον καθεύδων. καὶ ἐγείρουσιν αὐτὸν καὶ λέγουσιν αὐτῷ, Διδάσκαλε, οὐ μέλει σοι ὅτι ἀπολλύμεθα; 4:39 καὶ διεγερθεὶς ἐπετίμησεν τῷ ἀνέμῳ καὶ εἶπεν τῇ θαλάσσῃ, Σιώπα, πεφίμωσο. καὶ ἐκόπασεν ὁ ἄνεμος καὶ ἐγένετο γαλήνη μεγάλη. 4:40 καὶ εἶπεν αὐτοῖς, Τί δειλοί ἐστε; οὔπω ἔχετε πίστιν; 4:41 καὶ ἐφοβήθησαν φόβον μέγαν καὶ ἔλεγον πρὸς ἀλλήλους, Τίς ἄρα οὗτός ἐστιν ὅτι καὶ ὁ ἄνεμος καὶ ἡ θάλασσα ὑπακούει αὐτῷ; 5:1 Καὶ ἦλθον εἰς τὸ πέραν τῆς θαλάσσης εἰς τὴν χώραν τῶν Γερασηνῶν. 5:2 καὶ ἐξελθόντος αὐτοῦ ἐκ τοῦ πλοίου εὐθὺς ὑπήντησεν αὐτῷ ἐκ τῶν μνημείων ἄνθρωπος ἐν πνεύματι ἀκαθάρτῳ, 5:3 ὃς τὴν κατοίκησιν εἶχεν ἐν τοῖς μνήμασιν, καὶ οὐδὲ ἁλύσει οὐκέτι οὐδεὶς ἐδύνατο αὐτὸν δῆσαι 5:4 διὰ τὸ αὐτὸν πολλάκις πέδαις καὶ ἁλύσεσιν δεδέσθαι καὶ διεσπάσθαι ὑπ' αὐτοῦ τὰς ἁλύσεις καὶ τὰς πέδας συντετρῖφθαι, καὶ οὐδεὶς ἴσχυεν αὐτὸν δαμάσαι· 5:5 καὶ διὰ παντὸς νυκτὸς καὶ ἡμέρας ἐν τοῖς μνήμασιν καὶ ἐν τοῖς ὄρεσιν ἦν κράζων καὶ κατακόπτων ἑαυτὸν λίθοις.

³TP².¹⁶.³(6–10) CM: ἰδὼν τὸν Ἰησοῦν. MC.Dia: λέγει...ἔλεγεν. Jesus and the demoniac: the exorcism.
⁴TP².¹⁶.³.¹(6–7) CM: ἰδών. MC: κράξας...λέγει. SPAC: ὁρκίζω...μή (adjuration—a directive). The demoniac's supplication.
⁴TP².¹⁶.³.²(8) CM: ἔλεγεν. MC: Ibid. SPAC: ἔξελθε. Jesus' response: he commands the demon to depart (SPAC).
⁴TP².¹⁶.³.³(9) MC.Dia: ἐπηρώτα...λέγει. SPAC: question/answer. The demon's name.
⁵TP².¹⁶.³.³.¹(9a) MC: ἐπηρώτα. SPAC: question. Jesus asks the demon's name.
⁵TP².¹⁶.³.³.²(9b) MC: λέγει. SPAC: answer. The demon gives its name.
⁴TP².¹⁶.³.⁴(10) MC: παρεκάλει. SPAC: Ibid. (a directive). The demon's request.
³TP².¹⁶.⁴(11) CM: ἀγέλη. The flock of pigs.
³TP².¹⁶.⁵(12) CM, MC, SPAC: παρεκάλεσαν. The demons' request for asylum.
³TP².¹⁶.⁶(13a) CM: ἐπέτρεψεν (P) αὐτοῖς. Jesus accedes to the requests.
³TP².¹⁶.⁷(13b) EMr: (S) ἐξελθόντα. CM: Ibid. and χοίρους. The demon leaves.
³TP².¹⁶.⁸(14–17) EMr:(S) = CM: οἱ βόσκοντες...ἦλθον. CM(P): Ἰησοῦν. SPAC: report & παρακαλεῖν. The pig herders, town and country people come to see and ask Jesus to leave.

1 2 3 4

5:6 καὶ ἰδὼν τὸν Ἰησοῦν ἀπὸ μακρόθεν ἔδραμεν καὶ
προσεκύνησεν αὐτῷ 5:7 καὶ κράξας φωνῇ μεγάλῃ λέγει,
Τί ἐμοὶ καὶ σοί, Ἰησοῦ υἱὲ τοῦ θεοῦ τοῦ ὑψίστου;
ὁρκίζω σε τὸν θεόν, μή με βασανίσῃς.
5:8 ἔλεγεν γὰρ αὐτῷ,
Ἔξελθε τὸ πνεῦμα τὸ ἀκάθαρτον ἐκ τοῦ ἀνθρώπου.
5:9 καὶ ἐπηρώτα αὐτόν,
Τί ὄνομά σοι;
καὶ λέγει αὐτῷ,
Λεγιὼν ὄνομά μοι, ὅτι πολλοί ἐσμεν.
5:10 καὶ παρεκάλει αὐτὸν πολλὰ ἵνα
μὴ αὐτὰ ἀποστείλῃ ἔξω τῆς χώρας. (1, 2)
5:11 Ἦν δὲ ἐκεῖ πρὸς τῷ ὄρει ἀγέλη χοίρων μεγάλη
βοσκομένη· 5:12 καὶ παρεκάλεσαν αὐτὸν λέγοντες,
Πέμψον ἡμᾶς εἰς τοὺς χοίρους, ἵνα εἰς αὐτοὺς
εἰσέλθωμεν.
5:13 καὶ ἐπέτρεψεν αὐτοῖς. καὶ ἐξελθόντα τὰ πνεύματα
τὰ ἀκάθαρτα εἰσῆλθον εἰς τοὺς χοίρους, καὶ ὥρμησεν ἡ
ἀγέλη κατὰ τοῦ κρημνοῦ εἰς τὴν θάλασσαν, ὡς δισχίλιοι,
καὶ ἐπνίγοντο ἐν τῇ θαλάσσῃ. 5:14 καὶ οἱ βόσκοντες
αὐτοὺς ἔφυγον καὶ ἀπήγγειλαν εἰς τὴν πόλιν καὶ εἰς
τοὺς ἀγρούς· καὶ ἦλθον ἰδεῖν τί ἐστιν τὸ γεγονός 5:15
καὶ ἔρχονται πρὸς τὸν Ἰησοῦν καὶ θεωροῦσιν τὸν
δαιμονιζόμενον καθήμενον ἱματισμένον καὶ σωφρονοῦντα,
τὸν ἐσχηκότα τὸν λεγιῶνα, καὶ ἐφοβήθησαν. 5:16 καὶ
διηγήσαντο αὐτοῖς οἱ ἰδόντες πῶς ἐγένετο τῷ
δαιμονιζομένῳ καὶ περὶ τῶν χοίρων. 5:17 καὶ ἤρξαντο
παρακαλεῖν αὐτὸν
ἀπελθεῖν ἀπὸ τῶν ὁρίων αὐτῶν. (1, 2)

³TP².¹⁶·⁹(18–20) EMr:(S) πλοῖον. CM: αὐτὸν ὁ δαιμονισθείς. SPAC: request and response. Jesus sends the healed man to his family to tell of the Lord's mercy on him.
 ⁴TP².¹⁶·⁹·¹(18) CM, MC, SPAC: παρεκάλει. The man beseeches Jesus to let him be with Jesus.
 ⁴TP².¹⁶·⁹·²(19) CM, MC: λέγει. SPAC: ὕπαγε...ἀπάγγειλον (directives). Jesus sends him home to announce what the Lord has done for him.
 ⁴TP².¹⁶·⁹·³(20) CM, SPAC: κηρύσσειν. (proclamation—an assertive). The man proclaims Jesus instead of following Jesus' command.
²TP².¹⁷(21–43) EMr:(S) εἰς τὸ πέραν...θάλασσαν. Two healings in the area of the West bank of Galilee.
 ³TP².¹⁷·¹(21–24) CM: ὄχλος...αὐτὸν...'Ιάϊρος. CM(P): θυγάτριον. SPAC: παρακαλεῖ (a request whose intended perlocution is Jesus' agreement to heal). Jairus beseeches Jesus to lay hands on his daughter.
 ³TP².¹⁷·²(25–34) CM: γυνὴ...'Ιησοῦ. Jesus heals the hemorrhaging woman.
 ⁴TP².¹⁷·²·¹(25–29) CM: γυνή (P) 'Ιησοῦ. MC.Mon: ἔλεγεν. SPAC: ἐάν (assertion about the future). The sick woman and her interior monologue about healing.
 ⁴TP².¹⁷·²·²(30) CM: 'Ιησοῦς. MC: ἔλεγεν. SPAC: question. Jesus' response and question to the crowd about the toucher.
 ⁴TP².¹⁷·²·³(31) CM: οἱ μαθηταί. MC: ἔλεγον. SPAC: question. The disciples' skepticism towards Jesus' question.

1 2 3 4
5:18 καὶ ἐμβαίνοντος αὐτοῦ εἰς τὸ πλοῖον παρεκάλει
αὐτὸν ὁ δαιμονισθεὶς
   ἵνα μετ' αὐτοῦ ᾖ. (1, 2)
5:19 καὶ οὐκ ἀφῆκεν αὐτόν, ἀλλὰ λέγει αὐτῷ,
Ὕπαγε εἰς τὸν οἶκόν σου πρὸς τοὺς σοὺς καὶ
ἀπάγγειλον αὐτοῖς ὅσα ὁ κύριός σοι πεποίηκεν καὶ
ἠλέησέν σε.
5:20 καὶ ἀπῆλθεν καὶ ἤρξατο κηρύσσειν ἐν τῇ Δεκαπόλει
ὅσα ἐποίησεν αὐτῷ ὁ Ἰησοῦς, καὶ πάντες ἐθαύμαζον.
5:21 Καὶ διαπεράσαντος τοῦ Ἰησοῦ [ἐν τῷ πλοίῳ] πάλιν
εἰς τὸ πέραν συνήχθη ὄχλος πολὺς ἐπ' αὐτόν, καὶ ἦν
παρὰ τὴν θάλασσαν. 5:22 καὶ ἔρχεται εἷς τῶν
ἀρχισυναγώγων, ὀνόματι Ἰάϊρος, καὶ ἰδὼν αὐτὸν πίπτει
πρὸς τοὺς πόδας αὐτοῦ 5:23 καὶ παρακαλεῖ αὐτὸν πολλὰ
λέγων ὅτι
   Τὸ θυγάτριόν μου ἐσχάτως ἔχει, ἵνα ἐλθὼν ἐπιθῇς
   τὰς χεῖρας αὐτῇ ἵνα σωθῇ καὶ ζήσῃ.
5:24 καὶ ἀπῆλθεν μετ' αὐτοῦ. Καὶ ἠκολούθει αὐτῷ ὄχλος
πολύς καὶ συνέθλιβον αὐτόν. 5:25 καὶ γυνὴ οὖσα ἐν
ῥύσει αἵματος δώδεκα ἔτη 5:26 καὶ πολλὰ παθοῦσα ὑπὸ
πολλῶν ἰατρῶν καὶ δαπανήσασα τὰ παρ' αὐτῆς πάντα καὶ
μηδὲν ὠφεληθεῖσα ἀλλὰ μᾶλλον εἰς τὸ χεῖρον ἐλθοῦσα,
5:27 ἀκούσασα περὶ τοῦ Ἰησοῦ, ἐλθοῦσα ἐν τῷ ὄχλῳ
ὄπισθεν ἥψατο τοῦ ἱματίου αὐτοῦ· 5:28 ἔλεγεν γὰρ ὅτι
* Ἐὰν ἅψωμαι κἂν τῶν ἱματίων αὐτοῦ σωθήσομαι. (2
PN)
5:29 καὶ εὐθὺς ἐξηράνθη ἡ πηγὴ τοῦ αἵματος αὐτῆς καὶ
ἔγνω τῷ σώματι ὅτι ἴαται ἀπὸ τῆς μάστιγος.
5:30 καὶ εὐθὺς ὁ Ἰησοῦς ἐπιγνοὺς ἐν ἑαυτῷ τὴν ἐξ
αὐτοῦ δύναμιν ἐξελθοῦσαν ἐπιστραφεὶς ἐν τῷ ὄχλῳ
ἔλεγεν,
   Τίς μου ἥψατο τῶν ἱματίων;
5:31 καὶ ἔλεγον αὐτῷ οἱ μαθηταὶ αὐτοῦ,
   Βλέπεις τὸν ὄχλον συνθλίβοντά σε, καὶ λέγεις,
      Τίς μου ἥψατο;

⁴TP².¹⁷·²·⁴(32) CM: περιεβλέπετο. Jesus looks for the healed person.
⁴TP².¹⁷·²·⁵(33) CM: γυνή. SN: πᾶσαν τὴν ἀλήθειαν (for 25–29). The woman's response.
⁴TP².¹⁷·²·⁶(34) CM: εἶπεν. MC: Ibid. SPAC: σέσωκεν ...ὕπαγε...ἴσθι (declaratives). Jesus' blessing and healing.

³TP².¹⁷·³(35–43) EMr:(T) Ἔτι. CM: ἔρχονται...Ἰησοῦς ...ἀρχισυναγώγῳ. Jesus raises Jairus's daughter from death.
⁴TP².¹⁷·³·¹(35–37). EMr:(S) συνακολουθῆσαι (37). MC: λέγοντες...λέγει. SPAC: (35) assertion and question; (36) commands. On the way to the house Jesus exhorts the father to believe after the report of his daughter's death.
⁴TP².¹⁷·³·²(38–43) EMr:(S) οἶκον. The miracle in the house.
⁵TP².¹⁷·³·²·¹(38–40a) EMr:(S) Implied—in the house but not where the girl is. CM: αὐτοῖς. SPAC: τί, καθεύδει (question and assertion). The crowd laughs at Jesus' claim that the girl is not dead.
⁵TP².¹⁷·³·²·²(40b–43) EMr:(S) ὅπου ἦν τὸ παιδίον. Jesus heals the girl in private.
⁶TP².¹⁷·³·²·²·¹(40b) CM: πατέρα...μητέρα ...αὐτοῦ. Jesus, the parents, and the three go to the girl.
⁶TP².¹⁷·³·²·²·²(41) CM: λέγει αὐτῇ. SPAC: κουμ (a declarative). Jesus commands her to rise.
⁶TP².¹⁷·³·²·²·³(42a) CM: τὸ κοράσιον. The little girl rises.
⁶TP².¹⁷·³·²·²·⁴(42b) CM: ἐξέστησαν. The onlookers wonder.
⁶TP².¹⁷·³·²·²·⁵(43) CM, MC: διεστείλατο...εἶπεν δοθῆναι. SPAC: Ibid. Jesus' commands concerning the miracle and the girl's food.

1 2 3 4

5:32 καὶ περιεβλέπετο ἰδεῖν τὴν τοῦτο ποιήσασαν. 5:33 ἡ
δὲ γυνὴ φοβηθεῖσα καὶ τρέμουσα, εἰδυῖα ὃ γέγονεν αὐτῇ,
ἦλθεν καὶ προσέπεσεν αὐτῷ καὶ εἶπεν αὐτῷ πᾶσαν τὴν
ἀλήθειαν. 5:34 ὁ δὲ εἶπεν αὐτῇ,
   Θυγάτηρ, ἡ πίστις σου σέσωκέν σε· ὕπαγε εἰς
   εἰρήνην καὶ ἴσθι ὑγιὴς ἀπὸ τῆς μάστιγός σου.
5:35 Ἔτι αὐτοῦ λαλοῦντος ἔρχονται ἀπὸ τοῦ
ἀρχισυναγώγου λέγοντες ὅτι
   Ἡ θυγάτηρ σου ἀπέθανεν· τί ἔτι σκύλλεις τὸν
   διδάσκαλον;
5:36 ὁ δὲ Ἰησοῦς παρακούσας τὸν λόγον λαλούμενον
λέγει τῷ ἀρχισυναγώγῳ,
   Μὴ φοβοῦ, μόνον πίστευε.
5:37 καὶ οὐκ ἀφῆκεν οὐδένα μετ' αὐτοῦ συνακολουθῆσαι
εἰ μὴ τὸν Πέτρον καὶ Ἰάκωβον καὶ Ἰωάννην τὸν ἀδελφὸν
Ἰακώβου. 5:38 καὶ ἔρχονται εἰς τὸν οἶκον τοῦ
ἀρχισυναγώγου, καὶ θεωρεῖ θόρυβον καὶ κλαίοντας καὶ
ἀλαλάζοντας πολλά, 5:39 καὶ εἰσελθὼν λέγει αὐτοῖς,
   Τί θορυβεῖσθε καὶ κλαίετε; τὸ παιδίον οὐκ ἀπέθανεν
   ἀλλὰ καθεύδει.
5:40 καὶ κατεγέλων αὐτοῦ. αὐτὸς δὲ ἐκβαλὼν πάντας
παραλαμβάνει τὸν πατέρα τοῦ παιδίου καὶ τὴν μητέρα
καὶ τοὺς μετ' αὐτοῦ, καὶ εἰσπορεύεται ὅπου ἦν τὸ
παιδίον. 5:41 καὶ κρατήσας τῆς χειρὸς τοῦ παιδίου λέγει αὐτῇ,
   Ταλιθα κουμ,
ὅ ἐστιν μεθερμηνευόμενον
     Τὸ κοράσιον, (3 HS)
   σοὶ λέγω,
     ἔγειρε. (3 HS)
5:42 καὶ εὐθὺς ἀνέστη τὸ κοράσιον καὶ περιεπάτει· ἦν
γὰρ ἐτῶν δώδεκα. καὶ ἐξέστησαν [εὐθὺς] ἐκστάσει
μεγάλῃ. 5:43 καὶ διεστείλατο αὐτοῖς πολλὰ ἵνα
   μηδεὶς γνοῖ τοῦτο, (1, 2)
καὶ εἶπεν
   δοθῆναι αὐτῇ φαγεῖν. (1, 2)

²TP²·¹⁸(6:1–13) EMr:(S) πατρίδα. CM: οἱ μαθηταί. Jesus and his disciples minister in his town and the surrounding villages.
   ³TP²·¹⁸·¹(1–6a) EMr:(S) συναγωγῇ (T) σαββάτου. Jesus' rejection in the synagogue.
     ⁴TP²·¹⁸·¹·¹(1–2a) CM: αὐτῷ οἱ μαθηταί. Jesus and his disciples enter the synagogue.
     ⁴TP²·¹⁸·¹·²(2b–3) CM: πολλοί. MC.Mon λέγοντες. SPAC: questions. The crowd's negative response to Jesus.
     ⁴TP²·¹⁸·¹·³(4) CM: ἔλεγεν. MC: Ibid. SPAC: answer. Jesus' comment on their rejection of him: proverb about the rejected prophet.
     ⁴TP²·¹⁸·¹·⁴(5–6a) CM: ἀρρώστοις ἐπιθείς. SPAC: report. Jesus can only heal a few sick.
   ³TP²·¹⁸·²(6b–13) EMr: (S) τὰς κώμας κύκλῳ. The mission of the twelve.
     ⁴TP²·¹⁸·²·¹(6b) CM: περιῆγεν. Jesus teaches in surrounding villages.
     ⁴TP²·¹⁸·²·²(7–9) CM: προσκαλεῖται τ. δώδεκα. SPAC: παρήγγειλεν. Jesus instructs the twelve about what to take and wear on their mission.
     ⁴TP²·¹⁸·²·³(10–11) CM, MC: ἔλεγεν. Jesus instructs them further about the mission.
        ⁵TP²·¹⁸·²·³·¹(10) CM: οἰκίαν. SPAC: μένετε. They are to stay in one home.
        ⁵TP²·¹⁸·²·³·²(11) CM: τόπος. SPAC: ἐκτινάξατε. He commands them to shake off the dust under their feet if people will not receive them and listen.
     ⁴TP²·¹⁸·²·⁴(12–13) EMr:(S) ἐξελθόντες. CM: Ibid. SPAC: κηρύσσειν. The twelve on mission.

1 2 3 4

6:1 Καὶ ἐξῆλθεν ἐκεῖθεν καὶ ἔρχεται εἰς τὴν πατρίδα αὐτοῦ, καὶ ἀκολουθοῦσιν αὐτῷ οἱ μαθηταὶ αὐτοῦ. 6:2 καὶ γενομένου σαββάτου ἤρξατο διδάσκειν ἐν τῇ συναγωγῇ, καὶ πολλοὶ ἀκούοντες ἐξεπλήσσοντο λέγοντες,
Πόθεν τούτῳ ταῦτα, καὶ τίς ἡ σοφία ἡ δοθεῖσα τούτῳ, καὶ αἱ δυνάμεις τοιαῦται διὰ τῶν χειρῶν αὐτοῦ γινόμεναι; 6:3 οὐχ οὗτός ἐστιν ὁ τέκτων, ὁ υἱὸς τῆς Μαρίας καὶ ἀδελφὸς Ἰακώβου καὶ Ἰωσῆτος καὶ Ἰούδα καὶ Σίμωνος; καὶ οὐκ εἰσὶν αἱ ἀδελφαὶ αὐτοῦ ὧδε πρὸς ἡμᾶς;
καὶ ἐσκανδαλίζοντο ἐν αὐτῷ.
6:4 καὶ ἔλεγεν αὐτοῖς ὁ Ἰησοῦς ὅτι
Οὐκ ἔστιν προφήτης ἄτιμος εἰ μὴ ἐν τῇ πατρίδι αὐτοῦ καὶ ἐν τοῖς συγγενεῦσιν αὐτοῦ καὶ ἐν τῇ οἰκίᾳ αὐτοῦ.
6:5 καὶ οὐκ ἐδύνατο ἐκεῖ ποιῆσαι οὐδεμίαν δύναμιν, εἰ μὴ ὀλίγοις ἀρρώστοις ἐπιθεὶς τὰς χεῖρας ἐθεράπευσεν.
6:6 καὶ ἐθαύμαζεν διὰ τὴν ἀπιστίαν αὐτῶν.
Καὶ περιῆγεν τὰς κώμας κύκλῳ διδάσκων. 6:7 καὶ προσκαλεῖται τοὺς δώδεκα καὶ ἤρξατο αὐτοὺς ἀποστέλλειν δύο δύο καὶ ἐδίδου αὐτοῖς ἐξουσίαν τῶν πνευμάτων τῶν ἀκαθάρτων, 6:8 καὶ παρήγγειλεν αὐτοῖς ἵνα
μηδὲν αἴρωσιν εἰς ὁδὸν εἰ μὴ ῥάβδον μόνον, μὴ ἄρτον, μὴ πήραν, μὴ εἰς τὴν ζώνην χαλκόν, 6:9 ἀλλὰ ὑποδεδεμένους σανδάλια, καὶ μὴ ἐνδύσησθε δύο χιτῶνας. (1, 2)
6:10 καὶ ἔλεγεν αὐτοῖς,
Ὅπου ἐὰν εἰσέλθητε εἰς οἰκίαν, ἐκεῖ μένετε ἕως ἂν ἐξέλθητε ἐκεῖθεν. 6:11 καὶ ὃς ἂν τόπος μὴ δέξηται ὑμᾶς μηδὲ ἀκούσωσιν ὑμῶν, ἐκπορευόμενοι ἐκεῖθεν ἐκτινάξατε τὸν χοῦν τὸν ὑποκάτω τῶν ποδῶν ὑμῶν εἰς μαρτύριον αὐτοῖς.
6:12 Καὶ ἐξελθόντες ἐκήρυξαν ἵνα μετανοῶσιν, 6:13 καὶ δαιμόνια πολλὰ ἐξέβαλλον, καὶ ἤλειφον ἐλαίῳ πολλοὺς ἀρρώστους καὶ ἐθεράπευον.

²TP².¹⁹(14–29) EMr:(implied) Sometime during Jesus' ministry after his baptism by John (after the sending of the 12?). CM: Ἡρώδης. The story of Herod's relation to Jesus and John.
³TP².¹⁹.¹(14–16) EMr:(SmPr) After Herod's execution of John. CM: Ἡρώδης...ἔλεγον (P) αὐτοῦ...Ἰωάννης. Herod's speculation about Jesus and John based on that of the people.
⁴TP².¹⁹.¹.¹(14a) CM: Ἡρώδης (P) αὐτοῦ. MC: ἤκουσεν. Herod hears about Jesus.
⁴TP².¹⁹.¹.²(14b) CM: ἔλεγον. MC: Ibid. SPAC: assertion. The opinion of some: Jesus is John the baptist *redivivus*.
⁴TP².¹⁹.¹.³(15a) CM: ἄλλοι. MC: ἔλεγον. SPAC: assertion. The opinion of others: Jesus is Elijah.
⁴TP².¹⁹.¹.⁴(15b) CM: ἄλλοι. MC: ἔλεγον. SPAC: assertion. The opinion of others: Jesus is a prophet.
⁴TP².¹⁹.¹.⁵(16) CM: Ἡρώδης. MC: ἀκούσας...ἔλεγεν. SPAC: assertion. Herod hears of their opinions and accepts the John *redivivus* hypothesis.
³TP².¹⁹.²(17–29) EMr:(SmPr) Before Herod's execution of John. CM: Ἰωάννην...Ἡρώδῃ. CONJ: γάρ. SPAC: Ibid—an explanation. Story of Herod's execution of John as an explanation of vv. 14–16.
⁴TP².¹⁹.².¹(17–20) EMr:(S) φυλακῇ. CM: ἔδησεν αὐτὸν...Ἡρώδῃ. John is arrested and converses with Herod, and Herodias wants to kill him.
⁵TP².¹⁹.².¹.¹(17) CM: Αὐτός, (P) Ἰωάννην. Herod has John arrested because of Herodias.
⁵TP².¹⁹.².¹.²(18) CM: ἔλεγεν...Ἰωάννης...Ἡρώδῃ. SPAC: accusation. John criticizes Herod's marriage.
⁵TP².¹⁹.².¹.³(19) CM: Ἡρωδιάς. Herodias wants to kill John.
⁵TP².¹⁹.².¹.⁴(20) CM: Ἡρώδης. MC: ἤκουεν. CONJ: γάρ. The reason for Herodias's inability to kill John: Herod fears, admires and hears him gladly.

1 2 3 4

6:14 Καὶ ἤκουσεν ὁ βασιλεὺς Ἡρώδης, φανερὸν γὰρ ἐγένετο τὸ ὄνομα αὐτοῦ, καὶ ἔλεγον ὅτι Ἰωάννης ὁ βαπτίζων ἐγήγερται ἐκ νεκρῶν καὶ διὰ τοῦτο ἐνεργοῦσιν αἱ δυνάμεις ἐν αὐτῷ.
6:15 ἄλλοι δὲ ἔλεγον ὅτι Ἠλίας ἐστίν· ἄλλοι δὲ ἔλεγον ὅτι προφήτης ὡς εἷς τῶν προφητῶν.
6:16 ἀκούσας δὲ ὁ Ἡρώδης ἔλεγεν, Ὃν ἐγὼ ἀπεκεφάλισα Ἰωάννην, οὗτος ἠγέρθη.
6:17 Αὐτὸς γὰρ ὁ Ἡρώδης ἀποστείλας ἐκράτησεν τὸν Ἰωάννην καὶ ἔδησεν αὐτὸν ἐν φυλακῇ διὰ Ἡρῳδιάδα τὴν γυναῖκα Φιλίππου τοῦ ἀδελφοῦ αὐτοῦ, ὅτι αὐτὴν ἐγάμησεν· 6:18 ἔλεγεν γὰρ ὁ Ἰωάννης τῷ Ἡρώδῃ ὅτι Οὐκ ἔξεστίν σοι ἔχειν τὴν γυναῖκα τοῦ ἀδελφοῦ σου.
6:19 ἡ δὲ Ἡρῳδιὰς ἐνεῖχεν αὐτῷ καὶ ἤθελεν αὐτὸν ἀποκτεῖναι, καὶ οὐκ ἠδύνατο· 6:20 ὁ γὰρ Ἡρώδης ἐφοβεῖτο τὸν Ἰωάννην, εἰδὼς αὐτὸν ἄνδρα δίκαιον καὶ ἅγιον, καὶ συνετήρει αὐτόν, καὶ ἀκούσας αὐτοῦ πολλὰ ἠπόρει, καὶ ἡδέως αὐτοῦ ἤκουεν.

⁴TP².¹⁹.².²(21–29) EMr:(T) ἡμέρας...γενεσίοις. CM: μεγιστᾶσιν...πρώτοις (P):'Ιωάννου. The birthday execution.
⁵TP².¹⁹.².².¹(21) EMr:(S) δεῖπνον. CM: μεγιστᾶσιν, etc. The dinner and guests.
⁵TP².¹⁹.².².²(22–23) EMr:(S) εἰσελθούσης. CM: θυγατρός. Herodias's daughter dances, and Herod makes a promise/oath to her.
⁶TP².¹⁹.².².².¹(22) MC: εἶπεν. SPAC: αἴτησόν...δώσω (promise—a commissive). Herod makes a promise to Herodias.
⁶TP².¹⁹.².².².²(23) MC: ὤμοσεν. SPAC: Ibid. Herod describes the limits of his oath.
⁵TP².¹⁹.².².³(24) EMr:(S) ἐξελθοῦσα...μητρί. CM:Ibid. SPAC: τί and answer. Mother and daughter confer.
⁵TP².¹⁹.².².⁴(25–26) EMr:(S) εἰσελθοῦσα. CM: Ibid. SPAC: ᾐτήσατο—request. The daughter asks for John's head.
⁵TP².¹⁹.².².⁵(27) EMr:(S) σπεκουλάτορα...ἀπελθών. CM: Ibid. SPAC: ἐπέταξεν. A policeman cuts John's head off.
⁵TP².¹⁹.².².⁶(28) EMr:(S) ἤνεγκεν. CM: Ibid. The head is brought.
⁵TP².¹⁹.².².⁷(29) EMr:(S) οἱ μαθηταί...ἦλθον. CM: Ibid. John's disciples bury him.
²TP².²⁰(30–31) EMr:(S) συνάγονται οἱ ἀπόστολοι...'Ιησοῦν. CM: Ibid. MC: ἀπήγγειλαν. SN: ὅσα...ὅσα. SPAC: δεῦτε. The apostles return to Jesus and are instructed to go to a deserted place.

1 2 3 4

6:21 Καὶ γενομένης ἡμέρας εὐκαίρου ὅτε Ἡρῴδης τοῖς γενεσίοις αὐτοῦ δεῖπνον ἐποίησεν τοῖς μεγιστᾶσιν αὐτοῦ καὶ τοῖς χιλιάρχοις καὶ τοῖς πρώτοις τῆς Γαλιλαίας, 6:22 καὶ εἰσελθούσης τῆς θυγατρὸς αὐτοῦ Ἡρῳδιάδος καὶ ὀρχησαμένης ἤρεσεν τῷ Ἡρῴδῃ καὶ τοῖς συνανακειμένοις. εἶπεν ὁ βασιλεὺς τῷ κορασίῳ,
Αἴτησόν με ὃ ἐὰν θέλῃς, καὶ δώσω σοι·
6:23 καὶ ὤμοσεν αὐτῇ [πολλά],
Ὅ τι ἐάν με αἰτήσῃς δώσω σοι ἕως ἡμίσους τῆς βασιλείας μου.
6:24 καὶ ἐξελθοῦσα εἶπεν τῇ μητρὶ αὐτῆς,
Τί αἰτήσωμαι;
ἡ δὲ εἶπεν,
Τὴν κεφαλὴν Ἰωάννου τοῦ βαπτίζοντος.
6:25 καὶ εἰσελθοῦσα εὐθὺς μετὰ σπουδῆς πρὸς τὸν βασιλέα ᾐτήσατο λέγουσα,
Θέλω ἵνα ἐξαυτῆς δῷς μοι ἐπὶ πίνακι τὴν κεφαλὴν Ἰωάννου τοῦ βαπτιστοῦ.
6:26 καὶ περίλυπος γενόμενος ὁ βασιλεὺς διὰ τοὺς ὅρκους καὶ τοὺς ἀνακειμένους οὐκ ἠθέλησεν ἀθετῆσαι αὐτήν· 6:27 καὶ εὐθὺς ἀποστείλας ὁ βασιλεὺς σπεκουλάτορα ἐπέταξεν
ἐνέγκαι τὴν κεφαλὴν αὐτοῦ. (1, 2)
καὶ ἀπελθὼν ἀπεκεφάλισεν αὐτὸν ἐν τῇ φυλακῇ 6:28 καὶ ἤνεγκεν τὴν κεφαλὴν αὐτοῦ ἐπὶ πίνακι καὶ ἔδωκεν αὐτὴν τῷ κορασίῳ, καὶ τὸ κοράσιον ἔδωκεν αὐτὴν τῇ μητρὶ αὐτῆς. 6:29 καὶ ἀκούσαντες οἱ μαθηταὶ αὐτοῦ ἦλθον καὶ ἦραν τὸ πτῶμα αὐτοῦ καὶ ἔθηκαν αὐτὸ ἐν μνημείῳ.
6:30 Καὶ συνάγονται οἱ ἀπόστολοι πρὸς τὸν Ἰησοῦν καὶ ἀπήγγειλαν αὐτῷ πάντα ὅσα ἐποίησαν καὶ ὅσα ἐδίδαξαν.
6:31 καὶ λέγει αὐτοῖς,
Δεῦτε ὑμεῖς αὐτοὶ κατ' ἰδίαν εἰς ἔρημον τόπον καὶ ἀναπαύσασθε ὀλίγον.
ἦσαν γὰρ οἱ ἐρχόμενοι καὶ οἱ ὑπάγοντες πολλοί, καὶ οὐδὲ φαγεῖν εὐκαίρουν.

²TP².²¹(32–33) EMr:(S) ἔρημον τόπον. CM: ἀπῆλθον. The trip to the deserted place.
²TP².²²(34–44) EMr:(S) ἐξελθών. The deserted place: teaching and feeding.
   ³TP².²².¹(34) CM: ὄχλον. Jesus' compassion and teaching.
   ³TP².²².²(35–44) EMr:(T) ὥρας πόλλης. CM: οἱ μαθηταί. The feeding miracle late in the day.
     ⁴TP².²².².¹(35–38) CM: οἱ μαθηταί (P): αὐτούς. MC.Dia: ἔλεγεν...ἀποκριθείς. Jesus and the disciples discuss the crowd's meal.
        ⁵TP².²².².¹.¹(35–36) MC: ἔλεγον. SPAC: ἔρημός...ἀπόλυσον (assertion & directive). The disciples tell Jesus to send the people away.
        ⁵TP².²².².¹.²(37a) MC: εἶπεν. SPAC: δότε. Jesus tells the disciples to feed them.
        ⁵TP².²².².¹.³(37b) MC: λέγουσιν. SPAC: question. The disciples question Jesus about how to feed the crowds.
        ⁵TP².²².².¹.⁴(38a) MC: λέγει. SPAC: question & ὑπάγετε. Jesus questions them about the loaves they have.
        ⁵TP².²².².¹.⁵(38b) MC: λέγουσιν. SPAC: assertion. The disciples carry out his request.
     ⁴TP².²².².²(39) CM: ἐπέταξεν αὐτοῖς. SPAC: Ibid. Jesus commands the crowds to sit in companies.
     ⁴TP².²².².³(40) CM: ἀνέπεσαν. The crowds sit in 50's and 100's.
     ⁴TP².²².².⁴(41) CM: λαβών...μαθηταῖς (P) αὐτοῖς. SPAC: εὐλόγησεν. Jesus blesses the bread and gives it to the disciples who distribute it, and then Jesus divides the fish for all.
     ⁴TP².²².².⁵(42) CM: ἔφαγον. The crowds eat and are satisfied.
     ⁴TP².²².².⁶(43) CM: ἦραν. The disciples gather the leftovers.

A Linguistic Outline of Mark 211

1 2 3 4

6:32 καὶ ἀπῆλθον ἐν τῷ πλοίῳ εἰς ἔρημον τόπον κατ᾽ ἰδίαν. 6:33 καὶ εἶδον αὐτοὺς ὑπάγοντας καὶ ἐπέγνωσαν πολλοί καὶ πεζῇ ἀπὸ πασῶν τῶν πόλεων συνέδραμον ἐκεῖ καὶ προῆλθον αὐτούς. 6:34 καὶ ἐξελθὼν εἶδεν πολὺν ὄχλον καὶ ἐσπλαγχνίσθη ἐπ᾽ αὐτούς, ὅτι ἦσαν ὡς πρόβατα μὴ ἔχοντα ποιμένα, καὶ ἤρξατο διδάσκειν αὐτοὺς πολλά. 6:35 Καὶ ἤδη ὥρας πολλῆς γενομένης προσελθόντες αὐτῷ οἱ μαθηταὶ αὐτοῦ ἔλεγον ὅτι
Ἔρημός ἐστιν ὁ τόπος καὶ ἤδη ὥρα πολλή· 6:36 ἀπόλυσον αὐτούς, ἵνα ἀπελθόντες εἰς τοὺς κύκλῳ ἀγροὺς καὶ κώμας ἀγοράσωσιν ἑαυτοῖς τί φάγωσιν.
6:37 ὁ δὲ ἀποκριθεὶς εἶπεν αὐτοῖς,
Δότε αὐτοῖς ὑμεῖς φαγεῖν.
καὶ λέγουσιν αὐτῷ,
Ἀπελθόντες ἀγοράσωμεν δηναρίων διακοσίων ἄρτους καὶ δώσομεν αὐτοῖς φαγεῖν;
6:38 ὁ δὲ λέγει αὐτοῖς,
Πόσους ἄρτους ἔχετε; ὑπάγετε ἴδετε.
καὶ γνόντες λέγουσιν,
Πέντε, καὶ δύο ἰχθύας.
6:39 καὶ ἐπέταξεν αὐτοῖς
ἀνακλῖναι πάντας συμπόσια συμπόσια ἐπὶ τῷ χλωρῷ χόρτῳ. (1, 2)
6:40 καὶ ἀνέπεσαν πρασιαὶ πρασιαὶ κατὰ ἑκατὸν καὶ κατὰ πεντήκοντα. 6:41 καὶ λαβὼν τοὺς πέντε ἄρτους καὶ τοὺς δύο ἰχθύας ἀναβλέψας εἰς τὸν οὐρανὸν εὐλόγησεν καὶ κατέκλασεν τοὺς ἄρτους καὶ ἐδίδου τοῖς μαθηταῖς [αὐτοῦ] ἵνα παρατιθῶσιν αὐτοῖς, καὶ τοὺς δύο ἰχθύας ἐμέρισεν πᾶσιν. 6:42 καὶ ἔφαγον πάντες καὶ ἐχορτάσθησαν, 6:43 καὶ ἦραν κλάσματα δώδεκα κοφίνων πληρώματα καὶ ἀπὸ τῶν ἰχθύων.

⁴TP².²².².⁷(44) CM: οἱ φαγόντες. The number of men eating: 5000.
²TP².²³(45–52) EMr:(S) ἐμβῆναι...Βηθσαϊδάν (T) εὐθύς. An episode on land and sea: Jesus prays on the mountain and walks on the sea.
³TP².²³.¹(45) CM: ἠνάγκασεν (P) μαθητάς. Jesus sends the disciples to Bethsaida.
³TP².²³.²(46) EMr:(S) ἀπῆλθεν...ὄρος. CM: Ibid. Jesus goes to a mountain to pray.
³TP².²³.³(47) EMr: ὀψίας...θαλάσσης...γῆς. CM: πλοῖον...αὐτός. The disciples are in the boat, and Jesus is on the land.
³TP².²³.⁴(48–52) EMr:(T) τετάρτην...νυκτός (S) ἔρχεται πρὸς αὐτούς. CM: Ibid. SPAC: θαρσεῖτε. Jesus, walking on the sea, comes to the disciples.
⁴TP².²³.⁴.¹(48) CM: ἔρχεται. Jesus comes to the disciples walking on the sea.
⁴TP².²³.⁴.²(49–50a) CM: οἱ δέ. The disciples think it is a ghost.
⁴TP².²³.⁴.³(50b) CM: λέγει αὐτοῖς. SPAC: directive, assertion, directive. Jesus identifies himself and tells them not to fear.
⁴TP².²³.⁴.⁴(51) EMr, CM: ἀνέβη...ἄνεμος. The wind calms as Jesus enters the boat.
⁴TP².²³.⁴.⁵(52) CM: συνῆκαν. CONJ: γάρ. Narrator explains the disciples' amazement: they do not understand the loaves.
²TP².²⁴(6:53–7:23) EMr:(S) Γεννησαρέτ...χώραν. Jesus healing and arguing about the law in the Genessaret region.
³TP².²⁴.¹(53–56) CM: αὐτῶν...ἐπιγνόντες. Jesus healing the sick in villages and fields.
⁴TP².²⁴.¹.¹(53–54) EMr:(S) προσωρμίσθησαν. CM: Ibid. Leaving the boat.
⁴TP².²⁴.¹.²(55) EMr: (S) χώραν. CM: περιέδραμον. SPAC: ἐστίν (assertion). The crowds gather the sick.

1 2 3 4

6:44 καὶ ἦσαν οἱ φαγόντες [τοὺς ἄρτους] πεντακισχίλιοι ἄνδρες.
6:45 Καὶ εὐθὺς ἠνάγκασεν τοὺς μαθητὰς αὐτοῦ ἐμβῆναι εἰς τὸ πλοῖον καὶ προάγειν εἰς τὸ πέραν πρὸς Βηθσαϊδάν, ἕως αὐτὸς ἀπολύει τὸν ὄχλον. 6:46 καὶ ἀποταξάμενος αὐτοῖς ἀπῆλθεν εἰς τὸ ὄρος προσεύξασθαι. 6:47 καὶ ὀψίας γενομένης ἦν τὸ πλοῖον ἐν μέσῳ τῆς θαλάσσης, καὶ αὐτὸς μόνος ἐπὶ τῆς γῆς. 6:48 καὶ ἰδὼν αὐτοὺς βασανιζομένους ἐν τῷ ἐλαύνειν, ἦν γὰρ ὁ ἄνεμος ἐναντίος αὐτοῖς, περὶ τετάρτην φυλακὴν τῆς νυκτὸς ἔρχεται πρὸς αὐτοὺς περιπατῶν ἐπὶ τῆς θαλάσσης· καὶ ἤθελεν παρελθεῖν αὐτούς. 6:49 οἱ δὲ ἰδόντες αὐτὸν ἐπὶ τῆς θαλάσσης περιπατοῦντα ἔδοξαν ὅτι φάντασμά ἐστιν, καὶ ἀνέκραξαν 6:50 πάντες γὰρ αὐτὸν εἶδον καὶ ἐταράχθησαν. ὁ δὲ εὐθὺς ἐλάλησεν μετ' αὐτῶν, καὶ λέγει αὐτοῖς,
Θαρσεῖτε, ἐγώ εἰμι· μὴ φοβεῖσθε.
6:51 καὶ ἀνέβη πρὸς αὐτοὺς εἰς τὸ πλοῖον καὶ ἐκόπασεν ὁ ἄνεμος, καὶ λίαν [ἐκ περισσοῦ] ἐν ἑαυτοῖς ἐξίσταντο· 6:52 οὐ γὰρ συνῆκαν ἐπὶ τοῖς ἄρτοις, ἀλλ' ἦν αὐτῶν ἡ καρδία πεπωρωμένη.
6:53 Καὶ διαπεράσαντες ἐπὶ τὴν γῆν ἦλθον εἰς Γεννησαρὲτ καὶ προσωρμίσθησαν. 6:54 καὶ ἐξελθόντων αὐτῶν ἐκ τοῦ πλοίου εὐθὺς ἐπιγνόντες αὐτὸν 6:55 περιέδραμον ὅλην τὴν χώραν ἐκείνην καὶ ἤρξαντο ἐπὶ τοῖς κραβάττοις τοὺς κακῶς ἔχοντας περιφέρειν ὅπου ἤκουον ὅτι
ἐστίν.
6:56 καὶ ὅπου ἂν εἰσεπορεύετο εἰς κώμας ἢ εἰς πόλεις ἢ εἰς ἀγρούς, ἐν ταῖς ἀγοραῖς ἐτίθεσαν τοὺς ἀσθενοῦντας καὶ παρεκάλουν αὐτὸν ἵνα
κἂν τοῦ κρασπέδου τοῦ ἱματίου αὐτοῦ ἅψωνται· (1, 2)
καὶ ὅσοι ἂν ἥψαντο αὐτοῦ ἐσῴζοντο.

4TP2.24.1.3(56) EMr:(S) εἰσεπορεύετο εἰς κώμας. CM: Ibid.
SPAC: παρεκάλουν. Jesus healing.
3TP2.24.2(7:1–13) EMr:(S) συνάγονται...Φαρισαῖοι...
γραμματέων. CM: Ibid. Jesus' legal debate with the Pharisees.
4TP2.24.2.1(1–4) CM: Φαρισαῖοι (P): μαθητῶν. Pharisaic and Jewish customs.
4TP2.24.2.2(5–13) CM: = MC.Dia: ἐπηρωτῶσιν...εἶπεν, etc. SPAC: Question/Answer. Jesus' debate with the Pharisees.
5TP2.24.2.2.1(5) MC: ἐπηρωτῶσιν. SPAC: Ibid. The Pharisees question Jesus about his disciples' breaking the tradition by their eating practices.
5TP2.24.2.2.2(6–13) MC: εἶπεν, etc. SPAC: answer. Jesus' response to the Pharisees.
6TP2.24.2.2.2.1(6–8) MC: εἶπεν. SPAC: ἐπροφήτευσεν ... περὶ ὑμῶν. The first stage of the answer: Jesus applies Isaiah's prophecy to the Pharisees' rejection of God's commandment.
6TP2.24.2.2.2.2(9–13) SN: παρόμοια τοιαῦτα. MC: ἔλεγεν. SPAC: Answer. The second stage of the answer: Jesus gives an example of Pharisaical traditions resulting in the rejection of God's commandment. One example among many such examples.
7TP2.24.2.2.2.2.1(9) CM: ἀθετεῖτε. SPAC: assertion. Jesus argues that the Pharisees and scribes reject the command of God.
7TP2.24.2.2.2.2.2(10) CM: Μωϋσῆς. CONJ: γάρ. SPAC: Supporting assertion (frame 2); commands (frame 3 OT—τίμα...τελευτάτω). An assertion in support of 9. Jesus quotes Moses to support his position.
7TP2.24.2.2.2.2.3(11–13) CM: ὑμεῖς. MC: λέγετε. SPAC: assertion (frame 2); assertion (ἐάν, etc. on frame 3); vow—a performative—(κορβᾶν in

1 2 3 4

7:1 Καὶ συνάγονται πρὸς αὐτὸν οἱ Φαρισαῖοι καί τινες τῶν γραμματέων ἐλθόντες ἀπὸ Ἱεροσολύμων. 7:2 καὶ ἰδόντες τινὰς τῶν μαθητῶν αὐτοῦ ὅτι κοιναῖς χερσίν, τοῦτ' ἔστιν ἀνίπτοις, ἐσθίουσιν τοὺς ἄρτους 7:3⁻οἱ γὰρ Φαρισαῖοι καὶ πάντες οἱ Ἰουδαῖοι ἐὰν μὴ πυγμῇ νίψωνται τὰς χεῖρας οὐκ ἐσθίουσιν, κρατοῦντες τὴν παράδοσιν τῶν πρεσβυτέρων, 7:4 καὶ ἀπ' ἀγορᾶς ἐὰν μὴ βαπτίσωνται οὐκ ἐσθίουσιν, καὶ ἄλλα πολλά ἐστιν ἃ παρέλαβον κρατεῖν, βαπτισμοὺς ποτηρίων καὶ ξεστῶν καὶ χαλκίων [καὶ κλινῶν] ⁻ 7:5 καὶ ἐπερωτῶσιν αὐτὸν οἱ Φαρισαῖοι καὶ οἱ γραμματεῖς,
    Διὰ τί οὐ περιπατοῦσιν οἱ μαθηταί σου κατὰ τὴν παράδοσιν τῶν πρεσβυτέρων, ἀλλὰ κοιναῖς χερσὶν ἐσθίουσιν τὸν ἄρτον;
7:6 ὁ δὲ εἶπεν αὐτοῖς,
    Καλῶς ἐπροφήτευσεν Ἡσαΐας περὶ ὑμῶν τῶν ὑποκριτῶν, ὡς γέγραπται [ὅτι]
        Οὗτος ὁ λαὸς τοῖς χείλεσίν με τιμᾷ, ἡ δὲ καρδία αὐτῶν πόρρω ἀπέχει ἀπ' ἐμοῦ· 7:7 μάτην δὲ σέβονταί με διδάσκοντες διδασκαλίας ἐντάλματα ἀνθρώπων. (3 OT)
7:8 ἀφέντες τὴν ἐντολὴν τοῦ θεοῦ κρατεῖτε τὴν παράδοσιν τῶν ἀνθρώπων.
7:9 Καὶ ἔλεγεν αὐτοῖς, Καλῶς ἀθετεῖτε τὴν ἐντολὴν τοῦ θεοῦ, ἵνα τὴν παράδοσιν ὑμῶν στήσητε. 7:10 Μωϋσῆς γὰρ εἶπεν,
    Τίμα τὸν πατέρα σου καὶ τὴν μητέρα σου, (3 OT)
καί,
    Ὁ κακολογῶν πατέρα ἢ μητέρα θανάτῳ τελευτάτω. (3 OT)
7:11 ὑμεῖς δὲ λέγετε,
    Ἐὰν εἴπῃ ἄνθρωπος τῷ πατρὶ ἢ τῇ μητρί,
        Κορβᾶν,
ὅ ἐστιν,
        Δῶρον, ὃ ἐὰν ἐξ ἐμοῦ ὠφεληθῇς,

frame 4). The leaders' teaching about κορβᾶν rejects the word of God for the sake of tradition.

³TP²·²⁴·³(14–16) SN: παραβολήν (17). CM: προσκαλεσάμενος ...ὄχλον. MC.Mon: εἶπεν, AA: ἀκούσατε...σύνετε. SPAC: Ibid. and the parable. Jesus gives the crowd a parable and calls them to hear and understand it. Continuation of the answer to the Pharisees' question.

³TP²·²⁴·⁴(17–23) SN: παραβολήν (see 14–16). EM:(T) ὅτε (S) εἰσῆλθεν...οἶκον. CM: μαθηταί. MC.Dia: ἐπηρώτων...λέγει. SPAC: Ibid. (question, answer) & an interpretation (οὐ νοεῖτε). Jesus interprets the parable for his disciples.

⁴TP²·²⁴·⁴·¹(17) CM, MC: ἐπηρώτων. SPAC: Ibid. The disciples ask about the parable.

⁴TP²·²⁴·⁴·²(18–19a) CM, MC: λέγει. SPAC: Answer. What goes into the body.

⁴TP²·²⁴·⁴·³(19b) CM: καθαρίζων. The narrator interprets Jesus' answer: he cleanses all foods.

⁴TP²·²⁴·⁴·⁴(20–23) CM, MC: ἔλεγεν. SPAC: Answer. SN: οἱ διαλογισμοὶ οἱ κακοί (for πορνεῖαι...ἀφροσύνη). Jesus continues his answer by pointing to what comes out of the heart.

²TP²·²⁵(24–30) EM:(S) Ἐκεῖθεν...Τύρου. Jesus exorcises in the Tyre region.

³TP²·²⁵·¹(24) EM:(S) εἰσελθών...οἰκίαν. CM: Ibid. Jesus tries to remain concealed.

³TP²·²⁵·²(25–29) CM: ἐλθοῦσα. MC.Dia: ἠρώτα...ἔλεγεν. A Syrophoenecian woman asks Jesus to exorcise her daughter's demon.

⁴TP²·²⁵·²·¹(25–26) MC: ἠρώτα. CM: Ibid. SPAC: Ibid. The woman asks Jesus to exorcise her daughter.

1 2 3 4

7:12 οὐκέτι ἀφίετε αὐτὸν οὐδὲν ποιῆσαι τῷ πατρὶ ἢ τῇ μητρί, 7:13 ἀκυροῦντες τὸν λόγον τοῦ θεοῦ τῇ παραδόσει ὑμῶν ᾗ παρεδώκατε· καὶ παρόμοια τοιαῦτα πολλὰ ποιεῖτε.
7:14 Καὶ προσκαλεσάμενος πάλιν τὸν ὄχλον ἔλεγεν αὐτοῖς,
Ἀκούσατέ μου πάντες καὶ σύνετε. 7:15 οὐδέν ἐστιν ἔξωθεν τοῦ ἀνθρώπου εἰσπορευόμενον εἰς αὐτὸν ὃ δύναται κοινῶσαι αὐτόν, ἀλλὰ τὰ ἐκ τοῦ ἀνθρώπου ἐκπορευόμενά ἐστιν τὰ κοινοῦντα τὸν ἄνθρωπον. (2 PN)
7:17 Καὶ ὅτε εἰσῆλθεν εἰς οἶκον ἀπὸ τοῦ ὄχλου, ἐπηρώτων αὐτὸν οἱ μαθηταὶ αὐτοῦ τὴν παραβολήν. 7:18 καὶ λέγει αὐτοῖς,
Οὕτως καὶ ὑμεῖς ἀσύνετοί ἐστε; οὐ νοεῖτε ὅτι πᾶν τὸ ἔξωθεν εἰσπορευόμενον εἰς τὸν ἄνθρωπον οὐ δύναται αὐτὸν κοινῶσαι 7:19 ὅτι οὐκ εἰσπορεύεται αὐτοῦ εἰς τὴν καρδίαν ἀλλ' εἰς τὴν κοιλίαν, καὶ εἰς τὸν ἀφεδρῶνα ἐκπορεύεται, (2 PN)
καθαρίζων πάντα τὰ βρώματα; 7:20 ἔλεγεν δὲ ὅτι
Τὸ ἐκ τοῦ ἀνθρώπου ἐκπορευόμενον, ἐκεῖνο κοινοῖ τὸν ἄνθρωπον. 7:21 ἔσωθεν γὰρ ἐκ τῆς καρδίας τῶν ἀνθρώπων οἱ διαλογισμοὶ οἱ κακοὶ ἐκπορεύονται, πορνεῖαι, κλοπαί, φόνοι, 7:22 μοιχεῖαι, πλεονεξίαι, πονηρίαι, δόλος, ἀσέλγεια, ὀφθαλμὸς πονηρός, βλασφημία, ὑπερηφανία, ἀφροσύνη· 7:23 πάντα ταῦτα τὰ πονηρὰ ἔσωθεν ἐκπορεύεται καὶ κοινοῖ τὸν ἄνθρωπον. (2 PN)
7:24 Ἐκεῖθεν δὲ ἀναστὰς ἀπῆλθεν εἰς τὰ ὅρια Τύρου. καὶ εἰσελθὼν εἰς οἰκίαν οὐδένα ἤθελεν γνῶναι, καὶ οὐκ ἠδυνήθη λαθεῖν· 7:25 ἀλλ' εὐθὺς ἀκούσασα γυνὴ περὶ αὐτοῦ, ἧς εἶχεν τὸ θυγάτριον αὐτῆς πνεῦμα ἀκάθαρτον, ἐλθοῦσα προσέπεσεν πρὸς τοὺς πόδας αὐτοῦ· 7:26 ἡ δὲ γυνὴ ἦν Ἑλληνίς, Συροφοινίκισσα τῷ γένει· καὶ ἠρώτα αὐτὸν ἵνα
τὸ δαιμόνιον ἐκβάλῃ ἐκ τῆς θυγατρὸς αὐτῆς. (1, 2)

⁴TP².²⁵.².²(27) MC: ἔλεγεν. CM: Ibid. SPAC: ἄφες...γάρ (refusal with explanation). Jesus responds with the saying about the dogs and children.
⁴TP².²⁵.².³(28) MC: λέγει. CM: Ibid. SPAC: ἀπεκρίθη (a counter argument). The woman continues the image of dogs and children.
⁴TP².²⁵.².⁴(29) MC: εἶπεν. CM: Ibid. SPAC: ὕπαγε, ἐξελήλυθεν (a declarative). Jesus accedes to her request and argument by exorcising her daughter.
³TP².²⁵.³(30) EMr:(S) ἀπελθοῦσα...οἶκον. CM: Ibid. The woman goes to her house and finds her daughter free of the demon.
²TP².²⁶(7:31-8:9) EMr:(S) θάλασσαν...Δεκαπόλεως. Two miracles by the sea of Galilee on the Decapolis side.
³TP².²⁶.¹(31-37) CM: φέρουσιν...κωφόν. Healing of the deaf and dumb man.
⁴TP².²⁶.¹.¹(31-32) EM:(S) φέρουσιν. CM: Ibid. (P): κωφόν. MC: παρακαλοῦσιν. SPAC: Ibid. People beseech Jesus to heal the deaf and dumb man.
⁴TP².¹⁶.¹.²(33-35) EM:(S) ἀπολαβόμενος. CM: αὐτόν. SPAC: εφφαθα (a declarative). Alone, Jesus heals the man.
⁴TP².²⁶.¹.³(36-37) CM: αὐτοῖς. Jesus commands the crowd to be silent, but they disobey.
⁵TP².²⁶.¹.³.¹(36) MC: διεστείλατο. SPAC: Ibid. & ἐκήρυσσον. Jesus' command to be silent is disobeyed by the crowd which proclaims instead.
⁵TP².²⁶.¹.³.²(37) MC: λέγοντες. SPAC: proclamation (36). The onlookers proclaim Jesus' healing of the deaf and dumb.

1 2 3 4

7:27 καὶ ἔλεγεν αὐτῇ,
Ἄφες πρῶτον χορτασθῆναι τὰ τέκνα, οὐ γάρ ἐστιν
καλὸν λαβεῖν τὸν ἄρτον τῶν τέκνων καὶ τοῖς
κυναρίοις βαλεῖν.
7:28 ἡ δὲ ἀπεκρίθη καὶ λέγει αὐτῷ,
Κύριε, καὶ τὰ κυνάρια ὑποκάτω τῆς τραπέζης
ἐσθίουσιν ἀπὸ τῶν ψιχίων τῶν παιδίων.
7:29 καὶ εἶπεν αὐτῇ,
Διὰ τοῦτον τὸν λόγον ὕπαγε, ἐξελήλυθεν ἐκ τῆς
θυγατρός σου τὸ δαιμόνιον.
7:30 καὶ ἀπελθοῦσα εἰς τὸν οἶκον αὐτῆς εὗρεν τὸ
παιδίον βεβλημένον ἐπὶ τὴν κλίνην καὶ τὸ δαιμόνιον
ἐξεληλυθός.
7:31 Καὶ πάλιν ἐξελθὼν ἐκ τῶν ὁρίων Τύρου ἦλθεν διὰ
Σιδῶνος εἰς τὴν θάλασσαν τῆς Γαλιλαίας ἀνὰ μέσον τῶν
ὁρίων Δεκαπόλεως. 7:32 καὶ φέρουσιν αὐτῷ κωφὸν καὶ
μογιλάλον καὶ παρακαλοῦσιν αὐτὸν ἵνα
ἐπιθῇ αὐτῷ τὴν χεῖρα. (1, 2)
7:33 καὶ ἀπολαβόμενος αὐτὸν ἀπὸ τοῦ ὄχλου κατ' ἰδίαν
ἔβαλεν τοὺς δακτύλους αὐτοῦ εἰς τὰ ὦτα αὐτοῦ καὶ
πτύσας ἥψατο τῆς γλώσσης αὐτοῦ, 7:34 καὶ ἀναβλέψας
εἰς τὸν οὐρανὸν ἐστέναξεν καὶ λέγει αὐτῷ,
Εφφαθα,
ὅ ἐστιν,
Διανοίχθητι.
7:35 καὶ [εὐθέως] ἠνοίγησαν αὐτοῦ αἱ ἀκοαί, καὶ ἐλύθη ὁ
δεσμὸς τῆς γλώσσης αὐτοῦ καὶ ἐλάλει ὀρθῶς. 7:36 καὶ
διεστείλατο αὐτοῖς ἵνα
μηδενὶ λέγωσιν· (1, 2)
ὅσον δὲ αὐτοῖς διεστέλλετο, αὐτοὶ μᾶλλον περισσότερον
ἐκήρυσσον. 7:37 καὶ ὑπερπερισσῶς ἐξεπλήσσοντο
λέγοντες,
Καλῶς πάντα πεποίηκεν, καὶ τοὺς κωφοὺς ποιεῖ
ἀκούειν καὶ [τοὺς] ἀλάλους λαλεῖν.

³TP².²⁶.²(8:1–9) EMr:(T) ἡμέραις. The feeding of the 4000.
⁴TP².²⁶.².¹(1–5) CM: μαθητάς, (P): ὄχλου. MC.Dia: λέγει...ἀπεκρίθησαν, etc. Jesus discusses the situation with the disciples.
⁵TP².²⁶.².¹.¹(1–3) CM: προσκαλεσάμενος...μαθητάς. MC: λέγει. SPAC: Σπλαγχνίζομαι...ὅτι (expression of compassion with explanation). Jesus' compassion on the crowd because of their hunger.
⁵TP².²⁶.².¹.²(4) CM: ἀπεκρίθησαν. MC: Ibid. SPAC: Πόθεν. The disciples answer with a skeptical question about the ability of anyone to feed so many in the wilderness.
⁵TP².²⁶.².¹.³(5) CM: ἠρώτα...εἶπαν. MC: Ibid. SPAC: Ibid. Jesus questions them about the bread they have, and they answer him.
⁴TP².²⁶.².²(6a) CM: παραγγέλλει, (P) ὄχλῳ. MC: Ibid. SPAC: Ibid. Jesus commands the crowd to recline.
⁴TP².²⁶.².³(6b–7) CM: λαβών...μαθηταῖς, (P) ὄχλῳ. Jesus gives the disciples bread and fish to distribute to the crowd.
⁴TP².²⁶.².⁴(8–9) CM: ἔφαγον...ἦραν; ἀπέλυσεν. The 4000 eat and are satisfied; the disciples gather the leftovers; and Jesus dismisses the crowds.
²TP².²⁷(10–12) EM:(T) εὐθύς (S) ἐμβάς...πλοῖον ... Δαλμανουθά. CM: Ibid. & Φαρισαῖοι. The Pharisees seek a sign from Jesus in the Dalmanutha region.
³TP².²⁷.¹(10) CM: ἐμβάς...μαθητῶν. Jesus and the disciples go to Dalmanutha.
³TP².²⁷.²(11–12) CM: Φαρισαῖοι...αὐτῷ. The Pharisees ask for a sign and are refused.
⁴TP².²⁷.².¹(11) MC: συζητεῖν. SPAC: request. The request for a sign.
⁴TP².²⁷.².²(12) MC: λέγει. SPAC: question & ἀμὴν λέγω. Jesus asserts solemnly that there will be no sign.

1 2 3 4

8:1 Ἐν ἐκείναις ταῖς ἡμέραις πάλιν πολλοῦ ὄχλου ὄντος καὶ μὴ ἐχόντων τί φάγωσιν, προσκαλεσάμενος τοὺς μαθητὰς λέγει αὐτοῖς, 8:2 Σπλαγχνίζομαι ἐπὶ τὸν ὄχλον, ὅτι ἤδη ἡμέραι τρεῖς προσμένουσίν μοι καὶ οὐκ ἔχουσιν τί φάγωσιν· 8:3 καὶ ἐὰν ἀπολύσω αὐτοὺς νήστεις εἰς οἶκον αὐτῶν, ἐκλυθήσονται ἐν τῇ ὁδῷ· καί τινες αὐτῶν ἀπὸ μακρόθεν ἥκασιν. 8:4 καὶ ἀπεκρίθησαν αὐτῷ οἱ μαθηταὶ αὐτοῦ ὅτι Πόθεν τούτους δυνήσεταί τις ὧδε χορτάσαι ἄρτων ἐπ' ἐρημίας; 8:5 καὶ ἠρώτα αὐτούς, Πόσους ἔχετε ἄρτους; οἱ δὲ εἶπαν, Ἑπτά. 8:6 καὶ παραγγέλλει τῷ ὄχλῳ ἀναπεσεῖν ἐπὶ τῆς γῆς· (1, 2) καὶ λαβὼν τοὺς ἑπτὰ ἄρτους εὐχαριστήσας ἔκλασεν καὶ ἐδίδου τοῖς μαθηταῖς αὐτοῦ ἵνα παρατιθῶσιν, καὶ παρέθηκαν τῷ ὄχλῳ. 8:7 καὶ εἶχον ἰχθύδια ὀλίγα· καὶ εὐλογήσας αὐτὰ εἶπεν καὶ ταῦτα παρατιθέναι. 8:8 καὶ ἔφαγον καὶ ἐχορτάσθησαν, καὶ ἦραν περισσεύματα κλασμάτων ἑπτὰ σπυρίδας. 8:9 ἦσαν δὲ ὡς τετρακισχίλιοι. καὶ ἀπέλυσεν αὐτούς. 8:10 Καὶ εὐθὺς ἐμβὰς εἰς τὸ πλοῖον μετὰ τῶν μαθητῶν αὐτοῦ ἦλθεν εἰς τὰ μέρη Δαλμανουθά. 8:11 Καὶ ἐξῆλθον οἱ Φαρισαῖοι καὶ ἤρξαντο συζητεῖν αὐτῷ, ζητοῦντες παρ' αὐτοῦ σημεῖον ἀπὸ τοῦ οὐρανοῦ, πειράζοντες αὐτόν. 8:12 καὶ ἀναστενάξας τῷ πνεύματι αὐτοῦ λέγει, Τί ἡ γενεὰ αὕτη ζητεῖ σημεῖον; ἀμὴν λέγω ὑμῖν, εἰ δοθήσεται τῇ γενεᾷ ταύτῃ σημεῖον. (3 HS)

²TP².²⁸(13–21) EM: (S) ἀπῆλθεν...πέραν. CM: Ibid. & ἐπελάθοντο. MC.Dia: διεστέλλετο...διελογίζοντο...λέγει. SPAC: διεστέλλετο. Jesus and the disciples discuss the leaven of the Pharisees and Herod during a crossing to Bethsaida.
³TP².²⁸·¹(13–14) EM:(S) ἐμβάς. CM: ἐμβάς...ἐπελάθοντο. Description of the sea journey and lack of bread.
³TP².²⁸·²(15) CM = MC: διεστέλλετο. SPAC: Ibid. (warning—a directive). Jesus warns the disciples about the leaven.
³TP².²⁸·³(16) CM=MC: διελογίζοντο. SPAC: Ibid. (assertion). Report of the reaction to Jesus' warning.
³TP².²⁸·⁴(17–21) CM=MC.Dia: λέγει...λέγουσιν. SPAC: Question/Answer. Dialogue about Jesus' warning in relation to the feedings.
⁴TP².²⁸·⁴·¹(17–19a) MC: λέγει. SPAC: five questions. Jesus asks the disciples about their lack of understanding and examines their memory about the meals.
⁴TP².²⁸·⁴·²(19b) MC: λέγουσιν. SPAC: answer. The disciples remember the twelve baskets.
⁴TP².²⁸·⁴·³(20a) MC: Implied. SPAC: question. Jesus questions them about the other meal.
⁴TP².²⁸·⁴·⁴(20b) MC: λέγουσιν. SPAC: answer. The disciples remember the seven baskets.
⁴TP².²⁸·⁴·⁵(21) MC: ἔλεγον. SPAC: question. Jesus questions their continuing lack of understanding.
²TP².²⁹(22–26) EMr:(S) Βηθσαϊδάν. The healing of the blind man in Bethsaida.
³TP².²⁹·¹(22) CM: ἔρχονται...φέρουσιν...τυφλόν. MC: παρακαλοῦσιν. SPAC: Ibid. (request). People beseech Jesus to heal the blind man by touching.
³TP².²⁹·²(23–26) EMr:(S) ἔξω...κώμης. CM=MC.Dia: ἐπηρώτα...ἔλεγεν, etc. Jesus heals the blind man outside the city.
⁴TP².²⁹·²·¹(23) CM, MC: ἐπηρώτα. SPAC: Ibid. Jesus spits in his eyes, lays on hands, and questions him about the healings.

1 2 3 4

8:13 καὶ ἀφεὶς αὐτοὺς πάλιν ἐμβὰς ἀπῆλθεν εἰς τὸ πέραν.
8:14 Καὶ ἐπελάθοντο λαβεῖν ἄρτους καὶ εἰ μὴ ἕνα ἄρτον οὐκ εἶχον μεθ' ἑαυτῶν ἐν τῷ πλοίῳ. 8:15 καὶ διεστέλλετο αὐτοῖς λέγων,
Ὁρᾶτε, βλέπετε ἀπὸ τῆς ζύμης τῶν Φαρισαίων καὶ τῆς ζύμης Ἡρῴδου.
8:16 καὶ διελογίζοντο πρὸς ἀλλήλους ὅτι
Ἄρτους οὐκ ἔχουσιν. (1, 2)
8:17 καὶ γνοὺς λέγει αὐτοῖς,
Τί διαλογίζεσθε ὅτι ἄρτους οὐκ ἔχετε; οὔπω νοεῖτε οὐδὲ συνίετε; πεπωρωμένην ἔχετε τὴν καρδίαν ὑμῶν; 8:18 ὀφθαλμοὺς ἔχοντες οὐ βλέπετε καὶ ὦτα ἔχοντες οὐκ ἀκούετε; καὶ οὐ μνημονεύετε, 8:19 ὅτε τοὺς πέντε ἄρτους ἔκλασα εἰς τοὺς πεντακισχιλίους, πόσους κοφίνους κλασμάτων πλήρεις ἤρατε;
λέγουσιν αὐτῷ,
Δώδεκα.
8:20 Ὅτε τοὺς ἑπτὰ εἰς τοὺς τετρακισχιλίους, πόσων σπυρίδων πληρώματα κλασμάτων ἤρατε;
καὶ λέγουσιν [αὐτῷ],
Ἑπτά.
8:21 καὶ ἔλεγεν αὐτοῖς,
Οὔπω συνίετε;
8:22 Καὶ ἔρχονται εἰς Βηθσαϊδάν. καὶ φέρουσιν αὐτῷ τυφλὸν καὶ παρακαλοῦσιν αὐτὸν ἵνα
αὐτοῦ ἅψηται. (1, 2)
8:23 καὶ ἐπιλαβόμενος τῆς χειρὸς τοῦ τυφλοῦ ἐξήνεγκεν αὐτὸν ἔξω τῆς κώμης καὶ πτύσας εἰς τὰ ὄμματα αὐτοῦ, ἐπιθεὶς τὰς χεῖρας αὐτῷ ἐπηρώτα αὐτόν,
Εἴ τι βλέπεις;

⁴TP².²⁹.².²(24) CM, MC: ἔλεγεν. SPAC: answer. The man's response: people appear as walking trees.
⁴TP².²⁹.².³(25) CM: ἐπέθηκεν. Jesus lays hands on his eyes, and he sees clearly.
⁴TP².²⁹.².⁴(26) CM: ἀπέστειλεν. MC: λέγων. SPAC: μηδέ. Jesus sends him home and commands him to avoid the village.

¹TP³(8:27–10:52) EM:(S) ὁδῷ (Indications of a journey [with the same marker] also appear in: 9:33, 34; 10:17, 32, 46. 8:27 is first occurrence of Jesus on a ὁδός. 10:32, 33 show that the journey will end in Jerusalem). Jesus' journey to Jerusalem.
²TP³·¹(8:27–9:29) EMr:(S) κώμας...Φιλίππου. Esoteric teaching about the Messiah, public teaching, and public exorcism in the Caesarea Philippi region.
³TP³·¹·¹(8:27–9:1) EMr:(T) Implied: Six days before the transfiguration (see 9:2). Teaching in the Caesarea Philippi region about the Messiah and discipleship.
⁴TP³·¹·¹·¹(27–33) CM: Ἰησοῦς...μαθηταί. Jesus teaches the disciples alone.
⁵TP³·¹·¹·¹·¹(27–30) MC.Dia: ἐπηρώτα...εἶπαν. The disciples answer Jesus' questions about his identity.
⁶TP³·¹·¹·¹·¹·¹(27–28) CM=MC.Dia: ἐπηρώτα; εἶπαν. SPAC: Question/Answer. First question and answer: the public's opinion of Jesus.
⁶TP³·¹·¹·¹·¹·²(29) MC.Dia: ἐπηρώτα...ἀποκριθείς. SPAC: Question and Answer (an assertion). CM: Πέτρος. Second question about the disciples' opinion of Jesus with Peter's answer.
⁷TP³·¹·¹·¹·¹·²·¹(29a) CM: ἐπηρώτα. MC, SPAC: Ibid. Jesus asks about his disciples' views of him.

1 2 3 4

8:24 καὶ ἀναβλέψας ἔλεγεν,
    Βλέπω τοὺς ἀνθρώπους ὅτι ὡς δένδρα ὁρῶ
    περιπατοῦντας.
8:25 εἶτα πάλιν ἐπέθηκεν τὰς χεῖρας ἐπὶ τοὺς ὀφθαλμοὺς
    αὐτοῦ, καὶ διέβλεψεν καὶ ἀπεκατέστη καὶ ἐνέβλεπεν
    τηλαυγῶς ἅπαντα.
8:26 καὶ ἀπέστειλεν αὐτὸν εἰς οἶκον αὐτοῦ λέγων,
    Μηδὲ εἰς τὴν κώμην εἰσέλθῃς.
8:27 Καὶ ἐξῆλθεν ὁ Ἰησοῦς καὶ οἱ μαθηταὶ αὐτοῦ εἰς τὰς
    κώμας Καισαρείας τῆς Φιλίππου· καὶ ἐν τῇ ὁδῷ ἐπηρώτα
    τοὺς μαθητὰς αὐτοῦ λέγων αὐτοῖς,
        Τίνα με (2, 3)
    λέγουσιν οἱ ἄνθρωποι
        εἶναι; (2, 3)
8:28 οἱ δὲ εἶπαν αὐτῷ λέγοντες [ὅτι]
        Ἰωάννην τὸν βαπτιστήν, (2, 3)
    καὶ ἄλλοι,
        Ἡλίαν, (2, 3)
    ἄλλοι δὲ ὅτι
        εἷς τῶν προφητῶν. (2, 3)
8:29 καὶ αὐτὸς ἐπηρώτα αὐτούς,
        Ὑμεῖς δὲ
            τίνα με (2, 3)
        λέγετε
            εἶναι; (2, 3)

⁷TP³·¹·¹·¹·¹·²·²(29b) CM: ἀποκριθείς. MC, SPAC: Ibid. Peter's answer.
⁶TP³·¹·¹·¹·¹·³(30) CM: ἐπετίμησεν. MC: Ibid. SPAC: Ibid. Jesus warns them not to divulge his identity.
⁵TP³·¹·¹·¹·²(31–32a) CM: διδάσκειν. MC: Ibid. SPAC: Ibid (teaching). SN: λόγον. Jesus' open passion teaching.
⁵TP³·¹·¹·¹·³(32b–33) EMr:(S) προσλαβόμενος…αὐτόν. CM: Ibid. (P) μαθητάς. SPAC: ἐπιτιμᾶν (twice) ὕπαγε. MC: λέγει. Peter rebukes Jesus after the passion teaching and is in turn rebuked.
⁴TP³·¹·¹·²(8:34–9:1) MC.Mon: προσκαλεσάμενος…εἶπεν. CM: ὄχλον…μαθηταῖς. Jesus teaches the crowd and disciples about following him.
⁵TP³·¹·¹·²·¹(8:34–8:38) MC: εἶπεν. The first part of Jesus' speech.
⁶TP³·¹·¹·²·¹·¹(34b) CM: τις. SPAC: ἀπαρνησάσθω. The cost of following behind Jesus.
⁶TP³·¹·¹·²·¹·²(35) CM: ὅς. CONJ: γάρ. SPAC: two assertions. Saving and losing one's life.
⁶TP³·¹·¹·²·¹·³(36) CM: ἄνθρωπον. SPAC: τί (question). CONJ: γάρ. A person gaining the whole world at the price of their life.
⁶TP³·¹·¹·²·¹·⁴(37) SPAC: τί. CM: ἄνθρωπος. CONJ: γάρ. What can a person give for their lost life?
⁶TP³·¹·¹·²·¹·⁵(38) CM: ὅς. SPAC: assertion. CONJ: γάρ. The relation to Jesus will determine the future judgment of the person.
⁵TP³·¹·¹·²·²(9:1) MC: ἔλεγεν. CM: τίνες. SPAC: Ἀμήν. Second part of Jesus' speech to the crowds and disciples: some will not die before the Kingdom comes.

1 2 3 4

ἀποκριθεὶς ὁ Πέτρος λέγει αὐτῷ,
Σὺ εἶ ὁ Χριστός.
8:30 καὶ ἐπετίμησεν αὐτοῖς ἵνα
μηδενὶ λέγωσιν περὶ αὐτοῦ. (1, 2)
8:31 Καὶ ἤρξατο διδάσκειν αὐτοὺς ὅτι
δεῖ τὸν υἱὸν τοῦ ἀνθρώπου πολλὰ παθεῖν καὶ
ἀποδοκιμασθῆναι ὑπὸ τῶν πρεσβυτέρων καὶ τῶν
ἀρχιερέων καὶ τῶν γραμματέων καὶ ἀποκτανθῆναι καὶ
μετὰ τρεῖς ἡμέρας ἀναστῆναι· (2 PN)
8:32 καὶ παρρησίᾳ τὸν λόγον ἐλάλει. καὶ προσλαβόμενος
ὁ Πέτρος αὐτὸν ἤρξατο ἐπιτιμᾶν αὐτῷ. 8:33 ὁ δὲ
ἐπιστραφεὶς καὶ ἰδὼν τοὺς μαθητὰς αὐτοῦ ἐπετίμησεν
Πέτρῳ καὶ λέγει,
Ὕπαγε ὀπίσω μου, Σατανᾶ, ὅτι οὐ φρονεῖς τὰ τοῦ
θεοῦ ἀλλὰ τὰ τῶν ἀνθρώπων.
8:34 Καὶ προσκαλεσάμενος τὸν ὄχλον σὺν τοῖς μαθηταῖς
αὐτοῦ εἶπεν αὐτοῖς,
Εἴ τις θέλει ὀπίσω μου ἀκολουθεῖν, ἀπαρνησάσθω
ἑαυτὸν καὶ ἀράτω τὸν σταυρὸν αὐτοῦ καὶ ἀκολουθείτω
μοι. 8:35 ὃς γὰρ ἐὰν θέλῃ τὴν ψυχὴν αὐτοῦ σῶσαι
ἀπολέσει αὐτήν· ὃς δ' ἂν ἀπολέσει τὴν ψυχὴν αὐτοῦ
ἕνεκεν ἐμοῦ καὶ τοῦ εὐαγγελίου σώσει αὐτήν. 8:36 τί
γὰρ ὠφελεῖ ἄνθρωπον κερδῆσαι τὸν κόσμον ὅλον καὶ
ζημιωθῆναι τὴν ψυχὴν αὐτοῦ; 8:37 τί γὰρ δοῖ
ἄνθρωπος ἀντάλλαγμα τῆς ψυχῆς αὐτοῦ; 8:38 ὃς γὰρ
ἐὰν ἐπαισχυνθῇ με καὶ τοὺς ἐμοὺς λόγους ἐν τῇ
γενεᾷ ταύτῃ τῇ μοιχαλίδι καὶ ἁμαρτωλῷ, καὶ ὁ υἱὸς
τοῦ ἀνθρώπου ἐπαισχυνθήσεται αὐτόν, ὅταν ἔλθῃ ἐν
τῇ δόξῃ τοῦ πατρὸς αὐτοῦ μετὰ τῶν ἀγγέλων τῶν
ἁγίων. (2 PN)
9:1 Καὶ ἔλεγεν αὐτοῖς,
Ἀμὴν λέγω ὑμῖν ὅτι
εἰσίν τινες ὧδε τῶν ἑστηκότων οἵτινες οὐ μὴ
γεύσωνται θανάτου ἕως ἂν ἴδωσιν τὴν βασιλείαν
τοῦ θεοῦ ἐληλυθυῖαν ἐν δυνάμει. (3 PN, HS)

4TP3.1.1.3(2–13) EMr:(T) μετά...ἔξ (S) ὄρος. CM:
'Ιησοῦς...'Ιωάννην. The transfiguration six days later.
  5TP3.1.1.3.1(2–8) EM:(S) ἀναφέρει. The episode on the mountain.
    6TP3.1.1.3.1.1(2–3) CM: αὐτοῦ (P): the three. Jesus' transfiguration.
    6TP3.1.1.3.1.2(4) CM: 'Ηλίας...Μωϋσεῖ. Thisworldly vision of Moses, Elijah, and Jesus.
    6TP3.1.1.3.1.3(5) CM: λέγει. MC: Πέτρος. SPAC: ποιήσωμεν—recommendation (a directive). Peter suggests three tents.
    6TP3.1.1.3.1.4(6) CM: ἐγένοντο. CONJ: γάρ. The disciples' fear.
    6TP3.1.1.3.1.5(7) CM= MC: φωνή. SPAC: Assertion and directive (ἀκούετε). The voice (otherworldly) from the cloud identifies Jesus.
    6TP3.1.1.3.1.6(8) EMr:(T) ἐξάπινα. CM: 'Ιησοῦν μόνον. They see Jesus alone.
  5TP3.1.1.3.2(9–13) EMr:(S) καταβαινόντων...ὄρους. Conversations during the descent: the resurrection and the problem of Elijah.
    6TP3.1.1.3.2.1(9–10) CM= MC.Mon: διεστείλατο. SPAC: Ibid. & συζητοῦντες. Jesus' command not to reveal the episode until the resurrection, and the disciples' confusion.
    6TP3.1.1.3.2.2(11–13) CM= MC.Dia: ἐπηρώτων . . . λέγοντες . . . ἔφη. SPAC: question/answer. Question about Elijah, and Jesus' answer concerning Elijah and the Son of Man.
      7TP3.1.1.3.2.2.1(11) MC: ἐπηρώτων. SPAC: question. The disciples ask about the scribes' view of Elijah's return.
      7TP3.1.1.3.2.2.2(12–13) MC: SPAC: answer comprising an assertion, question, and assertion. Jesus answers them with teaching about Elijah's return, the Son of Man, and Elijah's already accomplished return.

1 2 3 4

9:2 Καὶ μετὰ ἡμέρας ἓξ παραλαμβάνει ὁ Ἰησοῦς τὸν Πέτρον καὶ τὸν Ἰάκωβον καὶ τὸν Ἰωάννην καὶ ἀναφέρει αὐτοὺς εἰς ὄρος ὑψηλὸν κατ' ἰδίαν μόνους. καὶ μετεμορφώθη ἔμπροσθεν αὐτῶν, 9:3 καὶ τὰ ἱμάτια αὐτοῦ ἐγένετο στίλβοντα λευκὰ λίαν οἷα γναφεὺς ἐπὶ τῆς γῆς οὐ δύναται οὕτως λευκᾶναι. 9:4 καὶ ὤφθη αὐτοῖς Ἠλίας σὺν Μωϋσεῖ, καὶ ἦσαν συλλαλοῦντες τῷ Ἰησοῦ. 9:5 καὶ ἀποκριθεὶς ὁ Πέτρος λέγει τῷ Ἰησοῦ,
 Ῥαββί, καλόν ἐστιν ἡμᾶς ὧδε εἶναι, καὶ ποιήσωμεν τρεῖς σκηνάς, σοὶ μίαν καὶ Μωϋσεῖ μίαν καὶ Ἡλίᾳ μίαν.
9:6 οὐ γὰρ ᾔδει τί ἀποκριθῇ ἔκφοβοι γὰρ ἐγένοντο. 9:7 καὶ ἐγένετο νεφέλη ἐπισκιάζουσα αὐτοῖς, καὶ ἐγένετο φωνὴ ἐκ τῆς νεφέλης,
 Οὗτός ἐστιν ὁ υἱός μου ὁ ἀγαπητός, ἀκούετε αὐτοῦ. (2 ON)
9:8 καὶ ἐξάπινα περιβλεψάμενοι οὐκέτι οὐδένα εἶδον ἀλλὰ τὸν Ἰησοῦν μόνον μεθ' ἑαυτῶν.
9:9 Καὶ καταβαινόντων αὐτῶν ἐκ τοῦ ὄρους διεστείλατο αὐτοῖς ἵνα
 μηδενὶ ἃ εἶδον διηγήσωνται, εἰ μὴ ὅταν ὁ υἱὸς τοῦ ἀνθρώπου ἐκ νεκρῶν ἀναστῇ. (1, 2 PN)
9:10 καὶ τὸν λόγον ἐκράτησαν πρὸς ἑαυτοὺς συζητοῦντες τί ἐστιν τὸ ἐκ νεκρῶν ἀναστῆναι. (1, 2)
9:11 καὶ ἐπηρώτων αὐτὸν λέγοντες,
 Ὅτι λέγουσιν οἱ γραμματεῖς ὅτι
  Ἠλίαν δεῖ ἐλθεῖν πρῶτον;
9:12 ὁ δὲ ἔφη αὐτοῖς,
 Ἠλίας μὲν ἐλθὼν πρῶτον ἀποκαθιστάνει πάντα· καὶ πῶς γέγραπται ἐπὶ τὸν υἱὸν τοῦ ἀνθρώπου ἵνα πολλὰ πάθῃ καὶ ἐξουδενηθῇ; (3 OT)
9:13 ἀλλὰ λέγω ὑμῖν ὅτι
 καὶ Ἠλίας ἐλήλυθεν, καὶ ἐποίησαν αὐτῷ ὅσα ἤθελον, καθὼς γέγραπται ἐπ' αὐτόν. (3 PN, HS)

4TP³·¹·¹·⁴(14–27) EMr:(S) ἐλθόντες. Jesus exorcises a resistant demon.
 5TP³·¹·¹·⁴·¹(14) CM: ἐλθόντες...μαθητὰς...γραμματεῖς (P): ὄχλον. The four return to the other disciples who are in the middle of a dispute.
 5TP³·¹·¹·⁴·²(15) EMr:(T) εὐθύς, (S) προστρέχοντες. CM: Ibid. MC: ἠσπάζοντο. The crowd sees and greets Jesus.
 5TP³·¹·¹·⁴·³(16–18) CM: εἷς, (P): υἱόν. MC.Dia: ἐπηρώτησεν...ἀπεκρίθη. SPAC: Ibid. A father answers Jesus' question about the dispute by explaining his son's possession.
 5TP³·¹·¹·⁴·⁴(19) CM: ὁ δέ...αὐτοῖς. MC: λέγει. SPAC: questions and φέρετε. Jesus bemoans the generation's unfaith and commands that the child be brought.
 5TP³·¹·¹·⁴·⁵(20) CM: ἤνεγκαν αὐτόν...πνεῦμα. The command is obeyed, and the spirit responds violently.
 5TP³·¹·¹·⁴·⁶(21–24) CM: ἐπηρώτησεν...εἶπεν, etc. MC.Dia: Ibid. SPAC: Ibid. and assertion (23) with an assertion (24) (πιστεύω) and request (βοήθει). Jesus' second dialogue with the father about his son.
  6TP³·¹·¹·⁴·⁶·¹(21a) MC: ἐπηρώτησεν. SPAC: Ibid. Jesus' asks about the length of the possession.
  6TP³·¹·¹·⁴·⁶·²(21b–22) MC: εἶπεν. SPAC: answer comprising an assertion and a conditional request (εἴ...βοήθησον). The father answers Jesus and asks for help.
  6TP³·¹·¹·⁴·⁶·³(23) MC, SPAC: εἶπεν (assertion). Jesus' response: all things are possible for the one who believes.
  6TP³·¹·¹·⁴·⁶·⁴(24) MC: ἔλεγεν. SPAC: assertion and request. The father's response to Jesus: help me in my unbelief.
 5TP³·¹·¹·⁴·⁷(25) CM: ὄχλος...πνεύματι. MC: ἐπετίμησεν. SPAC: Ibid. and ἐπιτάσσω (a declarative). Jesus rebukes and exorcises the demon.

1 2 3 4

9:14 Καὶ ἐλθόντες πρὸς τοὺς μαθητὰς εἶδον ὄχλον πολὺν περὶ αὐτοὺς καὶ γραμματεῖς συζητοῦντας πρὸς αὐτούς. 9:15 καὶ εὐθὺς πᾶς ὁ ὄχλος ἰδόντες αὐτὸν ἐξεθαμβήθησαν καὶ προστρέχοντες ἠσπάζοντο αὐτόν. 9:16 καὶ ἐπηρώτησεν αὐτούς,
 Τί συζητεῖτε πρὸς αὐτούς;
9:17 καὶ ἀπεκρίθη αὐτῷ εἷς ἐκ τοῦ ὄχλου,
 Διδάσκαλε, ἤνεγκα τὸν υἱόν μου πρὸς σέ, ἔχοντα πνεῦμα ἄλαλον· 9:18 καὶ ὅπου ἐὰν αὐτὸν καταλάβῃ ῥήσσει αὐτόν, καὶ ἀφρίζει καὶ τρίζει τοὺς ὀδόντας καὶ ξηραίνεται· καὶ εἶπα τοῖς μαθηταῖς σου ἵνα αὐτὸ ἐκβάλωσιν, (2, 3)
 καὶ οὐκ ἴσχυσαν.
9:19 ὁ δὲ ἀποκριθεὶς αὐτοῖς λέγει,
 Ὦ γενεὰ ἄπιστος, ἕως πότε πρὸς ὑμᾶς ἔσομαι; ἕως πότε ἀνέξομαι ὑμῶν; φέρετε αὐτὸν πρός με.
9:20 καὶ ἤνεγκαν αὐτὸν πρὸς αὐτόν. καὶ ἰδὼν αὐτὸν τὸ πνεῦμα εὐθὺς συνεσπάραξεν αὐτόν, καὶ πεσὼν ἐπὶ τῆς γῆς ἐκυλίετο ἀφρίζων. 9:21 καὶ ἐπηρώτησεν τὸν πατέρα αὐτοῦ,
 Πόσος χρόνος ἐστὶν ὡς τοῦτο γέγονεν αὐτῷ;
ὁ δὲ εἶπεν,
 Ἐκ παιδιόθεν· 9:22 καὶ πολλάκις καὶ εἰς πῦρ αὐτὸν ἔβαλεν καὶ εἰς ὕδατα ἵνα ἀπολέσῃ αὐτόν· ἀλλ' εἴ τι δύνῃ, βοήθησον ἡμῖν σπλαγχνισθεὶς ἐφ' ἡμᾶς.
9:23 ὁ δὲ Ἰησοῦς εἶπεν αὐτῷ,
 Τὸ Εἰ δύνῃ, πάντα δυνατὰ τῷ πιστεύοντι.
9:24 εὐθὺς κράξας ὁ πατὴρ τοῦ παιδίου ἔλεγεν,
 Πιστεύω· βοήθει μου τῇ ἀπιστίᾳ.
9:25 ἰδὼν δὲ ὁ Ἰησοῦς ὅτι ἐπισυντρέχει ὄχλος, ἐπετίμησεν τῷ πνεύματι τῷ ἀκαθάρτῳ λέγων αὐτῷ,
 Τὸ ἄλαλον καὶ κωφὸν πνεῦμα, ἐγὼ ἐπιτάσσω σοι, ἔξελθε ἐξ αὐτοῦ καὶ μηκέτι εἰσέλθῃς εἰς αὐτόν. (3 HS)

⁵TP³·¹·¹·⁴·⁸(26) CM: κράξας...πολλούς. MC: λέγειν. SPAC: Ibid. (assertion). The successful exorcism and the crowd's remark.
⁵TP³·¹·¹·⁴·⁹(27) CM: ᾿Ιησοῦς. Jesus raises the demoniac.
⁴TP³·¹·¹·⁵(28–29) EMr:(S) οἶκον. CM: εἰσελθόντος...μαθηταί. MC.Dia: ἐπηρώτων...εἶπεν. SPAC: Ibid. In private Jesus explains the disciples' failure to exorcise the demon.

²TP³·²(30–50) EMr:(S) Κακεῖθεν...Γαλιλαίας. The journey through Galilee.
³TP³·²·¹(30–32) EMr:(S) παραπορεύοντο. SN: ῥῆμα. CM: παραπορεύοντο. MC.Mon: ἐδίδασκεν. SPAC: Ibid. CONJ: γάρ. Passion teaching on a private journey through Galilee.
³TP³·²·²(33–50) EMr:(S) ἦλθον...Καφαρναούμ...οἰκίᾳ. CM: Ibid. Conversations of Jesus with his disciples in a house.
⁴TP³·²·²·¹(33–37) CM: Jesus and οἱ δέ. MC.Mon: ἐπηρώτα. SPAC: Ibid., a conditional command (35) (εἴ τις θέλει...ἔσται) and an (37) assertion. Jesus questions the disciples about their argument and gives the answer to their question by using the example of the child.
⁵TP³·²·²·¹·¹(33) CM, MC: ἐπηρώτα. SPAC. Ibid. Jesus questions the disciples about their argument.
⁵TP³·²·²·¹·²(34) CM, MC, SPAC: διελέχθησαν. They are silent: the narrator describes their argument about who is greatest.
⁵TP³·²·²·¹·³(35) CM, MC: λέγει. SPAC: conditional directive (εἴ...ἔσται). Jesus' response: whoever will be first will be last and a servant of all.
⁵TP³·²·²·¹·⁴(36–37) CM, MC: εἶπεν. SPAC: assertion. Jesus continues his response with teaching about receiving a child in his name.

1 2 3 4

9:26 καὶ κράξας καὶ πολλὰ σπαράξας ἐξῆλθεν· καὶ ἐγένετο ὡσεὶ νεκρός, ὥστε τοὺς πολλοὺς λέγειν ὅτι Ἀπέθανεν.
9:27 ὁ δὲ Ἰησοῦς κρατήσας τῆς χειρὸς αὐτοῦ ἤγειρεν αὐτόν, καὶ ἀνέστη. 9:28 καὶ εἰσελθόντος αὐτοῦ εἰς οἶκον οἱ μαθηταὶ αὐτοῦ κατ' ἰδίαν ἐπηρώτων αὐτόν,
Ὅτι ἡμεῖς οὐκ ἠδυνήθημεν ἐκβαλεῖν αὐτό;
9:29 καὶ εἶπεν αὐτοῖς,
Τοῦτο τὸ γένος ἐν οὐδενὶ δύναται ἐξελθεῖν εἰ μὴ ἐν προσευχῇ.
9:30 Κἀκεῖθεν ἐξελθόντες παρεπορεύοντο διὰ τῆς Γαλιλαίας, καὶ οὐκ ἤθελεν ἵνα τις γνοῖ· 9:31 ἐδίδασκεν γὰρ τοὺς μαθητὰς αὐτοῦ καὶ ἔλεγεν αὐτοῖς ὅτι
Ὁ υἱὸς τοῦ ἀνθρώπου παραδίδοται εἰς χεῖρας ἀνθρώπων, καὶ ἀποκτενοῦσιν αὐτόν, καὶ ἀποκτανθεὶς μετὰ τρεῖς ἡμέρας ἀναστήσεται.(2 PN)
9:32 οἱ δὲ ἠγνόουν τὸ ῥῆμα, καὶ ἐφοβοῦντο αὐτὸν ἐπερωτῆσαι.
9:33 Καὶ ἦλθον εἰς Καφαρναούμ. καὶ ἐν τῇ οἰκίᾳ γενόμενος ἐπηρώτα αὐτούς,
Τί ἐν τῇ ὁδῷ διελογίζεσθε;
9:34 οἱ δὲ ἐσιώπων, πρὸς ἀλλήλους γὰρ διελέχθησαν ἐν τῇ ὁδῷ
Τίς μείζων.
9:35 καὶ καθίσας ἐφώνησεν τοὺς δώδεκα καὶ λέγει αὐτοῖς,
Εἴ τις θέλει πρῶτος εἶναι, ἔσται πάντων ἔσχατος καὶ πάντων διάκονος.
9:36 καὶ λαβὼν παιδίον ἔστησεν αὐτὸ ἐν μέσῳ αὐτῶν καὶ ἐναγκαλισάμενος αὐτὸ εἶπεν αὐτοῖς,
9:37 Ὃς ἂν ἓν τῶν τοιούτων παιδίων δέξηται ἐπὶ τῷ ὀνόματί μου, ἐμὲ δέχεται· καὶ ὃς ἂν ἐμὲ δέχηται, οὐκ ἐμὲ δέχεται ἀλλὰ τὸν ἀποστείλαντά με.

4TP3.2.2.2(38–50) CM: Ἰωάννης. MC.Dia: "Ἔφη...εἶπεν. Jesus responds to John's comment about non-disciple exorcists who use Jesus' name and includes other comments on discipleship.
    5TP3.2.2.2.1(38) CM: Ἰωάννης. MC: "Ἔφη. SPAC: report. John's comment about the stranger-exorcist.
    5TP3.2.2.2.2(39–50) CM: Ἰησοῦς. MC: εἶπεν. Jesus responds and continues with remarks on discipleship.
        6TP3.2.2.2.2.1(39–40) CM: αὐτόν...ὅς. SPAC: command (μή) & two supporting arguments (γάρ). Jesus comments on the stranger.
        6TP3.2.2.2.2.2(41) CM: ὅς...ὑμᾶς. SPAC: ἀμήν. CONJ: γάρ. The relation of the water giver to Christ's followers.
        6TP3.2.2.2.2.3(42) CM: ὅς...τῶν μικρῶν. SPAC: assertion. Relation of a tempter to the little ones who believe.
        6TP3.2.2.2.2.4(43–48) CM: σε. SPAC: directives and assertions. The relationship of the disciples to their bodies and to everlasting life.
            7TP3.2.2.2.2.4.1(43) CM: χείρ. SPAC: ἀπόκοψον...ἐστίν (conditional directive and assertion). The hand and life or hell.
            7TP3.2.2.2.2.4.2(45) CM: πούς. SPAC: ἀπόκοψον...ἐστίν (conditional directive and assertion). The foot and life or hell.
            7TP3.2.2.2.2.4.3(47–48) CM: ὀφθαλμος. SPAC: ἔκβαλε...ἐστίν (conditional directive and assertion). The eye and the kingdom or hell.
        6TP3.2.2.2.2.5(49–50) CM: πᾶς...ἅλας. CONJ: γάρ. SPAC: assertions (ἁλισθήσεται...καλόν) and directives (ἔχετε...εἰρηνεύετε). The salt sayings.

1 2 3 4

9:38 Ἔφη αὐτῷ ὁ Ἰωάννης,
Διδάσκαλε, εἴδομέν τινα ἐν τῷ ὀνόματί σου
ἐκβάλλοντα δαιμόνια, καὶ ἐκωλύομεν αὐτόν, ὅτι οὐκ
ἠκολούθει ἡμῖν.
9:39 ὁ δὲ Ἰησοῦς εἶπεν,
Μὴ κωλύετε αὐτόν. οὐδεὶς γάρ ἐστιν ὃς ποιήσει
δύναμιν ἐπὶ τῷ ὀνόματί μου καὶ δυνήσεται ταχὺ
κακολογῆσαί με· 9:40 ὃς γὰρ οὐκ ἔστιν καθ' ἡμῶν,
ὑπὲρ ἡμῶν ἐστιν. 9:41 Ὃς γὰρ ἂν ποτίσῃ ὑμᾶς
ποτήριον ὕδατος ἐν ὀνόματι ὅτι Χριστοῦ ἐστε, ἀμὴν
λέγω ὑμῖν ὅτι
οὐ μὴ ἀπολέσῃ τὸν μισθὸν αὐτοῦ. (3 PN, HS)
9:42 Καὶ ὃς ἂν σκανδαλίσῃ ἕνα τῶν μικρῶν τούτων
τῶν πιστευόντων [εἰς ἐμέ], καλόν ἐστιν αὐτῷ μᾶλλον
εἰ περίκειται μύλος ὀνικὸς περὶ τὸν τράχηλον αὐτοῦ
καὶ βέβληται εἰς τὴν θάλασσαν. 9:43 Καὶ ἐὰν
σκανδαλίζῃ σε ἡ χείρ σου, ἀπόκοψον αὐτήν· καλόν
ἐστίν σε κυλλὸν εἰσελθεῖν εἰς τὴν ζωὴν ἢ τὰς δύο
χεῖρας ἔχοντα ἀπελθεῖν εἰς τὴν γέενναν, εἰς τὸ πῦρ
τὸ ἄσβεστον. 9:45 καὶ ἐὰν ὁ πούς σου σκανδαλίζῃ σε,
ἀπόκοψον αὐτόν· καλόν ἐστίν σε εἰσελθεῖν εἰς τὴν
ζωὴν χωλὸν ἢ τοὺς δύο πόδας ἔχοντα βληθῆναι εἰς
τὴν γέενναν. 9:47 καὶ ἐὰν ὁ ὀφθαλμός σου σκανδαλίζῃ
σε, ἔκβαλε αὐτόν· καλόν σέ ἐστιν μονόφθαλμον
εἰσελθεῖν εἰς τὴν βασιλείαν τοῦ θεοῦ ἢ δύο
ὀφθαλμοὺς ἔχοντα βληθῆναι εἰς τὴν γέενναν, 9:48
ὅπου ὁ σκώληξ αὐτῶν οὐ τελευτᾷ καὶ τὸ πῦρ οὐ
σβέννυται. 9:49 πᾶς γὰρ πυρὶ ἁλισθήσεται. 9:50 Καλὸν
τὸ ἅλας· ἐὰν δὲ τὸ ἅλας ἄναλον γένηται, ἐν τίνι
αὐτὸ ἀρτύσετε; ἔχετε ἐν ἑαυτοῖς ἅλα καὶ εἰρηνεύετε
ἐν ἀλλήλοις. (2 PN)

²TP³·³(10:1–52) EMr:(S) Ἐκεῖθεν...ὅρια...Ἰουδαίας...
Ἰορδάνου. The Journey through Judea and Perea.
   ³TP³·³·¹(1–9) EMr:(S) πρὸς αὐτόν. Jesus teaches the crowd and argues with Pharisees.
      ⁴TP³·³·¹·¹(1) CM: ὄχλοι...αὐτόν. SN: ἐδίδασκεν ὡς εἰώθει. Jesus teaches the crowd.
      ⁴TP³·³·¹·²(2–9) CM: Φαρισαῖοι. MC.Dia: ἐπηρώτων...εἶπεν, etc. SPAC: Ibid. (argument). The argument about divorce with the Pharisees.
         ⁵TP³·³·¹·²·¹(2) CM: Φαρισαῖοι. MC: ἐπηρώτων. SPAC: Question. The Pharisees ask: is divorce legal?
         ⁵TP³·³·¹·²·²(3) CM: ὁ δέ. MC: εἶπεν. SPAC: Question. Jesus responds with a question about the commandment concerning divorce.
         ⁵TP³·³·¹·²·³(4) CM: οἱ δέ. MC: εἶπαν. SPAC: Answer. The Pharisees answer Jesus' question by quoting the law correctly.
         ⁵TP³·³·¹·²·⁴(5–9) CM: ὁ δέ. MC: εἶπεν. SPAC: Answer comprising an assertion (5), another assertion (6–8a), a conclusion (8b: ὥστε) based on the prior assertion and a final conclusion (9: οὖν) based on 6–8. Jesus answers their question (2) by rejecting divorce.
   ³TP³·³·²(10–16) EMr:(S) οἰκίαν. SN: τούτου. CM: μαθηταὶ...αὐτόν. Jesus teaches the disciples privately about divorce and about entering the kingdom.
      ⁴TP³·³·²·¹(10–12) MC: λέγει. SPAC: answer. Jesus answers the disciples' question about the divorce debate.
      ⁴TP³·³·²·²(13–16) CM: προσέφερον, (P) παιδία. MC.Mon: εἶπεν. SPAC: ἄφετε...μὴ κωλύετε...ἐστίν (two directives, an assertion) ἀμήν (solemn assertion). Jesus responds to the disciples' rebuke of those wanting Jesus to touch the children, and Jesus blesses the children.

1 2 3 4

10:1 Καὶ ἐκεῖθεν ἀναστὰς ἔρχεται εἰς τὰ ὅρια τῆς Ἰουδαίας [καὶ] πέραν τοῦ Ἰορδάνου, καὶ συμπορεύονται πάλιν ὄχλοι πρὸς αὐτόν, καὶ ὡς εἰώθει πάλιν ἐδίδασκεν αὐτούς. 10:2 καὶ προσελθόντες Φαρισαῖοι ἐπηρώτων αὐτὸν εἰ ἔξεστιν ἀνδρὶ γυναῖκα ἀπολῦσαι, πειράζοντες αὐτόν. 10:3 ὁ δὲ ἀποκριθεὶς εἶπεν αὐτοῖς, Τί ὑμῖν ἐνετείλατο Μωϋσῆς;
10:4 οἱ δὲ εἶπαν,
Ἐπέτρεψεν Μωϋσῆς βιβλίον ἀποστασίου γράψαι καὶ ἀπολῦσαι. (2 PN)
10:5 ὁ δὲ Ἰησοῦς εἶπεν αὐτοῖς,
Πρὸς τὴν σκληροκαρδίαν ὑμῶν ἔγραψεν ὑμῖν τὴν ἐντολὴν ταύτην. 10:6 ἀπὸ δὲ ἀρχῆς κτίσεως ἄρσεν καὶ θῆλυ ἐποίησεν αὐτούς· 10:7 ἕνεκεν τούτου καταλείψει ἄνθρωπος τὸν πατέρα αὐτοῦ καὶ τὴν μητέρα [καὶ προσκολληθήσεται πρὸς τὴν γυναῖκα αὐτοῦ], 10:8 καὶ ἔσονται οἱ δύο εἰς σάρκα μίαν· ὥστε οὐκέτι εἰσὶν δύο ἀλλὰ μία σάρξ. 10:9 ὃ οὖν ὁ θεὸς συνέζευξεν ἄνθρωπος μὴ χωριζέτω. (2 PN)
10:10 Καὶ εἰς τὴν οἰκίαν πάλιν οἱ μαθηταὶ περὶ τούτου ἐπηρώτων αὐτόν. 10:11 καὶ λέγει αὐτοῖς,
Ὃς ἂν ἀπολύσῃ τὴν γυναῖκα αὐτοῦ καὶ γαμήσῃ ἄλλην μοιχᾶται ἐπ' αὐτήν· 10:12 καὶ ἐὰν αὐτὴ ἀπολύσασα τὸν ἄνδρα αὐτῆς γαμήσῃ ἄλλον μοιχᾶται.
10:13 Καὶ προσέφερον αὐτῷ παιδία ἵνα αὐτῶν ἅψηται· οἱ δὲ μαθηταὶ ἐπετίμησαν αὐτοῖς. 10:14 ἰδὼν δὲ ὁ Ἰησοῦς ἠγανάκτησεν καὶ εἶπεν αὐτοῖς,
Ἄφετε τὰ παιδία ἔρχεσθαι πρός με, μὴ κωλύετε αὐτά, τῶν γὰρ τοιούτων ἐστὶν ἡ βασιλεία τοῦ θεοῦ. 10:15 ἀμὴν λέγω ὑμῖν,
ὃς ἂν μὴ δέξηται τὴν βασιλείαν τοῦ θεοῦ ὡς παιδίον, οὐ μὴ εἰσέλθῃ εἰς αὐτήν. (3 PN, HS)
10:16 καὶ ἐναγκαλισάμενος αὐτὰ κατευλόγει τιθεὶς τὰς χεῖρας ἐπ' αὐτά.

³TP³·³·³(17–31) EMr:(S) ἐκπορευομένου...ὁδόν. An episode on the road about riches and discipleship.
⁴TP³·³·³·¹(17–22) CM: προσδραμών. MC.Dia: ἐπηρώτα...εἶπεν. SPAC: Ibid. A conversation with a rich man about everlasting life.
⁵TP³·³·³·¹·¹(17–19) CM: ἐπηρώτα...εἶπεν. MC: Ibid. SPAC: Ibid. The rich man questions Jesus who answers.
⁶TP³·³·³·¹·¹·¹(17) CM: ἐπηρώτα. MC, SPAC: Ibid. The man's question to Jesus about inheriting everlasting life.
⁶TP³·³·³·¹·¹·²(18–19) CM: εἶπεν. MC: Ibid. SN: ἐντολάς. SPAC: answer (comprising a question and 2 assertions). Jesus' response: he rejects the "good" designation and recites six commandments.
⁵TP³·³·³·¹·²(20) CM: ὁ δὲ ἔφη. MC: Ibid. SPAC: Ibid. (assertion). The man answers that he has kept these commandments.
⁵TP³·³·³·¹·³(21) CM: Ἰησοῦς. MC: εἶπεν. SPAC: assertion and commands. Jesus loves him and commands him to sell all that he has and give to the poor.
⁵TP³·³·³·¹·⁴(22) CM: στυγνάσας. The rich man leaves sorrowing.
⁴TP³·³·³·²(23–27) CM: Ἰησοῦς...μαθηταῖς. MC.Dia: λέγει...ἀποκριθείς. Jesus discusses wealth, salvation, and the Kingdom with his disciples.
⁵TP³·³·³·²·¹(23) CM: λέγει. MC: Ibid. SPAC: assertion. Jesus comments on the difficulty of the rich entering the Kingdom of God.
⁵TP³·³·³·²·²(24a) CM: μαθηταί. The disciples are amazed at Jesus' claim.
⁵TP³·³·³·²·³(24b–25) CM: Ἰησοῦς...λέγει. SPAC: assertion. Jesus responds to their amazement by repeating the claim and adding the saying about the camel going through the needle's eye.

A Linguistic Outline of Mark 239

1 2 3 4

10:17 Καὶ ἐκπορευομένου αὐτοῦ εἰς ὁδὸν προσδραμὼν εἷς καὶ γονυπετήσας αὐτὸν ἐπηρώτα αὐτόν, Διδάσκαλε ἀγαθέ, τί ποιήσω ἵνα ζωὴν αἰώνιον κληρονομήσω;
10:18 ὁ δὲ Ἰησοῦς εἶπεν αὐτῷ, Τί
  με (2, 3)
λέγεις
  ἀγαθόν; (2, 3)
οὐδεὶς ἀγαθὸς εἰ μὴ εἷς ὁ θεός. 10:19 τὰς ἐντολὰς οἶδας·
  Μὴ φονεύσῃς, Μὴ μοιχεύσῃς, Μὴ κλέψῃς, Μὴ ψευδομαρτυρήσῃς, Μὴ ἀποστερήσῃς, Τίμα τὸν πατέρα σου καὶ τὴν μητέρα. (3 ΟΤ)
10:20 ὁ δὲ. ἔφη αὐτῷ,
  Διδάσκαλε, ταῦτα πάντα ἐφυλαξάμην ἐκ νεότητός μου.
10:21 ὁ δὲ Ἰησοῦς ἐμβλέψας αὐτῷ ἠγάπησεν αὐτὸν καὶ εἶπεν αὐτῷ,
  Ἕν σε ὑστερεῖ· ὕπαγε, ὅσα ἔχεις πώλησον καὶ δὸς [τοῖς] πτωχοῖς, καὶ ἕξεις θησαυρὸν ἐν οὐρανῷ, καὶ δεῦρο ἀκολούθει μοι.
10:22 ὁ δὲ στυγνάσας ἐπὶ τῷ λόγῳ ἀπῆλθεν λυπούμενος· ἦν γὰρ ἔχων κτήματα πολλά.
10:23 Καὶ περιβλεψάμενος ὁ Ἰησοῦς λέγει τοῖς μαθηταῖς αὐτοῦ,
  Πῶς δυσκόλως οἱ τὰ χρήματα ἔχοντες εἰς τὴν βασιλείαν τοῦ θεοῦ εἰσελεύσονται.
10:24 οἱ δὲ μαθηταὶ ἐθαμβοῦντο ἐπὶ τοῖς λόγοις αὐτοῦ. ὁ δὲ Ἰησοῦς πάλιν ἀποκριθεὶς λέγει αὐτοῖς,
  Τέκνα, πῶς δύσκολόν ἐστιν εἰς τὴν βασιλείαν τοῦ θεοῦ εἰσελθεῖν· 10:25 εὐκοπώτερόν ἐστιν κάμηλον διὰ [τῆς] τρυμαλιᾶς [τῆς] ῥαφίδος διελθεῖν ἢ πλούσιον εἰς τὴν βασιλείαν τοῦ θεοῦ εἰσελθεῖν.

5TP3.3.3.2.4(26) CM: οἱ δὲ...λέγοντες. MC: Ibid. SPAC: τίς. The disciples ask themselves who can be saved.
5TP3.3.3.2.5(27) CM: ᾽Ιησοῦς. MC: λέγει. SPAC: assertion. Jesus affirms that all things are possible with God.
4TP3.3.3.3(28–31) EMr:(T) ἤρξατο. CM: Πέτρος. MC.Dia: λέγειν...ἔφη. Jesus responds to Peter's comment about the disciples' self sacrifice.
    5TP3.3.3.3.1(28) MC: λέγειν. SPAC: assertion. Peter describes the disciples' commitment to Jesus.
    5TP3.3.3.3.2(29–31) MC: ἔφη. SPAC: ἀμὴν λέγω (solemn assertion). Jesus describes the disciples' reward and the reversal of the first and last.
3TP3.3.4(32–52) EMr:(S) ὁδῷ ἀναβαίνοντες...῾Ιεροσόλυμα. Passion and authority teaching for the disciples while on the Jerusalem road and the healing of Bartimaeus.
    4TP3.3.4.1(32–34) CM: αὐτούς...δώδεκα. The third passion teaching.
        5TP3.3.4.1.1(32a) EMr: (S) implied (by 32b) A place where others are with the twelve. CM: αὐτούς. The wondering of Jesus' followers.
        5TP3.3.4.1.2(32b–33) EMr:(S) παραλαβών...δώδεκα. CM: Ibid. MC.Mon λέγειν. SN: τὰ μέλλοντα. SPAC: λέγειν τὰ μέλλοντα. Jesus teaches about his passion and resurrection.
    4TP3.3.4.2(35–40) EMr:(S) προσπορεύοντο. CM: ᾽Ιάκωβος...᾽Ιωάννης. MC.Dia: λέγοντες...εἶπεν. James and John ask to be on Jesus' right hand in his glory.
        5TP3.3.4.2.1(35) CM, MC: λέγοντες. SPAC: θέλομεν. The sons of Zebedee ask Jesus to grant a request.

A Linguistic Outline of Mark 241

1 2 3 4

10:26 οἱ δὲ περισσῶς ἐξεπλήσσοντο λέγοντες πρὸς ἑαυτούς,
Καὶ τίς δύναται σωθῆναι;
10:27 ἐμβλέψας αὐτοῖς ὁ Ἰησοῦς λέγει,
Παρὰ ἀνθρώποις ἀδύνατον, ἀλλ' οὐ παρὰ θεῷ· πάντα γὰρ δυνατὰ παρὰ τῷ θεῷ.
10:28 Ἤρξατο λέγειν ὁ Πέτρος αὐτῷ,
Ἰδοὺ ἡμεῖς ἀφήκαμεν πάντα καὶ ἠκολουθήκαμέν σοι.
10:29 ἔφη ὁ Ἰησοῦς,
Ἀμὴν λέγω ὑμῖν,
οὐδείς ἐστιν ὃς ἀφῆκεν οἰκίαν ἢ ἀδελφοὺς ἢ ἀδελφὰς ἢ μητέρα ἢ πατέρα ἢ τέκνα ἢ ἀγροὺς ἕνεκεν ἐμοῦ καὶ ἕνεκεν τοῦ εὐαγγελίου, 10:30 ἐὰν μὴ λάβῃ ἑκατονταπλασίονα νῦν ἐν τῷ καιρῷ τούτῳ οἰκίας καὶ ἀδελφοὺς καὶ ἀδελφὰς καὶ μητέρας καὶ τέκνα καὶ ἀγροὺς μετὰ διωγμῶν, καὶ ἐν τῷ αἰῶνι τῷ ἐρχομένῳ ζωὴν αἰώνιον. 10:31 πολλοὶ δὲ ἔσονται πρῶτοι ἔσχατοι καὶ [οἱ] ἔσχατοι πρῶτοι. (3 PN, HS)
10:32 Ἦσαν δὲ ἐν τῇ ὁδῷ ἀναβαίνοντες εἰς Ἱεροσόλυμα, καὶ ἦν προάγων αὐτοὺς ὁ Ἰησοῦς, καὶ ἐθαμβοῦντο οἱ δὲ ἀκολουθοῦντες ἐφοβοῦντο. καὶ παραλαβὼν πάλιν τοὺς δώδεκα ἤρξατο αὐτοῖς λέγειν τὰ μέλλοντα αὐτῷ συμβαίνειν, 10:33 ὅτι
Ἰδοὺ ἀναβαίνομεν εἰς Ἱεροσόλυμα, καὶ ὁ υἱὸς τοῦ ἀνθρώπου παραδοθήσεται τοῖς ἀρχιερεῦσιν καὶ τοῖς γραμματεῦσιν καὶ κατακρινοῦσιν αὐτὸν θανάτῳ καὶ παραδώσουσιν αὐτὸν τοῖς ἔθνεσιν 10:34 καὶ ἐμπαίξουσιν αὐτῷ καὶ ἐμπτύσουσιν αὐτῷ καὶ μαστιγώσουσιν αὐτὸν καὶ ἀποκτενοῦσιν, καὶ μετὰ τρεῖς ἡμέρας ἀναστήσεται. (2 PN)
10:35 Καὶ προσπορεύονται αὐτῷ Ἰάκωβος καὶ Ἰωάννης οἱ υἱοὶ Ζεβεδαίου λέγοντες αὐτῷ,
Διδάσκαλε, θέλομεν ἵνα ὃ ἐὰν αἰτήσωμέν σε ποιήσῃς ἡμῖν.

⁵TP³·³·⁴·²·²(36) CM, MC: εἶπεν. SPAC: τί. Jesus asks about the request.
⁵TP³·³·⁴·²·³(37) CM, MC: εἶπαν. SPAC: δός (a request, (35) αἰτήσωμεν). They want to sit on Jesus' right and left hand in his glory.
⁵TP³·³·⁴·²·⁴(38) CM, MC: εἶπεν. SPAC: οὐκ (assertion) & question. Jesus asserts their lack of knowledge and asks them about their readiness to suffer.
⁵TP³·³·⁴·²·⁵(39a) CM, MC: εἶπαν. SPAC: assertion. They assert their readiness.
⁵TP³·³·⁴·²·⁶(39b–40). CM, MC: εἶπεν. SPAC: assertion. Jesus accepts their assertion but defers their request for the places in glory to God's decision.
⁴TP³·³·⁴·³(41–45) EMr: προσκαλεσάμενος. CM: οἱ δέκα. MC: re: 35–40, ἀκουσάντες. MC.Mon: λέγει. Jesus responds to the ten's anger with teaching about authority among the disciples.
⁵TP³·³·⁴·³·¹(41) MC: ἀκουσάντες. CM: οἱ δέκα. The ten get angry with James and John.
⁵TP³·³·⁴·³·²(42–45) CM, MC: λέγει. SPAC: teaching comprising assertion (οἴδατε), conditional directives (ἄν...ἔσται), supporting argument (γάρ). Jesus teaches about authority among the disciples.
⁴TP³·³·⁴·⁴(46–52) EMr:(S) Ἰεριχώ. The healing near Jericho on the road.
⁵TP³·³·⁴·⁴·¹(46a) EMr:(S) ἔρχονται. The approach to Jericho.
⁵TP³·³·⁴·⁴·²(46b–52) EMr:(S) ἐκπορευομένου. Leaving Jericho: the healing.
⁶TP³·³·⁴·⁴·²·¹(46b) CM: αὐτοῦ...τυφλός. Jesus, the disciples, the crowds, and Bartimaeus.
⁶TP³·³·⁴·⁴·²·²(47–48) CM, MC.Dia: ἀκούσας...ἐπετίμων... ἔκραζεν. SPAC: ἐστίν (assertion) ἐλέησον and ἐπετίμων. The blind man asks for Jesus' mercy and is rebuked by the crowd.

1 2 3 4

10:36 ὁ δὲ εἶπεν αὐτοῖς,
  Τί θέλετέ [με] ποιήσω ὑμῖν;
10:37 οἱ δὲ εἶπαν αὐτῷ,
  Δὸς ἡμῖν ἵνα εἷς σου ἐκ δεξιῶν καὶ εἷς ἐξ
  ἀριστερῶν καθίσωμεν ἐν τῇ δόξῃ σου.
10:38 ὁ δὲ Ἰησοῦς εἶπεν αὐτοῖς,
  Οὐκ οἴδατε τί αἰτεῖσθε. δύνασθε πιεῖν τὸ ποτήριον ὃ
  ἐγὼ πίνω ἢ τὸ βάπτισμα ὃ ἐγὼ βαπτίζομαι βαπτισθῆναι;
10:39 οἱ δὲ εἶπαν αὐτῷ,
  Δυνάμεθα.
ὁ δὲ Ἰησοῦς εἶπεν αὐτοῖς,
  Τὸ ποτήριον ὃ ἐγὼ πίνω πίεσθε καὶ τὸ βάπτισμα ὃ
  ἐγὼ βαπτίζομαι βαπτισθήσεσθε, 10:40 τὸ δὲ καθίσαι
  ἐκ δεξιῶν μου ἢ ἐξ εὐωνύμων οὐκ ἔστιν ἐμὸν δοῦναι,
  ἀλλ' οἷς ἡτοίμασται.
10:41 Καὶ ἀκούσαντες οἱ δέκα ἤρξαντο ἀγανακτεῖν περὶ
Ἰακώβου καὶ Ἰωάννου. 10:42 καὶ προσκαλεσάμενος αὐτοὺς
ὁ Ἰησοῦς λέγει αὐτοῖς,
  Οἴδατε ὅτι οἱ δοκοῦντες ἄρχειν τῶν ἐθνῶν
  κατακυριεύουσιν αὐτῶν καὶ οἱ μεγάλοι αὐτῶν
  κατεξουσιάζουσιν αὐτῶν. 10:43 οὐχ οὕτως δέ ἐστιν
  ἐν ὑμῖν, ἀλλ' ὃς ἂν θέλῃ μέγας γενέσθαι ἐν ὑμῖν,
  ἔσται ὑμῶν διάκονος, 10:44 καὶ ὃς ἂν θέλῃ ἐν ὑμῖν
  εἶναι πρῶτος ἔσται πάντων δοῦλος· 10:45 καὶ γὰρ ὁ
  υἱὸς τοῦ ἀνθρώπου οὐκ ἦλθεν διακονηθῆναι ἀλλὰ
  διακονῆσαι καὶ δοῦναι τὴν ψυχὴν αὐτοῦ λύτρον ἀντὶ
  πολλῶν.
10:46 Καὶ ἔρχονται εἰς Ἰεριχώ. καὶ ἐκπορευομένου
αὐτοῦ ἀπὸ Ἰεριχὼ καὶ τῶν μαθητῶν αὐτοῦ καὶ ὄχλου
ἱκανοῦ ὁ υἱὸς Τιμαίου Βαρτιμαῖος, τυφλὸς προσαίτης,
ἐκάθητο παρὰ τὴν ὁδόν. 10:47 καὶ ἀκούσας ὅτι
Ἰησοῦς ὁ Ναζαρηνός ἐστιν
ἤρξατο κράζειν καὶ λέγειν,
  Υἱὲ Δαυὶδ Ἰησοῦ, ἐλέησόν με.

⁶TP³·³·⁴·⁴·²·³(49a) CM=MC: εἶπεν. SPAC: φωνήσατε. Jesus commands them to bring Bartimaeus.
⁶TP³·³·⁴·⁴·²·⁴(49b) CM=MC: φωνοῦσιν. SPAC: θάρσει. Jesus' order is carried out.
⁶TP³·³·⁴·⁴·²·⁵(50) EMr:(S) ἦλθεν. CM: Ibid. Bartimaeus comes to Jesus.
⁶TP³·³·⁴·⁴·²·⁶(51–52a) CM=MC.Dia: ἀποκριθείς...εἶπεν. Jesus honors his request for healing.
⁷TP³·³·⁴·⁴·²·⁶·¹(51a) MC: εἶπεν. SPAC: τί. Jesus asks the blind man for his request.
⁷TP³·³·⁴·⁴·²·⁶·²(51b) MC: εἶπεν. SPAC: request ἵνα). He requests healing.
⁷TP³·³·⁴·⁴·²·⁶·³(52) MC: εἶπεν. SPAC: ὕπαγε (command); σέσωκεν (a declarative). Jesus heals him.
⁶TP³·³·⁴·⁴·²·⁷(52b) CM: ἠκολούθει. Bartimaeus receives his sight and follows Jesus.
¹TP⁴(11:1–16:8) EMr:(S) Ἱεροσόλυμα...Βηθανίαν. Jesus in Jerusalem and environs.
²TP⁴·¹(11:1–11) EMr:(T) ὀψίας...ὥρας. First day in Jerusalem and environs.
³TP⁴·¹·¹(1–3) CM: ἀποστέλλει...μαθητῶν. MC.Mon: λέγει. SPAC: ὑπάγετε (command and an assertion about the future). Jesus sends the two to get the colt.
³TP⁴·¹·²(4–6) EMr:(S) ἀπῆλθον. CM: Ibid. The two obey Jesus' will.
⁴TP⁴·¹·²·¹(4) CM: ἀπῆλθον (P) πῶλον. The two find the colt.
⁴TP⁴·¹·²·²(5–6) CM: τινες. MC.Dia: ἔλεγον...εἶπαν. SPAC: τί. The two explain matters in response to the bystanders' question.
³TP⁴·¹·³(7–8) EMr:(S) φέρουσιν. CM: Ibid. & Ἰησοῦν...πολλοί. The preparation of the colt and road.

1 2 3 4

10:48 καὶ ἐπετίμων αὐτῷ πολλοὶ ἵνα
σιωπήσῃ· (1, 2)
ὁ δὲ πολλῷ μᾶλλον ἔκραζεν,
Υἱὲ Δαυίδ, ἐλέησόν με.
10:49 καὶ στὰς ὁ Ἰησοῦς εἶπεν,
Φωνήσατε αὐτόν.
καὶ φωνοῦσιν τὸν τυφλὸν λέγοντες αὐτῷ,
Θάρσει, ἔγειρε, φωνεῖ σε.
10:50 ὁ δὲ ἀποβαλὼν τὸ ἱμάτιον αὐτοῦ ἀναπηδήσας ἦλθεν
πρὸς τὸν Ἰησοῦν. 10:51 καὶ ἀποκριθεὶς αὐτῷ ὁ Ἰησοῦς
εἶπεν,
Τί σοι θέλεις ποιήσω;
ὁ δὲ τυφλὸς εἶπεν αὐτῷ,
Ραββουνι, ἵνα ἀναβλέψω.
10:52 καὶ ὁ Ἰησοῦς εἶπεν αὐτῷ,
Ὕπαγε, ἡ πίστις σου σέσωκέν σε.
καὶ εὐθὺς ἀνέβλεψεν καὶ ἠκολούθει αὐτῷ ἐν τῇ ὁδῷ.
11:1 Καὶ ὅτε ἐγγίζουσιν εἰς Ἱεροσόλυμα εἰς Βηθφαγὴ
καὶ Βηθανίαν πρὸς τὸ Ὄρος τῶν Ἐλαιῶν, ἀποστέλλει δύο
τῶν μαθητῶν αὐτοῦ 11:2 καὶ λέγει αὐτοῖς,
Ὑπάγετε εἰς τὴν κώμην τὴν κατέναντι ὑμῶν, καὶ
εὐθὺς εἰσπορευόμενοι εἰς αὐτὴν εὑρήσετε πῶλον
δεδεμένον ἐφ' ὃν οὐδεὶς οὔπω ἀνθρώπων ἐκάθισεν·
λύσατε αὐτὸν καὶ φέρετε. 11:3 καὶ ἐάν τις ὑμῖν εἴπῃ,
(2 PN)
Τί ποιεῖτε τοῦτο;
εἴπατε,
Ὁ κύριος αὐτοῦ χρείαν ἔχει,
καὶ εὐθὺς αὐτὸν ἀποστέλλει πάλιν ὧδε. (2 PN)
11:4 καὶ ἀπῆλθον καὶ εὗρον πῶλον δεδεμένον πρὸς θύραν
ἔξω ἐπὶ τοῦ ἀμφόδου καὶ λύουσιν αὐτόν. 11:5 καί τινες
τῶν ἐκεῖ ἑστηκότων ἔλεγον αὐτοῖς,
Τί ποιεῖτε λύοντες τὸν πῶλον;
11:6 οἱ δὲ εἶπαν αὐτοῖς καθὼς εἶπεν ὁ Ἰησοῦς, καὶ
ἀφῆκαν αὐτούς. 11:7 καὶ φέρουσιν τὸν πῶλον πρὸς τὸν
Ἰησοῦν καὶ ἐπιβάλλουσιν αὐτῷ τὰ ἱμάτια αὐτῶν, καὶ
ἐκάθισεν ἐπ' αὐτόν.

³TP⁴·¹·⁴(9–10) EMr:(S)=CM: οἱ προάγοντες...ἀκολουθοῦντες. MC.Mon: ἔκραζον. SPAC: Εὐλογημένος...ὡσαννά. The people surrounding Jesus respond to him with praise and blessing.
³TP⁴·¹·⁵(11a) EMr:(S) εἰσῆλθεν... ἱερόν. CM: Ibid. Jesus' entry into the temple.
³TP⁴·¹·⁶(11b) EMr:(S) ἐξῆλθεν. CM: Ibid. Return to Bethany.
²TP⁴·²(12–19) EMr:(T) τῇ ἐπαύριον...ὀψέ (19). The second day in Jerusalem and environs.
³TP⁴·²·¹(12–14) EMr:(S) ἐλθόντων ἀπὸ Βηθανίας. CM: αὐτῶν. The cursing of the fig tree.
⁴TP⁴·²·¹·¹(12–13a) EMr:(S) μακρόθεν. Jesus sees the fig tree.
⁴TP⁴·²·¹·²(13b–14) EMr:(S) ἐλθών. MC.Mon: εἶπεν. SPAC: curse—a declarative (21: καταράσω—an SN for 14). Jesus curses the tree.
³TP⁴·²·²(15–18) EMr:(S) Ἱεροσόλυμα. The temple cleansing and teaching about the temple.
⁴TP⁴·²·²·¹(15–16) EMr:(S) ἱερόν. CM: εἰσελθών...πωλούντων. Jesus cleanses the temple.
⁴TP⁴·²·²·²(17) MC.Mon: ἐδίδασκεν...ἔλεγεν αὐτοῖς. CM: Ibid. SPAC: Ibid. Jesus' teaching about the temple's purpose and present condition.
⁴TP⁴·²·²·³(18) CM: ἀρχιερεῖς...γραμματεῖς. SN: διδαχῇ. The authorities' deadly reaction.
⁴TP⁴·²·²·⁴(19) EMr:(S) ἐξεπορεύοντο. CM: Ibid. Leaving Jerusalem.
²TP⁴·³(20–25) EMr:(T) πρωΐ (S) παραπορευόμενοι (end of the third day is unclear). Approaching Jerusalem they see the fig tree withered, and Jesus teaches about prayer.
³TP⁴·³·¹(20) CM: εἶδον. The disciples see the withered tree.

A Linguistic Outline of Mark 247

1 2 3 4
11:8 καὶ πολλοὶ τὰ ἱμάτια αὐτῶν ἔστρωσαν εἰς τὴν ὁδόν, ἄλλοι δὲ στιβάδας κόψαντες ἐκ τῶν ἀγρῶν. 11:9 καὶ οἱ προάγοντες καὶ οἱ ἀκολουθοῦντες ἔκραζον, Ὡσαννά· Εὐλογημένος ὁ ἐρχόμενος ἐν ὀνόματι κυρίου· 11:10 Εὐλογημένη ἡ ἐρχομένη βασιλεία τοῦ πατρὸς ἡμῶν Δαυίδ· Ὡσαννὰ ἐν τοῖς ὑψίστοις.
11:11 Καὶ εἰσῆλθεν εἰς Ἱεροσόλυμα εἰς τὸ ἱερόν καὶ περιβλεψάμενος πάντα, ὀψίας ἤδη οὔσης τῆς ὥρας, ἐξῆλθεν εἰς Βηθανίαν μετὰ τῶν δώδεκα.
11:12 Καὶ τῇ ἐπαύριον ἐξελθόντων αὐτῶν ἀπὸ Βηθανίας ἐπείνασεν. 11:13 καὶ ἰδὼν συκῆν ἀπὸ μακρόθεν ἔχουσαν φύλλα ἦλθεν, εἰ ἄρα τι εὑρήσει ἐν αὐτῇ, καὶ ἐλθὼν ἐπ᾽ αὐτὴν οὐδὲν εὗρεν εἰ μὴ φύλλα· ὁ γὰρ καιρὸς οὐκ ἦν σύκων. 11:14 καὶ ἀποκριθεὶς εἶπεν αὐτῇ,
Μηκέτι εἰς τὸν αἰῶνα ἐκ σοῦ μηδεὶς καρπὸν φάγοι.
καὶ ἤκουον οἱ μαθηταὶ αὐτοῦ.
11:15 Καὶ ἔρχονται εἰς Ἱεροσόλυμα. καὶ εἰσελθὼν εἰς τὸ ἱερὸν ἤρξατο ἐκβάλλειν τοὺς πωλοῦντας καὶ τοὺς ἀγοράζοντας ἐν τῷ ἱερῷ, καὶ τὰς τραπέζας τῶν κολλυβιστῶν καὶ τὰς καθέδρας τῶν πωλούντων τὰς περιστερὰς κατέστρεψεν, 11:16 καὶ οὐκ ἤφιεν ἵνα τις διενέγκῃ σκεῦος διὰ τοῦ ἱεροῦ. 11:17 καὶ ἐδίδασκεν καὶ ἔλεγεν αὐτοῖς,
Οὐ γέγραπται ὅτι
Ὁ οἶκός μου οἶκος προσευχῆς κληθήσεται πᾶσιν τοῖς ἔθνεσιν; (3 OT, PN)
ὑμεῖς δὲ πεποιήκατε αὐτὸν σπήλαιον λῃστῶν.
11:18 καὶ ἤκουσαν οἱ ἀρχιερεῖς καὶ οἱ γραμματεῖς καὶ ἐζήτουν πῶς αὐτὸν ἀπολέσωσιν ἐφοβοῦντο γὰρ αὐτόν, πᾶς γὰρ ὁ ὄχλος ἐξεπλήσσετο ἐπὶ τῇ διδαχῇ αὐτοῦ.
11:19 Καὶ ὅταν ὀψὲ ἐγένετο, ἐξεπορεύοντο ἔξω τῆς πόλεως.
11:20 Καὶ παραπορευόμενοι πρωῒ εἶδον τὴν συκῆν ἐξηραμμένην ἐκ ῥιζῶν.

³TP⁴·³·²(21–25) CM: Πέτρος...αὐτῷ. MC.Dia: λέγει...ἀποκριθείς. Peter and Jesus' conversation about the tree.
    ⁴TP⁴·³·²·¹(21) CM: Πέτρος. MC: λέγει. SN: (for 13b–14) κατηράσω. SPAC: assertion. Peter's remark about the withered tree.
    ⁴TP⁴·³·²·²(22–25) CM: Ἰησοῦς. MC: ἀποκριθείς...λέγει. SPAC: ἔχετε (directive)... ἀμήν (solemn assertion)...διὰ τοῦτο (assertion/directive as a conclusion to preceding premise [23]). Jesus responds to Peter with teaching about faithful prayer.
        ⁵TP⁴·³·²·²·¹(22) SPAC: ἔχετε. Jesus exhorts: have faith in God.
        ⁵TP⁴·³·²·²·²(23) SPAC: ἀμὴν λέγω (solemn assertion); Ἄρθητι (declarative). Jesus asserts the possibilities open to faith.
        ⁵TP⁴·³·²·²·³(24) SPAC: διὰ τοῦτο (conclusion based on 23) πιστεύετε (directive). A directive about prayer based on 23.
        ⁵TP⁴·³·²·²·⁴(25) SPAC: conditional directive (ὅταν...ἀφίετε). Jesus exhorts them about forgiveness and prayer.
²TP⁴·⁴(11:27–12:44) EMr:(S) Ἱεροσόλυμα...ἱερῷ. Controversies in the temple.
    ³TP⁴·⁴·¹(11:27–12:34) SPAC: Questions (12:34). People question Jesus.
        ⁴TP⁴·⁴·¹·¹(11:27–12:12) CM: ἀρχιερεῖς...πρεσβύτεροι. Debate about Jesus' authority with Jesus' parable as an additional response to the leaders.
            ⁵TP⁴·⁴·¹·¹·¹(27–33) MC.Dia: ἔλεγον, etc. The debate about authority.
                ⁶TP⁴·⁴·¹·¹·¹·¹(27–30) CM=MC.Dia: ἔλεγον...εἶπεν. SPAC: Question/Answer. SN: ταῦτα (for 11:15–17). The first dialogue about the source of Jesus' authority with two questions.

1 2 3 4

11:21 καὶ ἀναμνησθεὶς ὁ Πέτρος λέγει αὐτῷ,
Ῥαββί, ἴδε ἡ συκῆ ἣν κατηράσω ἐξήρανται.
11:22 καὶ ἀποκριθεὶς ὁ Ἰησοῦς λέγει αὐτοῖς,
Ἔχετε πίστιν θεοῦ. 11:23 ἀμὴν λέγω ὑμῖν ὅτι
ὃς ἂν εἴπῃ τῷ ὄρει τούτῳ,
Ἄρθητι καὶ βλήθητι εἰς τὴν θάλασσαν,
καὶ μὴ διακριθῇ ἐν τῇ καρδίᾳ αὐτοῦ ἀλλὰ πιστεύῃ
ὅτι ὃ λαλεῖ γίνεται, ἔσται αὐτῷ. (3 PN, HS)
11:24 διὰ τοῦτο λέγω ὑμῖν,
πάντα ὅσα προσεύχεσθε καὶ αἰτεῖσθε, πιστεύετε
ὅτι ἐλάβετε, καὶ ἔσται ὑμῖν. 11:25 καὶ ὅταν
στήκετε προσευχόμενοι, ἀφίετε εἴ τι ἔχετε κατά
τινος, ἵνα καὶ ὁ πατὴρ ὑμῶν ὁ ἐν τοῖς οὐρανοῖς
ἀφῇ ὑμῖν τὰ παραπτώματα ὑμῶν. (3 PN, HS)
11:27 Καὶ ἔρχονται πάλιν εἰς Ἱεροσόλυμα. καὶ ἐν τῷ
ἱερῷ περιπατοῦντος αὐτοῦ ἔρχονται πρὸς αὐτὸν οἱ
ἀρχιερεῖς καὶ οἱ γραμματεῖς καὶ οἱ πρεσβύτεροι 11:28
καὶ ἔλεγον αὐτῷ,
Ἐν ποίᾳ ἐξουσίᾳ ταῦτα ποιεῖς; ἢ τίς σοι ἔδωκεν τὴν
ἐξουσίαν ταύτην ἵνα ταῦτα ποιῇς;
11:29 ὁ δὲ Ἰησοῦς εἶπεν αὐτοῖς,
Ἐπερωτήσω ὑμᾶς ἕνα λόγον, καὶ ἀποκρίθητέ μοι καὶ
ἐρῶ ὑμῖν
ἐν ποίᾳ ἐξουσίᾳ ταῦτα ποιῶ· (2, 3)
11:30 τὸ βάπτισμα τὸ Ἰωάννου ἐξ οὐρανοῦ ἦν ἢ ἐξ
ἀνθρώπων; ἀποκρίθητέ μοι.
11:31 καὶ διελογίζοντο πρὸς ἑαυτοὺς λέγοντες,
Ἐὰν εἴπωμεν,
Ἐξ οὐρανοῦ,
ἐρεῖ,
Διὰ τί [οὖν] οὐκ ἐπιστεύσατε αὐτῷ;
11:32 ἀλλὰ εἴπωμεν,
Ἐξ ἀνθρώπων—
ἐφοβοῦντο τὸν ὄχλον· ἅπαντες γὰρ εἶχον τὸν Ἰωάννην
ὄντως ὅτι προφήτης ἦν.

6TP4.4.1.1.1.2(31–32) CM: πρὸς ἑαυτούς. MC.Dia: διελογίζοντο. SPAC: assertion (of a dilemma). The leaders' dilemma involved in answering Jesus' question.
6TP4.4.1.1.1.3(33) CM=MC.Dia: ἀποκριθέντες...λέγει. SN: ταῦτα (for 11:15–17). SPAC: Ibid. (two answers). Second stage of the dialogue between Jesus and the authorities: their respective answers to each other's questions.
5TP4.4.1.1.2(12:1–12) EMr:(T) ἤρξατο. CM: ἤρξατο...αυτοῖς. Jesus' parable to the leaders with their response.
6TP4.4.1.1.2.1(1–11) CM=MC.Mon: ἤρξατο...λαλεῖν, CM: (P) αὐτοῖς. SN: παραβολαῖς...παραβολήν (1, 12). SPAC: Ibid. (parabolic teaching). Jesus' parable.
7TP4.4.1.1.2.1.1(1) CM: ἄνθρωπος. The vineyard and the planter.
7TP4.4.1.1.2.1.2(2–3) EMr:(T) καιρῷ. CM: δοῦλον. He sends a slave who is treated badly.
7TP4.4.1.1.2.1.3(4) CM: ἄλλον δοῦλον. Another slave is beaten and dishonored.
7TP4.4.1.1.2.1.4(5a) CM: ἄλλον. Another slave is killed.
7TP4.4.1.1.2.1.5(5b) CM: ἄλλους. Other slaves are beaten or killed.
7TP4.4.1.1.2.1.6(6–8) CM: υἱὸν ἀγαπητόν. MC.Mon: λέγων...εἶπαν. SPAC: (7) assertions & directive. The beloved son episode containing two predictions, each the negation of the other.
7TP4.4.1.1.2.1.7(9) CM: κύριος. SPAC: τί & Answer. Jesus (as narrator) asks the leaders a question and answers it himself: judgment on the tenant farmers.
7TP4.4.1.1.2.1.8(10–11) CM=MC. ἀνέγνωτε. SN: γραφήν. SPAC: οὐδέ. Rhetorical question to the leaders by Jesus who quotes Ps 118.
6TP4.4.1.1.2.2(12) EMr:(S) ἀπῆλθον =CM. The leader's response to the parable and their departure.

1 2 3 4

11:33 καὶ ἀποκριθέντες τῷ Ἰησοῦ λέγουσιν,
Οὐκ οἴδαμεν.
καὶ ὁ Ἰησοῦς λέγει αὐτοῖς,
Οὐδὲ ἐγὼ λέγω ὑμῖν
ἐν ποίᾳ ἐξουσίᾳ ταῦτα ποιῶ. (2, 3)
12:1 Καὶ ἤρξατο αὐτοῖς ἐν παραβολαῖς λαλεῖν,
Ἀμπελῶνα ἄνθρωπος ἐφύτευσεν καὶ περιέθηκεν
φραγμὸν καὶ ὤρυξεν ὑπολήνιον καὶ ᾠκοδόμησεν
πύργον καὶ ἐξέδετο αὐτὸν γεωργοῖς καὶ ἀπεδήμησεν.
12:2 καὶ ἀπέστειλεν πρὸς τοὺς γεωργοὺς τῷ καιρῷ
δοῦλον ἵνα παρὰ τῶν γεωργῶν λάβῃ ἀπὸ τῶν καρπῶν
τοῦ ἀμπελῶνος· 12:3 καὶ λαβόντες αὐτὸν ἔδειραν καὶ
ἀπέστειλαν κενόν. 12:4 καὶ πάλιν ἀπέστειλεν πρὸς
αὐτοὺς ἄλλον δοῦλον· κἀκεῖνον ἐκεφαλίωσαν καὶ
ἠτίμασαν. 12:5 καὶ ἄλλον ἀπέστειλεν· κἀκεῖνον
ἀπέκτειναν, καὶ πολλοὺς ἄλλους, οὓς μὲν δέροντες,
οὓς δὲ ἀποκτέννοντες. 12:6 ἔτι ἕνα εἶχεν υἱὸν
ἀγαπητόν· ἀπέστειλεν αὐτὸν ἔσχατον πρὸς αὐτοὺς
λέγων ὅτι
Ἐντραπήσονται τὸν υἱόν μου.
12:7 ἐκεῖνοι δὲ οἱ γεωργοὶ πρὸς ἑαυτοὺς εἶπαν ὅτι
Οὗτός ἐστιν ὁ κληρονόμος· δεῦτε ἀποκτείνωμεν
αὐτόν, καὶ ἡμῶν ἔσται ἡ κληρονομία.
12:8 καὶ λαβόντες ἀπέκτειναν αὐτόν καὶ ἐξέβαλον
αὐτὸν ἔξω τοῦ ἀμπελῶνος. 12:9 τί [οὖν] ποιήσει ὁ
κύριος τοῦ ἀμπελῶνος; ἐλεύσεται καὶ ἀπολέσει τοὺς
γεωργούς καὶ δώσει τὸν ἀμπελῶνα ἄλλοις. 12:10 οὐδὲ
τὴν γραφὴν ταύτην ἀνέγνωτε,
Λίθον ὃν ἀπεδοκίμασαν οἱ οἰκοδομοῦντες, οὗτος
ἐγενήθη εἰς κεφαλὴν γωνίας· 12:11 παρὰ κυρίου
ἐγένετο αὕτη καὶ ἔστιν θαυμαστὴ ἐν ὀφθαλμοῖς
ἡμῶν; (3 OT) (2 PN: $\underset{n}{1}$11)
12:12 Καὶ ἐζήτουν αὐτὸν κρατῆσαι, καὶ ἐφοβήθησαν τὸν
ὄχλον, ἔγνωσαν γὰρ ὅτι πρὸς αὐτοὺς τὴν παραβολὴν
εἶπεν. καὶ ἀφέντες αὐτὸν ἀπῆλθον.

⁴TP⁴·⁴·¹·²(13–17) EMr:(S) πρὸς αὐτόν. The debate about the tribute to Caesar.
  ⁵TP⁴·⁴·¹·²·¹(13) CM: ἀποστέλλουσιν. Unnamed figures send agents to trap Jesus in his speech.
    ⁶TP⁴·⁴·¹·²·¹·¹(14–17) CM: Φαρισαίων... Ἡρῳδιανῶν. MC.Dia: λέγουσιν...εἶπεν, etc. SPAC: Assertion with a question and response. The agents arrive and are amazed by Jesus' response.
    ⁶TP⁴·⁴·¹·²·¹·²(14) CM=MC: λέγουσιν. SPAC: οἴδαμεν...γάρ...ἔξεστιν (assertion with supporting assertion and a question). The description of Jesus and accompanying question about the tribute.
    ⁶TP⁴·⁴·¹·²·¹·³(15) CM=MC: εἶπεν. SPAC: question and command. Jesus' first response.
    ⁶TP⁴·⁴·¹·²·¹·⁴(16a) CM: ἤνεγκαν. They carry out his command.
    ⁶TP⁴·⁴·¹·²·¹·⁵(16b) CM=MC: λέγει. SPAC: Question. Jesus questions them about the coin.
    ⁶TP⁴·⁴·¹·²·¹·⁶(16c) CM: οἱ δὲ εἶπαν. MC: Ibid. SPAC: answer. They respond to Jesus.
    ⁶TP⁴·⁴·¹·²·¹·⁷(17a) CM=MC: εἶπεν. SPAC: response. Jesus' second response: he answers their question about the tax to Caesar.
    ⁶TP⁴·⁴·¹·²·¹·⁸(17b) CM: ἐξεθαύμαζον. Narrator's report about the leaders' amazement.
⁴TP⁴·⁴·¹·³(18–27) EMr:(S)= CM: ἔρχονται Σαδδουκαῖοι. MC.Dia: ἐπηρώτων...ἔφη. SPAC: Question/Answer. The question about the resurrection.
  ⁵TP⁴·⁴·¹·³·¹(18–23) MC: ἐπηρώτων. SPAC: An assertion (ἔγραψεν) about Scripture (19), a narrative (20–22), a question based on the narrative (23a) and an assertion grounding the question (γάρ). The Sadducees' arrival and their narrative question to Jesus about Levirate marriage and the resurrection.

1 2 3 4

12:13 Καὶ ἀποστέλλουσιν πρὸς αὐτόν τινας τῶν Φαρισαίων καὶ τῶν Ἡρῳδιανῶν ἵνα αὐτὸν ἀγρεύσωσιν λόγῳ. 12:14 καὶ ἐλθόντες λέγουσιν αὐτῷ,
Διδάσκαλε, οἴδαμεν ὅτι ἀληθὴς εἶ καὶ οὐ μέλει σοι περὶ οὐδενός· οὐ γὰρ βλέπεις εἰς πρόσωπον ἀνθρώπων, ἀλλ' ἐπ' ἀληθείας τὴν ὁδὸν τοῦ θεοῦ διδάσκεις· ἔξεστιν δοῦναι κῆνσον Καίσαρι ἢ οὔ; δῶμεν ἢ μὴ δῶμεν;
12:15 ὁ δὲ εἰδὼς αὐτῶν τὴν ὑπόκρισιν εἶπεν αὐτοῖς, Τί με πειράζετε; φέρετέ μοι δηνάριον ἵνα ἴδω.
12:16 οἱ δὲ ἤνεγκαν. καὶ λέγει αὐτοῖς,
Τίνος ἡ εἰκὼν αὕτη καὶ ἡ ἐπιγραφή;
οἱ δὲ εἶπαν αὐτῷ,
Καίσαρος.
12:17 ὁ δὲ Ἰησοῦς εἶπεν αὐτοῖς,
Τὰ Καίσαρος ἀπόδοτε Καίσαρι καὶ τὰ τοῦ θεοῦ τῷ θεῷ.
καὶ ἐξεθαύμαζον ἐπ' αὐτῷ.
12:18 Καὶ ἔρχονται Σαδδουκαῖοι πρὸς αὐτόν, οἵτινες λέγουσιν
ἀνάστασιν μὴ εἶναι, (1, 2)
καὶ ἐπηρώτων αὐτὸν λέγοντες,
12:19 Διδάσκαλε, Μωϋσῆς ἔγραψεν ἡμῖν ὅτι (3 OT: 19) ἐάν τινος ἀδελφὸς ἀποθάνῃ καὶ καταλίπῃ γυναῖκα καὶ μὴ ἀφῇ τέκνον, ἵνα λάβῃ ὁ ἀδελφὸς αὐτοῦ τὴν γυναῖκα καὶ ἐξαναστήσῃ σπέρμα τῷ ἀδελφῷ αὐτοῦ.
12:20 ἑπτὰ ἀδελφοὶ ἦσαν· καὶ ὁ πρῶτος ἔλαβεν γυναῖκα καὶ ἀποθνῄσκων οὐκ ἀφῆκεν σπέρμα· 12:21 καὶ ὁ δεύτερος ἔλαβεν αὐτὴν καὶ ἀπέθανεν μὴ καταλιπὼν σπέρμα· καὶ ὁ τρίτος ὡσαύτως· 12:22 καὶ οἱ ἑπτὰ οὐκ ἀφῆκαν σπέρμα. ἔσχατον πάντων καὶ ἡ γυνὴ ἀπέθανεν. 12:23 ἐν τῇ ἀναστάσει [ὅταν ἀναστῶσιν] τίνος αὐτῶν ἔσται γυνή; οἱ γὰρ ἑπτὰ ἔσχον αὐτὴν γυναῖκα. (2 PN)

5TP4.4.1.3.2(24–27) MC: ἔφη. SN: γραφάς (for 26b); τοῦτο (for 25–27). SPAC: answer comprising a question (οὐ) expecting an affirmative response with three supporting assertions (25 [γάρ], 26, 27a) and conclusion (πολὺ πλανᾶσθε). Jesus answers in support of the reality of the resurrection.
 6TP4.4.1.3.2.1(24) SPAC: οὐ. Jesus questions them about their lack of understanding of the scriptures and God's power.
 6TP4.4.1.3.2.2(25) SPAC: ὅταν (assertion). CONJ: γάρ. Jesus describes the absence of marriage in the resurrection.
 6TP4.4.1.3.2.3(26) SPAC: περὶ δέ (26a: assertion) οὐκ ἀνέγνωτε (26b: question). Jesus asserts the reality of the resurrection and supports it with a question about a statement of God.
 6TP4.4.1.3.2.4(27) SPAC: two assertions. Jesus affirms the nature of God and reaffirms the Sadducees' error.
4TP4.4.1.4(28–34) SN: καλῶς ἀπεκρίθη (for 18–27). EMr:(S) προσελθὼν εἷς. CM: Ibid. MC.Dia: ἐπηρώτησεν…εἶπεν. The incident of the understanding Scribe.
 5TP4.4.1.4.1(28–31) CM=MC: ἐπηρώτησεν…ἀπεκρίθη. SPAC: Question/Answer. The scribe's question about the greatest commandment and Jesus' answer incorporating the two greatest commandments.
 5TP4.4.1.4.2(32–33) CM=MC: εἶπεν. SN:…ἐπ' ἀληθείας εἶπες (29–31). SPAC: assertion. The scribe responds to Jesus' answer by restating the two commandments and asserting their superiority to ritual sacrifice.
 5TP4.4.1.4.3(34a) CM=MC: εἶπεν. SN: νουνεχῶς ἀπεκρίθη. (for 32–33). SPAC: assertion. Jesus' approving response to the Scribe and his remark in vv. 32–33.
 5TP4.4.1.4.4(34b) CM: οὐδεὶς. SPAC: ἐπηρωτῆσαι. SN: Ibid. (for 11:27–12:34a). Narrator's comment about the absence of any further questions.

1 2 3 4

12:24 ἔφη αὐτοῖς ὁ Ἰησοῦς,
Οὐ διὰ τοῦτο πλανᾶσθε μὴ εἰδότες τὰς γραφὰς μηδὲ τὴν δύναμιν τοῦ θεοῦ; 12:25 ὅταν γὰρ ἐκ νεκρῶν ἀναστῶσιν οὔτε γαμοῦσιν οὔτε γαμίζονται, ἀλλ' εἰσὶν ὡς ἄγγελοι ἐν τοῖς οὐρανοῖς. 12:26 περὶ δὲ τῶν νεκρῶν ὅτι ἐγείρονται οὐκ ἀνέγνωτε ἐν τῇ βίβλῳ (2 PN) Μωϋσέως ἐπὶ τοῦ βάτου πῶς εἶπεν αὐτῷ ὁ θεὸς λέγων,
Ἐγὼ ὁ θεὸς Ἀβραὰμ καὶ [ὁ] θεὸς Ἰσαὰκ καὶ [ὁ] θεὸς Ἰακώβ; (3 OT)
12:27 οὐκ ἔστιν θεὸς νεκρῶν ἀλλὰ ζώντων· πολὺ πλανᾶσθε.
12:28 Καὶ προσελθὼν εἷς τῶν γραμματέων ἀκούσας αὐτῶν συζητούντων, ἰδὼν ὅτι καλῶς ἀπεκρίθη αὐτοῖς ἐπηρώτησεν αὐτόν,
Ποία ἐστὶν ἐντολὴ πρώτη πάντων;
12:29 ἀπεκρίθη ὁ Ἰησοῦς ὅτι
Πρώτη ἐστίν,
Ἄκουε, Ἰσραήλ, κύριος ὁ θεὸς ἡμῶν κύριος εἷς ἐστιν, 12:30 καὶ ἀγαπήσεις κύριον τὸν θεόν σου ἐξ ὅλης τῆς καρδίας σου καὶ ἐξ ὅλης τῆς ψυχῆς σου καὶ ἐξ ὅλης τῆς διανοίας σου καὶ ἐξ ὅλης τῆς ἰσχύος σου. (3 OT)
12:31 δευτέρα αὕτη,
Ἀγαπήσεις τὸν πλησίον σου ὡς σεαυτόν. (3 OT)
μείζων τούτων ἄλλη ἐντολὴ οὐκ ἔστιν.
12:32 καὶ εἶπεν αὐτῷ ὁ γραμματεύς,
Καλῶς, διδάσκαλε, ἐπ' ἀληθείας εἶπες ὅτι
εἷς ἐστιν καὶ οὐκ ἔστιν ἄλλος πλὴν αὐτοῦ· 12:33 καὶ τὸ ἀγαπᾶν αὐτὸν ἐξ ὅλης τῆς καρδίας καὶ ἐξ ὅλης τῆς συνέσεως καὶ ἐξ ὅλης τῆς ἰσχύος καὶ τὸ ἀγαπᾶν τὸν πλησίον ὡς ἑαυτὸν περισσότερόν ἐστιν πάντων τῶν ὁλοκαυτωμάτων καὶ θυσιῶν.
12:34 καὶ ὁ Ἰησοῦς ἰδὼν [αὐτὸν] ὅτι νουνεχῶς ἀπεκρίθη εἶπεν αὐτῷ,
Οὐ μακρὰν εἶ ἀπὸ τῆς βασιλείας τοῦ θεοῦ.

³TP⁴·⁴·²(35–44) SPAC: Questions & Teaching. Jesus raises questions in the temple and teaches.
⁴TP⁴·⁴·²·¹(35–37) CM: ᾽Ιησοῦς. Jesus asks about the Christ.
⁵TP⁴·⁴·²·¹·¹(35–37a) CM=MC.Mon: ἀποκριθείς...ἔλεγεν διδάσκων. SPAC: διδάσκων (teaching comprising: a question [35b], an assertion [36], an assertion [37a] and an accompanying question [37a]). Jesus asks about the scribal view of the Messiah and quotes David on the issue.
⁶TP⁴·⁴·²·¹·¹·¹(35) SPAC: πῶς. Jesus asks about the scribes' opinion of the Messiah being the Son of David.
⁶TP⁴·⁴·²·¹·¹·²(36) SPAC: assertion. Jesus quotes David's reference to the Lord's statement to "my Lord (or Master)."
⁶TP⁴·⁴·²·¹·¹·³(37) SPAC: assertion and question. Jesus questions how the Messiah can be both David's Lord (Master) and his Son.
⁵TP⁴·⁴·²·¹·²(37b) CM: ὄχλον. MC: ἤκουεν. The crowd's approving response to Jesus.
⁴TP⁴·⁴·²·²(38–40) SN: διδαχῇ. MC: ἔλεγεν, AA: βλέπετε. SPAC: Warning. Jesus' warning about certain scribes.
⁴TP⁴·⁴·²·³(41–44) EMr:(S) καθίσας...γαζοφυλακίου. Episode by the temple treasury.
⁵TP⁴·⁴·²·³·¹(41–42) CM: ὄχλος...πλούσιοι...χήρα. Narrator's report about Jesus' perception of the contributors.
⁵TP⁴·⁴·²·³·²(43–44) EMr:(S) προσκαλεσάμενος...μαθητάς. CM: Ibid. SPAC: ἀμήν. MC.Mon: εἶπεν. Jesus' comment to the disciples about who gave the most.

1 2 3 4
καὶ οὐδεὶς οὐκέτι ἐτόλμα αὐτὸν ἐπερωτῆσαι.
12:35 Καὶ ἀποκριθεὶς ὁ Ἰησοῦς ἔλεγεν διδάσκων ἐν τῷ ἱερῷ,
  Πῶς λέγουσιν οἱ γραμματεῖς ὅτι
    ὁ Χριστὸς υἱὸς Δαυίδ ἐστιν;
  12:36 αὐτὸς Δαυὶδ εἶπεν ἐν τῷ πνεύματι τῷ ἁγίῳ,
    Εἶπεν κύριος τῷ κυρίῳ μου, (3 OT)
    Κάθου ἐκ δεξιῶν μου, ἕως ἂν θῶ τοὺς ἐχθρούς σου ὑποκάτω τῶν ποδῶν σου. (4 SOT)
  12:37 αὐτὸς Δαυὶδ λέγει αὐτὸν
    κύριον, (2, 3)
    καὶ πόθεν αὐτοῦ ἐστιν υἱός;
καὶ [ὁ] πολὺς ὄχλος ἤκουεν αὐτοῦ ἡδέως.
12:38 Καὶ ἐν τῇ διδαχῇ αὐτοῦ ἔλεγεν,
  Βλέπετε ἀπὸ τῶν γραμματέων τῶν θελόντων ἐν στολαῖς περιπατεῖν καὶ ἀσπασμοὺς ἐν ταῖς ἀγοραῖς 12:39 καὶ πρωτοκαθεδρίας ἐν ταῖς συναγωγαῖς καὶ πρωτοκλισίας ἐν τοῖς δείπνοις, 12:40 οἱ κατεσθίοντες τὰς οἰκίας τῶν χηρῶν καὶ προφάσει μακρὰ προσευχόμενοι· οὗτοι λήμψονται περισσότερον κρίμα. (2 PN)
12:41 Καὶ καθίσας κατέναντι τοῦ γαζοφυλακίου ἐθεώρει πῶς ὁ ὄχλος βάλλει χαλκὸν εἰς τὸ γαζοφυλάκιον. καὶ πολλοὶ πλούσιοι ἔβαλλον πολλά· 12:42 καὶ ἐλθοῦσα μία χήρα πτωχὴ ἔβαλεν λεπτὰ δύο, ὅ ἐστιν κοδράντης. 12:43 καὶ προσκαλεσάμενος τοὺς μαθητὰς αὐτοῦ εἶπεν αὐτοῖς,
  Ἀμὴν λέγω ὑμῖν ὅτι
    ἡ χήρα αὕτη ἡ πτωχὴ πλεῖον πάντων ἔβαλεν τῶν βαλλόντων εἰς τὸ γαζοφυλάκιον· 12:44 πάντες γὰρ ἐκ τοῦ περισσεύοντος αὐτοῖς ἔβαλον, αὕτη δὲ ἐκ τῆς ὑστερήσεως αὐτῆς πάντα ὅσα εἶχεν ἔβαλεν ὅλον τὸν βίον αὐτῆς. (3 HS, PN)

²TP⁴·⁵(13:1–37) EMr:(S) ἐκ τοῦ ἱεροῦ (1), κατέναντι τοῦ ἱεροῦ (3). Discourses in view of the Temple.
³TP⁴·⁵·¹(1–2) EMr:(S) ἐκπορευομένου. CM: εἷς. MC.Dia: λέγει…εἶπεν. SPAC: assertion (1: ἴδε), question with related assertion (2: βλέπεις…οὐ μή). Jesus' prophecy of temple destruction in response to a disciple's comment.
³TP⁴·⁵·²(3–37) EMr:(S) ὄρος τῶν ἐλαιῶν…ἱεροῦ. CM: Πέτρος … ᾽Ανδρέας. MC.Dia: ἐπηρώτα. SPAC: Question/Answer. Jesus' response to the four's question about the time of the temple's end.
⁴TP⁴·⁵·²·¹(3–4) CM=MC: ἐπηρώτα. SPAC: Ibid. SN: ταῦτα & πάντα (for 13:2). The four ask Jesus about the end of the temple.
⁴TP⁴·⁵·²·²(5–37) CM=MC.Mon: λέγειν. SPAC: Ibid. (answer—an assertion about the future). Jesus' apocalyptic answer.
⁵TP⁴·⁵·²·²·¹(5–8) SN: ἀρχὴ ὠδίνων ταῦτα (for 5–8). SPAC: Ibid. (assertion). EMa:(T) Ibid. CM: τις. The beginning of the birth pangs.
⁶TP⁴·⁵·²·²·¹·¹(5–6) SPAC: βλέπετε (frame 2), ἐγώ (assertion in frame 3). Warning against people claiming to be Jesus.
⁶TP⁴·⁵·²·²·¹·²(7–8) SPAC: μὴ θροεῖσθε. EM:(T) ὅταν. Jesus tells the four not to be alarmed at wars and rumors of wars.

1 2 3 4

13:1 Καὶ ἐκπορευομένου αὐτοῦ ἐκ τοῦ ἱεροῦ λέγει αὐτῷ
εἷς τῶν μαθητῶν αὐτοῦ,
Διδάσκαλε, ἴδε ποταποὶ λίθοι καὶ ποταπαὶ οἰκοδομαί.
13:2 καὶ ὁ Ἰησοῦς εἶπεν αὐτῷ,
Βλέπεις ταύτας τὰς μεγάλας οἰκοδομάς; οὐ μὴ ἀφεθῇ
ὧδε λίθος ἐπὶ λίθον ὃς οὐ μὴ καταλυθῇ. (2 PN)
13:3 Καὶ καθημένου αὐτοῦ εἰς τὸ Ὄρος τῶν Ἐλαιῶν
κατέναντι τοῦ ἱεροῦ ἐπηρώτα αὐτὸν κατ' ἰδίαν Πέτρος
καὶ Ἰάκωβος καὶ Ἰωάννης καὶ Ἀνδρέας,
13:4 Εἰπὸν ἡμῖν πότε ταῦτα ἔσται καὶ τί τὸ σημεῖον
ὅταν μέλλῃ ταῦτα συντελεῖσθαι πάντα;
13:5 ὁ δὲ Ἰησοῦς ἤρξατο λέγειν αὐτοῖς, (2 PN: 5-37)
Βλέπετε μή τις ὑμᾶς πλανήσῃ· 13:6 πολλοὶ ἐλεύσονται
ἐπὶ τῷ ὀνόματί μου λέγοντες ὅτι
Ἐγώ εἰμι,
καὶ πολλοὺς πλανήσουσιν. 13:7 ὅταν δὲ ἀκούσητε
πολέμους καὶ ἀκοὰς πολέμων, μὴ θροεῖσθε· δεῖ
γενέσθαι, ἀλλ' οὔπω τὸ τέλος. 13:8 ἐγερθήσεται γὰρ
ἔθνος ἐπ' ἔθνος καὶ βασιλεία ἐπὶ βασιλείαν, ἔσονται
σεισμοὶ κατὰ τόπους, ἔσονται λιμοί· ἀρχὴ ὠδίνων
ταῦτα.

5TP4.5.2.2.2(9–13) EMa:(T) time before the τέλος (13). SPAC: βλέπετε. CM: the four disciples and persecutors. Jesus warns the four about enemies.
   6TP4.5.2.2.2.1(9–11) SPAC: μὴ προμεριμνᾶτε...λαλεῖτε. CM: παραδώσουσιν. Courts and trials for the four who will speak by the Holy Spirit.
   6TP4.5.2.2.2.2(12) CM: ἀδελφὸς...πατήρ...τέκνα. SPAC: assertion. Family members attack disciples.
   6TP4.5.2.2.2.3(13) CM: πάντων. SPAC: assertion and directive (13b). The four, hated by all, are exhorted to endure to the end.
5TP4.5.2.2.3(14–27) EMa:(T) ὅταν, ἐν ἐκείναις τ. ἡμέραις (14,17,19). The "those days" period including the abomination figure, tribulation, and the parousia after the tribulation.
   6TP4.5.2.2.3.1(14–23) EMr:(T) θλῖψις (as a part of ἐκείναις τ. ἡμέραις (17=19,24). The tribulation: Abomination figure in Judea; false Christs.
      7TP4.5.2.2.3.1.1(14–17) SPAC: φευγέτωσαν, νοείτω (frame 1), οὐαί (an expressive). EMr: (S) ὅπου οὐ δεῖ. CM: ἴδητε, βδέλυγμα. Prediction of an episode with an Abomination figure including a series of directives to the disciples to flee. Narrator intrudes with a directive to the reader.

1 2 3 4

13:9 βλέπετε δὲ ὑμεῖς ἑαυτούς· παραδώσουσιν ὑμᾶς εἰς συνέδρια καὶ εἰς συναγωγὰς δαρήσεσθε καὶ ἐπὶ ἡγεμόνων καὶ βασιλέων σταθήσεσθε ἕνεκεν ἐμοῦ εἰς μαρτύριον αὐτοῖς. 13:10 καὶ εἰς πάντα τὰ ἔθνη πρῶτον δεῖ κηρυχθῆναι τὸ εὐαγγέλιον. 13:11 καὶ ὅταν ἄγωσιν ὑμᾶς παραδιδόντες, μὴ προμεριμνᾶτε τί λαλήσητε, ἀλλ' ὃ ἐὰν δοθῇ ὑμῖν ἐν ἐκείνῃ τῇ ὥρᾳ τοῦτο λαλεῖτε· οὐ γάρ ἐστε ὑμεῖς οἱ λαλοῦντες ἀλλὰ τὸ πνεῦμα τὸ ἅγιον. 13:12 καὶ παραδώσει ἀδελφὸς ἀδελφὸν εἰς θάνατον καὶ πατὴρ τέκνον, καὶ ἐπαναστήσονται τέκνα ἐπὶ γονεῖς καὶ θανατώσουσιν αὐτούς· 13:13 καὶ ἔσεσθε μισούμενοι ὑπὸ πάντων διὰ τὸ ὄνομά μου. ὁ δὲ ὑπομείνας εἰς τέλος οὗτος σωθήσεται.
13:14 Ὅταν δὲ ἴδητε τὸ βδέλυγμα τῆς ἐρημώσεως ἑστηκότα ὅπου οὐ δεῖ,
ὁ ἀναγινώσκων νοείτω,
τότε οἱ ἐν τῇ Ἰουδαίᾳ φευγέτωσαν εἰς τὰ ὄρη, 13:15 ὁ [δὲ] ἐπὶ τοῦ δώματος μὴ καταβάτω μηδὲ εἰσελθάτω ἆραί τι ἐκ τῆς οἰκίας αὐτοῦ, 13:16 καὶ ὁ εἰς τὸν ἀγρὸν μὴ ἐπιστρεψάτω εἰς τὰ ὀπίσω ἆραι τὸ ἱμάτιον αὐτοῦ.
13:17 οὐαὶ δὲ ταῖς ἐν γαστρὶ ἐχούσαις καὶ ταῖς θηλαζούσαις ἐν ἐκείναις ταῖς ἡμέραις.

7TP4.5.2.2.3.1.2(18–20) EMr(T) αἱ ἡμέραι ἐκεῖναι θλῖψις. SN: θλῖψις. SPAC: προσεύχεσθε. CM: Ibid. & θεός, ἐκλεκτούς. The time of tribulation in reference to God and the elect.
7TP4.5.2.2.3.1.3(21–23) EMr:(T) τότε (Some point in the θλῖψις which is itself part of ἐκείναις τ. ἡμέραις). SPAC: μή...βλέπετε (frame 2); ἴδε (frame 3). SN: πάντα. MC: εἴπῃ. CM: τις, ὑμεῖς. Warning against false Christs and false prophets.
6TP4.5.2.2.3.2(24–27) EMr:(T) ἐν ἐκείναις...μετὰ τ. θλῖψιν τότε, τότε. CM: ὄψονται, ἐκλεκτούς, υἱόν. The return of the Son of Man in great power and glory after the tribulation in "those days."
5TP4.5.2.2.4(28–29) EMa:(T) ὅταν: The time of all the end events. SN: παραβολήν (for 28–29); οὕτως (for 28); ταῦτα (for 5–27). SPAC: μάθετε. A fig tree parable compares knowledge of the harvest based on natural signs with knowledge of the end time based on the preceding events (5–27).
5TP4.5.2.2.5(30–31) EMa:(T) μεχρὶς οὗ. SN: ταῦτα πάντα, λόγοι (for 5–27). SPAC: ᾿Αμήν. CM(P): γενεά. Jesus comments on his own words in relation to the four's generation.
5TP4.5.2.2.6(32) EMa:(T) ἡμέρας, ὥρας. CM: οὐδείς, ἄγγελοι, υἱός, πατήρ. SPAC: assertion. Only the Father knows the end time.
5TP4.5.2.2.7(33–37) EMa:(T) ὁ καιρός. SPAC: βλέπετε. Watching for the end.
6TP4.5.2.2.7.1(33) CONJ: γάρ. SPAC: βλέπετε & assertion (of the reason for watching). CM: the four. The time is unknown.

1 2 3 4

13:18 προσεύχεσθε δὲ ἵνα
μὴ γένηται χειμῶνος· (2, 3)
13:19 ἔσονται γὰρ αἱ ἡμέραι ἐκεῖναι θλῖψις οἵα οὐ γέγονεν τοιαύτη ἀπ' ἀρχῆς κτίσεως ἣν ἔκτισεν ὁ θεὸς ἕως τοῦ νῦν καὶ οὐ μὴ γένηται. 13:20 καὶ εἰ μὴ ἐκολόβωσεν κύριος τὰς ἡμέρας, οὐκ ἂν ἐσώθη πᾶσα σάρξ· ἀλλὰ διὰ τοὺς ἐκλεκτοὺς οὓς ἐξελέξατο ἐκολόβωσεν τὰς ἡμέρας. 13:21 καὶ τότε ἐάν τις ὑμῖν εἴπῃ,
  Ἴδε ὧδε ὁ Χριστός, Ἴδε ἐκεῖ,
μὴ πιστεύετε· 13:22 ἐγερθήσονται γὰρ ψευδόχριστοι καὶ ψευδοπροφῆται καὶ δώσουσιν σημεῖα καὶ τέρατα πρὸς τὸ ἀποπλανᾶν, εἰ δυνατόν, τοὺς ἐκλεκτούς. 13:23 ὑμεῖς δὲ βλέπετε· προείρηκα ὑμῖν πάντα.
13:24 Ἀλλὰ ἐν ἐκείναις ταῖς ἡμέραις μετὰ τὴν θλῖψιν ἐκείνην ὁ ἥλιος σκοτισθήσεται, καὶ ἡ σελήνη οὐ δώσει τὸ φέγγος αὐτῆς, 13:25 καὶ οἱ ἀστέρες ἔσονται ἐκ τοῦ οὐρανοῦ πίπτοντες, καὶ αἱ δυνάμεις αἱ ἐν τοῖς οὐρανοῖς σαλευθήσονται. 13:26 καὶ τότε ὄψονται τὸν υἱὸν τοῦ ἀνθρώπου ἐρχόμενον ἐν νεφέλαις μετὰ δυνάμεως πολλῆς καὶ δόξης. 13:27 καὶ τότε ἀποστελεῖ τοὺς ἀγγέλους καὶ ἐπισυνάξει τοὺς ἐκλεκτοὺς [αὐτοῦ] ἐκ τῶν τεσσάρων ἀνέμων ἀπ' ἄκρου γῆς ἕως ἄκρου οὐρανοῦ. 13:28 Ἀπὸ δὲ τῆς συκῆς μάθετε τὴν παραβολήν· ὅταν ἤδη ὁ κλάδος αὐτῆς ἁπαλὸς γένηται καὶ ἐκφύῃ τὰ φύλλα, γινώσκετε ὅτι ἐγγὺς τὸ θέρος ἐστίν· 13:29 οὕτως καὶ ὑμεῖς, ὅταν ἴδητε ταῦτα γινόμενα, γινώσκετε ὅτι ἐγγύς ἐστιν ἐπὶ θύραις.
13:30 ἀμὴν λέγω ὑμῖν ὅτι
  οὐ μὴ παρέλθῃ ἡ γενεὰ αὕτη μέχρις οὗ ταῦτα πάντα γένηται. 13:31 ὁ οὐρανὸς καὶ ἡ γῆ παρελεύσονται, οἱ δὲ λόγοι μου οὐ μὴ παρελεύσονται. (3 HS)
13:32 Περὶ δὲ τῆς ἡμέρας ἐκείνης ἢ τῆς ὥρας οὐδεὶς οἶδεν, οὐδὲ οἱ ἄγγελοι ἐν οὐρανῷ οὐδὲ ὁ υἱός, εἰ μὴ ὁ πατήρ.

⁶TP⁴·⁵·²·²·⁷·²(34) CM: ἄνθρωπος. CONJ: ὡς. SPAC: Ibid. (assertion of a simile). Simile of the departed lord and his domestic slaves.
⁶TP⁴·⁵·²·²·⁷·³(35–36) SPAC: γρηγορεῖτε. CM: ὁ κύριος & the four. CONJ: οὖν. Conclusion about the necessity for waking based on the insertion of the four into the parable as the slaves.
⁶TP⁴·⁵·²·²·⁷·⁴(37) CM: ὑμῖν, πᾶσιν. SPAC: γρηγορεῖτε. Directive addressed to the four and to all. Perhaps includes "all" with the CM of the four in Mk 13.
²TP⁴·⁶(14:1–11) EMr:(T) πάσχα...ἡμέρας. The period two days before the passover.
³TP⁴·⁶·¹(1–2) CM: ἀρχιερεῖς, γραμματεῖς. SPAC: μή (directive). The High Priests, etc. plot to kill Jesus.
³TP⁴·⁶·²(3–9) EMr:(S) Βηθανίᾳ. CM: γυνή, αὐτόν. The anointing of Jesus.
⁴TP⁴·⁶·²·¹(3) CM: γυνή. The woman anoints Jesus.
⁴TP⁴·⁶·²·²(4–9) CM: ἀγανακτοῦντες. MC.Dia: Ibid. & εἶπεν. SPAC: question and answer. Some disciples question the woman's deed and Jesus responds to them.
⁵TP⁴·⁶·²·²·¹(4–5a) CM, MC ἀγανακτοῦντες. SPAC: εἰς τί...γάρ (question and assertion grounding the question's expected answer [that the ointment was wasted]). Some disciples are angry about the woman's use of the nard.
⁵TP⁴·⁶·²·²·²(5b) CM: αὐτῇ. They are angry with the woman.
⁵TP⁴·⁶·²·²·³(6–9) CM, MC: εἶπεν. SPAC: ἄφετε...τί...καλόν (assertion)...7 γάρ (assertion grounding 6)...8 ὅ (assertion)...9 ἀμὴν λέγω. Jesus' response to the disciples.
³TP⁴·⁶·³(10–11) EMr:(S) ἀπῆλθεν πρός. CM: εἷς...ἀρχιερεῖς. Judas betrays Jesus.

1 2 3 4

13:33 βλέπετε, ἀγρυπνεῖτε· οὐκ οἴδατε γὰρ πότε ὁ καιρός ἐστιν. 13:34 ὡς ἄνθρωπος ἀπόδημος ἀφεὶς τὴν οἰκίαν αὐτοῦ καὶ δοὺς τοῖς δούλοις αὐτοῦ τὴν ἐξουσίαν ἑκάστῳ τὸ ἔργον αὐτοῦ καὶ τῷ θυρωρῷ ἐνετείλατο ἵνα
    γρηγορῇ. (2, 3)
13:35 γρηγορεῖτε οὖν· οὐκ οἴδατε γὰρ πότε ὁ κύριος τῆς οἰκίας ἔρχεται, ἢ ὀψὲ ἢ μεσονύκτιον ἢ ἀλεκτοροφωνίας ἢ πρωΐ, 13:36 μὴ ἐλθὼν ἐξαίφνης εὕρῃ ὑμᾶς καθεύδοντας. 13:37 ὃ δὲ ὑμῖν λέγω πᾶσιν λέγω,
    γρηγορεῖτε. (3 HS)
14:1 Ἦν δὲ τὸ πάσχα καὶ τὰ ἄζυμα μετὰ δύο ἡμέρας. καὶ ἐζήτουν οἱ ἀρχιερεῖς καὶ οἱ γραμματεῖς πῶς αὐτὸν ἐν δόλῳ κρατήσαντες ἀποκτείνωσιν· 14:2 ἔλεγον γάρ, Μὴ ἐν τῇ ἑορτῇ, μήποτε ἔσται θόρυβος τοῦ λαοῦ. 14:3 Καὶ ὄντος αὐτοῦ ἐν Βηθανίᾳ ἐν τῇ οἰκίᾳ Σίμωνος τοῦ λεπροῦ, κατακειμένου αὐτοῦ ἦλθεν γυνὴ ἔχουσα ἀλάβαστρον μύρου νάρδου πιστικῆς πολυτελοῦς, συντρίψασα τὴν ἀλάβαστρον κατέχεεν αὐτοῦ τῆς κεφαλῆς.
14:4 ἦσαν δέ τινες ἀγανακτοῦντες πρὸς ἑαυτούς, Εἰς τί ἡ ἀπώλεια αὕτη τοῦ μύρου γέγονεν; 14:5 ἠδύνατο γὰρ τοῦτο τὸ μύρον πραθῆναι ἐπάνω δηναρίων τριακοσίων καὶ δοθῆναι τοῖς πτωχοῖς· καὶ ἐνεβριμῶντο αὐτῇ. 14:6 ὁ δὲ Ἰησοῦς εἶπεν, Ἄφετε αὐτήν· τί αὐτῇ κόπους παρέχετε; καλὸν ἔργον ἠργάσατο ἐν ἐμοί. 14:7 πάντοτε γὰρ τοὺς πτωχοὺς ἔχετε μεθ' ἑαυτῶν καὶ ὅταν θέλητε δύνασθε αὐτοῖς εὖ ποιῆσαι, ἐμὲ δὲ οὐ πάντοτε ἔχετε. 14:8 ὃ ἔσχεν ἐποίησεν· προέλαβεν μυρίσαι τὸ σῶμά μου εἰς τὸν ἐνταφιασμόν. 14:9 ἀμὴν δὲ λέγω ὑμῖν, ὅπου ἐὰν κηρυχθῇ τὸ εὐαγγέλιον εἰς ὅλον τὸν κόσμον, καὶ ὃ ἐποίησεν αὕτη λαληθήσεται εἰς μνημόσυνον αὐτῆς. (3 PN, HS)
14:10 Καὶ Ἰούδας Ἰσκαριὼθ ὁ εἷς τῶν δώδεκα ἀπῆλθεν πρὸς τοὺς ἀρχιερεῖς ἵνα αὐτὸν παραδοῖ αὐτοῖς.

²TP⁴·⁷(12–72) EMr:(T) πρώτῃ ἡμέρᾳ τ. ἀζύμων. The first day of unleavened bread.
³TP⁴·⁷·¹(12–16) CM: αὐτῷ οἱ μαθηταί. Jesus has the two prepare the passover.
⁴TP⁴·⁷·¹·¹(12–15) EMr:(S) implied: outside the city (13). MC.Dia: λέγουσιν, λέγει. SPAC: Question/Answer & ὑπάγετε. Jesus directs the preparations.
⁵TP⁴·⁷·¹·¹·¹(12) CM, MC: λέγουσιν. SPAC: ποῦ. The disciples question Jesus about the place of the passover meal.
⁵TP⁴·⁷·¹·¹·²(13–15) CM,MC: λέγει. SPAC: ὑπάγετε...ἀκολουθήσατε...εἴπατε...δείξει (assertion)...ἑτοιμάσατε. Jesus sends the two to prepare the passover.
⁴TP⁴·⁷·¹·²(16) EMr:(S) ἐξῆλθον...πόλιν. CM: Ibid. The disciples go into the city to prepare the meal.
³TP⁴·⁷·²(17–25) EMr:(T) ὀψίας (S) ἔρχεται (κατάλυμα 14). CM: Ibid. & δώδεκα. In the upper room.
⁴TP⁴·⁷·²·¹(17–21) MC.Dia: εἶπεν, λέγειν, etc. Jesus foretells the betrayal of the Son of Man.
⁵TP⁴·⁷·²·¹·¹(17) CM: ἔρχεται...δώδεκα. They come to the place prepared for the passover.
⁵TP⁴·⁷·²·¹·²(18) CM, MC: εἶπεν. SPAC: ἀμὴν λέγω. Jesus asserts the existence of a betrayer.
⁵TP⁴·⁷·²·¹·³(19) CM, MC: λέγειν. SPAC: μήτι. The disciples ask "Is it I?"
⁵TP⁴·⁷·²·¹·⁴(20–21) CM, MC: εἶπεν. SPAC: εἷς (assertion)...γέγραπται (assertion) ...οὐαί (woe— an expressive) ...καλόν (assertion). Jesus responds with an assertion about his death and the destiny of the betrayer.
⁴TP⁴·⁷·²·²(22–25) EMr:(T) ἐσθιόντων αὐτῶν. MC.Mon: εἶπεν. SPAC: εὐλογήσας, εὐχαριστήσας, λάβετε. The Lord's supper.

A Linguistic Outline of Mark 267

1 2 3 4

14:11 οἱ δὲ ἀκούσαντες ἐχάρησαν καὶ ἐπηγγείλαντο αὐτῷ ἀργύριον δοῦναι. καὶ ἐζήτει πῶς αὐτὸν εὐκαίρως παραδοῖ.
14:12 Καὶ τῇ πρώτῃ ἡμέρᾳ τῶν ἀζύμων, ὅτε τὸ πάσχα ἔθυον, λέγουσιν αὐτῷ οἱ μαθηταὶ αὐτοῦ,
Ποῦ θέλεις ἀπελθόντες ἑτοιμάσωμεν ἵνα φάγῃς τὸ πάσχα;
14:13 καὶ ἀποστέλλει δύο τῶν μαθητῶν αὐτοῦ καὶ λέγει αὐτοῖς,
Ὑπάγετε εἰς τὴν πόλιν, καὶ ἀπαντήσει ὑμῖν ἄνθρωπος κεράμιον ὕδατος βαστάζων· ἀκολουθήσατε αὐτῷ 14:14 καὶ ὅπου ἐὰν εἰσέλθῃ εἴπατε τῷ οἰκοδεσπότῃ ὅτι (2 PN)
Ὁ διδάσκαλος λέγει,
Ποῦ ἐστιν τὸ κατάλυμά μου ὅπου τὸ πάσχα μετὰ τῶν μαθητῶν μου φάγω;
14:15 καὶ αὐτὸς ὑμῖν δείξει ἀνάγαιον μέγα ἐστρωμένον ἕτοιμον· καὶ ἐκεῖ ἑτοιμάσατε ἡμῖν (2 PN).
14:16 καὶ ἐξῆλθον οἱ μαθηταὶ καὶ ἦλθον εἰς τὴν πόλιν καὶ εὗρον καθὼς εἶπεν αὐτοῖς καὶ ἡτοίμασαν τὸ πάσχα. 14:17 Καὶ ὀψίας γενομένης ἔρχεται μετὰ τῶν δώδεκα. 14:18 καὶ ἀνακειμένων αὐτῶν καὶ ἐσθιόντων ὁ Ἰησοῦς εἶπεν,
Ἀμὴν λέγω ὑμῖν ὅτι
εἷς ἐξ ὑμῶν παραδώσει με ὁ ἐσθίων μετ' ἐμοῦ. (3 PN, HS)
14:19 ἤρξαντο λυπεῖσθαι καὶ λέγειν αὐτῷ εἷς κατὰ εἷς,
Μήτι ἐγώ;
14:20 ὁ δὲ εἶπεν αὐτοῖς,
Εἷς τῶν δώδεκα, ὁ ἐμβαπτόμενος μετ' ἐμοῦ εἰς τὸ τρύβλιον. 14:21 ὅτι
ὁ μὲν υἱὸς τοῦ ἀνθρώπου ὑπάγει (3 OT)
καθὼς γέγραπται περὶ αὐτοῦ, οὐαὶ δὲ τῷ ἀνθρώπῳ ἐκείνῳ δι' οὗ ὁ υἱὸς τοῦ ἀνθρώπου παραδίδοται καλὸν αὐτῷ εἰ οὐκ ἐγεννήθη ὁ ἄνθρωπος ἐκεῖνος.
14:22 Καὶ ἐσθιόντων αὐτῶν λαβὼν ἄρτον εὐλογήσας ἔκλασεν καὶ ἔδωκεν αὐτοῖς καὶ εἶπεν,

5TP4.7.2.2.1(22) CM, MC: εἶπεν. CM: ἄρτον. SPAC: εὐλογήσας...λάβετε...τοῦτο (assertion). Jesus commands them to eat the loaf.
5TP4.7.2.2.2(23) CM: ποτήριον. SPAC: εὐχαριστήσας. Jesus takes the cup and gives thanks.
5TP4.7.2.2.3(24–25) CM, MC: εἶπεν. SPAC: τοῦτο (assertion)...ἀμὴν λέγω. Jesus describes the nature of the cup and makes a claim about his drinking of the fruit of the vine in the kingdom.
3TP4.7.3(26–31) EMr:(S) ἐξῆλθον, ἐλαιῶν. CM: Ἰησοῦς, αὐτοῖς. MC.Poly: λέγει, ἔφη, ἐλάλει, ἔλεγον. Jesus foretells the disciples' falling away on the way to Gethsemane.
4TP4.7.3.1(26) CM: ἐξῆλθον. Jesus and the disciples come to the Mt. of Olives.
4TP4.7.3.2(27–28) CM, MC: λέγει. SPAC: ὅτι (assertion)...ὅτι γέγραπται (assertion as a basis of the first one)...ἀλλά (assertion). Jesus predicts the falling away of the disciples, bases it in scripture, and then contrasts that with a future relationship of himself and the disciples in Galilee.
4TP4.7.3.3(29) CM, MC: ἔφη. SPAC: οὐκ (denial of an assertion). Peter denies that he will fall away.
4TP4.7.3.4(30) CM, MC: λέγει. SPAC: ἀμὴν λέγω. Jesus predicts Peter's threefold denial of him.
4TP4.7.3.5(31a) CM, MC: ἐλάλει. SPAC: οὐ μή (denial). Peter denies that he will ever deny Jesus.
4TP4.7.3.6(31b) CM, MC: ἔλεγον. SPAC: denial. SN: ὡσαύτως (for 31a). All the disciples speak as Peter did.
3TP4.7.4(32–52) EMr:(S) χωρίον. Γηθσημανί. The Gethsemane episode. Jesus' prayer and arrest.
4TP4.7.4.1(32–42) CM: μαθηταῖς αὐτοῦ. The prayer in proximity to the disciples.
5TP4.7.4.1.1(32) EMr:(S) ὧδε. MC: λέγει. SPAC: καθίσατε. The disciples are commanded to sit while Jesus prays.

1 2 3 4

Λάβετε, τοῦτό ἐστιν τὸ σῶμά μου.
14:23 καὶ λαβὼν ποτήριον εὐχαριστήσας ἔδωκεν αὐτοῖς, καὶ ἔπιον ἐξ αὐτοῦ πάντες. 14:24 καὶ εἶπεν αὐτοῖς, Τοῦτό ἐστιν τὸ αἷμά μου τῆς διαθήκης τὸ ἐκχυννόμενον ὑπὲρ πολλῶν. 14:25 ἀμὴν λέγω ὑμῖν ὅτι οὐκέτι οὐ μὴ πίω ἐκ τοῦ γενήματος τῆς ἀμπέλου ἕως τῆς ἡμέρας ἐκείνης ὅταν αὐτὸ πίνω καινὸν ἐν τῇ βασιλείᾳ τοῦ θεοῦ. (3 PN, HS)
14:26 Καὶ ὑμνήσαντες ἐξῆλθον εἰς τὸ Ὄρος τῶν Ἐλαιῶν.
14:27 Καὶ λέγει αὐτοῖς ὁ Ἰησοῦς ὅτι
Πάντες σκανδαλισθήσεσθε, ὅτι γέγραπται,
Πατάξω τὸν ποιμένα, καὶ τὰ πρόβατα διασκορπισθήσονται. (3 OT)
14:28 ἀλλὰ μετὰ τὸ ἐγερθῆναί με προάξω ὑμᾶς εἰς τὴν Γαλιλαίαν. (2 PN: 27-28)
14:29 ὁ δὲ Πέτρος ἔφη αὐτῷ,
Εἰ καὶ πάντες σκανδαλισθήσονται, ἀλλ᾽ οὐκ ἐγώ.
14:30 καὶ λέγει αὐτῷ ὁ Ἰησοῦς,
Ἀμὴν λέγω σοι ὅτι
σὺ σήμερον ταύτῃ τῇ νυκτὶ πρὶν ἢ δὶς ἀλέκτορα φωνῆσαι τρίς με ἀπαρνήσῃ. (3 HS)
14:31 ὁ δὲ ἐκπερισσῶς ἐλάλει,
Ἐὰν δέῃ με συναποθανεῖν σοι, οὐ μή σε ἀπαρνήσομαι. ὡσαύτως δὲ καὶ πάντες ἔλεγον.
14:32 Καὶ ἔρχονται εἰς χωρίον οὗ τὸ ὄνομα Γεθσημανί καὶ λέγει τοῖς μαθηταῖς αὐτοῦ,
Καθίσατε ὧδε ἕως προσεύξωμαι.
14:33 καὶ παραλαμβάνει τὸν Πέτρον καὶ [τὸν] Ἰάκωβον καὶ [τὸν] Ἰωάννην μετ᾽ αὐτοῦ καὶ ἤρξατο ἐκθαμβεῖσθαι καὶ ἀδημονεῖν 14:34 καὶ λέγει αὐτοῖς,
Περίλυπός ἐστιν ἡ ψυχή μου ἕως θανάτου· μείνατε ὧδε καὶ γρηγορεῖτε.
14:35 καὶ προελθὼν μικρὸν ἔπιπτεν ἐπὶ τῆς γῆς καὶ προσηύχετο ἵνα
εἰ δυνατόν ἐστιν παρέλθῃ ἀπ᾽ αὐτοῦ ἡ ὥρα, (1, 2)

5TP4.7.4.1.2(33–42) EMr:(S) προσλάμβανει τ. Πέτρον...'Ιωάννην. CM: Ibid. Jesus and the three in the place of prayer.
  6TP4.7.4.1.2.1(33–34) EMr:(S) μείνατε ὧδε. SPAC: Ibid. and assertion (περίλυπος). Jesus leaves the three.
  6TP4.7.4.1.2.2(35–36) EMr:(S) προελθών. MC: προσηύχατο. SPAC: Ibid. Jesus' prayer.
  6TP4.7.4.1.2.3(37–38) EMr:(S) ἔρχεται. SPAC: two questions, γρηγορεῖτε and an assertion (38b). Jesus finds the three sleeping.
  6TP4.7.4.1.2.4(39) EMr:(S) ἀπελθών. Jesus prays again.
  6TP4.7.4.1.2.5(40) EMr:(S) ἐλθών. Jesus finds the three asleep again.
  6TP4.7.4.1.2.6(41–42) EMr:(S) ἔρχεται. MC: λέγει. SPAC: Ibid. (assertion) & ἄγωμεν. Jesus finds the three asleep the third time and describes the approach of his betrayer.
4TP4.7.4.2(43–52) CM: 'Ιούδας...ὄχλος. The betrayer and crowd arrive and arrest Jesus.
  5TP4.7.4.2.1(43–44) CM: 'Ιούδας, ὄχλος. MC: λέγων. SPAC: Ibid. (assertion and directive [κρατήσατε]). The crowd's arrival with Judas.
  5TP4.7.4.2.2(45) CM=MC: λέγει. SPAC: Greeting/assertion. Judas identifies Jesus.
  5TP4.7.4.2.3(46–47) CM: οἱ δέ, εἷς. The arrest and wounding of the slave.
  5TP4.7.4.2.4(48–49) MC.Mon: εἶπεν. SPAC: Question, assertion, and directive: πληρωθῶσιν. Jesus criticizes the arresters' actions.

1 2 3 4

14:36 καὶ ἔλεγεν,
Αββα ὁ πατήρ, πάντα δυνατά σοι· παρένεγκε τὸ ποτήριον τοῦτο ἀπ' ἐμοῦ· ἀλλ' οὐ τί ἐγὼ θέλω ἀλλὰ τί σύ.
14:37 καὶ ἔρχεται καὶ εὑρίσκει αὐτοὺς καθεύδοντας, καὶ λέγει τῷ Πέτρῳ,
Σίμων, καθεύδεις; οὐκ ἴσχυσας μίαν ὥραν γρηγορῆσαι; 14:38 γρηγορεῖτε καὶ προσεύχεσθε, ἵνα μὴ ἔλθητε εἰς πειρασμόν· τὸ μὲν πνεῦμα πρόθυμον ἡ δὲ σὰρξ ἀσθενής.
14:39 καὶ πάλιν ἀπελθὼν προσηύξατο τὸν αὐτὸν λόγον εἰπών. 14:40 καὶ πάλιν ἐλθὼν εὗρεν αὐτοὺς καθεύδοντας, ἦσαν γὰρ αὐτῶν οἱ ὀφθαλμοὶ καταβαρυνόμενοι καὶ οὐκ ᾔδεισαν τί ἀποκριθῶσιν αὐτῷ. 14:41 καὶ ἔρχεται τὸ τρίτον καὶ λέγει αὐτοῖς,
Καθεύδετε τὸ λοιπὸν καὶ ἀναπαύεσθε· ἀπέχει· ἦλθεν ἡ ὥρα, ἰδοὺ παραδίδοται ὁ υἱὸς τοῦ ἀνθρώπου εἰς τὰς χεῖρας τῶν ἁμαρτωλῶν. 14:42 ἐγείρεσθε ἄγωμεν· ἰδοὺ ὁ παραδιδούς με ἤγγικεν.
14:43 Καὶ εὐθὺς ἔτι αὐτοῦ λαλοῦντος παραγίνεται Ἰούδας εἷς τῶν δώδεκα καὶ μετ' αὐτοῦ ὄχλος μετὰ μαχαιρῶν καὶ ξύλων παρὰ τῶν ἀρχιερέων καὶ τῶν γραμματέων καὶ τῶν πρεσβυτέρων. 14:44 δεδώκει δὲ ὁ παραδιδοὺς αὐτὸν σύσσημον αὐτοῖς λέγων,
Ὃν ἂν φιλήσω αὐτός ἐστιν, κρατήσατε αὐτὸν καὶ ἀπάγετε ἀσφαλῶς.
14:45 καὶ ἐλθὼν εὐθὺς προσελθὼν αὐτῷ λέγει,
Ραββί,
καὶ κατεφίλησεν αὐτόν· 14:46 οἱ δὲ ἐπέβαλον τὰς χεῖρας αὐτῷ καὶ ἐκράτησαν αὐτόν. 14:47 εἷς δέ [τις] τῶν παρεστηκότων σπασάμενος τὴν μάχαιραν ἔπαισεν τὸν δοῦλον τοῦ ἀρχιερέως καὶ ἀφεῖλεν αὐτοῦ τὸ ὠτάριον. 14:48 καὶ ἀποκριθεὶς ὁ Ἰησοῦς εἶπεν αὐτοῖς,
Ὡς ἐπὶ λῃστὴν ἐξήλθατε μετὰ μαχαιρῶν καὶ ξύλων συλλαβεῖν με;

5TP4.7.4.2.5(50–52) CM: πάντες, νεανίσκος. The disciples and the naked young man flee.
3TP4.7.5(53–72) EMr:(S) πρός. The trial and denial.
4TP4.7.5.1(53) CM: Ἰησοῦν, ἀρχιερέα...γραμματεῖς. Jesus is brought to the High Priest.
4TP4.7.5.2(54) EMr:(S) αὐλήν. CM: Πέτρος. Peter follows Jesus into the court of the High Priest.
4TP4.7.5.3(55–65) CM: ἀρχιερεῖς...Ἰησοῦν. The trial of Jesus.
   5TP4.7.5.3.1(55) CM: συνέδριον. The Sanhedrin seeks witnesses against Jesus.
   5TP4.7.5.3.2(56) CM: πολλοί. SPAC: ἐψευδομαρτύρουν. The false witnesses give conflicting testimony.
   5TP4.7.5.3.3(57–58). CM: τινες. MC.Mon: λέγοντες. SPAC: ἐψευδομαρτύρουν (accusation). Some of the false witnesses' testimony.
   5TP4.7.5.3.4(59) CM: αὐτῶν. The narrator comments on their conflicting testimony.
   5TP4.7.5.3.5(60–62) CM: ἀρχιερεύς, Ἰησοῦν. MC.Dia: ἐπηρώτησεν, ἀπεκρίνατο. SPAC: Question/Question/Answer. The High Priest elicits Jesus' statement of his identity.
      6TP4.7.5.3.5.1(60) CM, MC: λέγων. SPAC: τί...καταμαρτυροῦσιν. The High Priest questions Jesus about the witness against him.
      6TP4.7.5.3.5.2(61a) CM: οὐκ ἀπεκρίνατο. Jesus does not answer.
      6TP4.7.5.3.5.3(61b) CM, MC: ἐπηρώτα. SPAC: Ibid. The High Priest asks Jesus if he is the Christ, the Son of the Blessed One.
      6TP4.7.5.3.5.4(62) CM, MC: εἶπεν. SPAC: assertions. Jesus answers affirmatively and asserts that they will see the Son of Man.

1 2 3 4

14:49 καθ' ἡμέραν ἤμην πρὸς ὑμᾶς ἐν τῷ ἱερῷ διδάσκων καὶ οὐκ ἐκρατήσατέ με· ἀλλ' ἵνα πληρωθῶσιν αἱ γραφαί. 14:50 καὶ ἀφέντες αὐτὸν ἔφυγον πάντες. 14:51 Καὶ νεανίσκος τις συνηκολούθει αὐτῷ περιβεβλημένος σινδόνα ἐπὶ γυμνοῦ, καὶ κρατοῦσιν αὐτόν· 14:52 ὁ δὲ καταλιπὼν τὴν σινδόνα γυμνὸς ἔφυγεν. 14:53 Καὶ ἀπήγαγον τὸν Ἰησοῦν πρὸς τὸν ἀρχιερέα, καὶ συνέρχονται πάντες οἱ ἀρχιερεῖς καὶ οἱ πρεσβύτεροι καὶ οἱ γραμματεῖς. 14:54 καὶ ὁ Πέτρος ἀπὸ μακρόθεν ἠκολούθησεν αὐτῷ ἕως ἔσω εἰς τὴν αὐλὴν τοῦ ἀρχιερέως καὶ ἦν συγκαθήμενος μετὰ τῶν ὑπηρετῶν καὶ θερμαινόμενος πρὸς τὸ φῶς. 14:55 οἱ δὲ ἀρχιερεῖς καὶ ὅλον τὸ συνέδριον ἐζήτουν κατὰ τοῦ Ἰησοῦ μαρτυρίαν εἰς τὸ θανατῶσαι αὐτόν, καὶ οὐχ ηὕρισκον· 14:56 πολλοὶ γὰρ ἐψευδομαρτύρουν κατ' αὐτοῦ, καὶ ἴσαι αἱ μαρτυρίαι οὐκ ἦσαν. 14:57 καί τινες ἀναστάντες ἐψευδομαρτύρουν κατ' αὐτοῦ λέγοντες 14:58 ὅτι
 Ἡμεῖς ἠκούσαμεν αὐτοῦ λέγοντος ὅτι
  Ἐγὼ καταλύσω τὸν ναὸν τοῦτον τὸν χειροποίητον καὶ διὰ τριῶν ἡμερῶν ἄλλον ἀχειροποίητον οἰκοδομήσω (3 PN)
14:59 καὶ οὐδὲ οὕτως ἴση ἦν ἡ μαρτυρία αὐτῶν. 14:60 καὶ ἀναστὰς ὁ ἀρχιερεὺς εἰς μέσον ἐπηρώτησεν τὸν Ἰησοῦν λέγων,
 Οὐκ ἀποκρίνη οὐδέν τί οὗτοί σου καταμαρτυροῦσιν;
14:61 ὁ δὲ ἐσιώπα καὶ οὐκ ἀπεκρίνατο οὐδέν. πάλιν ὁ ἀρχιερεὺς ἐπηρώτα αὐτὸν καὶ λέγει αὐτῷ,
 Σὺ εἶ ὁ Χριστὸς ὁ υἱὸς τοῦ εὐλογητοῦ;
14:62 ὁ δὲ Ἰησοῦς εἶπεν,
 Ἐγώ εἰμι, καὶ ὄψεσθε τὸν υἱὸν τοῦ ἀνθρώπου ἐκ δεξιῶν καθήμενον τῆς δυνάμεως καὶ ἐρχόμενον μετὰ τῶν νεφελῶν τοῦ οὐρανοῦ. (2 PN)

5TP4.7.5.3.6(63–64) CM=MC: λέγει, ὑμῖν. SPAC: questions.
The High Priest speaks to the Sanhedrin and elicits the
condemnation of Jesus.
5TP4.7.5.3.7(65) CM: τινες, ὑπηρέται. SPAC: προφήτευσον.
Certain people including guards mock and beat Jesus.
4TP4.7.5.4(66–72) CM: Πέτρου. Peter denies Jesus.
  5TP4.7.5.4.1(66–68a) EMr:(S) κάτω, αὐλῇ. CM: μία. MC.Dia:
λέγει, ἠρνήσατο. SPAC: Ibid. Peter's first denial.
    6TP4.7.5.4.1.1(66–67) CM: Πέτρου...μία. MC: λέγει.
SPAC: accusation. The High Priest's maidservant
claims Peter was with Jesus.
    6TP4.7.5.4.1.2(68a) CM, MC: λέγων. SPAC: ἠρνήσατο.
Peter denies the accusation.
  5TP4.7.5.4.2(68b–72) EMr:(S) προαύλιον. CM: ἐξῆλθεν. Peter
in the forecourt: his denials.
    6TP4.7.5.4.2.1(68b) CM: ἐξῆλθεν. Peter withdraws into
the forecourt.
    6TP4.7.5.4.2.2(69–70a) CM: παιδίσκη, (P): παρεστῶσιν.
MC.Dia: λέγειν, ἠρνεῖτο. The maidservant's second
accusation and Peter's second denial.
      7TP4.7.5.4.2.2.1(69) CM: παιδίσκη. MC: λέγειν.
SPAC: accusation (an assertive). The maidservant
accuses Peter again.
      7TP4.7.5.4.2.2.2(70a) CM, MC, SPAC: ἠρνεῖτο. Peter
denies Jesus again.
    6TP4.7.5.4.2.3(70b–71) EMr:(T) μικρόν. CM: παρεστῶτες.
MC.Dia: ἔλεγον...ἀναθηματίζειν. SPAC: Ibid. The
bystanders accuse Peter, and he denies Jesus on oath.
      7TP4.7.5.4.2.3.1(70b) CM, MC: ἔλεγον. SPAC:
accusation and supporting assertion (γάρ). The
bystanders' charge.
      7TP4.7.5.4.2.3.2(71) CM, MC, SPAC: ἀναθεματίζειν.
Peter denies Jesus on oath.
    6TP4.7.5.4.2.4(72) EMr:(T) εὐθύς. CM: ἀλέκτωρ, Πέτρος.
SPAC: assertion (εἶπεν). Peter remembers Jesus'
prediction at the second cockcrow.

1 2 3 4

14:63 ὁ δὲ ἀρχιερεὺς διαρρήξας τοὺς χιτῶνας αὐτοῦ λέγει,
Τί ἔτι χρείαν ἔχομεν μαρτύρων; 14:64 ἠκούσατε τῆς βλασφημίας· τί ὑμῖν φαίνεται;
οἱ δὲ πάντες κατέκριναν αὐτὸν ἔνοχον εἶναι θανάτου.
14:65 Καὶ ἤρξαντό τινες ἐμπτύειν αὐτῷ καὶ περικαλύπτειν αὐτοῦ τὸ πρόσωπον καὶ κολαφίζειν αὐτὸν καὶ λέγειν αὐτῷ,
Προφήτευσον,
καὶ οἱ ὑπηρέται ῥαπίσμασιν αὐτὸν ἔλαβον.
14:66 Καὶ ὄντος τοῦ Πέτρου κάτω ἐν τῇ αὐλῇ ἔρχεται μία τῶν παιδισκῶν τοῦ ἀρχιερέως 14:67 καὶ ἰδοῦσα τὸν Πέτρον θερμαινόμενον ἐμβλέψασα αὐτῷ λέγει,
Καὶ σὺ μετὰ τοῦ Ναζαρηνοῦ ἦσθα τοῦ Ἰησοῦ.
14:68 ὁ δὲ ἠρνήσατο λέγων,
Οὔτε οἶδα οὔτε ἐπίσταμαι σὺ τί λέγεις.
καὶ ἐξῆλθεν ἔξω εἰς τὸ προαύλιον [καὶ ἀλέκτωρ ἐφώνησεν]. 14:69 καὶ ἡ παιδίσκη ἰδοῦσα αὐτὸν ἤρξατο πάλιν λέγειν τοῖς παρεστῶσιν ὅτι
Οὗτος ἐξ αὐτῶν ἐστιν.
14:70 ὁ δὲ πάλιν ἠρνεῖτο. καὶ μετὰ μικρὸν πάλιν οἱ παρεστῶτες ἔλεγον τῷ Πέτρῳ,
Ἀληθῶς ἐξ αὐτῶν εἶ, καὶ γὰρ Γαλιλαῖος εἶ.
14:71 ὁ δὲ ἤρξατο ἀναθεματίζειν καὶ ὀμνύναι ὅτι
Οὐκ οἶδα τὸν ἄνθρωπον τοῦτον ὃν λέγετε.
14:72 καὶ εὐθὺς ἐκ δευτέρου ἀλέκτωρ ἐφώνησεν. καὶ ἀνεμνήσθη ὁ Πέτρος τὸ ῥῆμα ὡς εἶπεν αὐτῷ ὁ Ἰησοῦς ὅτι
Πρὶν ἀλέκτορα φωνῆσαι δὶς τρίς με ἀπαρνήσῃ·
καὶ ἐπιβαλὼν ἔκλαιεν.

²TP⁴·⁸(15:1–47) EMr:(T) εὐθὺς πρωΐ...προσάββατον (42). The day before the Sabbath. Jesus' condemnation and death.
³TP⁴·⁸·¹(1) EMr:(S) ἀπήνεγκαν. CM: ἀρχιερεῖς...Πιλάτῳ. Jesus taken to Pilate by the Sanhedrin.
³TP⁴·⁸·²(2–15) EMr:(S) Implied: outside the αὐλά (16). CM: Πιλᾶτος. Jesus tried before Pilate.
⁴TP⁴·⁸·²·¹(2–5) CM: αὐτόν, Πιλᾶτος, ἀρχιερεῖς. MC.Dia: ἐπηρώτησεν, λέγει, κατηγόρουν, ἐπηρώτα. SPAC: Ibid. Pilate questions Jesus, receives an answer, and hears accusations against him.
⁵TP⁴·⁸·²·¹·¹(2a) CM, MC: ἐπηρώτησεν. SPAC: Ibid. Pilate asks Jesus if he is King of the Jews.
⁵TP⁴·⁸·²·¹·²(2b) CM, MC: SPAC: answer. Jesus answers.
⁵TP⁴·⁸·²·¹·³(3) CM: κατηγόρουν. SPAC: Ibid. The chief priests bring accusations against Jesus.
⁵TP⁴·⁸·²·¹·⁴(4) CM, MC: SPAC: question & assertion. Pilate again questions Jesus and remarks on the accusers.
⁵TP⁴·⁸·²·¹·⁵(5) CM: ἀπεκρίθη. Jesus is silent.
⁴TP⁴·⁸·²·²(6–15) CM: ἀπέλυεν, (P) Βαραββᾶς, τὸν Βασιλέα. Pilate and the crowd decide Jesus' fate.
⁵TP⁴·⁸·²·²·¹(6–7) CM(P): αὐτοῖς. Pilate's custom and his custody of Barabbas.
⁵TP⁴·⁸·²·²·²(8–9) EMr:(S) ἀναβάς. CM: ὄχλος. MC.Dia: αἰτεῖσθαι, ἀπεκρίθη. SPAC: Ibid. Pilate's first conversation with the crowd. His question is not answered immediately.
⁵TP⁴·⁸·²·²·³(10–11) CM: ἀρχιερεῖς. CONJ: γάρ. Narrator's remark about Pilate's knowledge of the High Priests and the priests' action with the crowd.
⁵TP⁴·⁸·²·²·⁴(12–14) CM, MC.Dia: ἔλεγεν, ἔκραξαν, ἔλεγεν. SPAC: 2 Questions/Answers. The crowd demands Jesus' death by crucifixion.
⁶TP⁴·⁸·²·²·⁴·¹(12) CM, MC: ἔλεγεν. SPAC: τί. Pilate questions the crowd about the "King of the Jews."

1 2 3 4

15:1 Καὶ εὐθὺς πρωῒ συμβούλιον ποιήσαντες οἱ ἀρχιερεῖς μετὰ τῶν πρεσβυτέρων καὶ γραμματέων καὶ ὅλον τὸ συνέδριον, δήσαντες τὸν Ἰησοῦν ἀπήνεγκαν καὶ παρέδωκαν Πιλάτῳ. 15:2 καὶ ἐπηρώτησεν αὐτὸν ὁ Πιλᾶτος,
 Σὺ εἶ ὁ βασιλεὺς τῶν Ἰουδαίων;
ὁ δὲ ἀποκριθεὶς αὐτῷ λέγει,
 Σὺ λέγεις.
15:3 καὶ κατηγόρουν αὐτοῦ οἱ ἀρχιερεῖς πολλά. 15:4 ὁ δὲ Πιλᾶτος πάλιν ἐπηρώτα αὐτὸν λέγων,
 Οὐκ ἀποκρίνῃ οὐδέν; ἴδε πόσα σου κατηγοροῦσιν.
15:5 ὁ δὲ Ἰησοῦς οὐκέτι οὐδὲν ἀπεκρίθη, ὥστε θαυμάζειν τὸν Πιλᾶτον.
15:6 Κατὰ δὲ ἑορτὴν ἀπέλυεν αὐτοῖς ἕνα δέσμιον ὃν παρῃτοῦντο. 15:7 ἦν δὲ ὁ λεγόμενος Βαραββᾶς μετὰ τῶν στασιαστῶν δεδεμένος οἵτινες ἐν τῇ στάσει φόνον πεποιήκεισαν. 15:8 καὶ ἀναβὰς ὁ ὄχλος ἤρξατο αἰτεῖσθαι καθὼς ἐποίει αὐτοῖς. 15:9 ὁ δὲ Πιλᾶτος ἀπεκρίθη αὐτοῖς λέγων,
 Θέλετε ἀπολύσω ὑμῖν τὸν βασιλέα τῶν Ἰουδαίων;
15:10 ἐγίνωσκεν γὰρ ὅτι διὰ φθόνον παραδεδώκεισαν αὐτὸν οἱ ἀρχιερεῖς. 15:11 οἱ δὲ ἀρχιερεῖς ἀνέσεισαν τὸν ὄχλον ἵνα μᾶλλον τὸν Βαραββᾶν ἀπολύσῃ αὐτοῖς. 15:12 ὁ δὲ Πιλᾶτος πάλιν ἀποκριθεὶς ἔλεγεν αὐτοῖς,
 Τί οὖν [θέλετε] ποιήσω [ὃν λέγετε] τὸν βασιλέα τῶν Ἰουδαίων;

6TP4.8.2.2.4.2(13) CM, MC: ἔκραξαν. SPAC: answer & σταύρωσον (directive). The crowd's answer: crucify him.
6TP4.8.2.2.4.3(14a) CM, MC: ἔλεγεν. SPAC: τί. Pilate questions them about Jesus' guilt.
6TP4.8.2.2.4.4(14b) CM, MC: ἔκραξαν. SPAC: answer & σταύρωσον. The crowd again demands Jesus' crucifixion.
5TP4.8.2.2.5(15) CM: Πιλᾶτος, Βαραββᾶν, Ἰησοῦν. Pilate releases Barabbas and hands Jesus over to be crucified.
3TP4.8.3(16–20a) EMr:(S) ἔσω τ. αὐλῆς. CM: στρατιῶται, σπεῖραν, (P): αὐτόν. SPAC: ἀσπάζεσθαι. The soldiers mock Jesus.
3TP4.8.4(20b–21) EMr:(S) ἐξάγουσιν. CM: Ibid. (P) αὐτόν, Σίμωνα. Jesus taken to be crucified with Simon of Cyrene carrying the cross.
3TP4.8.5(22–41) EMr:(S) Γολγοθάν. On Golgotha.
4TP4.8.5.1(22–23) EMr:(T) Implied: before the third hour. The time immediately before the third hour: Jesus given myrrh wine.
4TP4.8.5.2(24–32) EMr:(T) ὥρᾳ τρίτῃ. The crucifixion in the third hour and following (until the sixth hour).
5TP4.8.5.2.1(24–27) CM: σταυροῦσιν, λῃστάς. SPAC: βασιλεύς (written assertion). The soldiers and the crucified ones.
5TP4.8.5.2.2(29–30) CM: παραπορευόμενοι. SPAC: οὐά (an expressive); σῶσον. The revilers challenge Jesus to save himself.

1 2 3 4

15:13 οἱ δὲ πάλιν ἔκραξαν,
Σταύρωσον αὐτόν.
15:14 ὁ δὲ Πιλᾶτος ἔλεγεν αὐτοῖς,
Τί γὰρ ἐποίησεν κακόν;
οἱ δὲ περισσῶς ἔκραξαν,
Σταύρωσον αὐτόν.
15:15 ὁ δὲ Πιλᾶτος βουλόμενος τῷ ὄχλῳ τὸ ἱκανὸν ποιῆσαι ἀπέλυσεν αὐτοῖς τὸν Βαραββᾶν, καὶ παρέδωκεν τὸν Ἰησοῦν φραγελλώσας ἵνα σταυρωθῇ.
15:16 Οἱ δὲ στρατιῶται ἀπήγαγον αὐτὸν ἔσω τῆς αὐλῆς, ὅ ἐστιν πραιτώριον, καὶ συγκαλοῦσιν ὅλην τὴν σπεῖραν.
15:17 καὶ ἐνδιδύσκουσιν αὐτὸν πορφύραν καὶ περιτιθέασιν αὐτῷ πλέξαντες ἀκάνθινον στέφανον· 15:18 καὶ ἤρξαντο ἀσπάζεσθαι αὐτόν,
Χαῖρε, βασιλεῦ τῶν Ἰουδαίων·
15:19 καὶ ἔτυπτον αὐτοῦ τὴν κεφαλὴν καλάμῳ καὶ ἐνέπτυον αὐτῷ καὶ τιθέντες τὰ γόνατα προσεκύνουν αὐτῷ. 15:20 καὶ ὅτε ἐνέπαιξαν αὐτῷ, ἐξέδυσαν αὐτὸν τὴν πορφύραν καὶ ἐνέδυσαν αὐτὸν τὰ ἱμάτια αὐτοῦ. καὶ ἐξάγουσιν αὐτὸν ἵνα σταυρώσωσιν αὐτόν.
15:21 Καὶ ἀγγαρεύουσιν παράγοντά τινα Σίμωνα Κυρηναῖον ἐρχόμενον ἀπ' ἀγροῦ, τὸν πατέρα Ἀλεξάνδρου καὶ Ῥούφου, ἵνα ἄρῃ τὸν σταυρὸν αὐτοῦ. 15:22 καὶ φέρουσιν αὐτὸν ἐπὶ τὸν Γολγοθᾶν τόπον, ὅ ἐστιν μεθερμηνευόμενον Κρανίου Τόπος. 15:23 καὶ ἐδίδουν αὐτῷ ἐσμυρνισμένον οἶνον· ὃς δὲ οὐκ ἔλαβεν. 15:24 καὶ σταυροῦσιν αὐτὸν καὶ διαμερίζονται τὰ ἱμάτια αὐτοῦ, βάλλοντες κλῆρον ἐπ' αὐτὰ τίς τί ἄρῃ. 15:25 ἦν δὲ ὥρα τρίτη καὶ ἐσταύρωσαν αὐτόν. 15:26 καὶ ἦν ἡ ἐπιγραφὴ τῆς αἰτίας αὐτοῦ ἐπιγεγραμμένη,
Ὁ βασιλεὺς τῶν Ἰουδαίων.
15:27 Καὶ σὺν αὐτῷ σταυροῦσιν δύο λῃστάς, ἕνα ἐκ δεξιῶν καὶ ἕνα ἐξ εὐωνύμων αὐτοῦ.
15:29 Καὶ οἱ παραπορευόμενοι ἐβλασφήμουν αὐτὸν κινοῦντες τὰς κεφαλὰς αὐτῶν καὶ λέγοντες,

5TP4.8.5.2.3(31–32a) CM: ἀρχιερεῖς, γραμματέων. SN: ὁμοίως (for 29–30). SPAC: ἐμπαίζοντες (content of the SPAC in 31b, 32a including καταβάτω). The leaders challenge him to prove his messianic identity.
5TP4.8.5.2.4(32b) CM: συνεσταυρωμένοι. SPAC: ὠνείδιζον. The two robbers revile Jesus.
4TP4.8.5.3(33) EMr:(T) ἕκτης. Darkness at noon.
4TP4.8.5.4(34–41) EMr:(T) ἐνάτῃ. Three p.m. until evening: Jesus' death with the accompanying events and onlookers.
5TP4.8.5.4.1(34) CM: Ἰησοῦς. MC: ἐβόησεν. SPAC: λεμα (question). Jesus' last words.
5TP4.8.5.4.2(35) CM, MC: ἔλεγον. SPAC: ἴδε interpretation of a text/saying—an assertive. Bystanders try to interpret Jesus' cry.
5TP4.8.5.4.3(36) CM, MC: λέγων. SPAC: ἄφετε ἴδωμεν. A bystander exhorts the others to see if Elijah will rescue Jesus.
5TP4.8.5.4.4(37) CM: ἐξέπνευσεν. The narrator describes Jesus' death.
5TP4.8.5.4.5(38) CM:(P) καταπέτασμα. The temple curtain is torn.
5TP4.8.5.4.6(39) CM: κεντυρίων. SN: οὕτως. (for 37 and 38?). SPAC: ἀληθῶς (confession/assertion). The centurion's confession.
5TP4.8.5.4.7(40–41) EMr:(S) μακρόθεν. CM: γυναῖκες, Σαλώμη. πολλαί. The women who followed Jesus watch.
3TP4.8.6(42–47) EMr:(T) ὀψίας, (S) ἐλθών. CM: Ἰωσήφ. Joseph buries Jesus.
4TP4.8.6.1(42–45) EMr:(S) πρὸς τ. Πιλᾶτον. CM: Ibid. SPAC: ᾐτήσατο (43) ἐπηρώτησεν (44). Joseph gives Pilate his request and Pilate agrees.

1 2 3 4

Οὐὰ ὁ καταλύων τὸν ναὸν καὶ οἰκοδομῶν ἐν τρισὶν ἡμέραις, 15:30 σῶσον σεαυτὸν καταβὰς ἀπὸ τοῦ σταυροῦ.
15:31 ὁμοίως καὶ οἱ ἀρχιερεῖς ἐμπαίζοντες πρὸς ἀλλήλους μετὰ τῶν γραμματέων ἔλεγον,
Ἄλλους ἔσωσεν, ἑαυτὸν οὐ δύναται σῶσαι· 15:32 ὁ Χριστὸς ὁ βασιλεὺς Ἰσραὴλ καταβάτω νῦν ἀπὸ τοῦ σταυροῦ, ἵνα ἴδωμεν καὶ πιστεύσωμεν.
καὶ οἱ συνεσταυρωμένοι σὺν αὐτῷ ὠνείδιζον αὐτόν.
15:33 Καὶ γενομένης ὥρας ἕκτης σκότος ἐγένετο ἐφ' ὅλην τὴν γῆν ἕως ὥρας ἐνάτης. 15:34 καὶ τῇ ἐνάτῃ ὥρᾳ ἐβόησεν ὁ Ἰησοῦς φωνῇ μεγάλῃ,
Ελωι ελωι λεμα σαβαχθανι;
ὅ ἐστιν μεθερμηνευόμενον
Ὁ θεός μου ὁ θεός μου, εἰς τί ἐγκατέλιπές με;
15:35 καί τινες τῶν παρεστηκότων ἀκούσαντες ἔλεγον,
Ἴδε Ἠλίαν φωνεῖ.
15:36 δραμὼν δέ τις [καὶ] γεμίσας σπόγγον ὄξους περιθεὶς καλάμῳ ἐπότιζεν αὐτόν λέγων,
Ἄφετε ἴδωμεν εἰ ἔρχεται Ἠλίας καθελεῖν αὐτόν.
15:37 ὁ δὲ Ἰησοῦς ἀφεὶς φωνὴν μεγάλην ἐξέπνευσεν.
15:38 Καὶ τὸ καταπέτασμα τοῦ ναοῦ ἐσχίσθη εἰς δύο ἀπ' ἄνωθεν ἕως κάτω. 15:39 Ἰδὼν δὲ ὁ κεντυρίων ὁ παρεστηκὼς ἐξ ἐναντίας αὐτοῦ ὅτι οὕτως ἐξέπνευσεν εἶπεν,
Ἀληθῶς οὗτος ὁ ἄνθρωπος υἱὸς θεοῦ ἦν.
15:40 Ἦσαν δὲ καὶ γυναῖκες ἀπὸ μακρόθεν θεωροῦσαι, ἐν αἷς καὶ Μαρία ἡ Μαγδαληνὴ καὶ Μαρία ἡ Ἰακώβου τοῦ μικροῦ καὶ Ἰωσῆτος μήτηρ καὶ Σαλώμη, 15:41 αἳ ὅτε ἦν ἐν τῇ Γαλιλαίᾳ ἠκολούθουν αὐτῷ καὶ διηκόνουν αὐτῷ, καὶ ἄλλαι πολλαὶ αἱ συναναβᾶσαι αὐτῷ εἰς Ἱεροσόλυμα.
15:42 Καὶ ἤδη ὀψίας γενομένης, ἐπεὶ ἦν παρασκευή ὅ ἐστιν προσάββατον, 15:43 ἐλθὼν Ἰωσὴφ [ὁ] ἀπὸ Ἁριμαθαίας εὐσχήμων βουλευτής, ὃς καὶ αὐτὸς ἦν προσδεχόμενος τὴν βασιλείαν τοῦ θεοῦ, τολμήσας

⁴TP⁴.⁸.⁶.²(46–47) EMr:(S) καθελών, μνημείῳ. CM: Ibid. & Μαρία ... Ἰωσῆτος. Joseph removes Jesus from the cross and puts him in the tomb with the two women looking on.
²TP⁴.⁹(16:1–8) EMr:(T) διαγενομένου, σαββάτου. The empty tomb and resurrection news on the day after the sabbath.
   ³TP⁴.⁹.¹(1) EMr:(T) σαββάτου. (S) Implied: Away from the tomb. CM: Μαρία...Σαλώμη. The three women buy spices when the sabbath is over.
   ³TP⁴.⁹.²(2–7) EMr:(T) λίαν...σαββάτων, (S) μνημείῳ. Early on the day after the Sabbath they go to the tomb and hear the resurrection news.
      ⁴TP⁴.⁹.²·¹(2–4) EMr:(S) Outside of the tomb. MC: ἔλεγον. SPAC: Ibid. (question) They discover the stone rolled away.
      ⁴TP⁴.⁹.²·²(5–7) EMr:(S) εἰς τ. μνημεῖον. CM: νεανίσκον. MC.Mon: λέγει. SPAC: μὴ ἐκθαμβεῖσθε...ἠγέρθη ὑπάγετε...προάγει (respectively: command, assertion, command, assertion). The angel in the tomb gives them the resurrection news.
   ³TP⁴.⁹.³(8) EMr:(S) ἀπὸ τ. μνημείου. Afraid, they speak to no one.

1 2 3 4

εἰσῆλθεν πρὸς τὸν Πιλᾶτον καὶ ᾐτήσατο τὸ σῶμα τοῦ Ἰησοῦ. 15:44 ὁ δὲ Πιλᾶτος ἐθαύμασεν εἰ ἤδη τέθνηκεν καὶ προσκαλεσάμενος τὸν κεντυρίωνα ἐπηρώτησεν αὐτὸν εἰ πάλαι ἀπέθανεν· (1, 2) 15:45 καὶ γνοὺς ἀπὸ τοῦ κεντυρίωνος ἐδωρήσατο τὸ πτῶμα τῷ Ἰωσήφ. 15:46 καὶ ἀγοράσας σινδόνα καθελὼν αὐτὸν ἐνείλησεν τῇ σινδόνι καὶ ἔθηκεν αὐτὸν ἐν μνημείῳ ὃ ἦν λελατομημένον ἐκ πέτρας καὶ προσεκύλισεν λίθον ἐπὶ τὴν θύραν τοῦ μνημείου. 15:47 ἡ δὲ Μαρία ἡ Μαγδαληνὴ καὶ Μαρία ἡ Ἰωσῆτος ἐθεώρουν ποῦ τέθειται. 16:1 Καὶ διαγενομένου τοῦ σαββάτου Μαρία ἡ Μαγδαληνὴ καὶ Μαρία ἡ [τοῦ] Ἰακώβου καὶ Σαλώμη ἠγόρασαν ἀρώματα ἵνα ἐλθοῦσαι ἀλείψωσιν αὐτόν. 16:2 καὶ λίαν πρωῒ τῇ μιᾷ τῶν σαββάτων ἔρχονται ἐπὶ τὸ μνημεῖον ἀνατείλαντος τοῦ ἡλίου. 16:3 καὶ ἔλεγον πρὸς ἑαυτάς,
Τίς ἀποκυλίσει ἡμῖν τὸν λίθον ἐκ τῆς θύρας τοῦ μνημείου;
16:4 καὶ ἀναβλέψασαι θεωροῦσιν ὅτι ἀποκεκύλισται ὁ λίθος· ἦν γὰρ μέγας σφόδρα. 16:5 καὶ εἰσελθοῦσαι εἰς τὸ μνημεῖον εἶδον νεανίσκον καθήμενον ἐν τοῖς δεξιοῖς περιβεβλημένον στολὴν λευκήν, καὶ ἐξεθαμβήθησαν. 16:6 ὁ δὲ λέγει αὐταῖς,
Μὴ ἐκθαμβεῖσθε· Ἰησοῦν ζητεῖτε τὸν Ναζαρηνὸν τὸν ἐσταυρωμένον· ἠγέρθη, οὐκ ἔστιν ὧδε· ἴδε ὁ τόπος ὅπου ἔθηκαν αὐτόν. 16:7 ἀλλὰ ὑπάγετε εἴπατε τοῖς μαθηταῖς αὐτοῦ καὶ τῷ Πέτρῳ ὅτι
Προάγει ὑμᾶς εἰς τὴν Γαλιλαίαν· ἐκεῖ αὐτὸν ὄψεσθε,
καθὼς εἶπεν ὑμῖν. (2 ON, PN)
16:8 καὶ ἐξελθοῦσαι ἔφυγον ἀπὸ τοῦ μνημείου, εἶχεν γὰρ αὐτὰς τρόμος καὶ ἔκστασις· καὶ οὐδενὶ οὐδὲν εἶπαν· ἐφοβοῦντο γάρ.

CHAPTER 4

THE GOVERNING SPEECH ACT AND THE EXEGESIS OF MARK

4.1. Introduction

The burden of this chapter is to show that text linguistics can help an interpreter to think about certain things in Mark in new ways. A text linguistic approach can contribute to the work of Markan scholarship by analyzing the text of Mark using the concept of a "governing speech act." Below I shall first relate the governing speech act of Mark to the texts of Mark 1:2–13, 14–15 and 8:27–9:1. Next, the relationship of the governing speech act to the genre of Mark will be discussed. Finally, the implications of the governing speech act for the Messianic Secret will be explored.

In the outline of Mark as presented in the previous chapter many references are made to speech acts in the text of Mark. These insights concerning speech acts in Mark are one of the basic contributions that this work can make to the exegetical discipline. As a written speech act, the entire text of Mark provides the interpretive frame for the speech acts that make up the units of conversation in the text. My conclusion is that the governing speech act of Mark intends to draw people into discipleship by leading them through the narrative world of the text.

Mark 1:2–13, 14–15 and 8:27–9:1 are examples of texts that contain speech acts that are subordinate to the governing speech act. Both complexes of texts contain usages of the word "gospel." Approaching Mark as a written speech act (an aspect of pragmatics) will also make a contribution to the understanding of Mark as a literary genre that is usually investigated using only syntax and semantics. To look at Mark as a governing speech act with actual effects on readers adds to the usual discussion of Mark as a genre. In this light Mark emerges as a text that changes hearers or readers. The speech act analysis helps hearers or readers to understand the Markan narrative world, including the motif of the Messianic Secret. I shall argue that the persuasive function of the Messianic Secret supports an understanding of Mark's governing speech act. The secrecy language actually reveals Jesus' identity to implied readers and to the audience. One can look at the secret as a narrative speech act whose illocution is initiating the reader into the secret.

4.2. The Governing Speech Act of Mark

The question raised and discussed in Chapter Two had to do with the function of the Markan narrative in the first century.[1] To approach the problem of function one should ask what kind of speech act governs the text of Mark. Text linguistics' use of the concept of speech acts to analyze texts is a tool that can enrich the work of Markan scholarship. As a governing speech act Mark has a rhetorical function. I use the term "governing" because the written act is larger than the usual speech acts, such as promises, warnings, whose basic building blocks are the sentence.[2] A speech act such as the command to the little girl "little girl, I say to you, arise" (5:41) is "governed" by the larger speech act of the

---

[1] See 2.3.4.

[2] See Rosengren 1987, 28ff. and the discussion of a governing speech act in 2.4.

Gospel. Jesus' words in 5:41 appear in communication Frame 2. The intended result ("perlocution" in the language of speech acts) of Jesus' command (a "supernatural" declarative) is the obedience of the little girl. The narrator (in Frame 1) in 5:42 shows that the command's intended result was carried out. Our claim in this work is that the speech act in 1:1 (in communication Frame 0) governs the other speech acts in Frames 1, 2, and beyond.[3] The "gospel narrative" speech act of 1:1 governs every other speech act in the text, including the reports that describe the narrative world. Mark therefore depicts the speech act in 5:41 as part of his use of language to exert a persuasive pull on the reader/hearer.

The frames clarify the interaction of the various speech acts in the text. This interaction is something that can make a contribution to the field of Markan studies because it has not been closely investigated before.[4] Text linguistics can help interpreters think about certain areas such as governing and governed speech acts that have been intuitively known but not extensively discussed. In the speech act we have named "gospel narrative," the author draws the reader into the world of the text and encourages him or her to accept the text as good news. The author makes statements about the world and attempts to change the reader. This point of view is in accord with literary theorists such as Suleiman, who argues that preachers, moralists and novelists are trying to say something about reality.[5] Novels, according to Lanser, communicate values and ways of seeing the world. The different communication frames ("narrative levels" in Lanser's terminology) comprise evaluative illocutions in the words of the author or characters that make "commentary and assertions about events, states, beings, values, problems, and ideas that have meaning in the historical world."[6] In the case of

---

[3]See 3.2.2, 3.3.2 above, and Appendix 1 below.
[4]Botha 1991 and du Plessis 1991 give bibliographical information on scholars who have used speech acts in investigations of NT texts.
[5]See Suleiman's remarks in 2.3.4.
[6]Lanser 1981, 292, 293.

Mark, the narrator creates narratives that sound like reports but actually involve a claim on the reader's life. This aspect of Mark has been approached in a similar way by many scholars. Bultmann, with his emphasis on Mark as kerygma, is a prime example.[7]

The characteristics of a textual written act were discussed above in 2.3.5. The "appeal factor" (including the many rhetorical figures),[8] the beginning and end of a text, the inscription (a meta-communicative marker because it mentions the author's name), the title in 1:1 (a Substition in a Meta-frame because it describes the contents of the text) including εὐαγγέλιον (gospel), and the sequence of the text that the reader experiences—all these contribute to an understanding of the function of Mark that I have chosen to call "gospel narrative." Mark's text encourages a complete allegiance to Jesus, faith in him, and a disciple/teacher relationship with Jesus. It pictures Jesus as a teacher sent by God and as the Son of God and Son of Man who dies on the cross, rises from the dead, and who will judge human beings after his return. The text of Mark probably served as a powerful attraction to anyone who heard it in the first century, whether or not they were part or became part of the Christian community.[9] The last imperative in Mk 13:37, γρηγορεῖτε (watch), helps prove that the audience of the text may be comprised of those who are drawn into the narrative world of the four disciples in chapter 13 (see the marker analysis). The imperative (a speech act) has as its perlocution the actual watching for Jesus on the part of the audience. The

---

[7]See Bultmann in 1.5.2, Strecker in 1.3.7.2, and all the other scholars discussed in the section on the reader and the Messianic Secret (1.3.6). See also Beardslee in 1.4.2 and Boers in 1.4.3.

[8]See "appeal factor," 2.3.5, and Tolbert 1989, index, for a set of rhetorical figures in Mark.

[9]The passionate negative response of certain pagans to the gospel (including Hierocles) is portrayed in Cook 1993. The ability of Christian texts to persuade hearers (including the Gospel of John's persuasion of Hilary of Poitiers) is the subject of Cook 1994.

communication is technically text-internal because it is in Frame 2, but when Jesus mentions "all" people in his statement he includes more than his own audience—namely, all people, including those who hear/read the text. Only the one who accepts the truth of the text will be interested in such watching.

The written act we have called a "gospel narrative" governs and unifies the other speech acts (or written acts) of the text such as dialogue, questions, curses, and reports. Indications of all these speech acts, including the textual speech act "gospel narrative," are contained in the analysis in Chapter Three. We have not given a name for the speech act in every Text Part, but have included a large number of names in the analysis. Reports comprise all the stories that constitute the narrative world. They are subordinated to the primary governing speech act "gospel narrative." The text as a written act exerts a strong pull on readers and hearers. This result can be intersubjectively checked by modern scholars looking at their and others' experience of religious literature. Scholars must then make an inference by analogy about the pragmatics of Mark's first century text. Since pragmatics considers users of the text, it can also treat users of the language within the text and not only the author and audience of the text itself. The frames of communication give an intimate portrait of the nature of the speech acts and their effects on the hearers.

Below, two groups of texts—1:2–13, 14–15 and 8:27–9:1—will be considered in relation to the governing speech act of Mark. Both contain usages of the word "gospel" and are illustrative of the power of the governing speech act.

4.2.1. Mk 1:2–13, 14–15 and the Governing Speech Act

The texts that follow the title in Mk 1:1, namely 1:2–13 and 1:14–15, contain speech acts that are directed or guided by 1:1. The first text sequence depicts John and Jesus in the wilderness (1:2–13). They are in the Jordan area of the wilderness in 1:2–11. The narrator concentrates on John alone in 1:2–8 before the period "in those days" in 1:9. The mention of Isaiah in 1:2–3 calls attention to a very powerful speech act in the ancient world called "prophecy." Mk 1:2–3, with its depiction of John (the "messenger") and Jesus ("thy face"), begins the depiction of the good news. Robbins notes that 1:2–3 raises the expectation that the next event will be the appearance of the messenger—what Robbins calls a "logical progression."[10]

The narrator's claim that Isaiah prophesied about John and Jesus is an example of an accepted mode of persuasion in the ancient world.[11] A number of intellectuals in late antiquity were persuaded by the argument that Jesus fulfilled OT prophecies. Others objected strenuously to that thesis. For example, Porphyry, the Platonist philosopher, objected to the conflation of prophets in Mk 1:2 and found the narrators of the Gospels to be ignorant in secular and divine matters.[12] Celsus and Julian both objected to the Christian practice of finding details of Jesus' life in ancient prophecies.[13] Prophecy was a form of assertion. In any speech act such as the prophecy in 1:2–3, one had to ask whether the recipient of the communication accepted the assertion as true or not. Though the records are slender, it is apparent that certain observers (hearers) of the Christian use of Hebrew prophecy were unpersuaded.

The speech act of proclamation plays a role in Mk 1:4–6, where John is the major character. The baptism of repentance is the explicit perlocution of John's speech. The hearers from Judea and Jerusalem confess their sins. Their confession and baptism are the intended perlocution of John's language. Mark does not analyze the reasons for John's success. Some of the verbal content of his proclamation appears in 1:7–8. The people from Judea and

---

[10] Robbins 1992, 79. He defines "logical progression" as the form of a perfectly conducted argument, advancing step by step (1992, 9).

[11] Cook 1994, 113–115.

[12] Harnack 1916, Frag. 9; discussed in Cook 1993, 247. Porphyry wrote in reference to this text in Mark: Evangelistae tam imperiti fuerunt homines, non solum in saecularibus, sed etiam in scripturis divinis, ut testimonium, quod alibi scriptum est, de alio ponerent propheta.

[13] References in Cook 1993, 238, 252, and 1994, 115.

Jerusalem are not described as having accepted this particular part of John's proclamation. Nor does Mark say that they rejected it. The audience's evaluation of John's proclamation in 1:7–8 would include observing Jesus' appearance and observing whether Jesus actually did baptize others with the Holy Spirit.

The next section (1:9–11) includes a reference to time (in those days) and place when Jesus travels from Nazareth to the Jordan river. The otherworldly voice in 1:11 makes an assertion about the identity of Jesus. The speech act is assertion. If a hearer rejects the assertion, then the speech act does not have persuasive force for that hearer. The author's claim in 1:1 is that the text is true. Celsus asks if a voice at Jesus' baptism proclaimed him to be son of God, if Jesus saw a bird flying toward him, and where a trustworthy witness was. There is no proof except for Jesus' word and those who were punished with him.[14] (Celsus is an example of a person who does not find the text in 1:9–11 (or its parallels) to be true or "good news.") The governing speech act encourages a reader to take 1:11 as a true assertion. "Divine speech," as in these words in Mark, was an accepted part of the Hellenistic world. Christians used the claim to have divine speech or words from God to persuade others to join their movement.[15] In Mk 1:11, the voice of God identifies Jesus. Oracles of other gods evaluated Jesus in a different light. Apollo's oracle, for example, called Jesus a "god who died in delusion." Hecate's oracle, when asked if Christ was god, replied that he was a "man of outstanding piety."[16] Both Apollo and Hecate take an approach to Jesus that is different from the otherworldly voice in 1:11. Consequently, the reader's response to 1:11 will be determined by the reader's response to the governing speech act in 1:1. If the text is good news, then Mk 1:11 can be accepted as a true assertion.

What remains unexplored is the set of cultural values that would encourage a person in the Greco-Roman world to be

---

[14]Cook 1993, 235 from Origen, *Contra Celsum* 1.41.
[15]Texts in Cook 1994, 121–125.
[16]Cook 1993, 248, 249.

willing to accept Jesus as God's beloved son, as opposed to those oracles of Apollo and Hecate who found the claim incredible. In other words, why are speech acts such as 1:1 and 1:11 effective on certain people and not others? Julian attributes his cure from the "disease" of Christianity to Zeus and the fates. Hecate's oracle describes the "error" of Christians as due to the fact that they were not "fated to know God."[17] Such explanations leave one unsatisfied.

In the next episode Jesus is driven to another part of the wilderness, away from John (1:12–13). Jesus' ability to resist Satan's temptations and survive the wilderness in the presence of wild animals fills out the picture of his identity as "Christ" and "Son of God." Here again the governing speech act defines this text as good news. A reader who rejects the governing speech act might consider the story in 1:12–13 to be a fabrication or myth, as in the case of Celsus who so evaluated certain Christian texts about Jesus.[18]

With Mk 1:14–15 a new sequence of text begins (1:14–8:26) in which Jesus ministers in Galilee and the surrounding area. 1:14–15 is transitional; that probably explains its occasional inclusion with the verses in 1:2–13 or with 1:16–20, according to Robbins.[19] Mk 1:1 begins a "qualitative progression" in which the reader begins to ask: "What are the characteristics of this message of good news, and what are the attributes of the Messiah (Son of God) who is associated with this message. The reader expects that the qualities of Jesus' character, action, and speech will

---

[17] Cook 1993, 249, 252.

[18] Origen, *Contra Celsum* 5.57; referred to in Cook 1994, 130, n. 52.

[19] Robbins 1994, 142. Robbins compares the repetition of "gospel" in Mk 1:1 and 1:14–15 with a similar repetition of important concepts in Xenophon, *Memorabilia* 4.1.1 and the ending of the introduction at 4.4.4–5. On the other hand, 1:14–15 contains a temporal reference and an occurrence of Jesus' name that separates it from the preceding narrative, and so Robbins compares it with the text that introduces Elijah's words in 1 Kings 17:1 (Robbins 1994, 142, 143). See the arguments above about the limits of Mark's "introduction" in 1.2.4.3.

emerge to answer these questions as the narrative progresses."[20] Robbins sees 1:14–20 as the first three step progression that elaborates the topic in 1:1. The ethos of Jesus becomes manifest in his speech and action. Jesus "announces a prophetic message and challenges people to adopt a particular system of thought and action in response to the message."[21] This is very close to an approach that uses speech acts to understand the ability of Markan language to persuade hearers or, in the case of the "pagans" such as Celsus, to fail to persuade and to actually repel hearers. The speech acts in Mk 1:14–15 include the assertion of the kingdom's nearness and the two imperatives to repent and believe in the gospel. The speech acts in 1:15 are an example of the reference of the phrase "gospel of God" in 1:14. The assertion in the first part of 1:15 is acceptable only to a person who regards positively the speech act 1:1. The perlocution of the imperatives is the hearers' repentance and faith in the gospel. The language itself exerts a persuasive pull on the reader, although it is of course not universally successful. The speech act we have called "gospel narrative" makes assertions (such as Jesus' about the kingdom in 1:15) about the world, and then encourages the hearers to respond appropriately. Mk 1:15 is a truth claim that actually molds hearers' response. The response can be positive, as in the case of the disciples who are called in 1:16–20. Robbins notes that Jesus' calls to the disciples in 1:17 and 1:20 elaborate the imperatives in 1:15.[22] A negative response appears in the persons of Jesus' antagonists, such as the Pharisees and Herodians in 3:6, or in non-Christian authors such as Celsus and Porphyry, who were scandalized by the traditions in the gospels. In Origen's terms, Jesus' words in 1:15 will make happy a hearer who accepts what is announced and who believes that something good is coming to himself or herself.[23]

---

[20]Robbins 1992, 79.
[21]Robbins 1992, 28, 29, 30.
[22]Robbins 1992, 28.
[23]See 2.3.4 and Appendix 1 for Origen.

Here a comparison between Robbins' socio-rhetorical method and the concept of a governing speech act can be drawn. The reader, for Robbins, expects qualities of Jesus' character to emerge as the narrative develops.[24] One important characteristic of an approach that uses speech acts is the intended effect (perlocution) of the language on the hearer or reader. Robbins does observe this aspect of Mark's language, but it is not his main emphasis: "Since no one in Mark's gospel fully adopts the system of thought and action taught and enacted by Jesus, the reader is the object of a special summons to perpetuate the system of thought and action 'to all nations for the sake of Jesus and the gospel.'"[25] Tolbert claims that the purpose of Mark is to persuade hearers to have faith in the Gospel of Jesus Christ and to follow in his way.[26] The word "good news" in 1:1 encourages every reader to decide that the text is actually true. In other words, is the text good news? The anonymous philosopher, mentioned above, is concerned to show that a narrative in Mark, such as 5:1–20, is either fiction, or if true, a joke.[27] Consequently, the situation is not as simple as Robbins appears to make it when he states that:

> The reader learns that Jesus is associated with a message of good news (1:1), that he is the Messiah (1:1), that he is the beloved Son of God (1:1, 11), that he is mightier than John the Baptist (1:7), that the Spirit of God has come upon him and can control him (1:10, 12), and that Satan is an adversary, the angels are allies, and wild beasts hold no power to destroy him (1:13).[28]

"Pagan" readers who objected to the claims of the Gospels did not "learn" these claims made in Mark. They were thoroughly

---

[24] Robbins 1992, 79, 82.
[25] Robbins 1992, 209.
[26] Tolbert's views on the purpose of the text are summarized in 1.4.4.
[27] For his views, see 2.3.4.
[28] Robbins 1992, 81.

unconvinced.[29] Robbins would have to restate his point with a qualifier such as "the reader learns that Mark claims...."

The governing speech act in Frame 0 (Mk 1:1) guides the interpretation of the other speech acts in 1:2–13 and 1:14–15.[30] Without 1:1, one could simply read 1:14–15 and remark that it is a curious phenomenon that certain people, such as the four disciples, responded positively to Jesus' preaching. One could also observe negative responses such as the one in 3:6 and note that it is also a curious phenomenon that certain people found Jesus' gospel to be repellent. The reader could stop there and avoid any "existential" or "personal" response. But 1:1 as a governing speech act indicates that every hearer of the text will experience its power to persuade or repulse. The "pagan" responses (e.g., Celsus) are indication enough of the apotreptic power of the language. Many people in late antiquity experienced the persuasive or protreptic power of the gospels (e.g., Hilary and Augustine's multitudes).[31]

4.2.2. Mk 8:27–9:1 and the Governing Speech Act

In the text analysis in Chapter Three above, Mk 8:27 begins a new section describing the journey to Jerusalem (^{1}TP^3 [8:27–10:52]). The spatial marker—ὁδός—coheres with the reasons for considering 8:27ff. to be the turning point in the text. Wrede makes the claim that one could put the confession of Peter in Mk 2, move the passion predictions to points earlier in the narrative, and put an exorcism in Mk 12 without disturbing the text.[32] One could do that, but the disciples' dawning understanding in texts such as 10:37 would not make as much sense if such experiences had occurred before Peter's confession. Placing 8:27ff. in Mk 2 would also destroy the subtle relationship of Herod's questions about Jesus' identity in 6:14–16 to the people's similar questions

---

[29]Cook 1993, 1994.
[30]On this function of governing speech acts in general, see 2.4.
[31]Cook 1993, 1994.
[32]Wrede 1971, 120.

in 8:28. The portrayal of the effect of Jesus' extensive ministry inside and outside Galilee on popular opinion about him helps explain the hypotheses about Jesus in 8:28. Mk 8:27ff., as it stands, introduces the travel section (8:27–10:52) and indicates that the journey is going to end in Jesus' passion. The verse's effect as a turning point in Jesus' ministry would be destroyed if placed earlier in the text. Aristotle describes a "plot" (μῦθος) as having components that cannot be moved: "... the component incidents must be so arranged that if one of them be transposed or removed, the unity of the whole is dislocated and destroyed. For if the presence or absence of a thing makes no visible difference, then it is not an integral part of the whole."[33] Mark probably would not satisfy Aristotle's definition of a good plot, because too many stories could be moved around. But texts such as 8:27ff. and the passion seem to be well glued into place.

Bickerman[34] calls the material in Mk 8:27ff. a "recognition scene." Using Aristotle's terms,[35] Bickerman described it as a μετάβασις μετὰ ἀναγνωρισμοῦ (transition with recognition) in the Gospel in a plot of complicated action (πεπληγμένη πρᾶξις). This judgment is shared by many scholars who see the passage as a major turning point (περιπέτεια).[36] An outline of Mark based on the disciples' perception of Jesus would have to describe 8:27ff. as a major change in the text. Thus, Bickerman seems correct in his judgment that there is a turning point here. In terms of the

---

[33]Aristotle, *Poetics* (8.4) 1451a (LCL translation).
[34]Bickermann [sic] 1923, 132.
[35]Aristotle, *Poetics* (c. 10) 1452a.
[36]Vielhauer 1975, 331 sees it as a major break which introduces the new theme of the passion. Pesch 1976, 37, has the same view as do Klostermann 1971, 78 and Maria Horstmann 1969, 8. Bultmann 1963, 350 calls it the beginning of a new epoch for the reader and the beginning of the "esoteric teaching about the Messiah" with the disciples representing the reader. Kuby 1958, 58 begins the second major division at 8:22, where the clarity of 8:27ff. is symbolized by the healing of the blind man. Wrede 1971, 115–119 disputed the importance of Mk 8:27ff. in the Gospel. Kümmel 1966, 61, 62 does not include it in his outline as a major break.

Text Parts' inter-relations, one can consider a motif such as the disciples' knowledge of Jesus in Mark, which could be expressed as a proposition. Kuby attempted this.[37] He remarked that from this point the disciples know Jesus is the Christ, although misunderstanding of him and his fate remains. Outlines that locate the break in Mark at 8:27 can also be linked to a branch of linguistics that uses the theory of action to analyze and structure texts.[38] The categories of classical drama, as in Bickerman's approach, Kuby's remarks about the disciples' relationship to Jesus, and the narrative categories used by some French structuralists, all make use of theories of human action. No matter how one approaches 8:27ff., it is a major text in the Gospel's structure.

Jesus is on the road with his disciples in 8:27–10:52. Mk 10:32, 33 show that the journey on the "road" will end in Jerusalem. From 8:27–9:29, they are in the region of Caesarea Philippi. Six days before the transfiguration (9:2) Jesus teaches his followers about the Messiah and discipleship (8:27–9:1). Due to the presence of the spatial markers, 8:27 begins a new section in the outline in Chapter Three. Tolbert sees the break at 8:22 and notes that two healings of the blind delineate the section in 8:22–10:52. This suggests that "Jesus can open the eyes of the blind, but cannot make his disciples see."[39] Bartimaeus, on the other hand, is healed by faith and follows Jesus on the road. He symbolizes the true follower of faith according to Tolbert.[40] Although I put 8:22–26 at the end of the Galilee and environs episode (1:14–8:26), Tolbert's insight is still useful here. The disciples do not see perfectly, but they see a little.

---

[37] Kuby 1958, 58 locates at 8:22 a change in the disciples' understanding of Jesus. Up to this point they do not understand who Jesus is. After this point they misunderstand the fact that he must suffer. See the outlines in Chapter One that use Jesus' relationship with his disciples to structure the text (1.2.4.1.1).

[38] See note 78.

[39] Tolbert 1989, 178, 179.

[40] Tolbert 1989, 191, 192.

Robbins states that Peter's answer to Jesus in 8:29 is a "new step in the elaboration of the 'gospel of Jesus *Christ*, the Son of God.'" In 8:27 the disciples are asked to "produce the information on the basis of their association with Jesus as disciple-companions." Peter's answer is "a restatement of a feature of Mark 1:1 in a setting that gathers together the thought and action from the intervening scenes and asks the disciples to relate that thought and action to their understanding of the identity of Jesus."[41] Here is a point that is critical to our approach of using a governing speech act and emphasizing the persuasive power of Mark's language. The text in 8:27–30 shows that Jesus' action and words left people in confusion about his identity. Those who perhaps saw the same healings and heard the same teachings ended up with these different inferences about Jesus' identity: he was thought to be John the Baptist, Elijah, or one of the prophets. Peter's answer (a speech act) in Frame 2 to Jesus' question (a speech act) does reflect the author's evaluation of Jesus in 1:1 in communication Frame 1. What remains unexplained in the text is why Peter was able to achieve that answer as opposed to the other onlookers. Robbins's words for Peter's conclusion, such as "produce information on the basis of their association with Jesus as disciple-companions," or "relate that thought and action to their understanding of the identity of Jesus," avoid grappling with the mystery of Peter's persuasion. Matthew (16:17) gives a supernatural explanation for Peter's view of Jesus. Bultmann simply notes that nothing in the narrative prepares for the confession of Peter: "...for Mark has neither depicted the recognition of Jesus as something newly won by him, as the fruit of his ministry or of his estimate of the outward and inward situation, nor has he pictured the recognition by the disciples as the outcome of some development."[42] Mark probably pictures "Christ" as being a word that Peter understands to refer to someone who does and says the kinds of things that Jesus does in the narrative. Others

---

[41]Robbins 1992, 38, 39.
[42]Bultmann 1963, 350.

such as the high priests do not share Peter's understanding of the word (15:32), because they refuse to apply it to Jesus. The High Priest is clear that he does not understand "Christ" or "Son of God" to describe Jesus (14:61, 64). So the definitions of the term "Christ" do not really answer the question about why Peter was persuaded but not the high priests or other onlookers.

Mark does not explain Peter's persuasion that Jesus is the Christ. In other words, Mark does not explain why Peter responded positively to the governing speech act in 1:1. That speech act encourages the reader to see Jesus' words and actions as words and action of the Christ, the Son of God. The text does not tell why some readers or hearers are persuaded and some not. Mark pictures Peter as being caught up by the power of the gospel. The narrator shows that some people are persuaded by Jesus and others simply are left in confusion. Peter does not see clearly. Though he was persuaded, he later denies Jesus (14:66–72) and is expected to rejoin the faithful after the resurrection (16:7). "Pagan" critics of Christianity were frustrated by the persuasive power of Christian language. The texts mentioned above (4.2.1) from the oracles of Hecate and Apollo used "fate" to explain Christian belief. Another oracle of Apollo counsels a husband who tries to recall his wife from Christian belief:

> You might perhaps find it easier to write on water in printed characters, or fly like a bird through the air spreading light wings to the breeze, than recall to her senses an impious, polluted wife. Let her go as she pleases, persisting in her vain delusions, singing in lamentation for a god who died in delusions, who was condemned by right-thinking judges, and killed in hideous fashion by the worst of deaths, a death bound with iron.[43]

According to the text, Peter ends up with something like that woman's "incurable belief."

---

[43] Augustine, *De Civ. Dei* 19.23. ET in Henry Bettenson's translation, 1972, 884, 885.

Jesus' teaching about his destiny (cross and resurrection) confuse Peter. Peter's rebuke of Jesus indicates that his understanding of the "Christ" was at variance with what Jesus was going to experience. Robbins notes that the disciples are asked to "learn an aspect of Jesus' identity in events that will happen to him rather than on the basis of events that they have already observed happen to him. They must anticipate both for themselves and for their teacher the significance of an identity that arises out of rejection and leads to public humiliation and death."[44] Peter's problems with understanding Jesus' suffering are perhaps reflected in some "pagan" responses to this material. Celsus found it objectionable. A god would avoid suffering that was foreknown. Anyone punished as a robber or murderer could be said to be not a robber but a god. Celsus also believed that the disciples invented the story that Jesus foreknew what happened to him.[45] The material in 8:31–33 was not at all persuasive to Celsus, and Peter had trouble with it himself. The speech act of teaching in 8:31 imparts good news about Jesus according to the governing act in 1:1. If Augustine is correct about the historical effect of the gospels, they exerted a very persuasive pull on the hearers. In Origen's terms, Jesus' cross and resurrection promise good to the hearer who believes it is true good news.[46]

Robbins sees 8:34–38 as including a proposition (8:34) with four steps that are rationales for the proposition (8:35, 36, 37, 38).[47] The rationales in 8:35, 36, and 37 have parallels in the Hellenistic philosophical tradition.[48] Mark may expect his audience to be aware of this—a pragmatic presupposition. Mark 8:38 represents biblical tradition from Daniel 7 and 11.

So in Mk 8:34–38, Mk 1:1 is developed to the point that Jesus and the gospel are "thoroughly intertwined" (8:35). The disciples

---

[44]Robbins 1992, 39.

[45]Origen, *Contra Celsum*, 2.17; 2.44; 2.13; discussed in Cook 1993, 236, 237, 238.

[46]Augustine's and Origen's texts are quoted in 2.3.4.

[47]Robbins 1994, 234, 235.

[48]Robbins 1994, 235–37.

are challenged to "accept an identity as disciples who are willing to gain life by losing it."[49] The "proposition" in 8:34 as a speech act is a conditional command. The perlocution would be actually denying oneself, taking up one's cross and following Jesus. As a speech act, 8:35 is two assertions. The perlocution of 8:35b accepts the assertion as true. The governing speech act in 1:1 defines all these verses to be "good news." In Origen's language a hearer who accepts them as good news for himself or herself will rejoice (2.3.4). If the gospel fails to persuade a hearer, then the hearer obviously does not believe that it is going to bring something good. In other words, the hearer does not believe that it is "good news."

One is still left wondering why Peter is convinced along with certain other hearers of the gospel. Words like those in Mk 8:27–9:1 helped Christianize the Greco-Roman world, according to Augustine (2.3.4). Peter's conviction that Jesus is the Christ is an example of the persuasive power of the language and action contained in the gospel. In Mark, Jesus' miracles and teaching succeed in persuading Peter—in accord with the speech act in 1:1. But miracles, or rather stories about the miracles of Jesus, including the miracle of the resurrection, were not successful in persuading all hearers (as in the case of Celsus, Hierocles, Julian, and others in the ancient world).[50] The language itself was able to draw people to faith in Jesus of Nazareth. Certain Christians, such as Origen, attributed this power of God.[51] It is not necessary to make this theological move to observe that the language of texts, such as Mark, actually changed the hearers' lives by persuading them that "good news" was present. This function of language illustrates the power of the governing speech act we have called "gospel narrative." The contribution of linguistics here, with its emphasis on the perlocution of the speech acts, is that the words are able to change people in analogy with political propaganda. This pragmatic dimension of

---

[49]Robbins 1992, 40, 41.
[50]Cook 1993, 1994, 109–11.
[51]Cook 1994, 121–25.

the language of the gospels should not be ignored. It was part of the social function of these texts to mold individuals and communities in the Greco-Roman world.

4.3. The Governing Speech Act and the Genre of Mark

Text linguistics' interest in describing the interaction of the governing and governed speech acts in Mark can aid in the description of Mark as a genre. The clear distinction between semantics and pragmatics can also contribute to the scholarly conversation. The discussion of the genre of Mark in 1.5 above ends with the remark that there seems to be little scholarly consensus in determining the nature of the genre "gospel." With form criticism, rhetoric, and text linguistics in the background, any adequate discussion of the genre of Mark should include references to the syntax (syntagmatic criteria), semantics and pragmatics of a "gospel."[52] If a definition of the genre leaves out linear or syntagmatic criteria, the definition needs broadening. If the definition leaves out a reference to the pragmatics or function of the text, then it also needs broadening. From a paradigmatic point of view, one can list characteristics of the text-syntax, text-semantics and text-pragmatics of Mark and different gospels.[53] An immediate question would be what to include in the pool of texts to be considered "gospels." I shall

---

[52]Syntax, semantics, and pragmatics correspond largely with form criticism's "form, content, and *Sitz im Leben*." See 2.4.

[53]Compare Hellholm 1982, 164 for a list of these aspects of apocalyptic texts. See further Hellholm 1991, 134ff., 149 for an analysis of Revelation from the point of view of text-syntax, text-semantics, and text-pragmatics. Burridge and Bryan (referred to in 1.5.4) have similar lists, although they are not concerned with the distinction between semantics and pragmatics. Burridge prefers to link function with content since it has to be inferred from the text itself in the case of the gospels (1992, 110). Nevertheless, a pragmatic approach to a text is different from a semantic approach even though pragmatics is far more difficult than semantics.

avoid that issue here and simply consider Mark with the other three canonical gospels in the background.

One of the sources of disagreement in the issue of finding analogies to the New Testament gospels is what precisely constitutes a "gospel" in the first place. In other words, which characteristics of form (text-syntax), content (semantics), and *Sitz im Leben* (pragmatics) are constitutive of a gospel? For example, does a Messianic Secret have to be explicitly present for a text to be considered a gospel? If so, then one would exclude almost any other Hellenistic text from consideration as a gospel. Consider Jonathan Z. Smith's definition that is referred to in 1.5.4 above: "A 'gospel' is a narrative of a son of god who appears among men as a riddle inviting misunderstanding." Here "son of god" is included in the content. "Narrative" is included as the form. "Misunderstanding" is the aspect of the *Sitz im Leben* which Smith includes. The lives (βίοι) of Pythagoras (by Iamblichus) and Apollonius (by Philostratus) are "gospels" (εὐαγγέλια) under this definition. Robert Guelich's definition (referred to in 1.5.4 above) that a gospel is a "...literary genre whose form and content consist of 'the gospel of Jesus Messiah, Son of God'" is based on his rejection of Hellenistic analogies to the New Testament gospel genre. His main element for content is "Jesus Messiah, Son of God," and his element for form is "gospel." Given such a definition, other Hellenistic texts (non-Christian) are automatically excluded from consideration as analogies to the canonical gospels. Guelich's position is a variation of Bultmann's picture (1.5.2) of the gospels as expanded cult legends or expansions of the Christian kerygma, with the death and resurrection of Christ being central. From the point of view of content, Bultmann places the death and resurrection of Christ as central, with kerygma or cult legend being the main elements of the *Sitz im Leben*. Drawing upon the definitions of some scholars mentioned in this section and in 1.5 the following paradigm is suggested:

4.3.1. Form or Text-Syntactic Elements of a Gospel

1. Narrative
2. Legends
3. Literary forms such as parables, miracles, wisdom sayings, and chreiai
4. Brief scenes
5. Dialogue with narrative summaries
6. Central turning point
7. Final recognition scene
8. Embedded communication frames
9. Episodes connected by loose temporal and spatial markers
10. Repetitive forms
11. Presignals such as inscriptions and titles (2.3.5)
12. Length

4.3.2. Content or Text-Semantic Elements of a Gospel

1. Story of a son of god
2. Jesus the Messiah (and Son of God)
3. Death and resurrection
4. Literary forms from the point of view of their content such as parables, miracles, wisdom sayings, and apophthegms/chreiai[54]
5. Teacher-student relationship (a portrayal of a religio-ethical teacher manifesting his adult role through interaction with those around him—Robbins)[55]

4.3.3. Sitz im Leben or Text-Pragmatic Elements of a Gospel

1. A text whose governing speech act is one which draws the reader into its narrative world and challenges the reader/hearer to accept the text as good news
2. A kerygma
3. A cult legend

---

[54] See Mack and Robbins 1989 for convincing proof that the gospels contain examples of chreia elaboration.

[55] Robbins 1992, 63.

4. A riddle inviting misunderstanding
5. Guidance for future generations ("teachers themselves show their disciples how they themselves do what they teach and lead them on by speech . . ."[56])
6. Rhetorical functions: apologetic;[57] epideictic (more specifically encomium);[58] deliberative (accepting the text as good news or not accepting it is a decision the audience makes)
7. Orientation by disorientation: challenging the audience's view of reality[59]

We will leave this paradigm as an alternative approach to defining what a gospel is. The question about the closest Hellenistic analogies to the New Testament gospels will probably remain controversial. Using the schema developed above, one can compare Mark to the *Vita Apollonii* by considering the content (text-semantics) and function (text-pragmatics) of the text.

---

[56]Xenophon *Memorabilia* (1.2.17) quoted in Robbins 1992, 64 with reference to a teacher transmitting a religio-ethical system to later generation through disciples.

[57]Burridge summarizes the work of many scholars who find this function in the gospels (1992, 216, 237).

[58]Philip L. Shuler finds evidence of a laudatory biography genre whose primary purpose is to praise (Shuler 1982, 37, 45, 85, discussed in Guelich 1983, 190ff., who finds Matthew to have little to do with such a genre of biography, since Matthew is about what God does in Jesus Messiah). Dihle 1983, 399 argues that the encomia of Isocrates and Xenophon are a specific genre, but are not an example of "biography." Bryan agrees that the functions of Mark include epideictic and deliberative rhetoric. Under "epideictic" he includes biographies "seeking to persuade their auditors to hold or reaffirm a point of view in the present, and celebrating a particular person." "Deliberative" texts "seek to persuade them [the auditors] to action in the future" (Bryan 1993, 60, 131).

[59]See Beardslee in 1.4.2.

4.3.4. The Content and Function of the Vita Apollonii and Mark

Robbins has an extensive discussion of the *Vita Apollonii* that focuses on the teaching and learning phases in the narrative in the context of an itinerant life. The motif of discipleship appears even though Apollonius did not summon disciples.[60] The disciples make the decision to follow Apollonius. Robbins outlines the text with references to the stages of teaching and learning: 1.1–20, Initial stage of the teacher/disciple relationship of Apollonius and Damis; 1.21–40, Initial Teaching; 2, Major Demonstration of the Superiority of the Teacher's System of Thought and Action through Encounter with King Phraotes; 3, Exploration of the Depths of the Teacher's System Through Mutual Learning from the Sages of India; 4–6, Foreshadowing of Arrest and Trial through Encounter and Exploration of the System with a Range of Public Groups. The texts from 1.21–6.43 depict an "intermediate" stage of teaching and learning.[61] In the initial phase a relationship is established between a teacher and a disciple. In the intermediate phase the teacher and disciple enter into a teaching and learning process.[62] The four parts of the intermediate phase correspond to Robbins's outline of Mark. The last part of the intermediate phase creates the stage for Apollonius's imprisonment, trial, and death.[63] These remarks of Robbins on *Apollonius* are primarily text-semantic. They focus on the content of the text and compare it to the content of Mark.

A pragmatic approach to the text can consider the reader's experience of the text. A comparison with an implied reader's experience of the *Vita Apollonii* (3rd CE, perhaps 217) is useful in an effort to understand the purpose of Mark, even though the text is later than Mark. Apollonius is pictured as a very special person. Apollonius released himself from a chain in the presence of Damis. Damis consequently understood Apollonius's

---

[60]Robbins 1992, 105–107.
[61]Robbins 1992, 148, 155.
[62]Robbins 1992, 125.
[63]Robbins 1992, 155; and see Robbins's outline in 1.2.3.

"...nature, that it was divine and greater than human."[64] Apollonius, however, calls the view of himself as a "God" an illusion (ἀπάτη, 8.7.7). The nature of all good people, according to Apollonius, has something of God. Apollonius claims: "A human being philosophizes about his/her nature and in what way it participates in the divine...and he/she is convinced that virtues come from God to him/her and that those who share in virtue are godlike and are divine."[65]

In answer to Domitian's question about why people call him "God," Apollonius states that every person who is considered good is honored with the name of "God" (θεοῦ ἐπωνυμίᾳ τιμᾶται, 8.5).[66] Apollonius also describes Lycurgus's being honored with the name of "God" by Apollo (8.7.7). Even more important, the disembodied soul of Apollonius (a swift horse out of its bonds) appears to a young man who is skeptical (8.31) about the immortality of the soul. Apollonius already had, in a Cretan tradition, ascended into heaven (8.30). The entire work defends Apollonius against the charge of wizardry (μάγος, γόης magician, wizard; see 1.2, 5.12, 8.7.2). The epilogue describes (8.31) Apollonius's purpose in life: A clear utterance of Apollonius with oracular authority established the mysteries of the soul (ἔστηκεν ὑπὲρ τῶν τῆς ψυχῆς ἀπορρητῶν), so that we might go joyously to the place that the Fates appoint. No tomb of Apollonius was found by the narrator, but his shrine at Tyana was marked by royal officers. The end of the text, therefore, makes no unique claims for the sovereignty of Apollonius over history or a last judgment or anything else along these lines. If anything, the fates are in control of the universe. The text, according to what one can glean from the epilogue, is to help people get through life joyously while accepting their fate-appointed destiny. Apollonius, exonerated from the charge of

---

[64] *Vita Ap.* 7.38: φύσεως, ὅτι θεία τε εἴη καὶ κρείττων ἀνθρώπου.

[65] *Vita Ap.* 8.7.7: φιλοσοφεῖ δὲ καὶ ὑπὲρ τῆς ἑαυτοῦ φύσεως καὶ ὅπη μετέχει τοῦ θείου...τάς τε ἀρετὰς θεόθεν ἥκειν ἐπ' αὐτὸν πέπεισται, καὶ τοὺς μετέχοντας ἀγχιθείους τε εἶναι καὶ θείους.

[66] Compare the discussion in Petzke 1970, 191ff.

wizardry, can help the reader live well. Hierocles' later work attacking Jesus and praising Apollonius does not claim divinity for Apollonius.[67] Hierocles' negative response to gospel traditions indicates his concern for their ability to persuade hearers.

In terms of the content, Mark and the *Vita Ap.* both contain miracle stories and exorcisms, among other narrative types. But the content of the portrayal of the figure of Apollonius and Jesus is different, since the text of Philostratus makes no universal claims about Apollonius's divinity or sovereignty.[68] The Gospel of Mark does make claims about Jesus being Son of God, Messiah, Son of Man, and world judge. Both texts may have similar functions (a question of pragmatics) if they are meant in part to give respective communities biographical information about a venerated figure. Gerd Petzke remarks that the *Vita Ap.* and the gospels are religious propaganda literature.[69] But the function of the *Vita Ap.*, on the one hand, is primarily to defend the hero from the charge of wizardry. The function of the Gospel of Mark (or part of the function), on the other hand, is to draw the reader into its narrative world and to challenge the reader to accept the text as good news.[70] If this is correct, then the Gospel of Mark has more of a "cultic" function than does the *Vita Ap.*[71]

---

[67]See Cook 1993, 244–46.

[68]Morton Smith (1978, 89–91) discusses the response to Hierocles' comparison of Apollonius with Christ by Eusebius (*The Treatise of Eusebius, the Son of Pamphilus, Against the Life of Apollonius of Tyana Written by Philostratus, Occasioned by the Parallel Drawn by Hierocles Between Him and Christ*) and Lactantius (in the *Div. Inst.* 5.2.12ff.).

[69]Petzke 1970, 62. Burridge 1992, 159 includes other bibliography on the *Life of Apollonius*.

[70]2.3.4 discusses the text as a speech act. See also 3.3.2 on the function of Mk 1:1 in clarifying the nature of the text.

[71]Talbert 1977, 101ff. compares the text with Mark because both are "cultic legends" in his terminology. But a cult of Apollonius in no way establishes the cultic nature of the *Vita Ap.*, though it does establish the possibility. The *Vita Ap.* 8.31 notes that there was a shrine for Apollonius at Tyana and that the emperors have not withheld honors from him. Alexander Severus had

This function is what I have called the "governing speech act" of the text and is a question of text-pragmatics.

4.3.5. Conclusion

One can use the tools of text linguistics to comment on the debate between Tolbert and Robbins concerning the genre of Mark.[72] The many interesting parallels that Tolbert finds between Mark and ancient novels are primarily stylistic or what I have called "text-syntactic": recognition scenes, dialogue within narrative summations, central turning points, and so forth. She argues that the *memorabilia* genre with its focus on the teacher cycle of Jesus and the disciples undervalues parts of Mark's story, such as biography's focus on the character of Jesus and aretalogy's focus on miracle working.[73] In addition, she argues, Xenophon's *Memorabilia* exhibits a much higher literary skill and philosophical acumen than Mark's text. On the other hand, Robbins concentrates on text-semantic aspects in his comparison of Mark and Xenophon's text. Both have a disciple-gathering teacher whose career as an adult is described along with the teacher's death and appointment of students to carry on his message. Certainly from the point of view of content or text-semantics, Mark is closer to the *Memorabilia* than to romance

---

statues of certain deified emperors and holy men placed in his private shrine, including Alexander the Great, Apollonius, Christ, Abraham and Orpheus (*SHA Alex. Sev.* 29.2, 31.5 and discussed with skepticism in R. MacMullen 1981, 190, n. 64—see also Talbert 1977, 107). According to Dio 78.18 (ed. LCL) Caracalla erected a shrine to Apollonius. Lactantius (*Div. Inst.* 5.3.14) notes that Apollonius has been worshiped by some as God and that his statue under the name of Hercules Alexicacus is honored by the inhabitants of Ephesus. The text of the *Vita Ap.* itself does not seem to support Talbert's analysis. Esser 1969 compares both texts by considering the units that are used such as miracle stories. For the "mimetic" function of narrative see Perrin 1974a, 37. See also Beardslee 1975 and Boers 1981.

[72] Their positions are summarized in 1.2.3 and 1.5.4.

[73] Tolbert 1989, 59; and see 1.5.4.

novels. But from the point of view of style or text-syntax, Tolbert makes many important comparisons to the popular novel of Xenophon of Ephesus. Rather than saying that one scholar is right and the other wrong, it seems preferable to note that both have made good contributions to the cause of investigating Mark's relationship to the literature of the Mediterranean world. I would propose to identify "gospel" as a subgenre of biography; although it has close parallels with both types of literature, it is not to be identified with either *memorabilia* or popular novels.

Hellholm[74] (using Hempfer's schema) describes "narrative" as a mode of writing, with "gospel" identified as a historical genre. Using the suggestions offered in 1.5.4 above by a variety of scholars (such as Talbert, Cancik, Berger, Hengel, Burridge, and Bryan), one can hypothesize that "gospel" is a sub-genre of "biography."[75] This leaves room for a recognition of the creative and somewhat unique nature of the various gospels while not attempting to divorce the sub-genre from its larger context of Hellenistic literature. The precise classification of the gospel genre is important, but more important is the continued attempt to draw analogies between the structure, semantics, and pragmatics of gospel texts and other Hellenistic texts. Martin Buss has argued that Gunkel's "essentialist" view of forms (an Aristotelian approach) should be replaced by "relationism." A form in such an approach is a pattern—"a system of relations that are an intrinsic part of reality." One of the relations that a pattern stands in is with an observer. A pattern is therefore

---

[74] Hellholm 1982, 169, where he applies Hempfer's schema (Hempfer 1973, 27ff.) to apocalyptic literature.

[75] Folkert Fendler's study is in accord with these results. The form of ancient biography is closest to that of the gospels. The Gospel of Mark can be called a special form of ancient biography. There are differences, such as the fact that the ancient biographies do not have a cultic use in religious communities, and that they are not anonymous (Fendler 1991, 78, 79). Fendler compares Mark with Philo's *Life of Moses*, Plutarch's *Aratus*, and Suetonius's *Divus Claudius* (Fendler 1991, 59–77) to arrive at his conclusions.

perspectival, and one can accept a variety of possible classifications. This is not nominalism, but a view that sees forms in the relation between the object and the observer. Therefore, scholars need not try to establish only one classification for the genre "gospel."[76] The attempt to completely divorce the gospels from Greco-Roman culture seems misguided and certainly unnecessary. One of text-linguistics' contributions to the debate about the genre of Mark is the clear distinction between semantics and pragmatics. The desire that Mark be viewed as a governing speech act with actual effects on readers changes the shape of the genre discussion. Mark becomes, in this vision, a dynamic text that changes hearers/readers.

4.4. The Messianic Secret and the Governing Speech Act in Mark

An important test case for our understanding of the governing speech act of Mark is the motif called the "Messianic Secret." From the point of view of semantics, one should analyze the texts that make up the motif and attempt to clearly define the motif. From a pragmatic point of view, one should attempt to determine the intended effect on the hearers of the "secret." A pragmatic approach also considers the speech acts that are combined to produce the motif. My goal is to show that the Messianic Secret confirms one of the main arguments of this work: the governing speech act of Mark intends to draw people into discipleship by leading them through the narrative world of the text. The narrative world includes the Messianic Secret with its picture of the unfolding of the identity of Jesus.

---

[76]Buss, 1993, 70, 71, 73. Compare Klaus Hempfer's evolutionary model of Gattung development which combines invariant features with variable ones (1973, 223–228). Hellholm (1980, 62–74) gives an overview of the entire issue. Burridge also has an evolutionary approach to genre that he derives from literary theorists (1992, 45). He rejects nominalism (every text is a unique genre) and Platonism (genres are ideal forms), although he does opt for one generic identification of the gospels as "lives" (1992, 32, 57, 240–59).

The discussion below has two focal points: the semantics and the pragmatics of the motif. Using a synchronic method that does not look at the motif in chronological development (first oral tradition, then editorial additions), Mark will be considered as a literary composition. This is in the effort to understand the semantics of the motif. One can analyze the motif on a more abstract level in Hellenistic literature just as one can consider a Greek word in its usage in a certain stage of Hellenistic Greek. Or one can look at the motif in its use in one text, just as one can analyze a word in its usage in a given text. I shall offer a definition of the motif that is tied to the flow of the narrative.

The pragmatics of the Messianic Secret considers the effect of the motif on the audience (hearers or readers). The motif consists of individual speech acts that will be summarized below. The speech acts are governed by an encompassing speech act I have called "gospel narrative." The commands to silence directed to the demons, for example, could be viewed as an interesting relic of the history of religion. But the governing speech act encourages the reader to see them as part of the good news for himself or herself.

The clarity about the semantics and pragmatics of the motif is the contribution text linguistics can make to prior work on the Messianic Secret. The persuasive power of the language of the "secret" exerts its pull on the audience of the text.

4.4.1. Semantics and the Motif

Below I shall consider the motif as a sign in analogy with a word. The analysis will focus on Mark as a literary composition and will not investigate different historical stages of the motif's development. One could compare an abstract version of the motif with other texts, but here only Mark will be used.

The Messianic Secret in Mark is a phenomenon that draws together a number of different parts of the text. It is a *signeme* that has generated much interest (see 1.3 above) among readers of Mark. Text linguistics can offer some insights into the nature of the problem. Being aware of whether one is using a synchronic (one temporal stage in a language) or diachronic (a language viewed through time) method on the level of *parole* (Mark alone), *langue* (Hellenistic Greek), or *langage* (many languages) can help. The categories just mentioned can be used on Mark viewed as tradition, redaction, or as a literary composition. To give a linguistic clarification to a textual motif is more difficult than to use linguistics to clarify words. A narrative motif, as used in this work, is a proposition about the characters that is true of a number of a text's parts, and can therefore be clearly inferred from those Text Parts. This definition should be taken only as a working one. It will serve the practical purpose here of using text linguistics to analyze the Messianic Secret in Mark.

Text linguistic researchers[77] have not been particularly interested in dealing with the problem of motif, although some French structuralists and others[78] have analyzed plots and elements of plots common to folk stories and other narratives. To establish the motif proposition's truth one needs to show that all or some of the Text Parts can generate the proposition. The motif has to be either explicitly present or the implied result of an analysis of the meanings of the Text Parts' words and sentences.

If one looks through ancient literature concerned with holy figures for similar phenomena to that of the Messianic Secret in Mark, one finds occasional references to figures who keep their identity secret. This more abstract motif is then analogous to a word that one investigates in all of its uses in Greek (*langue*), instead of looking only at its uses in a text such as Mark (*parole*). The abstract motif as a sign can have several meanings (*sememes*) and thus can have several references, such as Dionysus or Jesus.

---

[77]The closest Heger comes to including this important element in his work is his concept of an actantial presupposition chain, which refers to a text's ability to chain together a number of references to the same actor or object (Heger 1976, 299–302).

[78]Gülich and Raible 1977 discuss the narrative text models of Vladimir Propp, Claude Bremond, Tzvetan Todorov, Teun van Dijk, and Götz Wienold who attempt to find common elements in all narratives.

Consequently, on the level of an entire language (*langue*), one can consider a motif-proposition as a complex sign (*signifiant*) that could be described as in figure 4 below.

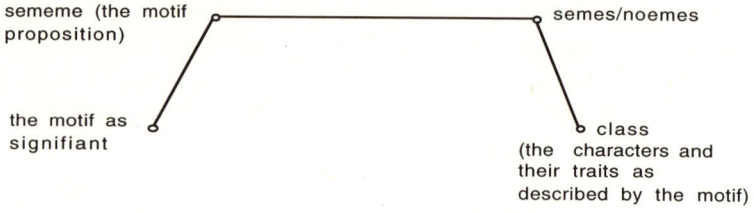

Fig. 4. The motif proposition as a complex sign

On the level of *langue* (one language) or *langage* (the system of all languages) the motif can appear in many texts. Bickerman attempts to give parallels, for example, to the secret messiah motif in other literature including the lives of saints, gods such as Dionysus of Euripides' *Bacchae*, prophets, and figures such as Baalschem, who are not recognized for a time by their onlookers even though the religious figures are aware of their own identity.[79] Here the motif is something like "a religious figure knows his/her identity, but keeps it secret for a time." This proposition would be the sign (or *signifiant*) with many possible meanings (*sememes*). The sign's referential meaning would be the "class" element of the trapezium. Jesus, Baalschem, and Dionysus are three members of the class.

On the level of *parole* one considers a motif as it appears in a given text such as Mark. My semantic analysis pictures the motif as a sign with one meaning (a "monosemized *signeme*"), given its context in Mark (see figure 5):

---

[79]Bickermann [*sic*] 1923, passim.

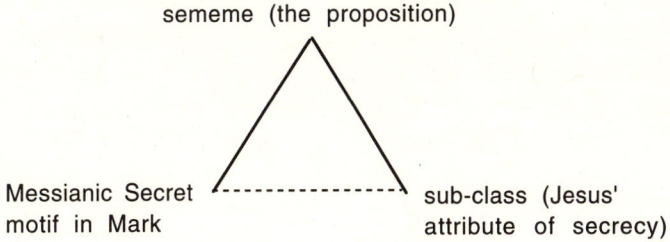

Fig. 5. The motif as a sign

The reference (sub-class) would be Jesus of Nazareth and his secret messiahship, and the meaning of the motif (*sememe*) would be the proposition expressing the Messianic Secret motif.[80] Dionysus and others would not appear in the sub-class because the context of the motif in Mark makes it clear that Jesus alone is the secret Messiah/Son of God. The proposition is composed of an ordered group of concepts (*semes/noemes* in the words of semantics).

4.4.2. The Definition of the Motif in Mark

A fundamental question in Markan scholarship is the meaning of the Messianic Secret motif (as a proposition), and what is its scope when one considers the Markan text as it stands.[81] Many articles and books on the Messianic Secret do not attempt to give a precise definition of the motif. With a vague motif one is at a loss to decide whether or not the Markan text sustains the motif. The works of Ulrich Luz, William Robinson, C. F. D. Moule, and Heikki Räisänen have attacked the notion of a general Messianic

---

[80]For a discussion of the sub-class or extension of a *signeme*, see the discussion in 2.2.3.

[81]C. F. D. Moule 1975, 247 pleads for the interpretation of Mark "as it stands" in addition to the other methods of criticism. This method we have called synchronic interpretation.

Secret in Mark which can be found in all parts of the text.[82] Räisänen, for example, concludes that only the commands to silence directed to the demons and the disciples can be considered to constitute the Messianic Secret (viz. that Jesus is the Son of God or Christ must be kept silent.)[83] If one defines the Messianic Secret this tightly, then Räisänen may be correct because such texts as the disciples' misunderstanding in 4:13 and 7:18[84] do not obviously relate to Jesus' identity. Other misunderstandings about Jesus' identity in Mark, such as 4:41, 6:52, and 8:14ff., Räisänen believes are cleared up after 8:29.[85] This fact, for Räisänen, goes against the belief that the Messianic Secret is only cleared up at the cross and resurrection. Furthermore, Räisänen claims,[86] the motif of the misunderstanding of the disciples does not need the Messianic Secret (as is the case in John), and the Messianic Secret does not have the paraenetic theme which the motif of misunderstanding has. The problem Räisänen uncovers is twofold: how to define the Messianic Secret; and how to marshal textual evidence for the Messianic Secret?

Both of these problems are acute in scholarship, and it seems clear that little progress will be made on resolving the Messianic Secret debate until scholars are willing to give clear definitions of the motif such that others can then look for pertinent evidence in the text. At least the following facts about the text will have to be taken into account in forming the motif-proposition.

---

[82]Luz 1965, Robinson 1973; Moule 1975; Räisänen 1990. See also the discussion in 1.3.

[83]Räisänen 1990, 242. 9:9 is Markan for Räisänen, but he finds it difficult to draw "connective lines from 9:9 to other parts of the secrecy complex" (1990, 185ff., 188).

[84]Räisänen 1990, 216. Räisänen does concede that the idea of parables as riddles may point to the same dynamics that contributed to the Messianic Secret (1990, 143, 245).

[85]Räisänen 1990, 217.

[86]Räisänen 1990, 242.

(1.) Of all the sixteen exorcisms and miracles only three have commands to silence, with the possible addition of 8:26 (see 1.3.2 above).

(2.) Jesus' identity is openly revealed as Son of Man, Son of God, or Son of David in 2:10, 2:28, 5:7 (without a crowd around), in 8:38, 10:45, 12:1-12 (almost openly), in 14:62, and 15:39.[87]

(3.) The statement in 9:9 does not refer to a theology of the cross, as Luz unconvincingly attempts to prove;[88] it refers to the resurrection by any straightforward exegesis.

(4.) Misunderstanding remains even after the resurrection (16:8).[89]

Räisänen says little more than that something important about Jesus could only be known in the time after his death and resurrection, and that Mark wanted to keep the Christological confession from a premature revelation.[90] Yet Räisänen, as T. A.

---

[87] Räisänen 1990, 224ff. and Moule 1975. G. H. Boobyer's attempt to avoid much of this evidence is unpersuasive in Boobyer, 1960. Kingsbury (I think successfully) disassociates the "Son of Man" and "Son of David" titles from the "Son of God" secret (1.3.5). An interesting point of disagreement between Kingsbury and Räisänen is the question whether 12:12 contradicts the parable theory in 4:11-12 (Räisänen 1990, 88, 89, 224; Kingsbury 1983 17, 114). Räisänen argues that the "intellectual understanding" that the opponents have in 12:12 contradicts 4:11-12. However, Kingsbury seems more correct, because it is quite clear that the leaders do not "repent" so Mark does not fully contradict himself.

[88] Luz, 1965, 26ff.

[89] Theodore Weeden 1971 and Frank Kermode 1979 both strongly emphasize the element of misunderstanding in Mark—sometimes to excess. On 16:8, see Horstmann 1969, 138.

[90] Räisänen 1976, 166-167. In his 1990 (254, 257) edition Räisänen sees the secret less as a religious conviction of Mark than as an expression of an argument between Hellenistic Christians (including Mark) and Palestinian wandering preachers (possibly a Q-group) that misunderstood the passion and resurrection.

Burkill before him, acknowledges that the element of openness is unavoidable in Mark.[91]

4.4.3. A Dynamic Understanding of the Motif

The question of Mark's intention in including the motif of secrecy (an issue of pragmatics) will be left aside. As it stands, the Gospel is complex in its presentation of the disciples' relationship to Jesus and in its portrayal of the revelation of Jesus' identity. The text seems to resist precise abstractions about the time and method of the revelation of Jesus' identity. At this point (along the lines of Räisänen and Kingsbury) I recommend the following version of the Messianic Secret: Jesus' identity as Christ and Son of God must be concealed temporarily; it becomes clearer as the text nears the cross and resurrection, but misunderstanding remains until the end. The advance over Wrede here is that the motif becomes dynamic instead of static. Instead of looking for an abstraction such as "Jesus' identity is not revealed until the resurrection," the flow of the narrative is taken into account. In text linguistic categories, Kingsbury works with a synchronic level, examining Mark as it stands. This method results in a convincing picture of the secret. The confusion between synchronic and diachronic approaches has tended to obscure the issue of reaching a clear understanding of the motif.[92] Crucial to the success of the above definition of the motif is the thesis that the "Son of David" title is an inadequate (but not false) understanding of Jesus.[93] Whether Kingsbury has

---

[91] Burkill 1963 gives clear evidence for the polarity of openness and hiddenness in Mark.

[92] Confusion between paradigmatic and syntagmatic approaches has also generated problems.

[93] In Mk 12:37 the πόθεν (how) is a word that is syntactically ambiguous. What kind of answer does the word demand when it is used in a question? The evidence shows that the word's use does not justify the claim that Jesus' answer means "the 'Son of David' is a wrong title" (see Lk 1:43, John 1:48, 6:5). The logical schema is how (πῶς) is it the case that S1 (a statement) is

successfully shown that "Son of Man" does not reveal Jesus' identity in itself (see also 1.3.5 above) will be controversial. "Son of Man" alone has several meanings (*sememes*).[94] In its use in Mark and some Jewish literature such as Enoch and the Targum to Ps 80, the term has a *seme* "unique being" and is therefore what

---

true given S2 (another statement) as in John 6:42, 8:33, 12:34, 14:9, and 1 Cor 15:12. In 1 Cor 15:12, S1 (no resurrection—15:12b) is false given S2 (15:12a—Paul's argument). In all the Johannine examples except 14:9, S1 (Jesus' statement) is true because something is wrong with S2 [the hearers' belief: e.g., John 12:34 ὁ Χριστός...αἰῶνα (the Christ...forever]). John 14:9 is perhaps the best logical parallel to Mark (although πῶς is the "how" word) because S1 (δεῖξον...πατέρα [show...the father]) is Philip's statement and S2 is Jesus' response. S1 is not totally wrong but is misconceived because in Jesus they have seen the Father. The scribes' conception of Son of David is misconceived, and one can only speculate exactly what their concept is. In Ps Sol 17:21 and *b. San.* 97a–98b the rabbis do not conceive the Son of David as a κύριος figure who must sit (after his death) at God's side for a period until his enemies are conquered. Klostermann (1971, on 12:37) and Pesch (1977 on 12:37) both agree in not seeing the text as a total rejection of the title. Achtemeier (1978, 128ff.) argues that Mark does not see Jesus as the Son of David. For a finely nuanced position, see Kingsbury 1983, 109ff.

[94]The rabbis (as is well known) used the term בר נשא for "human being" as in *p. Keth.* 12.35a, line 10: כמה דבר נשא אזל הוא אתי (as a person goes [dies], so will he come [rise from the dead]). In *p. Shevi.* 9.38d, line 28ff., Simeon ben Yochay uses the term to refer to humans including himself (text in Cook 1988, 143). That is one *sememe* of the expression. Str-B 1.485, 486, 956–959 still have one of the best collections of relevant texts for the use of the title for a supernatural being (another *sememe* of the expression). Texts in Ethiopic Enoch such as *walda be'si* ("Son of Man" in 69.29, 71.14) and *walda'egwāla-'emma-heyyaw* ("son of the offspring of the mother of the living" in 69.26, 27, 70.1, 71.17) certainly contain a *seme* "unique being." (I am indebted to Dr. Patrick Tiller for the notes on Enoch.) This *seme* is also present in the Targum to Ps 80:18 which has בר נש (who is a messianic king in 80:16 of the Targum). Kingsbury 1983, 166 ff. refers to much of the literature on the title.

logicians call a "definite description."⁹⁵ Because "Son of Man" alone could be understood to mean "human being," Jesus does not break the secrecy motif in 2:10, 28, and 8:38. His public claims to have the power to forgive (2:10), to have authority over the Sabbath (2:28), and his reference to a future return by the Son of Man that vindicates Jesus' words (8:38) do not in themselves reveal his identity as Messiah and Son of God. It is not the title but the claims Jesus attaches to the title that bother his opponents in the text of Mark (2:10, 28).⁹⁶ 8:38 causes no response in the narrative. In support of this position one can point to the only use in the canonical gospels of "Son of Man," where it appears in a mouth other than that of Jesus. John 12:34 reads:

Ἀπεκρίθη οὖν αὐτῷ ὁ ὄχλος· ἡμεῖς ἠκούσαμεν ἐκ τοῦ νόμου ὅτι ὁ χριστὸς μένει εἰς τὸν αἰῶνα, καὶ πῶς λέγεις σὺ ὅτι δεῖ ὑψωθῆναι τὸν υἱὸν τοῦ ἀνθρώπου; . . .

The crowd answered him: we have heard from the law that the Christ remains forever, and how do you say that the Son of Man must be lifted up?

The crowd cannot understand the import of the title "Son of Man"; they try to relate it to the more traditional title "Christ." They do understand the claim that Jesus makes about "the Son of Man," namely, that he must be lifted up. The ambiguous title "Son of Man" fits nicely the secrecy motif.

---

[95] A definite description would also be, e.g., "the author of Mark." The term is used in exegesis in Gibson 1981, 137–8 and can be defined in informal logic as (see Carnap 1956, 32) "an individual who is F such that only one individual is F." "F" is the definite description such as "Son of Man."

[96] Fendler 1991, 139 notes that Mk 2:10, 28 belong to the controversies which end with the indication in 3:6 of the rejection of Jesus by the opponents. The public statements of Jesus are therefore not "revelation."

The foregoing remarks concern the semantics of the motif in Mark. Semantics includes the question concerning the meaning of the Messianic Secret. In particular, the statements with Christological titles are important in determining the scope of the secret. Linguistics also brings needed precision to the synchronic/diachronic confusion in scholarship. A method that looks for tradition and redaction is diachronic. Kingsbury's and the above arguments hopefully show that a synchronic method that approaches the text of Mark as a literary unit yields good results.[97]

Aspects of the secrecy motif cohere well with the text analysis in Chapter Three above. The section entitled "Jesus' journey to Jerusalem" begins in 8:27 and ends at 10:52. Its beginning in 8:27ff. shows the agreement of the change in the episode markers—the appearance of Jesus on the "way"—with the new understanding of Jesus' identity by Peter.[98] From 8:27 onward the disciples have an awareness of Jesus' identity. During the same journey God tells several disciples who Jesus is and commands them to listen to his beloved son (9:7). During the journey the sons of Zebedee question Jesus (10:37) and illustrate their dawning but imperfect understanding of Jesus' identity. The person who comes closest to penetrating the secret of Jesus' identity, the "pagan" Centurion (15:39), does it in sight of the cross in the Jerusalem episode (11:1-16:8). That episode has the greatest concentration of spatial and temporal markers in all of Mark with its focus on the suffering in the last days of Jesus' life. Mark makes Jerusalem the place of the revelation of Jesus' identity as Son of God. After viewing Jesus' death, a "pagan" sees what others have not seen. Unlike the high priest (14:61-64), the centurion believes what he is saying (whatever he means by the words). The confession seems almost as "supernatural" or

---

[97]Though not ignoring the issue of the Markan redaction of many motifs in the Messianic Secret, Fendler sees it to be the unifying general theme of the Gospel (1991, 140-146).

[98]Koch has demonstrated the correspondence of "theme" and geography at this point in Mark (1983, 146-149).

unexplained as the knowledge of Jesus' identity by those demonically inspired voices of prostrate demoniacs (3:11).

The dynamic understanding of the secrecy motif seems an improvement upon attempts to reduce the Text Parts of Mark to a static proposition, such as "Jesus' identity remains secret until the resurrection." The contribution of text linguistics in this endeavor includes clarifying the issue by the use of categories including the following: synchronic approaches; diachronic approaches; *parole* (the text of Mark only); *langue* (other texts in Greek including Euripides' *Bacchae*, etc.); *langage* (texts from several languages); and all of the five previous categories in combination with the understanding of Mark on the level of tradition, redaction, or literary composition. The approach in this section is on the level of *parole* (Mark only) with a synchronic analysis of the Gospel on the level of Mark as a literary composition. Insistence on scholars defining the motif can lead to greater clarity.

Tolbert has a different view of the secrecy motif from the one expressed here. She writes: "Understanding the disciples' desire for glory and renown as a foil to Jesus' actions suggests a different construction for secrecy: Jesus' commands for silence and his attempts to stay hidden define his steadfast rejection of personal renown and glory."[99] She believes this alternative to be an improvement over Wrede since Jesus' messianic identity is not secret to Peter (8:29), the demons, or the scribes and Jerusalem leaders (12:12, 14:61–62). Her motif is defined very clearly. However, the fact that the leaders do not accept Jesus' messianic identity shows that they have not penetrated the secret. Consequently, the results of this study are slightly different from hers. But her view of the contrast between the secrecy surrounding Jesus' identity with the disciples' desire for renown is consistent with my approach. Robbins's study of Jesus the teacher does not use the motif of secrecy to understand Mark.[100] But his study does uncover a narrative progression in the use of

---

[99]Tolbert 1989, 227.

[100]Robbins 1992, 77–79.

the christological titles that coincides with his outline of the text.[101] My work is supportive of such a narrative development in the perception of Jesus' identity, but it does include the emphasis on secrecy.

Text linguistics also underlines the distinction between semantics and pragmatics. The appeal to the users of Mark's language (e.g., an implied or "real" reader) raises the question of the effect of the motif on people.

4.4.4. A Pragmatic Understanding of the Motif

The pragmatics of the motif can also be illuminated by linguistics. The scholars who use a concept of the reader in their work on the Messianic Secret (Dibelius, Tillesse, Bickerman, Ebeling, Dahl, Kingsbury; see 1.3.6 above) are working with pragmatics and have reached a consensus in the field: the motif functions to guide the implied reader into an experience, understanding and confession of Jesus. With such a definition the misunderstanding of the disciples, the obscurity of the parables, and the occasional motif of silence in the miracles can be loosely related to the Messianic Secret but not identified with it.[102] From a semantic point of view the motif keeps Jesus' identity secret until the story nears the cross and the resurrection. From a pragmatic point of view the motif is constantly revealing Jesus' identity to the narrator's audience. The secrecy language is not just a narrative description of the time of Jesus' revelation of himself, but it actually does reveal him to implied readers and to the actual audience. Therefore, one can call it a narrative speech act whose illocution is initiating the reader into the secret. The intended perlocution would be the actual understanding, experience, and confession of Jesus on the part of a real reader (or hearer).

The narrative speech act ("gospel narrative") governs the individual speech acts that make up the secret, including the

---

[101] Robbins 1992, 19–48, 184–185.
[102] Compare Kingsbury 1983, 22.

commands to silence directed to demons in 1:24–25,[103] 1:34, and 3:11, 12. The perlocution of the commands is the actual obedience of the demons to Jesus words. The narrator does not

---

[103]The meaning of the word φιμώθητι (be bound, be silenced) in Mk 1:25 can serve as an example of the problem of deciding the correct meaning of a word. The *sememe* of φιμώθητι (in Mark) is probably "be silent" and not "be bound" as E. Rohde translates (Rohde 1921, 424 using other texts). Rohde points to uses of the verb and noun where a magician binds gods, demons and ἄωρα (restless souls) to his/her purposes. Of course, such a use could be in the background (pragmatics) of Mark. A text in Kenyon 1893 pap 121.396 describes binding an ἄωρον to one's purposes (although φιμοτικόν here may mean a "silencing/muzzling formula"). In 121.968ff. φίμωσον is addressed to a god who is to "bind" a certain person for the magician: φίμωσον, ὑπόταξον καταδούλωσον τόν ᶠ τῷ ᶠ καὶ ποίησον αὐτὸν ὑπὸ τοὺς πόδας μοι ἐλθῇ (bind, subordinate, and enslave this one to that one and make him come under my feet). Here φίμωσον seems likely to have the *sememe* "bind" or "muzzle" rather than "silence," but it could also be a silence charm. LSJ φιμός (muzzle) gives more relevant material. A text in Audollent 1904, 15.24 has the verb used to silence mouths in a curse to be carried out by a god. Audollent 1904, 22.42 also has a use of φίμωσον where demons are to silence an accuser as in 23.2. See Audollent's index on 476ff.

The linguistic issue is whether the *sememe* "be silent" or "be bound" is correct. The other use of the verb in Mark (4:39) is accompanied by another verb for silence and so encourages the reader to use the silence *sememe* for 1:25. But Jesus could be binding a demonic sea and silencing it in 4:39, so there is still an ambiguity. Baldinger (1980, 149, 150) notes that when the syntagmatic environment (syntax or context) is not adequate to resolve an ambiguity one must turn to the situation or extraverbal context and get feedback from the speaker. In the Markan context "be silent" fits best since the demon has claimed knowledge of Jesus and expressed it publicly. This is an argument based on the immediate context. This choice is also supported by such texts as Mk 3:12, where Jesus silences the demons. The appeal to 3:12 is textually based, but appeals to a situation that is outside the situation of 1:25. 3:12 encourages the reader to believe that Jesus might have the intention to silence demons in 1:25. The claim about Jesus' intention is about an extraverbal context (in reference to 1:25).

indicate that they disobeyed. The command appears in communication Frame 2 in 1:24–25, but the narrator (Frame 1) reports the speech act in 1:34 and 3:11, 12. The speech act of confession/assertion appears in Frame 2 in 8:29 and is either true or false.[104] The confession/assertion in Frame 2 in 15:39 is also either true or false—whether the centurion means "Son of God" in a supernatural sense (as surely the demons do) or in the sense of a "virtuous king."[105] Jesus' command concerning the transfiguration in 9:9 appears in communication Frame 2, and the narrator does not mention the disciples' breaking the command. They do not repeat publicly, for example, the words of the voice from the cloud (9:7), "This is my son." Kingsbury's texts (see section 1.3.5 above) that he uses to argue for a secrecy motif concerning the Son of God are assertions that appear in Frames 0 and 2. The narrator's title in Frame 0 may contain the expression (1:1— if the longer text is original). The other uses of "Son of God" appear in communication Frame 2, as direct address to Jesus in the second person (1:11, 5:7, 14:61), in a third person description of Jesus (9:7), and in Jesus' parabolic speech about himself (12:6). God's identification of Jesus, an assertion (9:7), contains an imperative to "listen to him." The disciples listen to him, and thus the imperative's perlocution is satisfied.

---

[104]Wörner 1978, 52–54 reviews assertions. J. L. Austin, in a manuscript, called them "constatives" and made a long list of them (reference in Wörner 1978, 54, 55). Austin (1970, 250) distinguishes statements from many other types of speech acts by noting that they are either true or false.

[105]Robbins, (1992, 189–191) with reference to Dio Chrysostom 4.39–45, understands the centurion's use of "Son of God" to be analogous to "Son of Zeus." Compare Kingsbury 1983, 153, who does not distinguish the centurion's use of the expression from the other uses in Mark. Robbins works with a semantics on the level of Hellenistic Greek (*langue*), while Kingsbury works with a semantics on the level of Mark's text only (*parole*). Although he understands the Centurion's acclamation to be a confession of faith, Räisänen (1990, 239; Plutarch *Kleomenes* 39, 823e) calls attention to the onlookers of the crucified Kleomenes (with a snake wrapped around his head), who call him a "son of the gods" [θεῶν παῖς].

The otherworldly voice's identifications of Jesus in 1:11 and 9:7 are a form of "divine speech" that was very persuasive in drawing people into the Christian movement in late antiquity. Celsus objected to Jesus' use of a human voice to persuade people. In response to Celsus' objection that "The body of a god does not use that [Jesus'] method of persuasion," Origen notes that the Pythian and Didymean Apollo used a human voice (the Pythian priestess and the prophetess at Miletus). He then writes:

> "But how much superior to this was it for God to make use of a voice which effected conviction in those who heard in some indescribable way, because it was proclaimed with power [πολλῷ δὲ τούτου βέλτιον ἦν χρήσασθαι τὸν θεὸν φωνῇ ἐμποιούσῃ διὰ τὸ μετὰ δυνάμεως ἀπαγγέλλεσθαι ἄφατόν τινα πειθὼ τοῖς ἀκούουσιν]."[106]

Origen has extensive discussions on the power of Christian language to persuade many hearers.[107] He understands this power to be divinely given. The voice from heaven was not persuasive to all readers. Celsus's Jew composes a logical conundrum for the Christians: "If he wanted to be unnoticed, why was the voice from heaven heard, proclaiming him as Son of God? Yet if he did not want to be unnoticed why was he punished or why did he die?"[108] The voice from heaven was not persuasive to Celsus, as he makes clear with his other remarks denying that Jesus was a Son of God.[109] Origen challenged Celsus to find the source of the gospels' "persuasive power" (δύναμις πειστική). Origen's answer is that God gives this power.[110] One can hypothesize that statements in Mark such as 1:11 and 9:7 exerted the same persuasive force on hearers that the other

---

[106] *C. Cels.* 1.70 (ed. Koetschau); ET in Henry Chadwick 1959, 64. This text is discussed in Cook 1994, 125.
[107] Cook 1994, 122–125.
[108] *C. Cels.* 2.72; ET in Chadwick 1959, 121.
[109] Cook 1993, 236, 237.
[110] *C. Cels.* 1.62; discussed in Cook 1994, 122, 123.

Christian language exerted in Origen's observations. Origen is not just making a theological argument about persuasive force that was not based on the fact of the texts' ability to persuade hearers. Julian complained about the Christians' use of persuasion. Christians "do not look to the truth but to that which will persuade all men [τὸ πᾶσι πιθανὸν βλέποντες]."[111] Celsus believes that Jesus won over only ten sailors and tax collectors. But he then asks: "Is it not utterly ludicrous that when he was alive himself he convinced nobody; but now that he is dead, those who wish to do so convince multitudes?"[112] Given these comments by later authors on the persuasive force of Christian language, it seems to be a well grounded hypothesis that speech acts such as 1:11 and 9:7 exerted a strong pull on hearers.

The individual speech acts together serve to guide the reader/hearer into an understanding of Jesus and a confession of Jesus. The speech act we have named "gospel narrative" governs the smaller speech act units which all appear in communication Frames 1 and 2. Mk 1:1 is the narrator's truth claim (in Frame 0) concerning the text, namely that it is "good news" or "true good news." The concept of speech act implies that the Markan language is performing an action. A man who tells his parents that an object is "given to God" gives the object to God by virtue of his words. By narrating the good news with its secretive Messiah/Son of God, Mark draws a reader or hearer into the narrative. The reader or hearer has to respond to the truth claim in 1:1 (and consequently the rest of the text) positively or negatively. In other words, a reader has to determine if the centurion's assertion in 15:39 and the voice from the cloud's assertion (9:7) are true or false. The words of the text may actually effect a persuasive change in the reader. That is the

---

[111]Julian, *C. Gal.* 320c (LCL III, 410). Cook 1993, 254. Compare Cook 1994, 111, 112 with the reference to *C. Celsum* 3.55, Celsus's famous complaint about the Christians who proselytize women and children.

[112]Origen, *C. Celsum* 2.46.

intended perlocution of the "gospel narrative" speech act. It could and did occasionally fail.[113]

An understanding of Mark as a governing speech act that attempts to persuade the reader to become a disciple of Jesus can contribute to the understanding of Mark as a dynamic text. The structure of Mark given in Chapter Three includes many references to speech acts. Each one is subordinated to the governing speech act mentioned in 1:1. This includes the Messianic Secret, which is composed of speech acts such as commands. The text consists of an orderly sequence of speech acts that accomplish the governing speech act I have chosen to call a "gospel narrative."

4.4.5. Concluding Remarks on the Messianic Secret

The distinction between semantics and pragmatics offers a new angle on the nature of the secret. In terms of semantics, one can give a propositional form to the motif. Kingsbury was not concerned to establish a propositional form for the Messianic Secret, and in that respect text linguistics can offer some additional clarity. The secret is not just a literary characteristic of Mark, because a pragmatic approach emphasizes the actual effect of the language on the receivers of the language. The readers or hearers are not just "implied," but are people that actually used the text. This is a speculative enterprise, but it is aided by comments such as those of Origen and Augustine in 2.3.4. The various speech acts that make up the Messianic Secret are subordinate to the speech act in 1:1. They do, in a sense, "unpack" the governing speech act by showing how a reader is to come to trust that the words of the text of Mark are good news. The voice from heaven (1:11, 9:7) gives these speech acts a peculiar authority. The alleged "divine power" of the gospels to persuade people did not go unnoticed in antiquity. My

---

[113]For failure of the gospels to convince, see Cook 1993. For the success of Christian language to persuade hearers (including Hilary's conversion by the Gospel of John), see Cook 1994.

approach affirms the persuasive power of a text like Mark. The text is a dynamic object that is able to actually effect a change in its audience. The Messianic Secret serves as part of that textual function. One could therefore call the Messianic Secret a part of the strategy of Christian "propaganda." The fact that some people successfully resisted the persuasive pull of the gospels and Christian language that used gospel traditions simply illustrates my point.[114] The language of Mark and texts like it was able to exert a powerful attraction on many hearers. To repeat Augustine's words: "Through these texts the Christian religion has been disseminated through the whole world."[115]

---

[114]Cook 1993; 1994, 125.
[115]Aug. *De Cons. Evang.* 1.7.10 (CSEL 43.10).

CHAPTER FIVE

CONCLUSION

5.1. The Thesis of the Work

The text linguistic method presented in this work can increase the tools of historical critical exegesis. This thesis is well grounded by the evidence given in the previous chapters. The chapters provide a method for giving better reasons for the exegetical results. The insight that Mark has a speech act that governs the individual speech acts of the entire text builds on older insights, but it nevertheless offers a new way of conceiving the structure and persuasive power of the text.[1] Three topics were chosen in Chapter Four to illustrate the power of the governing speech act: texts in Mk 1:2–13, 14–15 and Mk 8:27–9:1; the genre of Mark; and the motif of the Messianic Secret. The governing speech act encourages the reader to accept the text as good news. The persuasive power of the speech act is illustrated by both the negative and positive responses to gospel language in late antiquity.[2] Mark's author makes statements about the world and attempts to change the reader or hearer. This understanding

---

[1] See 2.3.4, 2.3.5., 2.4, and 3.3.2 for the development of the concept of a governing speech act in Mark.

[2] See 2.3.4, 4.2.1, 4.2.2, and 4.4.4.

results in a dynamic picture of the text of Mark—a text that has the power to change its hearers and readers.

The texts in Mark 1:2–13, 14–15 and Mark 8:27–9:1 illustrate the ability of the speech act in Mark 1:1 to govern the speech acts in the rest of the text. The governing speech act indicates that readers will experience the power of the text to persuade (or to repulse, as in the case of the "pagan" critics of the NT). According to Augustine (see 2.3.4 above), words such as these helped "christianize" the Greco-Roman world. The disciples' persuasion (including Peter's confession in 8:27ff.) are examples of the persuasive force of the language. Like political propaganda, the words are able to change people. This casts a social light upon the interpretation of the gospels. People and their communities are drawn into the picture—a concern of pragmatics. The language does not just have meaning (the concern of semantics), but it has effects on people that can be investigated.

The question of Mark's genre can be cast in terms of the syntax, semantics, and pragmatics of gospel texts. The governing speech act illuminates the pragmatics of Mark's gospel—a text that draws the reader/hearer into its narrative world and persuades him or her to accept the text as good news. A comparison with a text such as the *Vita Apollonii* shows that the function of Mark has a different persuasive force from the text of Philostratus. Discussions of Mark's genre that leave out syntax, semantics, or pragmatics need to be broadened, and we have given an example of a set of criteria that are useful in describing the genre of Mark (see 4.3.1 above). One can describe the gospels as a subgenre of "biography" without ignoring their somewhat unique nature and without divorcing them from their surrounding context in Hellenistic literature.

The distinction between semantics and pragmatics also illuminates the Messianic Secret motif. From a semantic point of view, the motif is given a propositional form (see 4.4.3 above). From a pragmatic point of view, the motif is viewed in light of its effect on readers or hearers. The secret is not just a literary fact about the text, but is instead a method by which the text guides the readers or hearers into an understanding of Jesus and a confession of Jesus. The text could fail in this purpose (see 4.4.4 above). The narrator's claim to be telling true "good news" in Mark 1:1 is a speech act that governs the speech acts that make up the Messianic Secret. For example, the centurion's assertion in Mk 15:39 and the assertion by the voice from heaven in Mk 9:7 are not just interesting facts from the religious literature of the Greco-Roman world. Instead, because of the governing speech act, they are themselves speech acts that may have exerted a strong pull on readers and hearers (see 4.4.4 above). The secrecy motif, from this pragmatic point of view, is a dynamic object that contributes to Mark's ability to effect a change in the audience.

5.2. Semantics and Pragmatics

The work has analyzed semantics and pragmatics as being distinct approaches to the text of Mark. There is actually an overlap between both aspects of the text, since semantics (on the level of *langue* and *langage*) depends on isolating texts from the ancient culture and claiming that they illuminate or even create the possibility of understanding the Markan text. One begins with the text of Mark (*parole*), moves to other NT texts as closest to Mark's cultural background, then moves to the LXX, other Hellenistic texts, and then classical texts. This process involves the recognition that Mark's language behavior emerges from a cultural consensus about how to use words and larger signs. This cultural consensus can be expressed as a pragmatic presupposition of the most basic variety: "Mark expects his audience to be aware of the current linguistic usage and may assume awareness of LXX usage and so forth."[3] The lexicon we use to understand the text of Mark is based on a summary of ancient linguistic behavior by the lexicographer. An illustration of the above pragmatic presupposition from outside Mark is the

---

[3] This is my formulation.

word ἐπιούσιον in Mt 6:11.[4] The rarity of the word indicates that the ancient author probably had specific expectations about the audience being aware of the word's *sememe*, unless the author did not understand the word himself.

The pragmatic analysis of the Gospel's function (4.2 above) as a governing speech act is based on semantic evidence, such as the use of the word "gospel." But the claims made in that section are actually a large pragmatic presupposition about the function of the text as Mark conceived it. The pragmatic presupposition is indirectly accessible because of the presence of 1:1 and the other evidence drawn from the text. Nevertheless, the results are inherently more speculative than the results of semantics.

5.3. Text Linguistics and Exegesis

The linguistics used in this work has many roots in the movement known as "analytic philosophy." It also has roots in Hellenistic philosophy, as the footnotes have shown the careful reader. As I have attempted to make clear, the method sketched above does not attempt to "refute" all other methods of exegesis and replace them. My intention is only to enrich the tools of the historical critical exegete and to produce a method with some power in its own right. Richard Rorty has recently noted the juristic nature of much of analytic philosophy in which a scholar attempts to refute another philosopher's position in the same way that a law student does casebook studies.[5] This puts philosophers in an adversarial relationship with one another. Often a new method casts itself in an adversarial role with other work. Perhaps, that helps to highlight the differences between the new method and those old methods that the new one seeks to dislodge. Stephen Moore's work[6] is an example. Moore

---

[4]A TLG search on the word found no references to it outside of texts that depend on or interpret Matthew. The TLG does not include papyri, ostraka, and inscriptions.

[5]Rorty 1982, 227, 230, n. 3.

[6]Moore 1989.

appeals to an argument that claims that what we perceive is shaped by interpretive acts.[7] The conclusion is that there is no independent text to put constraints on readers' interpretations. This argument is similar to the empiricists' old argument from illusion in which problems in sense experience (such as seeing a stick that looks bent when placed half underwater) were taken to lead to the conclusion that we should no longer speak about objective physical objects. From such an argument Moore deduces a number of fascinating and almost wistful proposals for an exegesis without philosophical illusions (such as the one about there being an objective text that can overrule certain interpretations).[8] Moore's critique of "naive empiricism" or "hermeneutic realism" attempts to cast all unphilosophical critics in a negative light.[9] The argument mentioned above does not in itself establish Moore's conclusion (namely the conclusion that there is no "objective text"). Rather, the fact that interpretive experience is guided by various concepts shows that we experience literature under the influence of a number of different conventions and beliefs.

Rorty argues that there is no great difference between what physicists and critics do. He writes:

> The strong textualist simply asks himself the same question about a text which the engineer or the physicist asks himself about a puzzling physical object: how shall I describe this in order to get it to do what I want...the pragmatist reminds us that a new and useful vocabulary is just *that*, not a sudden unmediated vision of things or texts as they are.[10]

---

[7]Moore 1989, 116.
[8]Moore 1989, 128, 172.
[9]Moore 1989, 116.
[10]Rorty 1982, 153. In xlvi, n. 31 Rorty notes that a pragmatist "... regards all vocabularies as tools for accomplishing purposes and none as representations of how things really are...."

To draw a corollary with biblical studies: exegetes ask themselves questions about puzzling physical objects (texts): how shall we describe these texts in order to get them to do what we want? Text linguistics is another new vocabulary for attempting to say things about the historical meaning of ancient texts. It should be judged on its ability to get the texts to speak to us in what we take to be their original meaning. The fact that our perceptions of such ancient meanings are guided by modern presuppositions, beliefs, and concepts does not have to stop us from doing such work. Most of us surely do not "want" the texts to say anything that we can force them to say using some interpretive framework. We "want" the texts to provide constraints on what we say about them. Elisabeth Schüssler Fiorenza writes (quoting J. Hillis Miller) in this regard: "The ethics of reading which respects the rights of the text and assumes that the text being interpreted 'may say something different from what one wants or expects it to say,' is highly developed in biblical studies."[11]

Ethics has provided a very creative vocabulary for recent interpretation. Beardslee notes in a discussion of Schüssler Fiorenza's work that liberation theology does not necessarily reject historical exegesis, but demands more engagement on the part of the scholar with contemporary movements such as the emancipation of slaves and of freeborn women.[12] Schüssler Fiorenza argues for an ethics of historical reading that asks what kind of readings "...do justice to the text in its historical contexts." Such an approach limits the number of interpretations appropriate to the original text and asserts its "...original meanings over and against later dogmatic usurpations."[13] She also argues that scholars should adhere to an ethics of accountability that clarifies the "ethical consequences and political functions of biblical texts in their historical as well as in their contemporary

---

[11] Schüssler Fiorenza 1988, 5.
[12] Beardslee 1990, 24 with reference to Schüssler Fiorenza 1988, 7.
[13] Schüssler Fiorenza 1988, 14.

sociopolitical contexts."[14] According to Schüssler Fiorenza, historical sources are "perspectival discourse constructing their worlds and symbolic universes."[15] In terms of understanding the texts historically, the linguistic method of this book offers insight into how Mark constructs a narrative world—something that is Mark's symbolic universe in a sense. In addition, with regard to the historical context of the Gospel, text linguistics offers perspective on speech acts. What did the words do to their hearers? Such questions receive critical attention in work on the pragmatics of language. The political and ethical functions of the Markan discourse can be approached when one has analyzed the function of the language in terms of written acts/speech acts.

Instead of the adversarial role that some exegetes take when they adopt new methods I would argue that a "synergistic" understanding of different methods is more appropriate. Scholars can still argue from their own interpretive frameworks that certain interpretations are in error, but they can also accept new methods in part as a creative addition to the common task of interpretation. One such "synergistic" approach to exegesis is the "socio-rhetorical" method that Vernon K. Robbins has recently developed. Robbins uses the categories of inner texture, intertexture, social and cultural texture, and ideological texture to define the exegetical task.[16] Inner texture means intrinsic features of the text. The syntactic approach in this work involving the delimitation of the text into text sequences is an example of inner texture. Intertexture is the relation of a text with other texts. Semantics involves intertexture, since the interpreter has to use texts from the surrounding culture to understand the words in Mark. Social and cultural texture is the social environment in which a text exists. The social sciences are often used to understand this kind of texture.

In my work, pragmatics is a kind of social and cultural texture because in pragmatics the interpreter makes hypotheses

---

[14]Schüssler Fiorenza 1988, 15.
[15]Schüssler Fiorenza 1988, 13–14.
[16]Robbins 1992, xix–xxxviii.

about the author and audience. Ideological texture includes the ideology of the text, the ideology of the history of interpretation, and the modern interpreter's ideology. Interpretations that read Mark from a specific political point of view exhibit ideological texture.[17] Exegesis becomes stronger and more socially responsible when aided by linguistics, rhetoric, literary criticism, and ethics.

---

[17]As in Ched Myers's work (1990).

APPENDIX 1

The literature on εὐαγγέλιον (gospel) includes Friedrich 1935 (and his basis Schniewind 1927/1931), Deissmann 1923, 313ff., Nock 1972, 80ff., and Klostermann 1971, excursus to 1:1, Vielhauer 1975, 252ff., and Koester 1989 who traces the usage of the term for a written document to Marcion. Origen gives a useful discussion of the semantics and pragmatics of the term:

Ἔστι τοίνυν εὐαγγέλιον λόγος περιέχων ἀπαγγελίαν πραγμάτων κατὰ τὸ εὔλογον διὰ τὸ ὠφελεῖν εὐφραινόντων τὸν ἀκούοντα, ἐπὰν παραδέξηται τὸ ἀπαγγελλόμενον· οὐδὲν δ' ἧττον ὁ τοιοῦτος λόγος εὐαγγέλιόν ἐστιν, ἂν καὶ πρὸς τὴν σχέσιν τοῦ ἀκούοντος ἐξετάζηται. ἢ εὐαγγέλιον ἐστι λόγος περιέχων ἀγαθοῦ τῷ πιστεύοντι παρουσίαν ἢ λόγος ἐπαγγελλόμενος παρεῖναι ἀγαθὸν τὸ προσδοκώμενον....

A gospel then is a discourse containing an announcement of matters that with good reason make the hearer rejoice (because they help the hearer) when he/she accepts what is announced. Such a discourse is not any less a "gospel" if it is examined in relation to the hearer. Either a gospel is a discourse comprising the arrival of a good for the believer or a discourse that announces the arrival of an expected good.

(Origen, *in Joh.* ed. Preuschen 1903 I.5, 9/25–30) Origen's emphasis on the hearer corresponds to this work's concern for the speech act which constitutes "good news." Suidas (ad loc.) gives the following definition: τὰ κάλλιστα ἀπαγγέλλον (announcing the best things) and αἰτιατικῇ. εὐαγγελίζομαι δέ σοι χαράν (in the accusative: I give you the good news of joy). One could not ask for a better approach to the word as speech act. Hesychius, *Lexicon* (ad loc.) defines εὐαγγέλια with μηνύματα. κηρύγματα (information, proclamations) and *Etymologicum Magnum* defines the noun with τὸ ἀγαθὰς ἀγγελίας δωρούμενον. εὐαγγέλιον δέ μοι ἔστω (that which gives good announcements, let there be good news for me). All definitions (except Hesychius) agree on including the seme "good" or "joyful" in the definition of the content of what is announced. Origen's definition emphasizes the necessity of the message being believed if it is to bring joy. Friedrich discusses several instances of skepticism toward an εὐαγγέλιον, in Friedrich, 1935, 720. Appian, *Bella Civilia* 3.13.93 contains a use of εὐαγγέλιον where it turns out to be a false message of joy. Phil. *Vita Ap.* 8.27 gives a picture of an audience skeptical about Apollonius' εὐαγγέλιον of Domitian's murder, which they of course would be happy about.

The well known examples of the word used in relation to an emperor's birth or reign are: Dittenberger, *OGIS* 458, 40 (the Priene inscription about Augustus); Deissmann 1923, 313–314 (or Preisigke, *Sb.* 421)—an Egyptian person writing concerning G. Verus Maximus; *IG* III, #1.10 (an announcement concerning Septimius Geta [editor's completion of a lacuna]), and Josephus, *Bellum Judaicum* 4.618 and 656 about Vespasian. The meaning "good news" appears in a non-emperor context also in such places as LXX 2Reg 18: 20, 22, 27 and 4 Reg 7:9 (the εὐαγγελία form). Josephus, *Bellum Judaicum* 2.420 uses the word for the report of a revolt that Florus gets to suppress. Appian *Bella Civilia* 4.4.20 has the word used in conjunction with the good news of Cicero's murder. Heliod. *Aethiopica* 1.14 (18.17 ed. Bekker) has it refer to the death of an evil stepmother.

In early Christian literature the word begins to be used for a literary genre and as a general theological word for the Christian message. Mk 1:1 provides the impetus for this development where the word probably refers to the content of the book and

Appendix 1

is not a genre title (Vielhauer 1975, 255, 256). 1 Cor 15:1 has a use of the word for a short narrative of Jesus' death and resurrection. *Ign. Phil.* 9:2 gives a similar use where the word refers to Jesus' life (παρουσίαν), passion and resurrection. Vielhauer (1975, 254) refers to Did. 15:4, 2 Cl 8:5 and Justin *Apologia* 1.66.3 as the earliest use of the word for a literary product. Did 15:4 may, however, mean "good news" and not the literary "Gospel." To these examples Diogn. 11:6 should be added where the εὐαγγελίων πίστις (faith of the gospels) is used in conjunction with the law and the prophets. The gospel inscriptions are discussed in 3.2.1 and 3.3.1. The shorter form (ΚΑΤΑ ΜΑΡΚΟΝ—According to Mark) may result from the conception of one gospel in four forms (Vielhauer 1975, 255) although this is not certain. Irenaeus, *Adversus haereses* 3.11.8 discusses the τετράμορφον (four-form) gospel. Lampe (LPGL, ad loc. 556b, 1) gives other examples of the canonical view of four gospels especially calling attention to Athanasius, *Epistulae festales* 39,7 εὐαγγέλια τέσσαρα, κατὰ Ματθαῖον, κατὰ Μᾶρκον, κατὰ Λουκᾶν, κατὰ ᾿Ιωάννην...(four gospels: According to Matthew, According to Mark, According to Luke, According to John). The term came to be used for the genre which included all the non-canonical gospels (LPGL, 556, C) such as the Manichean κατὰ Θωμᾶν εὐαγγελιον (Gospel according to Thomas) in Cyril of Jerusalem, *Catecheses* 4.36. It also came to mean "book" in the physical sense though even then the genre meaning "good news" may not have completely disappeared. For this use Lampe (LPGL 558, G) quotes Evagrius Ponticus, *Practicus* B 97 (PG 40 1249D) ἐκέκτητο τις τῶν ἀδελφῶν εὐαγγέλιον μόνον, καὶ τοῦτο πωλήσας ἔδωκεν εἰς τροφὴν τοῖς πεινῶσιν (One of the brothers was the owner of only [one] a gospel, and selling it he gave it for food to the hungry).

APPENDIX 2

SUMMARY OF THE OUTLINE IN CHAPTER THREE

^{00}TP	^{0}TP	^{1}TP	^{2}TP
Superscript (Gospel According to Mark)	Mk 1:1	^{1}TP^{1}(1:2–13) John and Jesus in the wilderness	^{2}TP$^{1.1}$(1:2–11) John and Jesus at the Jordan ^{2}TP$^{1.2}$(12–13) Jesus' temptation in the wilderness away from John
		^{1}TP^{2}(1:14–8:26) Jesus' ministry in Galilee and environs	^{2}TP$^{2.1}$(14–15) Jesus' proclamation in Galilee ^{2}TP$^{2.2}$(16–20) Jesus' call of the first two disciples ^{2}TP$^{2.3}$(21–34) Jesus in Capernaum on the Sabbath ^{2}TP$^{2.4}$(35–38) Jesus and his disciples in a desolate place for prayer

00TP	0TP	1TP	2TP
			$2TP^{2.5}$(39–44) Jesus' preaching and exorcising in the synagogues and a leper healing
			$2TP^{2.6}$(45) The leper proclaims the word, and Jesus withdraws from the cities
			$2TP^{2.7}$(2:1–12) Jesus heals the paralytic
			$2TP^{2.8}$(13–14) Jesus by the sea
			$2TP^{2.9}$(15–22) Jesus defends eating with sinners and tax collectors
			$2TP^{2.10}$(2:23–3:6) Two Sabbath conflicts
			$2TP^{2.11}$(7–12) Healings and exorcisms by the sea
			$2TP^{2.12}$(13–19) Jesus chooses the twelve
			$2TP^{2.13}$(20–35) Jesus defends himself in the Beelzebul controversy and affirms his true family
			$2TP^{2.14}$(4:1–34) Jesus' parables of the word and kingdom by the sea
			$2TP^{2.15}$(35–41) Jesus stills the storm
			$2TP^{2.16}$(5:1–20) Jesus exorcises in the Gerasa region
			$2TP^{2.17}$(21–43) Two healings in the area of the West bank of Galilee

Summary of the Outline 345

00TP	0TP	1TP	2TP
			2TP2.18 (6:1–13) Jesus and his disciples minister in his town and the surrounding villages
			2TP2.19 (6:14–29) The story of Herod's relation to Jesus and John
			2TP2.20 (30–31) The apostles return to Jesus and are instructed to go to a deserted place
			2TP2.21 (32–33) The trip to the deserted place
			2TP2.22 (6:34–44) The deserted place: teaching and feeding
			2TP2.23 (45–52) An episode on land and sea: Jesus prays on the mountain and walks on the sea
			2TP2.24 (6:53–7:23) Jesus healing and arguing about the law in the Genessaret region
			2TP2.25 (7:24–30) Jesus exorcises in the Tyre region
			2TP2.26 (7:31–8:9) Two miracles by the sea of Galilee on the Decapolis side
			2TP2.27 (10–12) The Pharisees seek a sign from Jesus in the Dalmanutha region
			2TP2.28 (13–21) Jesus and the disciples discuss the leaven of the Pharisees and Herod during a crossing to Bethsaida

00TP	0TP	1TP	2TP
			2TP2.29(22–26) The healing of the blind man in Bethsaida
		1TP3(8:27–10:52) Jesus' journey to Jerusalem	2TP3.1(8:27–9:29) Esoteric teaching about the Messiah, public teaching and public exorcism in the Caesarea Philippi region 2TP3.2(30–50) The journey through Galilee 2TP3.3(10:1–52) The journey through Judea and Perea
		1TP4(11:1–16:8) Jesus in Jerusalem and environs	2TP4.1(11:1–11) First day in Jerusalem and environs 2TP4.2(11:12–19) Second day in Jerusalem and environs 2TP4.3(11:20–25) Approaching Jerusalem they see the fig tree withered, and Jesus teaches about prayer 2TP4.4(11:27–12:44) Controversies in the temple 2TP4.5(13:1–37) Discourses in view of the Temple 2TP4.6(14:1–11) The period two days before the passover 2TP4.7(14:12–72) The first day of unleavened bread.

⁰⁰TP	⁰TP	¹TP	²TP
			$^2TP^{4.8}$(15:1–47) The day before the Sabbath: Jesus' condemnation and death
			$^2TP^{4.9}$(16:1–8) The resurrection news on the day after the Sabbath

GLOSSARY

Character Markers. Character markers are those words that describe changes in the group of characters in a given Text Part. An example is the appearance of the words "Simon" and "Andrew" in Mk 1:16 (see 2.4.2.5).

Class. "Class" means a group of elements that exist in a logical class or set. A class corresponds to the reference (q.v.) of a sign. A word such as "angel," for example, can refer to a large "class" or set of beings. The use of class allows a linguist to investigate the referential dimension of a sign's meaning without having to decide if the elements of the class actually exist (see 2.2.2).

Diachronic. A diachronic approach considers a language's development through time (see Introduction).

Episode Markers. Episode markers are changes in time and place that appear in the text. An example of an episode marker is Ἱεροσόλυμα (Jerusalem) in Mk 11:1 (see 2.4.2.4).

Frame of Communication. A communication frame is the context in which communication takes place. One frame would be that of an author and her or his audience. Another frame would be that of a character speaking to other characters in a text (see Introduction and 2.4.1).

Gospel Narrative. "Gospel narrative" is a speech act which has its own peculiar illocutionary force in that it makes assertions about the world and encourages the allegiance of the reader (see 2.3.4).

Governing Speech Act. A governing speech act is the speech act that governs or organizes an entire text (see 2.4).

Illocution. An illocution is what is done "in" a speech act. Examples are assertion, command, and question (compare "perlocution" and 2.3.3).

Langage. The level of *langage* is the system of all languages. An example of an investigation on the level of *langage* would be considering the meaning of a sign such as "evil eye" in ancient Hebrew and Greek.

Langue. A sign on the level of *langue* includes all possible meanings of the sign in a given language (see Introduction).

Level. Levels are the different grades of an outline. Every outline uses some form of embedded levels or grades. For example "II.C.1" in an outline using Roman numerals would be on the third level of the outline. In an outline using the "legal" style (such as the one used in this work) "II.C.1" in the Roman outline would correspond to "2.3.1" (see 2.4.3).

Marker. A marker is an indicator or signal that helps a hearer to structure a speaker's communication by dividing it into its parts. The latter indicate that changes are being made in the linear flow of the text. A chapter title is an example of a marker that stands for or substitutes for a text sequence (see Introduction and 2.4.2).

Meta-Communicative Markers. These are markers that signal the beginning or end of a communication situation. In other words, they indicate that a communication is going to take place or stop. They are a form of speech referring to speech (see 2.4.2.1).

Meta-frame. The frame that governs an embedded frame is called a "meta-frame." In the narrator's "Jesus said to them" (1:17), for example, the words "Jesus said to them " appear in Frame 1. The words "Follow me" appear in Frame 2. Frame 2 is embedded in Frame 1 (see Introduction and 2.4.1).

Monosemized Sign. A word or other sign such as a phrase may have multiple meanings (*sememes*). When that word or *signifiant* appears on the level of *parole*, the context enables the reader to choose the correct meaning or *sememe* (see 2.2.2).

Motif. A motif is a proposition about the characters that is true of a number of the text's parts and therefore can be inferred from those Text Parts (see 4.4.1).

Noeme. A *noeme* is a *seme* that exists in two or more languages or in different stages of one language (see 2.2.2).

Parole. A sign on the level of *parole* is used in an actual context such as a word in a sentence of the Gospel of Mark (see Introduction).

Perlocution. A perlocution is "what is done 'by' a speech act," with a focus on what comes after the utterance has ceased. The perlocution is the act which the speaker causes to be performed (compare "illocution," and see 2.3.3).

Pragmatics. Pragmatics is the relation between a sign, its meaning, and the users of the sign and includes both the sender(s) and receiver(s) of the sign (see Introduction).

Reference. This dimension of meaning comprises the reality that a sign stands for. In the example from the Stoics given in 2.2 the sign or word "Dion" actually refers to a person. See also "class."

Semantics. Semantics is the relation of a sign and its meaning. "Meaning" includes both the sense and the reference of a sign (see Introduction).

Seme. A *seme* is an abstract entity of one language and means a "minimal unit of meaning" (see 2.2.2).

Sememe. A *sememe* is one of a signeme's meanings (see 2.2.2).

Sense. The sense of a given sign or word is its conceptual meaning. The concept is not the same as the reference. Sextus Empiricus speaks of the Stoics distinguishing the word, the concept in our understanding, and the reality referred to by the word. The reality referred to is the "reference" (q.v.) of the sign (see 2.2.).

Signeme. A *signeme* is a sign viewed from both its material aspect and its content (see 2.2.2).

Signifiant. A *signifiant* is the material substance of a sign (such as the sound or the ink marks on the page—see 2.2.2).

Signifié. A *signifié* is the content level of a sign (see 2.2.2).

Speech Act. The use of language to do something is called a "speech act." Ancient scholars were aware of the ability of language to act. "I baptize you" is an example of a speech act (see Introduction and 2.3.3).

Substitution Markers. A "substitution" is the replacement of one linguistic expression (*substituendum*) by another (*substituens*). In a substitution one sign (*substituens*) stands or substitutes for another (*substituendum*). "Parable," for example, in Mk 4:13 "substitutes" for the text in Mk 4:3–9 and is a substitution marker (see 2.4.2.2).

Synchronic. A synchronic approach considers a language at one point in its history over its entire breadth (see Introduction).

Syntax. Syntax is the relation between signs (see Introduction).

Text Part. "Text Part" is a given sequence of text.

Written Act. A written act is a textual speech act. Several criteria for analyzing entire texts as written acts are given in 2.3.5.

BIBLIOGRAPHY

Linguistic Works, the Theory of Literature, and Works of Social Science

Austin, J. L.
1975 *How to Do Things with Words. The William James Lectures Delivered at Harvard University in 1955.* 2nd ed. Cambridge: Harvard University Press (1st ed. 1962).
1970 "Performative Utterances." Pp. 233–252 in *Philosophical Papers.* Oxford: Oxford University Press.

Baldinger, Kurt
1980 *Semantic Theory. Towards a Modern Semantics.* Oxford: Blackwell.

Barr, James
1961 *The Semantics of Biblical Language.* London: Oxford University Press.

Brekle, Herbert E.
1972 *Semantik, Eine Einführung in die sprachwissenschaftliche Bedeutungslehre.* Uni Taschenbücher 102. München: Fink.

Brinker, Klaus
1983 "Textfunktionen. Ansätze zu ihrer Beschreibung." *Zeitschrift für Germanistische Linguistik* 11: 127–148.

Carnap, Rudolf
1956   *Meaning and Necessity. A Study in Semantics and Modal Logic.* Chicago: University of Chicago Press.

Coseriu, Eugenio
1984   "Georg von der Gabelentz und die synchronische Sprachwissenschaft." Pp. 3-35 in G. von der Gabelentz, 1901/1984.

Derrida, Jacques
1976   *Of Grammatology.* Trans. G. Spivak. Baltimore: Johns Hopkins University Press.

Dijk, Teun A. van
1972   *Some Aspects of Text Grammars. A Study in Theoretical Linguistics and Poetics.* The Hague/Paris: Mouton.
1977   *Text and Context, Explorations in the Semantics and Pragmatics of Discourse.* Longman Linguistics Library 21. London and New York: Longman.
1979   "New Developments and Problems in Textlinguistics." Pp. 509-523 in J. Petöfi, ed. 1979.
1985   "Semantic Discourse Analysis" Pp. 103-136 in T. van Dijk, ed. 1985.

Dijk, Teun A. van, ed.
1985   *Handbook of Discourse Analysis. Volume 2. Dimensions of Discourse.* London, et al.: Academic Press.

Dressler, Wolfgang
1973   *Einführung in die Textlinguistik.* Konzepte der Sprach und Literaturwissenschaft 13. Tübingen: Niemeyer.

Ferrara, A.
1985   "Pragmatics." Pp. 137-158 in T. van Dijk, ed. 1985.

Fotion, N.
1970   "Master Speech Acts." *Philosophical Quarterly* 21: 232-243.
1979   "Speech Activity and Language Use." in: *Philosophia. Philosophical Quarterly of Israel* 8: 614-638.

French-Strout, Ruth
1956 "The Development of the Catalog and Cataloging Codes." *Library Quarterly* 26: 254–275.

Gabelentz, Georg von der
1901/1984 *Die Sprachwissenschaft: Ihre Aufgaben, Methoden und bisherige Ergebnisse*. Tübinger Beiträge zur Linguistic 1. Tübingen: Narr (3rd edition, 2nd edition 1901).

Gibson, Arthur
1981 *Biblical Semantic Logic. A Preliminary Analysis*. New York: St. Martin's.

Goffman, Erving
1974 *Frame Analysis. An Essay on the Organization of Experience*. Cambridge, MA: Harvard University Press.

Greenberg, Ira A.
1968 *Psychodrama and Audience Attitude Change*. Beverly Hills: Thyrsus.

Grimes. Joseph
1975 *The Thread of Discourse*. Janua Linguarum Series Minor 207. The Hague: Mouton.

Grosse, Ernst U.
1976 *Text und Kommunikation. Eine linguistische Einführung in die Funktionen der Texte*. Stuttgart: Kohlhammer.

Gülich, Elisabeth, and Wolfgang Raible
1977 *Linguistische Textmodelle. Grundlagen und Möglichkeiten*. Uni-Taschenbücher 130. München: Fink.

Gülich, Elisabeth, Klaus Heger, and Wolfgang Raible
1979 *Linguistische Textanalyse. Überlegungen zur Gliederung von Texten*. Papiere zur Textlinguistik/Papers in Textlinguistics Band 8/Volume 8. Hamburg: Buske.

Harris, Zellig S.
1970 "Discourse Analysis." Pp. 313–348 in *Papers in Structural and Transformational Linguistics*. Formal Linguistics Series 1. Dordrecht: Reidel.

Harweg, Roland
1979 *Pronomina und Textkonstitution*. 2nd improved ed. München: Fink.

Heger, Klaus
1976 *Monem, Wort, Satz, und Text*. 2nd ed. Tübingen: Niemeyer.
1979 "Signemränge und Textanalyse." Pp. 1–71 in Gülich and Raible, eds. 1979.

Hellwig, Peter
1984 "TITULUS oder ÜBER DEN ZUSAMMENHANG VON TITELN UND TEXTEN. Titel sind ein Schlüssel zur Textkonstitution." *Zeitschrift für Germanistische Linguistik* 12: 1–20.

Hempfer, Klaus
1973 *Gattungstheorie. Information und Synthese*. Uni-Taschenbücher 133. München: Fink.
1981 "Präsuppositionen, Implikaturen und die Struktur wissenschaftlicher Argumentation." Pp. 309–342 in: Theo Bungarten, ed. *Wissenschaftssprache. Beiträge zur Methodologie, theoretischen Fundierung und Deskription*. München: Fink.

Husserl, Edmund
1970 "Zur Logik der Zeichen (Semiotik)." Pp. 340–73 in *Philosophie der Arithmetik, Logische und psychologische Untersuchungen, mit ergänzenden Texten (1890–1901)*. Gesammelte Werke vol. 12. Ed. L. Eley. Den Haag: Nijhoff, 1970, .

Iser, Wolfgang
1976 *Der Akt des Lesens. Theorie ästhetischer Wirkung*. Uni-Taschenbücher 636. München: Fink.

Kempson, Ruth M.
1975 *Presuppositions and the Delimitation of Semantics*. Cambridge Studies in Linguistics 15. Cambridge: Cambridge University Press.

Kermode, Frank
1979 *The Genesis of Secrecy, On the Interpretation of Narrative*. Cambridge, MA: Harvard University Press.

Kubczak, Hartmut
1975 *Das Verhältnis von Intension und Extension als sprachwissenschaftliches Problem*. Forschungsberichte des Instituts für deutsche Sprache Mannheim 23. Tübingen: Narr.
1978 *Die Metapher. Beiträge zur Interpretation und semantischen Struktur der Metapher auf der Basis einer referentialen Bedeutungsdefinition*. Heidelberg: Winter.

Kutschera, Franz von
1975 *Philosophy of Language*. Synthese Library 71. Boston: Reidel (Trans. of 2nd German ed.).

Lanser, Susan
1981 *The Narrative Act. Point of View in Prose Fiction*. Princeton: Princeton University Press.

Lausberg, Heinrich
1960 *Handbuch der Literarischen Rhetorik. Eine Grundlegung der Literaturwissenschaft*. München: Hüber.

Lorenz, Wolfgang, and Gerd Wotjak
1977 *Zum Verhältnis von Abbild und Bedeutung, Überlegungen im Grenzfeld zwischen Erkenntnistheorie und Semantik*. Sammlung Akademie-Verlag 39. Berlin: Akademie Verlag.

Louw, J. P.
1982 *Semantics of New Testament Greek*. Semeia Studies. Chico and Philadelphia: Scholars Press and Fortress.

McKnight, Edgar V.
1985 *The Bible and the Reader. An Introduction to Literary Criticism.* Philadelphia: Fortress.

Ogden, C. K., and I. A. Richards
1947 *The Meaning of Meaning.* London: Kegan Paul.

Petőfi, János, ed.
1979 *Text vs Sentence. Basic Questions of Textlinguistics. Second Part.* Papiere zur Textlinguistik/Papers in Textlinguistics 20.2. Hamburg: Buske.

Plett, Heinrich F.
1979 *Textwissenschaft und Textanalyse. Semiotik, Linguistic, Rhetorik.* Uni-Taschenbücher 328. 2nd ed. Heidelberg: Quelle & Meyer.

Pratt, Mary L.
1977 *Toward a Speech Act Theory of Literary Discourse.* Bloomington and London: Indiana University Press.

Quine, Willard van Orman
1961 "Meaning in Linguistics." Pp. 45–64 in *From a Logical Point of View. Nine Logico-Philosophical Essays.* 2nd rev. ed. New York, etc.: Harper and Row.

Raible, Wolfgang
1972 *Satz und Text. Untersuchungen zu vier romanischen Sprachen.* Beiheft zur *Zeitschrift für Romanische Philologie* 132. Tübingen: Niemeyer.
1980 "Was sind Gattungen. Eine Antwort aus semiotischer und textlinguistischer Sicht." *Poetica* 12: 320–349.
1981 Review of Lorenz and Wotjak, 1977. *Zeitschrift für Romanische Philologie* 97: 403–412.
1983 "Zur Einleitung." Pp. 1–24 in H. Stimm and W. Raible, eds., *Zur Semantik des Franzözischen. Beiträge zum Regensburger Romanistentag 1981. Zeitschrift für Französische Sprache und Literatur.* Beiheft N.F. 9. Wiesbaden: Steiner.

Rauh, Gisa
1978   Linguistische Beschreibung deiktischer Komplexität in narrativen Texten. Tübinger Beiträge zur Linguistik 106. Tübingen: Narr.

Rorty, Richard
1982   Consequences of Pragmatism (Essays: 1972–1980). Minneapolis: University of Minnesota Press.

Rosengren, Inger
1980   "Texttheorie." Pp. 275–286 in H. Althaus, et al., ed., Lexikon der Germanistischen Linguistik, Studienausgabe II. 2nd rev. ed. Tübingen: Niemeyer.
1987   "Hierarchisierung und Sequenzierung von Illokutionen: zwei interdependente Strukturierungsprinzipien bei der Textproduktion." Zeitschrift Phon. Sprachwiss. Kommunikationsforschung 40: 1–44.

Sadock, Jerry M.
1974   Toward a Linguistic Theory of Speech Acts. New York: Academic.

Saussure, Ferdinand de
1960   Cours de Linguistique Generale. Paris: Payot (lst ed. 1915).

Schifferin, D.
1987   Discourse Markers. Studies in Interactional Sociolinguistics 5. Cambridge, et al.: Cambridge University Press.

Schmidt, Siegfried J.
1973   Texttheorie. Uni-Taschenbücher 202. München: Fink.

Searle, John R.
1969   Speech Acts. London: Cambridge University Press.
1976   "A Classification of Illocutionary Acts." Language and Society 5:1–23.

Stalnaker, Robert C.
1973   "Pragmatics." Pp. 389–408 in J. Petöfi and D. Franck, eds. Präsuppositionen in Philosophie und Linguistik, Presuppositions in

Philosophy and Linguistics. Linguistische Forschungen 7. Frankfurt: Athenaeum.

Stebbing, Lizzie S.
1952 *A Modern Elementary Logic.* London: Methuen.

Suleiman, Susan
1977 "Le récit exemplaire." *Poétique* 32: 468–489.

Ullmann, Stephen
1957 *The Principles of Semantics.* Oxford: Blackwell.

Vasiliu, Emanuel
1979 "On Some Meanings of 'Coherence.'" Pp. 450–466 in Petöfi, ed. 1979.

Weimann, R.
1976 *Structure and Society in Literary History.* Charlottesville: University Press of Virginia.

White, Hugh C.
1988 "Introduction: Speech Act Theory and Literary Criticism." *Semeia (Speech Act Theory and Biblical Criticism)* 41: 1–24.

Wienold, Götz
1972 *Semiotik der Literatur.* Frankfurt am Main: Athenaeum.

Wörner, Markus H.
1978 *Performative und sprachliches Handeln. Ein Beitrag zu J. L. Austins Theorie der Sprechakte.* IKP Forschungsberichte I:64. Hamburg: Buske.

Wunderlich, Dieter
1979 *Foundations of Linguistics.* Cambridge Studies in Linguistics 22. Cambridge: Cambridge University Press.

Exegetical Works: Ancient

Cramer, J.
1844   *Catenae graecorum patrum in Novum Testamentum.* Vol 1. Oxford: Oxford University Press.

Origen
1903   *Origines Werke, Vierter Band. Der Johannes-Kommentar.* Ed. E. Preuschen. GCS 10. Leipzig: Hinrichs.

Theophylact
1864   *Opera Tomus Primus Ennarationes in Evangelium....*PG 123. Paris: J. Migne.

Exegetical Works and Works of NT Scholarship: Modern

Achtemeier, Paul J.
1975   *Mark.* Proclamation Commentaries. Philadelphia: Fortress.
1978   "'And he followed him': Miracles and Discipleship in Mark 10:46–52." *Semeia* 11: 115–145.
1990   "*Omne verbum sonat*: The New Testament and the Oral Environment of Late Western Antiquity." *JBL* 109: 3–27.

Aland, Kurt
1973   *Synopsis Quattuor Evangeliorum . . . edidit Kurt Aland.* 8th ed. Stuttgart: Württembergische Bibelanstalt.

Anderson, Hugh
1976   *The Gospel of Mark.* NCB. Greenwood, SC: Attic.

Baarlink, Heinrich
1977   *Anfängliches Evangelium. Ein Beitrag zur näheren Bestimmung der theologischen Motive im Markusevangelium.* Kampen: Kok.

Beardslee, William
1975   "Narrative Form in the New Testament and Process Theology." *Encounter* 36: 301–315.

| 1990 | "Ethics and Hermeneutics." Pp. 15–32 in *Text and Logos. The Humanistic Interpretation of the New Testament*. Ed. T. Jennings. Atlanta: Scholars Press. |

Bengel, Johann
| 1855 | *Gnomon Novi Testamenti, in quo ex nativa verborum vi, simplicitas, profunditas, concinnitas, salubritas sensuum coelestium indicatur*....Stuttgart: Steinkopf (Reprint of 3rd ed. 1773). |

Berger, Klaus
| 1984 | "Hellenistische Gattungen im Neuen Testament." *ANRW* II.25.2: 1034–1379. |

Best, Ernest
| 1965 | *The Temptation and the Passion. The Markan Soteriology*. Cambridge: Cambridge University Press. |

Betz, Hans-Dieter
| 1982 | "Gottmensch II (Griechisch-römische Antike und Urchristentum." *RAC* 12: 234–311. |

Bickermann [*sic*], Elias
| 1923 | "Das Messiasgeheimnis und die Komposition des Markusevangeliums." *ZNW* 22: 122–146. |

Bikerman [*sic*], Elie
| 1946 | "*Latens Deus*: La reconnaissance du Christ dans les évangiles." *HTR* 39: 169–188. |

Bilezikian, Gilbert G.
| 1977 | *The Liberated Gospel. A Comparison of the Gospel of Mark and Greek Tragedy*. Grand Rapids: Baker. |

Blatherwick, David
| 1970 | "The Markan Silhouette." *NTS* 17: 184–192. |

Blevins, James
| 1981 | *The Messianic Secret in Markan Research, 1901–1976*. Washington: University Press of America. |

Boers, Hendrikus W.
1981 "The Unity of the Gospel of Mark." *Scriptura* 4: 1–7.

Boobyer, G. H.
1959/1960 "The Secrecy Motif in St. Mark's Gospel." *NTS* 6: 225–235.

Botha, J. E.
1991 "The Case of Johannine Irony Reopened I: The Problematic Current Situation." *Neot* 25: 209–220.

Botha, J.
1994 *Subject to Whose Authority? Multiple Readings of Romans 13.* Emory Studies in Early Christianity 4. Atlanta: Scholars Press.

Branscomb, B. Harvie
1937 *The Gospel of Mark.* New York: Harper.

Bryan, Christopher
1993 *A Preface to Mark. Notes on the Gospel in Its Literary and Cultural Settings.* New York and Oxford: Oxford University Press.

Bultmann Rudolf
1963 *History of the Synoptic Tradition.* 3rd ed. New York: Harper and Row.

Burch, Ernest W.
1931 "Tragic Action in the Second Gospel: A Study in the Narrative of Mark." *JR* 11: 346–358.

Burkill, T. A.
1963 *Mysterious Revelation. An Examination of the Philosophy of St. Mark's Gospel.* Ithaca: Cornell University Press.

Burridge, Richard A.
1992 *What Are the Gospels? A Comparison with Graeco-Roman Biography.* SNTSMS 70. Cambridge: Cambridge University Press.

Buss, Martin J.
1988 "Potential and Actual Interactions between Speech Act Theory and Biblical Studies." *Semeia* (*Speech Act Theory and Biblical Criticism*) 41: 125–134.
1993 "Form Criticism." Pp. 69–85 in S. L. McKenzie, and S. R. Haynes, eds. *To Each Its Own Meaning.* Philadelphia: Westminster/John Knox.

Buss, Martin J.
Forthcoming *A History of Form Criticism.*

Butterworth, Robert
1972 "The Composition of Mark 1–12." *HeyJ* 13: 5–26.

Cancik, Hubert
1984a "Bios und Logos. Formengeschichtliche Untersuchungen zu Lukians *Demonax.*" Pp.115–130 in H. Cancik, ed. 1984.
1984b "Die Gattung Evangelium. Das Evangelium des Markus im Rahmen der antiken Historiographie." Pp. 85–113 in H. Cancik, ed. 1984.

Cancik, Hubert, ed.
1984 *Markus-Philologie. Historische, literargeschichtliche und stilistische Untersuchungen zum zweiten Evangelium.* WUNT 33. Tübingen: Mohr-Siebeck.

Carrington, Philip
1960 *According to Mark. A Running Commentary on the Oldest Gospel.* Cambridge: Cambridge University Press.

Carré, Henry B.
1928 "The Literary Structure of the Gospel of Mark." Pp. 105–126 in *Studies in Early Christianity*....Ed. S. J. Case. New York: Century.

Conzelmann, Hans
1957 "Gegenwart und Zukunft in den synoptischen Tradition." *ZTK* 54: 277–296.

1968	"Historie und Theologie in der synoptischen Passionsgeschichten." Pp. 37–53 in F. Viering, ed. *Zur Bedeutung des Todes Jesu*. Gütersloh: Mohn.

Conzelmann, Hans, and Andreas Lindemann
1977   *Arbeitsbuch zum Neuen Testament*. Uni-Taschenbücher 52. Tübingen: Mohr.

Cook, John G.
1988   "The Sparrow's Fall in Mt 10:29b." *ZNW* 79: 138–144.
1993   "Some Hellenistic Responses to the Gospels and Gospel Traditions." *ZNW* 84: 233–254.
1994   "The Protreptic Power of Early Christian Language: From John to Augustine." *VC* 48: 105–134.

Cranfield, C. E. B.
1959   *The Gospel According to St. Mark*. Cambridge Greek New Testament Commentary. Cambridge: Cambridge University Press.

Credner, Karl A.
1836   *Einleitung in das Neue Testament. Erster Teil. Erste Abtheilung*. Halle: Waisenhaus.

Dahl, Nils A.
1976   "The Purpose of Mark's Gospel." Pp. 52–65 in *Jesus in the Memory of the Early Church*. Minnesota: Augsburg.

Davies, W. D., and D. C. Allison,
1988   *The Gospel According to Saint Matthew*. Vol I. ICC. Edinburgh: Clark.

Dehn, Günther
1953   *Der Gottessohn. Eine Einführung in das Evangelium des Markus*. Hamburg: Furche.

Deissman, Adolf
1923   *Licht vom Osten. Das Neue Testament und die neuentdeckten Texte der hellenistisch-römischen Welt*. Tübingen: Mohr-Siebeck.

Delorme, Jean
1972 "Lecture de L'Évangile selon Saint Marc." *Cahiers Évangile* 54: 1-123.

Derrett, J. Duncan M.
1985 *The Making of Mark. The Scriptural Bases of the Earliest Gospel.* 2 Vols. Shipston-on-Stour: Drinkwater.

Dibelius, Martin
1961 *Die Formgeschichte des Evangelium.* 4th ed. Tübingen: Mohr-Siebeck.

Dihle, Albrecht
1983 "Die Evangelien und die griechische Biographie." Pp. 383-411 in P. Stuhlmacher, ed.

Dodd, C. H.
1932 "The Framework of the Gospel Narrative." *ET* 43: 396-400.

Dowd, Sharyn
1988 *Prayer, Power, and the Problem of Suffering: Mark 11:22-25 in the Context of Markan Theology.* SBLDS 105. Atlanta: Scholars Press.

Ebeling, Hans Jürgen
1939 *Das Messiasgeheimnis und die Botschaft des Marcus-Evangelisten.* Berlin: Töpelmann.

Esser, D.
1969 *Formgeschichtliche Studien zur hellenistischen und zur frühchristlichen Literatur, unter besonderer Berücksichtigung der vita Apollonii des Philostrat und der Evangelien.* Ev. theol. Diss. Bonn.

Farrer, Austin
1954 *St. Matthew and St. Mark.* Westminster (London): Dacre.

Faw, Chalmer E.
1957 "The Outline of Mark." *JBR* 25: 19-23.

Feine, Paul
1923   Einleitung in das Neue Testament. Leipzig: Quelle & Meyer.

Fendler, Folkert
1991   Studien zum Markusevangelium. Zur Gattung, Chronologie, Messiasgeheimnistheorie und Überlieferung des zweiten Evangeliums. GTA 49. Göttingen: Vandenhoeck.

Feneberg, Wolfgang
1974   Der Markusprolog; Studien zur Formbestimmung des Evangeliums. STANT 36. München: Kösel.

Fowler, Robert
1985   "Who is 'the Reader' in Reader Response Criticism?" Semeia 31: 5–23.

Frankemölle, Hubert
1982   "Kommunikatives Handeln in Gleichnissen Jesu. Historische-kritische und pragmatische Exegese. Eine kritische Sichtung." NTS 28: 61–90.

Friedrich, Gerhard
1935   "εὐαγγελίζομαι, κτλ." TWNT 2: 702–735.

Gnilka, Joachim
1961   Die Verstockung Israels. Isaias 6, 9–10 in der Theologie der Synoptiker. SANT 3. München: Kösel.
1978   Das Evangelium nach Markus. EKK 2.1. Neukirchen-Vluyn: Neukirchner Verlag.

Goguel, Maurice
1909   L'Évangile de Marc et ses Rapports avec Ceux de Mathieu et de Luc. Paris: Leroux.

Grant, F. C.
1951   "Mark." IB 7: 627–917.

Grob, Rudolf
1965   Einführung in das Markus Evangelium. Zürich: Zwingli.

Grundmann, Walter
1959   Das Evangelium nach Markus. THKNT 2. Berlin: Evangelische Verlaganstalt.

Grundmann, Walter, Franz Hesse, Marinus de Jonge, and Adam S. van der Woude
1974   "χρίω, χριστός, ἀντίχριστος, χρῖσμα, χριστιανός." TDNT 9: 493–580.

Guelich, Robert
1983   "The Gospel Genre." Pp. 183–219 in P. Stuhlmacher, ed.

Hadas, Moses, and Morton Smith
1965   Heroes and Gods: Spiritual Biographies in Antiquity. New York: Harper & Row.

Haenchen, Ernst
1966   Der Weg Jesus....Sammlung Töpelmann 2.16. Berlin: Töpelmann.

Hahn, Ferdinand
1963   Das Verständnis des Mission im Neuen Testament. WMANT 13. Neukirchen-Vluyn: Neukirchener Verlag.
1985   "Einige Überlegungen zu gegenwärtigen Aufgaben der Markusinterpretation." Pp. 173–197 in Der Erzähler des Evangeliums. Methodische Neuansätze in der Markusforschung. SBS 118/119. Ed. F. Hahn. Stuttgart: Katholisches Bibelwerk.

Harrison, Everett F.
1964   Introduction to the New Testament. Grand Rapids: Eerdmans.

Hartmann, Gerhard
1936   Der Aufbau des Markusevangeliums. Mit einem Anhang: Untersuchungen zur Echtheit des Marksusschlusses. NTAbh 17.2–3. Münster: Aschendorff.

Hartman, Lars
1983   "Survey of the Problem of Apocalyptic Genre." Pp. 329–343 in Hellholm, ed.

Hauck, Friedrich
1931   *Das Evangelium des Markus (Synoptiker I)*.THKNT 2. Leipzig: Deichert,.

Hawkin, David J.
1977   "The Symbolism and Structure of the Marcan Redaction." *EvQ* 49: 98–110.

Head, Peter M.
1991   "A Text Critical Study of Mark 1.1 'The Beginning of the Gospel of Jesus Christ.'" *NTS* 37: 621–629.

Hedrick, Charles W.
1983   "What Is a Gospel? Geography, Time and Narrative Structure." *Perspectives in Religious Studies* 10: 255–268.
1984   "The Role of 'Summary Statements' in the Composition of the Gospel of Mark: A Dialog with Karl Schmidt and Norman Perrin." *Nov T* 26: 289–311.

Heinrici, C. F. Georg
1913   *Die Bodenständigkeit der synoptischen Überlieferung vom Werke Jesu.* Berlin: Runge.

Hellholm, David
1980   *Das Visionenbuch des Hermas als Apokalypse. Formgeschichtliche und texttheoretische Studien zu einer literarischen Gattung.* ConBNT 13.1. Lund: Gleerup.
1982   "The Problem of Apocalyptic Genre and the Apocalypse of John." Pp. 157–198 in *SBLSP*. Ed. K. Richards. Chico, CA: Scholars Press.
1983   "Introduction." Pp. 1–6 in: Hellholm, ed.
1990   "The Visions He Saw, or: To Encode the Future in Writing. An Analysis of the Prologue of John's Apocalyptic Letter." Pp. 109–146 in *Text and Logos. The Humanistic Interpretation of the New Testament.* Ed. T. Jennings. Atlanta: Scholars Press.
1991   "Methodological Reflections on the Problem of Definition of Generic Texts." Pp. 135–163 in *Mysteries and Revelations.*

Apocalyptic Studies Since the Uppsala Colloquium. JSPSup 9. Ed. J. J. Collins and J. H. Charlesworth. Sheffield: Sheffield.

forthcoming "Probleme und Bedeutung Substitutioneller Gliederungsmerkmale für die Komposition des Matthäeusevangeliums."

Hellholm, David, ed.
1983   Apocalypticism in the Mediterranean World and the Near East. Proceedings of the International Colloquium on Apocalypticism Uppsala, August 12–17, 1979. Tübingen: Mohr.

Hengel, Martin
1985   Studies in the Gospel of Mark. Trans. J. Bowden. Philadelphia: Fortress.

Hilgenfeld, Adolf
1875   Historisch-kritische Einleitung in das Neue Testament. Leipzig: Fues.

Holladay, Carl
1977   Theios Aner in Hellenistic Judaism. A Critique of the Use of This Category in New Testament Christology. SBLDS 40. Missoula: Scholars Press.

Holtzmann, Heinrich J.
1863   Die synoptischen Evangelien. Ihr Ursprung und geschichtliche Charakter. Leipzig: Engelmann.

Horstmann, Maria
1969   Studien zur markinischen Christologie, Mk 8:27–9:13 als Zugang zum Christusbild des zweiten Evangeliums. Münster: Aschendorff.

Huby, Joseph
1948   Évangile selon Saint Marc. VS 2. Paris: Beauchesne.

Iersel, Bas van
1982   "De betekenis van Marcus vanuit zijn topografische structur." Tijdschrift voor Theologie 22: 117–138.

1983 "Locality, Structure and Meaning in Mark." *Linguistica Biblica* 53: 45–54.

Johnson, Sherman E.
1960 *A Commentary on the Gospel According to St. Mark.* London: Black.

Kalin, Everett
1975 "Early Traditions About Mark's Gospel, Canonical Status Emerges, the Story Grows." *Currents in Theology and Mission* 2: 332–341.

Keck, Leander
1965/66 "The Introduction to Mark's Gospel." *NTS* 12: 352–70.

Kee, Howard C.
1973 "Aretalogy and Gospel." *JBL* 92: 402–422.
1977 *Community of the New Age.* Philadelphia: Westminster.

Keil, C. F.
1879 *Commentar über die Evangelien des Markus und Lukas.* Leipzig: Dörffling.

Kingsbury, Jack Dean
1983 *The Christology of Mark's Gospel.* Philadelphia: Fortress (1989 paperback edition).

Klostermann, Erich
1971 *Das Markusevangelium.* HNT 3. 5th ed. Tübingen: Mohr-Siebeck.

Knigge, Heinz Dieter
1968 "The Meaning of Mark. The Exegesis of the Second Gospel." *Int* 22: 53–70.

Knopf, Rudolf
1919 *Einführung in das Neue Testament....*Sammlung Töpelmann 1.2. Gießen: Töpelmann.

Knopf, Rudolf, Hans Lietzmann, and Heinrich Wienel
1949 *Einführung in das Neue Testament. Bibelkunde des Neuen Testaments. Geschichte und Religion des Urchristentums*....Sammlung Töpelmann 2. 4th ed. Berlin: Töpelmann.

Koch, Dietrich Alex
1983 "Inhaltliche Gliederung und geographischer Aufriss im Markusevangelium." *NTS* 29: 145–166.

Koester, Helmut
1989 "From Kerygma-Gospel to Written Gospels." *NTS* 35: 361–381.

Kuby, A.
1958 "Zur Konzeption des Markus-Evangeliums." *ZNW* 49: 52–64.

Kümmel, Werner G.
1966 *Introduction to the New Testament*....London: SCM.

Lagrange, M.-J.
1947 *L'Évangile selon Saint Marc.* Paris: Lecoffre.

Lane, William
1974 *The Gospel According to Mark. The English Text with Introduction, Exposition and Notes.* NICNT 2. Grand Rapids: Eerdmans.

Lang, Friedrich G.
1977 "Kompositionsanalyse des Markusevangeliums." *ZTK* 74: 1–24.

Leon-Dufour, X.
1959 "Évangiles Synoptiques." Pp. 144–334 in *Introduction à la Bible.* Ed. A. Robert and A. Feuillet. Tournai: Desclée.

Lightfoot, Robert H.
1950 *The Gospel Message of St. Mark.* Oxford: Clarendon.

Lohmeyer, Ernst
1967 *Das Evangelium des Markus.* Göttingen: Vandenhoeck & Ruprecht.

Lohse, Eduard
1972 *Die Entstehung des Neuen Testaments.* Theologische Wissenschaft 4. Stuttgart, etc.: Kohlhammer.

Loisy, Alfred
1912 *L'Évangile selon Marc.* Paris: Nourry.

Lührmann, Dieter
1987 *Das Markusevangelium.* HNT 3. Tübingen: Mohr-Siebeck.

Luz, Ulrich
1965 "Das Geheimnismotiv und die markinische Christologie." *ZNW* 56: 9–30.

Mack, Burton, and Vernon K. Robbins
1989 *Patterns of Persuasion in the Gospels.* Sonoma: Polebridge.

Malbon, Elizabeth Struthers
1982 "Galilee and Jerusalem." *CBQ* 44: 242–255.
1986 *Narrative Space and Mythic Meaning in Mark.* San Francisco: Harper.
1993 "Echoes and Foreshadowing in Mark 4–8. Reading and Rereading." *JBL* 112: 211–230.

Marxsen, Willi
1969 *Mark the Evangelist. Studies on the Redaction History of the Gospel.* Nashville: Abingdon.

Merkel, Helmut
1978 *Bibelkunde des Neuen Testaments. Ein Arbeitsbuch.* Gütersloh: Mohn.

Metzger, Bruce M.
1968 *The Text of the New Testament. Its Transmission, Corruption, and Restoration.* New York and Oxford: Oxford University Press.

Minette de Tillesse, G.
1968 *Le Secret Messianique dans l'Évangile de Marc.* Paris: Cerf.

Montefiore, C. G.
1909   *The Synoptic Gospels . . . I.* London: MacMillan.

Moore, Stephen
1989   *Literary Criticism and the Gospels. The Theoretical Challenge.* New Haven: Yale University Press.

Moule, C. F. D.
1975   "On Defining the Messianic Secret of Mark." Pp. 230–252 in *Jesus und Paulus, Festschrift für Werner Georg Kümmel zum 70. Geburtstag.* Göttingen: Vandenhoeck & Ruprecht.

Myers, Ched
1990   *Binding the Strong Man: A Political Reading of Mark's Story of Jesus.* Maryknoll: Orbis.

Nestle, Eberhard, and Kurt Aland, et al., eds.
1979   *Novum Testamentum Graece.* Stuttgart: Deutsche Bibelstiftung (26th ed.).

Nock, Arthur D.
1972   "Early Gentile Christianity and Its Hellenistic Background." Pp. 49–133 in *A. D. Nock. Essays on Religion and the Ancient World, I.* Ed. E. Stewart. Oxford: Clarendon.

O'Day, Gail R.
1986   *Revelation in the Fourth Gospel. Narrative Mode and Theological Claim.* Philadelphia: Fortress.

Perrin, Norman
1974a   "Towards an Interpretation of the Gospel of Mark." Pp. 1–78 in H.-D. Betz, ed. *Christology and a Modern Pilgrimage. A Discussion with Norman Perrin.* Missoula: Scholars Press.
1974b   *A Modern Pilgrimage in New Testament Christology.* Philadelphia: Fortress.
1974c   *The New Testament. An Introduction. Proclamation and Parenesis, Myth and History.* New York: Harcourt.
1976   *Jesus and the Language of the Kingdom: Symbol and Metaphor in New Testament Interpretation.* Philadelphia: Fortress.

Pesch, Rudolf
1968 *Naherwartungen. Tradition und Redaktion in Mk 13.* Dusseldorf: Patmos.
1976/1977 *Das Markusevangelium I, II.* HTKNT. Freiburg, etc.: Herder.

Petersen, Norman
1978a "'Point of View' in Mark's Narrative." *Semeia* 12: 97–121.
1978b *Literary Criticism for New Testament Critics.* Philadelphia: Fortress.

Petzke, Gerd
1970 *Die Traditionen über Apollonius von Tyana und das Neue Testament.* SCHNT 1. Leiden: Brill.

Du Plessis, J. G.
1991 "Speech Act Theory and New Testament Interpretation with Special Reference to G. N. Leech's Pragmatic Principles." Pp. 129–142 in *Text and Interpretation. New Approaches in the Criticism of the New Testament.* Eds. P. J. Hartin and J. H. Petzer. NTTS 15. Leiden et al.: Brill.

Pokorný, Petr
1985 "Das Markus-Evangelium. Literarische und theologische Einteilung mit Forschungsbericht." *ANRW* II.25.3: 1969–2035.

Potterie, I. de la
1966 "De Compositione evangelii Marci." *VD* 44: 135–141.

Radermakers, J.
1974 "L'évangile de Marc. Structure et Théologie." Pp. 221–239 in *L'Évangile selon Marc. Tradition et Rédaction.* BETL 34. Ed. M. Sabbe. Gembloux: Leuven.

Räisänen, Heikki
1976 *Das Messiasgeheimnis im Markusevangelium. Ein redaktionskritischer Versuch.* Finnische Exegetische Gesellschaft 23. Helsinki: Finnish Exegetical Society.
1990 *The "Messianic Secret" in Mark.* Trans. C. Tuckett. Edinburgh: T. & T. Clark (extensive revision of the 1976 ed.).

Ramaroson, Léonard
 1975 "Le plan du second Évangile." *ScEs* 27: 219–233.

Rau, Gottfried
 1985 "Das Markus-Evangelium. Komposition und Intention der ersten Darstellung christlichen Mission." *ANRW* II.25.3: 2036–2257.

Rawlinson, A. E. J.
 1927 *St. Mark*....London: Methuen.

Reiser, Marius
 1984 "Der Alexanderroman und das Markusevangelium." Pp. 132–163 in H. Cancik, ed.

Rhoads, David, and Donald Mitchie
 1982 *Mark as Story. An Introduction to the Narrative of a Gospel.* Philadelphia: Fortress.

Riesenfeld, Harald
 1954 "Tradition und Redaktion im Markusevangelium." Pp. 157–164 in *Neutestamentliche Studien für Rudolf Bultmann, zu seinem siebzigsten Geburtstag am 20. August 1954.* BZNW 21. Berlin: Töpelmann.

Robinson, William
 1973 "The Quest for Wrede's Secret Messiah." *Int* 27: 10–30.

Robbins, Vernon K.
 1981 "Summons and Outline in Mark: The Three-Step Progression." *Nov T* 22: 97–114.
 1992 *Jesus the Teacher. A Socio-Rhetorical Interpretation of Mark.* Philadelphia: Fortress (original ed. 1984).
 1994 *New Boundaries in Old Territory.* Emory Studies in Early Christianity 3. New York et al.: Peter Lang.
 1994b "Socio-Rhetorical Criticism: Mary, Elizabeth, and the Magnificat as a Test Case." Pp. 164–209 in *The New Literary Criticism and the New Testament.* Eds. E. S. Malbon and E. V. McKnight. Sheffield: Sheffield Academic Press.

Ruddick, C. T.
1969 "Behold I Send my Messenger." *JBL* 88: 381–417.

Sawyerr, Harry
1961 "The Markan Framework." *SJT* 14: 279–294.

Schenke, Ludger
1986 "Der Aufbau des Markusevangeliums—ein hermeneutische Schlüssel?" *BN* 32: 54–82.

Schille, Gottfried
1957 "Bemerkungen zur Formgeschichte des Evangeliums. Rahmen und Aufbau des Markus-evangeliums." *NTS* 4: 1–24.

Schmid, Josef
1958 *Das Evangelium nach Markus*. RNT 2. 4th ed. Regensburg: Pustet.

Schmidt, Karl L.
1919 *Der Rahmen der Geschichte Jesu; literarkritische Untersuchungen zur ältesten Jesusüberlieferung*. Berlin: Trowitzsch.
1923 "Die Stellung der Evangelien in der allgemeinen Literaturgeschichte." Pp. 50–134 in *ΕΥΧΑΡΙΣΤΗΡΙΟΝ, FS H. Gunkel, II*. FRLANT 19.2. Göttingen: Vandenhoeck & Ruprecht.

Schniewind, Julius
1927–31 *Euangelion. Ursprung und erste Gestalt des Begriffes Evangelium*. BFChTh 2.13/25. Gütersloh: Bertelsmann.
1952 *Das Evangelium nach Markus*. NTD 1. Göttingen: Vandenhoeck.

Schüssler Fiorenza, Elisabeth
1988 "The Ethics of Biblical Interpretation: Decentering Biblical Scholarship." *JBL* 108: 3–17.
1990 *In Memory of Her. A Feminist Theological Reconstruction of Christian Origins*. New York: Crossroad.

Schweizer, Eduard
1964 "Die theologische Leistung des Markus." *EvT* 24 : 337–355.
1983 *Das Evangelium nach Markus*. NTD 1. Göttingen: Vandenhoeck.

Scott, M. Philip
1985 "Chiastic Structure: A Key to the Interpretation of Mark's Gospel." *BTB* 15: 17–26.

Shuler, Philip L.
1982 *A Genre for the Gospels: The Biographical Character of Matthew*. Philadelphia: Fortress.

Smith, Jonathan Z.
1975 "Good News is No News: Aretalogy and Gospel." Pp. 21–38 in *Christianity, Judaism and Other Greco-Roman Cults. Studies for Morton Smith at Sixty. Part One. New Testament*. SJLA 12.1. Ed. J. Neusner. Leiden: Brill.

Smith, Morton
1978 *Jesus the Magician*. New York: Harper.

Söding, Thomas
1987 *Glaube bei Markus. Glaube an das Evangelium, Gebetsglaube und Wunderglaube im Kontext der markinischen Basileiatheologie und Christologie*. SBB12. Stuttgart: Katholisches Bibelwerk.

Standaert, Benoît
1978 *L'Évangile selon Marc. Composition et Genre Literaire*. Bruges: Nijmegen.

Stock, Augustine
1985 "The Structure of Mark." *Bible Today* 23: 291–296.

Strecker, Georg
1964 "Zur Messiasgeheimnistheorie im Markusevangelium." Pp. 87–104 in *Studia Evangelica III*. TU 88. Ed. F. Cross. Berlin: Akademie.

1979   "Das Evangelium Jesu Christi." Pp. 183–228 in *Eschaton und Historie. Aufsätze.* Göttingen: Vandenhoeck & Ruprecht.

Stuhlmacher, Peter, ed.
1983   *Das Evangelium und die Evangelien. Vorträge vom Tübinger Symposium 1982.* WUNT 28. Tübingen: Mohr-Siebeck.

Swete, Henry B.
1913   *The Gospel According to Mark.* London: Macmillan.

Talbert, Charles
1977   *What Is a Gospel: The Genre of the Canonical Gospels.* Philadelphia: Fortress.

Taylor, Vincent
1966   *The Gospel According to St. Mark...* 2nd ed. London: Macmillan.

Tiede, David L.
1984   "Religious Propaganda and the Gospel Literature of the Early Christian Mission." *ANRW* II.25.2: 1705–1729

Tolbert, Mary Ann
1989   *Sowing the Gospel. Mark's World in Literary-Historical Perspective.* Minneapolis: Fortress.

Trocmé, Étienne
1963   *La Formation de L'Évangile selon Marc.* Paris: Presses Universitaires.

Vielhauer, Philipp
1975   *Geschichte der urchristlichen Literatur. Einleitung in das Neue Testament, die Apokryphen und die Apostolischen Väter.* Berlin/New York: De Gruyter.

Weeden, Theodore J.
1971   *Mark-Traditions in Conflict.* Philadelphia: Fortess (paper edition 1979).

Weiss, Bernhard
1889   *Lehrbuch der Einleitung in das Neue Testament.* Berlin: Hertz.

Weiss, Johannes
1907 "Markus." Pp. 67–229 in *Die Schriften des Neuen Testaments...Erster Band...* Ed. J. Weiss. Göttingen: Vandenhoeck.

Wellhausen, J.
1903 *Das Evangelium Marci.* Berlin: Reimer.
1911 *Einleitung in die drei ersten Evangelien.* 2nd ed. Berlin: Reimer.

Wettstein, Jacobus
1965 *Novum Testamentum Graecum Tomus I.* Graz: Akademische Drück-u. Verlaganstalt (lst ed. 1751).

Wikenhauser, Alfred
1959 *Einleitung in das Neue Testament.* 3rd ed. Basel, etc.: Herder.

Wikgren, Allen
1942 "ΑΡΧΗ ΤΟΥ ΕΥΑΓΓΕΛΙΟΥ." *JBL* 61: 11–20.

Wohlenberg, Gustav
1910 *Das Evangelium des Markus ausgelegt.* Kommentar zum Neuen Testament. Ed. T. Zahn. 2nd ed. Leipzig: Deichert.

Wrede, William
1971 *The Messianic Secret.* Cambridge: Clarke (lst ed. 1901).

Zehrer, F.
1969 *Synoptischer Kommentar zu den drei ersten Evangelien. Kindheitsgeschichte und Anfang des öffentlichen Wirkens Jesus (Mt 1,1–4,25; Mk 1,1–39; Lk 1,1–5,11).* Klosterneuburg: Klosterneuburger.

Greco-Roman Sources and Grammatical Works

Apuleius
1938 *Apulei Madaurensis Opera Quae Supersunt, Vol. III: De Philosophia Libri, Liber ΠΕΡΙ ΕΡΜΗΝΕΙΑΣ.* Ed. P. Thomas. Leipzig: Teubner.

Aristotle
1982   *Poetics*. Ed. and Tr. W. H. Fyfe. LCL. Cambridge, MA and London: Harvard University Press and Heinemann (rep. of 1927 ed.).

Audollent, A.
1904   *Defixionum Tabellae*....Paris: Fontemoing.

Augustine
1972   *City of God*. Trans. Henry Bettenson. Great Britain: Penguin.

Bauer, Walter
1957   *A Greek English Lexicon of the New Testament and Other Early Christian Literature*. Trans. and adapted by G. Arndt and F. Gingrich. Chicago: University of Chicago Press.
1971   *Griechisch-deutsches Wörterbuch zu den Schriften des Neuen Testaments*. 5th ed. Berlin: de Gruyter.

Berkowitz, Luci, and Karl A.Squitier, eds.
1990   *Thesaurus Linguae Graecae. Canon of Greek Authors and Works*. 3rd ed. New York and Oxford: Oxford University Press.

Blass, Friedrich, Albert Debrunner, and Robert Funk,
1961   *A Greek Grammar of the New Testament and Other Early Christian Literature*. Chicago: University of Chicago Press.

Brashear, William
1975   "Vier Berliner Zaubertexte." *Zeitschrift für Papyrologie und Epigraphik* 19: 25–33.

Butts, James R.
1987   "The 'Progymnasmata' of Theon: A New Text with Translation and Commentary." PhD Dissertation: Claremont Graduate School.

[Cicero]
1989   *Ad C. Herennium*....Ed. and tr. H. Caplan. LCL. Cambridge, MA and London: Harvard University Press and Heinemann.

Sancti Caecilii Cypriani
  1726   *Sancti Caecilii Cypriani Carthaginensis et martyris opera . . . Stephani Balizii*....Paris: Typographia Regia (Containing Ps. Cypr., Confess.).

Harnack, Adolf von
  1911   *Kritik des Neuen Testaments von einem griechischen Philosophen des 3. Jahrhunderts [Die im Apocriticus des Macarius Magnes enthaltene Streitschrift]*. TU 37/4. Leipzig: Hinrichs.
  1916   *Porphyrius "Gegen die Christen," 15 Bücher. Zeugnisse, Fragmente und Referate.* APAW.PH. Berlin: Verlag der könig. Akademie der Wissenschaften.

Hatch, E., and H. Redpath
  1897   *A Concordance to the Septuagint and the Other Greek Versions of the Old Testament I, II, III.* Oxford: Clarendon.

Julian
  1913/1923 *The Works of the Emperor Julian, I–III.* Ed. and trans. W. C. Wright. LCL. London and Cambridge: Heinemann and Harvard University Press.

Kenyon, Frederic
  1893   *Greek Papyri in the British Museum. Catalogue with Texts.* London: Trustees of the British Museum.

Lampe, G. W. H.
  1961–68   *A Patristic Greek Lexicon.* Oxford: Clarendon.

Lefkowitz, Mary R., and Maureen B. Fant
  1992   *Women's Life in Greece and Rome.* Baltimore: Johns Hopkins University Press.

Liddell, Henry, Robert Scott, and Henry Jones
  1940   *A Greek English Lexicon.* Oxford: Clarendon (reprinted 1976 with 1968 Supplement).

MacMullen, Ramsey
1981   *Paganism in the Roman Empire*. New Haven: Yale University Press.

Maltomini, Franco
1981   "Due Papiri Magici Inediti." *Studi Classici e Orientali* 31: 111–117.

Origen
1899   *Origenes Werke I, II*. Ed. P. Koetschau. GCS 2, 3. Leipzig: Hinrichs.

Origen
1953   *Origen: Contra Celsum. Translated with an Introduction and Notes*. Ed. and trans. H. Chadwick. Cambridge: Cambridge University Press

Papyri Greek and Egyptian
1981   *Papyri Greek and Egyptian. Edited by Various Hands in Honour of Eric Gardner Turner on the Occasion of his Seventieth Birthday*. Greco-Roman Memoirs 68. London: British Academy.

Pradel, Fritz
1907   *Griechische und süditalienische Gebete, Beschwörungen und Rezepte des Mittelalters*. Religionsgeschichtliche Versuche und Vorarbeiten 3.3. Giessen: Töpelmann.

Preisendanz, Karl
1973/74   *Papyri Graecae Magicae. Die Griechische Zauberpapyri, I, II*. Ed. E. Heitsch and A. Henrichs. Stuttgart: Teubner.

Reitzenstein, Richard
1904   *Poimandres. Studien zur Griechisch-Ägyptischen und Frühchristlichen Literatur*. Leipzig: Teubner.

Rohde, Erwin
1921   *Psyche. Seelencult und Unsterblichkeitsglaube der Griechen*. Tübingen: Mohr-Siebeck.

Spengel, L., ed.
1854 *Rhetores Graeci II.* Leipzig: Teubner.

Sullivan, M. W.
1967 *Apuleian Logic. The Nature, Sources, and Influence of Apuleius's Peri Hermeneias.* Studies in Logic and the Foundations of Mathematics. Amsterdam: North-Holland.

Thesaurus Linguae Graecae (*TLG*)
1987 *Thesaurus Linguae Graecae Pilot CD ROM #C.* Irvine: University of California.

Judaica

Strack, Hermann, and Paul Billerbeck (Str-B)
1956 *Kommentar zum Neuen Testament aus Talmud und Midrasch.*Vols. 1–4. München: Beck.

Talmud Jerushalmi
1920 *Talmud Jerushalmi.* Ed. Lamm. Berlin: Lamm (Reprint of the Krotoschin edition).

Coptica

Crum, W. E.
1922 "La Magie Copte. Nouveaux Textes." Pp. 537–544 in *Recueil d'Études Égyptologiques.* Bibliothèque de l'École des Hautes Etudes...Sciences Historiques et Philologiques 234. Paris: Champion, 1922.

GENERAL THEOLOGICAL SEMINARY
NEW YORK

DATE DUE			
NOV 04 1998			
MAY 0 5 2008			
			Printed in USA

HIGHSMITH #45230